MW01120571

Inclusive Education for Students With Intellectual Disabilities

A Volume in
International Advances in Education:
Global Initiatives for Equity and Social Justice

Series Editors:
Elinor L. Brown, *University of Kentucky*
Rhonda G. Craven, *Australian Catholic University*
George F. McLean, *The Council for Research
in Values and Philosophy*

International Advances in Education:
Global Initiatives for Equity and Social Justice

Elinor L. Brown, Rhonda G. Craven, and George F. McLean,
Series Editors

Inclusive Education for Students With Intellectual Disabilities (2015)
Edited by Rhonda G. Craven, Alexandre J. S. Morin, Danielle Tracey,
Philip D. Parker, and Hua Flora Zhong

Poverty, Class, and Schooling:
Global Perspectives on Economic Justice and Educational Equity (2014)
Edited by Elinor L. Brown, Paul C. Gorski, and Gabriella Lazaridis

Migrants and Refugees: Equitable Education for Displaced Populations (2013)
Edited by Elinor L. Brown and Anna Krasteva

Indigenous Peoples: Education and Equity (2013)
Edited by Rhonda G. Craven, Gawaian Bodkin-Andrews, and Janet Mooney

Communication and Language: Surmounting the Barriers
to Cross-Cultural Understanding (2013)
Edited by Alexander S. Yeung, Elinor L. Brown, and Cynthia Lee

Refugee and Immigrant Students: Achieving Equity in Education (2012)
Edited by Florence E. McCarthy and Margaret H. Vickers

Ethnicity and Race: Creating Educational Opportunities Around the Globe (2011)
Edited by Elinor L. Brown and Pamela E. Gibbons

Religion and Spirituality (2010)
Edited by Martin Dowson and Stuart Devenish

Inclusive Education for Students With Intellectual Disabilities

Edited by

Rhonda G. Craven
Australian Catholic University

Alexandre J. S. Morin
Australian Catholic University

Danielle Tracey
University of Western Sydney

Philip D. Parker
Australian Catholic University

and

Hua Flora Zhong
Australian Catholic University

Information Age Publishing, Inc.
Charlotte, North Carolina • www.infoagepub.com

Library of Congress Cataloging-in-Publication Data

CIP data for this book can be found on the Library of Congress website:
http://www.loc.gov/index.html

Paperback: 978-1-62396-998-1
Hardcover: 978-1-62396-999-8
E-Book: 978-1-68123-000-9

Copyright © 2015 IAP–Information Age Publishing, Inc.

Printed in the United States of America

CONTENTS

FOREWORD

Christophe Maïano
Université du Québec en Outaouais,
Campus of Saint-jérôme, Saint-Jérôme

This research monograph entitled *Inclusive Education for Students With Intellectual Disabilities* is dedicated to the identification of international strategies to promote successful education and positive psychosocial development of students (children, adolescents, and young adults) with intellectual disabilities (ID). More specifically, the main objective of this volume is to provide examples of effective theory, research, policy, and practice that were developed with the objective to best educate or intervene with students with ID in a wide range of countries, contexts, and educational settings.

Quite impressively, this objective is successfully reached by this volume, including contributions made by an impressive list of 31 scholars (e.g., professors, associate professors, PhD candidates, researchers, etc.) from a great variety of research areas (i.e., teacher education, educational psychology, special education and disability policy, special needs and inclusive education, health sciences) and an even more impressive list of countries (i.e., Australia, Austria, Canada, Finland, Ireland, Netherlands, Republic of China, Republic of Singapore, United States of America, New Zealand). As such, the contributions included in this book carry a rich potential to influence practice in this critically understudied but critical area and to generate ground breaking international dialogue designed to improve social equity and justice for students with ID.

Inclusive Education for Students With Intellectual Disabilities,
pp. ix–x

In this volume, the contributions have been grouped into four sections. The first section is centered on effective transition programs developed to facilitate future success and opportunities among students with ID. More specifically, in this section, chapters present multiple programs and practices developed with the objective to facilitate, for example, the transitions: into community-based work, from an inclusive day-care center to kindergarten, or from high school to adult life. The second section focuses on research conducted to facilitate the inclusion of students with ID through the development of supportive learning environments. For example, some of these supportive learning environments used technology solutions or learning networks and career opportunities. The third section focuses on self-determination and decision making, and on research that places the voices of students with ID at the forefront. Finally, the last section focuses on parents and educators as advocates for the inclusive education of students with ID. More precisely, this section describes the experiences, expectations or views of parents and teachers toward inclusive education for children with intellectual and developmental disabilities.

In this volume, the contributors highlight that ascertaining social justice and equity for students with ID represents a critically important international concern and that several initiatives or actions have been developed to attain this objective. These initiatives and actions are anchored into various theoretical and methodological perspectives, highly diverse cultural and educational settings, and as such provide an incredibly rich eye-opening, thought-provoking, and stimulating contribution to this area, showing that hope for improvements can take many forms. Readers (i.e., scholars, parents, policymakers, teachers, educators, psychologists, etc.) of this book will find many findings, strategies, or solutions to develop effective programs, practices, or educational policies to furthering positive education and psychosocial development of students with ID and will likely feel as invigorated as I was after my first reading of this volume.

SERIES INTRODUCTION

Elinor L. Brown, Rhonda G. Craven, and George F. McLean

International Advances in Education: Global Initiatives for Equity and Social Justice is an international research monograph series of scholarly works that primarily focus on empowering students (children, adolescents, and young adults) from diverse education, sociocultural, linguistic, religious, racial, ethnic, and socioeconomic settings to become nonexploited and nonexploitive contributing members of the global community. The series draws on the research and innovative practices of investigators, academics, and community organizers around the globe that have contributed to the evidence base for developing sound educational policies, practices, and programs that optimize all students' potential. Each themed volume includes multidisciplinary theory, research, and practices that provide an enriched understanding of the drivers of human potential via education to assist others in exploring, adapting, and replicating innovative strategies that enable *all* students to realize their full potential.

Increasing numbers of students internationally are being diagnosed with intellectual disabilities. This population of students and their families are at risk of being undervalued and stigmatized in contemporary society and their capacity to express self-determination may be limited. Since the release of the Salamanca Statement in 1994 (UNESCO), a large number of developed countries have established policies or laws to promote inclusive education, and a number of developing countries have started to reformulate their policies. With some key policy changes still emerging, it is apparent that meaningful advances for students with intellectual disabilities are yet to be fully realized. The goal of inclusive educa-

Inclusive Education for Students With Intellectual Disabilities,
pp. xi–xii

tion is to bolster the education of all students by promoting equal opportunities for all, and investing sufficient support, curriculum and pedagogy that cultivates high self-concepts, emphasizes students' strengths rather than weaknesses, and assists students to reach their optimal potential to make a contribution to society. In order to realize these goals for students with intellectual disabilities, it is essential to address their educational and psychosocial needs in educational contexts to foster their success and attainment of a high quality of life and opportunity.

As a social justice endeavor, inclusive education requires innovative and effective curriculum and pedagogy derived from research-based practice to achieve positive outcomes in educational and psychosocial development for students with intellectual disabilities. The process of identifying curriculum and pedagogy requires collaboration from multiple parties (i.e., parents, educators, students with intellectual disabilities, and policy-makers) and an appreciation of the different perspectives about what is important and effective in the delivery of inclusive education particularly for students with intellectual disabilities.

Research with the collaboration of universities, schools, and professionals is called for to (a) advance our understanding of the best educational practices and effective interventions within school settings for students with intellectual disabilities; and (b) offer learning opportunities for educators to develop innovative solutions to face the challenges of inclusive education. With a focus on empirically assessed educational and psycho-educative practice, this volume, with a series of subsections, offers insights and useful strategies to promote inclusive education for enhancing the educational and psychosocial development of students with intellectual disabilities globally.

VOLUME INTRODUCTION

**Rhonda G. Craven, Alexandre J. S. Morin,
Danielle Tracey, Philip D. Parker, and Hua Flora Zhong**

Students with intellectual disabilities often do not achieve their full potential which hampers them from leading happy, productive, and fulfilling lives. Given that education predicates life opportunities this is of dire concern. The concept of inclusive education has been largely embraced throughout the developed world, however, educators are still grappling with how best to implement inclusive education to the benefit of all. There is currently a paucity of research with students with intellectual disabilities that identifies strategies that seed success in educational and psychosocial developmental outcomes for this population that can inform effective intervention and practice. This dearth of research is impeding progress in addressing the educational and psychosocial disadvantage that students with intellectual disabilities encounter, the development of new solutions for enabling full potential, and ensuring that students with intellectual disabilities not only succeed but flourish.

This volume includes examples of theory, research, policy, and practice that will advance our understandings of how best to educate and more generally intervene within educational settings and promote social justice and equity. Importantly, this discussion transcends research methodology, context, and geographical locations and may lead to far-reaching applications. As such, the focus is placed on research-derived educational and psycho-educative practices that seed success for students with intellectual disabilities in inclusive educational settings and new directions in theory, research, and practice that can seed success and have implications for

Inclusive Education for Students With Intellectual Disabilities,
pp. xiii–xix

enhancing the education and psychosocial development of students with intellectual disabilities globally.

The themes of this volume include:

1. Promoting effective transition programs to facilitate future success and opportunities;
2. Pedagogy and learning environments that enhance social justice and educational outcomes;
3. Enabling self-determination and authentic participation in decision-making; and
4. The agency of parents and educators as advocates for the inclusive education of students with intellectual disabilities.

PROMOTING EFFECTIVE TRANSITION PROGRAMS TO FACILITATE FUTURE SUCCESS AND OPPORTUNITIES

Transition planning plays a vital role in preparing individuals with intellectual disabilities to be successful in the next phase of their lives. This section describes and critiques several programs that seek to enhance the transition of individuals with intellectual disabilities across developmental periods extending from early childhood to adulthood.

Claude Normand, Julie Ruel, and Lucie Leclair Arvisais' chapter presents the purpose and evaluation of an intensive early intervention program that aims to encourage equality among children in Canada. The intensive early intervention program prepares children for their transition to kindergarten by: stimulating child development and adaptation within an inclusive day-care setting; encouraging generalization of abilities to various contexts; and empowering parents. The program aims to develop inclusive practices by providing a subsidized trained early childhood educator, dispensing information and training, as well as interdisciplinary support and specialised services. The chapter concludes by describing the necessary conditions to build more inclusive communities for preschoolers with an intellectual or developmental disability through early intervention.

Tiffany Gallagher and Shelia Bennett's chapter provides an illustrative case of a Canadian school board that has attempted to provide a program for high school students with intellectual disabilities to assist them in transitioning successfully into the community workplace. This program is coordinated, collaborative, and belief driven on the part of high school teachers, job coaches, administrators, and community employers. The study concludes that opportunities for successful community engagement beyond high school for students with intellectual disabilities was achieved. The students with intellectual disabilities were also found to have social connectivity and were involved in environments where they could develop friendships and workplace networks.

Kathryn Best, LaRon Scott, and Colleen Thoma introduce the emerging concept of Universal Design for Transition (UDT) which is designed to help teachers and educational planners link academic content to transition planning and individualized instruction and goals. The chapter reports on the results of a national US survey to determine how secondary general educators, special educators, and transition specialists use elements of UDT in transition planning to impact students with disabilities in preparing for their lives after high school. The chapter concludes that the premise of the UDT research is helpful in preparing special education teachers and enhancing the academic performance of students with disabilities.

Soh Mee Choo and Levan Lim's chapter provides a retrospective case study using an action learning and research framework to illustrate an example of developing a transition program at a special school in Singapore. This study advances practice as transition planning has not been a formal and compulsory part of the special school experience for many students with disabilities in Singapore. The chapter contributes toward the understanding of the development work involved in setting up transition programs and provides key insights into the relevant processes and practices that contributed to its chronological development over a 3-year period.

PEDAGOGY AND LEARNING ENVIRONMENTS THAT ENHANCE SOCIAL JUSTICE AND EDUCATIONAL OUTCOMES

Inclusive education involves much more than placing individuals with special educational needs in regular classrooms. What happens in classrooms is critical for achieving authentic inclusion. This section provides valuable insights into how best to build effective inclusive pedagogy and learning environments.

Geert Van Hove, Elisabeth De Schauwer, and Inge Van de Putte take us on a journey based on "key incidents" observed by the authors and "narrative snapshots" derived from informal qualitative interviewing—about the lives of three young adults with an intellectual disability in the Flemish speaking part of Belgium. The three young adults followed an inclusive trajectory within their school career. As such, their stories teach us about the experience of participation and belonging throughout their inclusive trajectory. More specifically, the chapter encourages educators to: view people as "continuously becoming"; presume competence; and conceive education as a healthy mixture of qualification, socialization, and subjectivation. Educators are challenged to adopt a broad framework to inclusive education that opens up opportunities for multiple talents to assure that people with intellectual disabilities get the time and opportunities to become respected citizens.

Eija Kärnä's chapter introduces a supportive technology-enhanced learning environment that emphasizes the emergence of the strengths and creativity of children with autism spectrum disorders and intellectual disabilities. The environment is developed in the ongoing interdisciplinary research project based in Finland, "Children with Autism Spectrum Disorders as Creative Actors in a Strength-Based Technology-Enhanced Learning Environment." The environment is developed to be adaptable and transferrable and thus, it could be used in the future to support learning and inclusion of children with special educational needs in different educational contexts. The chapter presents the results of a mid-evaluation of the project and describes the participating teachers' and assistants' views on the adaptivity and transferability of the learning environment and on participants' inclusion in the project.

John Kubiak and Michael Shevlin highlight that people with intellectual disabilities continue to remain underrepresented in higher education both internationally and in Ireland, the site of the study. The chapter reports on the findings of a research project that examined how learning is experienced in college by students with intellectual disabilities. This learning is presented by four key categories: the cognitive stages of learning; self-regulation of learning; learning as collective meaning making, and the supportive environment and learning. The findings depict that learning for this group of individuals is far more sophisticated and multifaceted than previously thought. The findings have far-reaching implications for teaching and learning at all levels—primary, secondary, and tertiary. The chapter concludes that, if started early, the learning model outlined has the potential to enable all students to process information in a more active and reflective manner and to solve problems collectively.

ENABLING SELF-DETERMINATION AND AUTHENTIC PARTICIPATION IN DECISION MAKING

This section aims to cultivate practice that will enable people with intellectual disabilities to actively participate in processes where decisions are made about their futures. The chapters specifically advocate for this to occur in the transition from schooling to adulthood, and in research methodology that investigates the experience of people with intellectual disabilities.

Aino Äikäs' chapter focuses on the inclusion (and exclusion) of young adults in the decision-making process and the planning of their futures as they move out of upper secondary education in Finland. The chapter reports on a case study of a young adult called Oliver and consists of interviews from Oliver, his mother, and professionals who work closely with him. The results provide insight into how future planning was conducted and Oliver's personal experience in the process. The influence of the disability diagnosis in relation to educational decision making is addressed, as well as the significance of using the appropriate communication method in advocating educational excellence. In addition, Oliver's experience of disability itself and how the concept is experienced and interpreted are examined. Lastly, the chapter proposes how people with intellectual disability could be part of an inclusive decision-making process concerning their future planning in order to realize their full, unique potential.

Karrie Shogren and Michael Wehmeyer's chapter explores the emergence of strengths-based approaches to intellectual disability, and the role of positive psychology and self-determination in the implementation of such approaches. They postulate that the participation and learning support required by an individual can be identified by adopting a socioecological model to address the mismatch between personal capacities and environmental demands. The chapter introduces the third generation of inclusive practice, focused on the total education program—where, how, and what students are taught. Research on the role of self-determination in promoting valued post-school outcomes is described and the self-determined learning model of instruction is highlighted as a means to promote self-determination and student involvement in inclusive settings, building on student strengths to create strengths-based systems of supports.

Danielle Tracey, Rhonda G. Craven, and Herb Marsh's chapter highlights the imperative for the voices of children and young people with intellectual disabilities to be heard in matters that affect them. They identify the self-reporting of self-concept as one means to achieve this goal in both research and professional practice but explain that rigor in this area is still emerging with this population. The chapter critiques the evolution and current state of research into the self-concepts of children with mild intellectual disabilities and provides a clear demonstration of the gains that have been made in this important research area. The chapter encourages researchers to embrace validated measurement tools to further this line of investigation and do so in a way that empowers and respects the voices of children with mild intellectual disabilities. The central purpose of the chapter is to promote social justice, respect, and inclusion by critiquing and influencing both research and practice in this important area of psychosocial well-being.

THE AGENCY OF PARENTS AND EDUCATORS AS ADVOCATES FOR THE INCLUSIVE EDUCATION OF STUDENTS WITH INTELLECTUAL DISABILITIES

This section highlights the critical role that parents, educators, and other community members play in boosting the opportunity for inclusive education and its effectiveness for people with intellectual disabilities. A common theme addressed in this section is the limited capacity and barriers experienced by key stakeholders, which are particularly profound when families come from disadvantaged communities.

Meghan Burke recognizes the importance of parent advocacy driving inclusive education in the United States, but laments that parents encounter various barriers when advocating on behalf of their children with disabilities and this is exacerbated among low-income, minority, and non-English speaking families. The chapter discusses the historical importance of parent advocacy with respect to inclusion, and elucidates existing barriers around attitudes, knowledge, and logistics. A critique of the gaps in the existing research is provided. Finally, directions for future research and practice are discussed in the chapter. These include the need to develop an operational definition of advocacy, document the relation between parent advocacy and inclusion, and provide targeted support for marginalized populations.

Frances Lai Mui Lee, Alexander Seeshing Yeung, Danielle Tracey, Katrina Barker, and Jesmond Fan investigate the views toward inclusion held by teachers in Hong Kong. A sample of preprimary teachers were surveyed ($N = 436$) with regard to their perceptions of inclusive education. The main results indicated that special education teachers and their collaborating regular teachers in inclusive classrooms were higher in knowledge, efficacy, individualized curriculum, and lower in resistance than teachers in regular classrooms. All three teacher types showed similarly low scores for government support. More experienced teachers tended to have better knowledge about special education, but this difference was small. The chapter concludes by suggesting that resources are needed to develop regular teachers who teach in regular classrooms in order to promote inclusive education.

Michaela Kramann and Gottfried Biewer highlight parental views on the process of school placement in Austria where legal entitlements provide the opportunity for parents to choose whether their child with a disability attends an integrative or special school setting. Despite this apparent opportunity, the analyses of interviews with parents, reveals hidden institutional factors which undermine parents' school choice. The stories shared by parents indicate that special schools deliver a wide range of therapies and support, whereas mainstream schools confront parents with additional problems including: transport, missing day care in the afternoon, insufficient material equipment, and the need to persuade mainstream schools to receive children with disabilities. The authors' argue that only those parents who have the resources to engage in their children's school career in a certain way, are able to act as advocates for their children within a selective school system. As a result, the unequal conditions between inclusive and special classes are a barrier for societal development toward equity in education.

Llyween Couper's chapter provides insight into the pitfalls and successes that inclusion brings for those involved in the lives of children who are nonverbal and have autistic spectrum disorders. This chapter explores the frustrations, the challenges, and problems that arise for both the families and their school communities, with particular emphasis on the playground as an important context in children's lives. Set in New Zealand, the chapter provides a commentary on the relationship between the ministry of education and different government policies and current research. The chapter concludes that for many years there have been issues with funding, assessment, resources, and professional development which have served as barriers to the realization of inclusive education.

ACKNOWLEDGMENTS

The editorial efforts leading to the development of this collective work was realized in the context of, and made possible by, a grant from the Australian Research Council (DP140101559) awarded to Alexandre J. S. Morin, Rhonda G. Craven, and Danielle Tracey, and an early career research award from the Australian Research Council (DE14010080) given to Philip D. Parker.

PART I

**PROMOTING EFFECTIVE TRANSITION PROGRAMS
TO FACILITATE FUTURE SUCCESS AND OPPORTUNITIES**

CHAPTER 1

AN INTENSIVE EARLY INTERVENTION PROGRAM

Building Inclusive Communities and Transitioning to Kindergarten

Claude L. Normand, Julie Ruel, and Lucie Leclair Arvisais

While it is known that intensive early intervention (IEI) targeting children with an intellectual disability or autism spectrum disorder can help with developmental delay, it can also have a much broader social impact. Our chapter presents the purpose and results of an intensive early intervention program that aims to encourage equality among children. Implemented by a rehabilitation center in partnership with a regional association of day-care centers in western Quebec, Canada, this IEI program prepares children for their transition to kindergarten by stimulating child development and adaptation within an inclusive day-care setting. Furthermore, it favors social integration and the generalization of abilities to various contexts, like the home, school, and community. The IEI program empowers parents and helps them build partnerships with social and health services providers. Their participation in planning interventions and educational goals for their child prepares them for the collaboration that they will need to exercise within the school system. The

Inclusive Education for Students With Intellectual Disabilities,
pp. 3–24

program aims to develop inclusive practices in day-care centers by providing a subsidized trained early childhood educator for 20 hours per week to aid in the inclusion of the child attending day-care. The rehabilitation center (RC) dispenses information and training tailored to each day-care center (e.g., on special needs, intervention strategies, government funding), as well interdisciplinary support and specialized services. We outline transition practices and then conclude our chapter by describing the necessary conditions to build more inclusive communities for preschoolers with an intellectual or developmental disability through early intervention.

INTRODUCTION

My name is Emma and I have Down syndrome. I have wonderful parents who are always there for me. When I have to go to the doctor or the hospital, which is quite often, my mum is always by my side. I also have a sister that I love very much. We do all sorts of things together. When I was one, my mum found an opening for me at a day-care center near our home. Everybody was nice and thought I had an irresistible smile. As they got older, the other kids could walk faster, and it was hard for me to play with them, so I often sat alone, unable to keep my toys around me. That's why it was great when a new program made it possible for me to have special help at the day-care center. With an early childhood educator by my side, I could participate in the group activities, and I learned a lot!

My name is Logan. At birth, my doctor and my parents noticed that I wasn't a typically developing child: I have multiple disabilities. Since birth, I have visited many hospitals and seen many specialists. What a pain! Eventually, the doctors told my parents that I also had an intellectual disability. The most difficult part was that my parents could not find a day care for me because of my special needs. The day-care supervisors even said that it wasn't the right place for me and that they didn't know what they would do with me. Even though my parents were taking good care of me (my mum quit her job after I was born), I wanted to go to day care like my brother and the other children. I felt lonely and sad! But when I was 4 and a half, I got a surprise! A new program started, and a day care was willing to take me. I was so happy to be with other children. You can just imagine how my parents felt!

Intensive early intervention has shown promise in enhancing development for children with intellectual or behavioral disabilities or autism spectrum disorder (ASD) (Guralnick, 2007; Kaczmarek & Groark, 2007; Odom & Wolery, 2003; Pépin et al., 2006). Both Emma and Logan participated in an intensive early intervention program in western Quebec,

Canada. Their stories are told throughout this chapter. They are based on their experiences and their parents' experiences; however, the children's accounts are not verbatim.

The reported positive outcomes of IEI programs have prompted the Ministry of Health and Social Services in Quebec to offer 20 hours per week of intensive behavioral intervention to children with ASD until they are 5 years old. Rehabilitation centers (RC) for persons with an intellectual disability (ID) or ASD are mandated to implement these programs. Pavillon du Parc, a rehabilitation in western Quebec, has extended these 20 hours to children (2–5 year olds) diagnosed with an intellectual disability or a global developmental delay. However, only 5 hours of intensive stimulation are required by the provincial government for this population. This is the only RC in the province to have such a program.

Early intervention programs vary in intensity and duration throughout North America. Many are offered exclusively on a one-to-one basis, with a strong emphasis on the child's development. While most early interventions are offered by professionals in a clinical setting, at home, or both, this method presents numerous limitations. Not only does it deprive the child of interactions with peers for many hours each day, but it also may require a parent to be available as many as 40 hours per week to be trained and then follow the stimulation program. In other words, families may be obligated to make substantial financial and career sacrifices as a trade-off for their child's optimal development. Yet it is not clear how this method helps a child's transition to school.

A distinctive feature of the Pavillon du Parc's IEI program, in which Logan and Emma took part, is that it adheres to the Division for Early Childhood's recommended practices in early intervention (Sandall, McLean, & Smith, 2000). Because the program is child-centered, it begins with a comprehensive, interdisciplinary assessment of the child (Sandall, Hemmeter, Smith, & McLean, 2005). Timing, duration, and intensity are also crucial. The IEI is offered as early as possible, from the time of referral until the start of school, and for 20 hours per week (Guralnick, 2007; Pépin et al., 2006). It takes place in a naturalistic and inclusive setting (DeVore & Russell, 2007; Odom, Buysse, & Soukakou, 2011), as close as possible to the family's home, with typically developing infants, toddlers, and preschoolers, and is similar to what the child will experience in school. Furthermore, the IEI follows an interagency model embedded in the local service delivery model (Ramey, Ramey, & Lanzi, 2006) and is paired with an interdisciplinary team that includes the child's parents (Kaczmarek & Groark, 2007).

The IEI program's objectives are centered around the children, their families, and the day-care centers. The children-centered objectives are to enhance development, adaptation, social integration, generalization of abilities to various contexts (home, school, and community), and preparation for the transition to school. For parents, the IEI program focuses on empowerment and building partnerships with social and health services providers. Parents' participation in interdisciplinary planning of interventions and educational goals for their child prepares them for when they will need to work with school staff. Finally, the program aims to promote inclusive practices in day-care centers by providing subsidized access to a trained early childhood educator (ECE) for 20 hours per week to support the inclusion of the child attending day care. Information and training tailored to each day-care center (e.g., on special needs, intervention strategies, and government financial support) and joint interdisciplinary support and services are provided.

In this chapter, we will explain the IEI program objectives, structure, and organization within the services offered by this RC to children like Logan and Emma. We will also present the IEI program results: how it affected child development, what parents thought, and the program's effect on day-care centers. We will conclude with the favorable conditions for implementing IEI in naturalistic and inclusive environments and the successful transition to school.

PROGRAM OBJECTIVES

There are various types of early intervention programs that are expected to improve development and outcomes for children with intellectual or developmental disabilities. Many scientific literature reviews have been conducted to analyze the impact of these programs. They all reached the same conclusion: there is no strong evidence of a single most effective program for children with ASD or ID. Although progress can be made and the rate of development can increase, we have yet to determine how to achieve the best outcomes in terms of type of program and child or length and intensity of the intervention (Charman & Howlin, 2003; Corsello, 2005; Goldstein, 2002; Odom & Wolery, 2003; Pépin et al., 2006; Rogers, Reddy, Files-Hall, & Schaefer, 2005; Sandall et al., 2000; Sladeczek & Amar, 2006).

Child-Centered Objectives

Based on some evidence, certain conditions are associated with promising results. Early intervention should begin as early as possible, be very intensive, be tailored to the needs and abilities of each child, and be offered in a naturalistic setting (Childress, 2004; DeVore & Russell, 2007; Guralnick,

Neville, & Connor, 2008; Irwin, Lero, & Brophy, 2004; Pépin et al., 2006; Sandall, McLean, & Smith, 2000). Our RC's IEI program strives to meet all of these criteria. While the goal of early intervention is first and foremost to maximize the child's potential, it should also reduce the delay in development and contribute to positive outcomes, such as social inclusion.

The child-centered objectives of IEI include: (1) improving the child's cognitive, social, language, motor, and adaptive skills through individualized planning and intervention, with particular emphasis on autonomy and social and communication skills; (2) providing learning opportunities through peer behavior modelling and peer interactions; (3) enhancing and strengthening the child's adaptive behaviors; (4) facilitating transfer and generalization of skills from the day-care setting to the home and vice versa; (5) preparing the child's transition to kindergarten and helping him or her build lifelong skills; and (6) encouraging the child's peers, day-care staff, and other parents—and thus the community—to socially accept, integrate, and include the child.

Family-Centered Objectives

Parents of children with ID or ASD need to feel competent in raising their child (Guralnik, 2007). They want their efforts to be recognized and their expertise to be valued; they also want access to adequate services and to feel included in the intervention planning and implementation. The professionals involved with their child also need to consider parents' priorities and resources (Kemp, 2003). When a naturalistic environment like a day-care center is a part of their child's development, parents feel supported by an entire community (Ruel, Moreau, Normand, & Leclair Arvisais, 2010; Shonkoff, & Phillips, 2000).

IEI family-centered objectives include: (1) providing services that help the parents access day care; (2) helping parents trust others with the care of their child; (3) creating a stronger bond between parent and child through play, communication, and shared moments of leisure and stimulation; (4) offering child development strategies to parents; (5) reinforcing parents' expertise and abilities by making the most of embedded learning opportunities; (6) reassuring parents about the suitability of services for their child's special needs; (7) involving parents in every step of the interdisciplinary work; and (8) helping parents prepare their child's transition to school.

Inclusive Day-Care-Centered Objectives

It has been established that successful early intervention is not limited to supporting parents, overcoming disability, and improving child development (Jourdan-Ionescu, 2003; Pépin et al., 2006). The central goal of the RC's strategic planning, services, and research program is to build more inclusive communities. By offering IEI in day cares, it is helping to develop an inclusive community with services located in the community. It is also recognizing the relevance and effectiveness, for all children, of the services provided by government-subsidized day-care centers. Day cares are an ideal environment for all children to learn, socialize, and grow. Kaczmarek and Groark (2007) have found that day-care environments provide more opportunities for social interaction and using complex social strategies by children with or at risk for intellectual disabilities. It has also been shown that children's communication and imitation skills increase at a greater rate when they spend time interacting with other children, and that the use of play and routines in day care are effective early intervention strategies (Bricker, 2001; Childress, 2004; Ouellet, & Poliquin, 2006; Rousseau, Dionne, Dugas, & Ouellet, 2010; Sandall et al., 2000). It is thought that spending at least 20 hours per week from early childhood with other children facilitates social inclusion in other settings, for example on family outings and at school.

Our experience has shown that, as long as they are supported by a team of specialized professionals and by government policy (i.e. subsidies for children with impairments), day-care centers are able to include all children, regardless of their special needs. Children with disabilities can be included with their peers, and when needed, specialized services can be given in a regular day-care environment.

IEI aims to provide services that will: (1) encourage day-care centers to include children with intellectual or developmental disabilities; (2) recognize the importance of the role of day care in child development; (3) establish collaboration between day cares and the RC; (4) provide day-care centers with support and educational strategies on a regular basis; (5) enhance day-care staff's knowledge of the specific needs of children with disabilities; and (6) help day-care centers develop inclusive practices.

STRUCTURE OF THE INTENSIVE EARLY INTERVENTION PROGRAM

Finding or Creating an Inclusive Day-Care Environment

The majority of early education centers in Quebec are government subsidized: children can attend day care for as little as $7 a day. The provincial government created this network of subsidized and regulated day-care centers to make early education accessible to all children, especially those most at risk; to optimize their development; and to better prepare them for school.

Day cares receive additional funding to care for children with disabilities recognized by the Ministry of Health and Social Services. However, this additional funding does not cover the cost of an extra ECE to provide daily individual assistance or intervention for the child. For that reason, our RC provides additional funding. It has signed agreements with the regional association of day-care centers and independent day-care centers for IEI to be offered on their premises by one of its employees. Hence, individualized intervention is provided by an ECE trained and supported by the rehabilitation center's team of IEI professionals.

RC resources have made day care a possibility for Logan and many others who had been refused access to day care when their parents alone knocked on doors (Normand, Sallafranque-St-Louis, Ruel, Moreau, & Boyer, 2011). For some, like Emma, the RC's support may prevent exclusion from the group as the gap in development increases in comparison to the rest of the children. It may even go one step further by fostering full social participation. As mentioned, the RC is dedicated to building more inclusive communities. Its IEI programs are accessible largely because of its collaborative agreements with day-care centers. Each year, new resources are sought and agreements are signed between the RC and day-care centers. This means that more children, parents, and professionals in western Quebec become open to inclusion and develop relationships with families of children with ID or ASD.

> Every morning, the adapted transportation service picks me up and takes me to day care. It's like having my own private chauffeur. When I arrive, the other children greet me. Even their parents know me by now, and they say "Hello Logan!" Though it's hard for me to express myself, I make sounds, and they know it means that I like it here and that I'm happy to be part of the group. (Logan)

The majority of mothers reduce their working hours, refuse promotions, or quit their jobs to take care of a child with disabilities (Berthelot, Camirand, Tremblay, & Cardin, 2006; Conseil de la famille et de l'enfance, 2007). Providing IEI in a day care allows both parents to be available during regular working hours so they can reenter the workforce (Ruel et al., 2010), providing them with similar opportunities to other dual-income households, and possibly reducing the gap between their income and that of families with children without disabilities (Camirand & Aubin, 2004).

Although the day-care centers benefit from an ECE with specialized training for 4 hours a day, the day-care staff are strongly encouraged to keep the child with the group for the entire day. By doing so, they will come to realize that they have the necessary expertise and confidence to care for a child with special needs alongside the rest of the group. Hence, the majority of the children in our program attend full-time day care (i.e. 6 to 8 hours per day). Furthermore, the majority of day-care centers that have accepted a child with an intellectual or developmental disability into their programs decide to remain a part of the inclusion effort. They will often take in another child referred by the RC once the first child enters kindergarten. RC statistics show that we now have relationships with an increasing number of day-care centers, growing from a meagre 8 day-care centers in 2005 to 60 day-care centers plus 23 home-based day cares that accept children with a developmental delay, ID or ASD in 2013.

The Role of the Psychoeducator[1] and the Early Childhood Educator

An interdisciplinary team from the RC evaluates child development. The team comprises specialized professionals such as psychoeducators, occupational therapists, speech therapists, physical therapists, and psychologists from the RC—selected according to the child's profile. In line with the naturalistic nature of the IEI, the evaluation is completed in the child's home. Individualized IEI objectives are set by the interdisciplinary team in conjunction with the parents and day-care workers.

The psychoeducator is at the center of the intervention, ensuring collaboration between all of the parties involved in the child's development and harmonizing the pedagogical strategies between environments. Psychoeducators are also central in devising a work plan for the early childhood educator assigned to the case. They visit the day-care center weekly to observe the child, reevaluate objectives, and address any concerns from the ECE or other staff. They also meet with parents in the family home to address specific home-related issues (e.g. around bath time) and to continue the learning process in both the day care and the home environment.

The RC's psychoeducators foster a close relationship between the child, the family, and the day-care center. They have to take into consideration all of their needs while coordinating evaluations and programming with the interdisciplinary team (complementary services are given when necessary by an occupational, speech, or physical therapist and a psychologist from the rehabilitation center). When preparing the child's intervention plan (IP), they also have to take into account the day-care center's routine and planned activities for the group. This is a challenging task! The psychoeducator assigned to the case pays weekly visits to the day care and biweekly visits to the family home to observe the child, model strategies, intervene, reevaluate the objectives, and answer any concerns the ECE, other day-care workers, or parents may have.

The early childhood educator also has a key role. The RC provides training in intellectual and developmental disabilities before sending ECEs out to observe the target child in the day care for 2 weeks. The ECEs participate in the child evaluation and intervention plan, but their main responsibility is to provide 20 hours per week of intensive, individualized support and stimulation to the child within the regular activities and routines of day care. They are at the front line for implementing the developmental strategies outlined in the child's IP, and they are responsible for supporting and collaborating with the ECE in charge of the entire group of children as well as communicating with the parents on a daily basis. They are also required to complete observation reports, which they then share with the visiting psychoeducator and other members of the interdisciplinary team.

> I really like going to day care. I used to feel sad because people did not seem to understand what I wanted, so I sat down and refused to move. But my psychoeducator explained to the childcare educator the difference between "delays in expressive language" and "noncompliant behavior." Now that I know how to ask for juice or a toy, I feel a lot better. (Emma)

Cost and Human Resources

Having the psychoeducator and ECE work together allows intensive services to be provided to a larger number of children diagnosed with an ID or ASD. Each child receives frontline personal services for 20 hours per week from a trained ECE. The psychoeducator can then be assigned a larger caseload of children, and specialized services are provided by the RC only when necessary. The Pavillon du Parc RC was able to increase its mandated 5 hours per week of IEI to children with ID to 20 hours per week, which allowed them to offer the same level of service as the intensive behavioral intervention offered to children with ASD and their families. It has also greatly reduced waiting lists for these services. Meanwhile, specialists can devote more of their expertise to a greater array of environments. Moreover, this model widens the pool of early childhood educators who are formally trained to care for children with special needs (i.e., ID, ASD or developmental delay).

From Inclusive Day Care to School Inclusion

It appears that offering IEI in a naturalistic day-care environment better prepares children with ID or ASD for their transition to kindergarten

(Julien-Gauthier, Dionne, Lachance, & Lacharité, 2004). However, planning is the key to success in this first school transition (Pianta, Cox, Taylor, & Early, 1999; Pianta, & Kraft-Sayre, 2003; Ruel, Moreau, Bourdeau, & Lehoux, 2008). Children with special needs experience increased challenges during this period. The complexity of their needs in regard to their intellectual, motor, social, emotional and speech abilities must be taken into account, and the variety of workers involved in the process adds to the complexity. For children like Logan and Emma, transition planning with the IEI program team (which includes the parents) and the staff of the future school focused on several objectives:

- ensure continuity among the child's different life environments;
- ease the child's adaptation and integration into their new environment;
- support the school in preparation for welcoming each child and their individualities;
- adapt activities according to the child's needs; and
- encourage full participation of the parents and professionals who know the child (Ruel, 2011).

Transition planning allows parents and workers to benefit from shared knowledge. They are all keen to share what works and to explore innovative solutions to the complex situations they face. Sharing knowledge opens the lines of communication between the parents and the stakeholders in different sectors (Ruel, 2011) and adds to the quality of the transition (Therrien, 2008; Therrien & Goupil, 2009).

Planning strategies have been developed to specifically support the transition. One such strategy is a customized timeline of important dates and activities geared to prepare the child for school entry (Ruel et al., 2008; Tétreault, Beaupré, & Pelletier, 2004; Tétreault, Beaupré, Pomerleau, Courchesne, & Pelletier, 2006). Structured practices put in place by the IEI team help integrate these children in regular school environments (Ruel et al., 2008). Furthermore, the number of transition practices put in place also facilitates the children's adaptation to school in regard to their social and academic competencies (LoCasale-Crouch, Mashburn, Downer, & Pianta, 2008; Margetts, 2007).

RESULTS OF THE IEI PROGRAM

I spent only seven months in the program because it was time for me to go to school. At the end of the program, the specialists did a second assessment. What a surprise! My results improved in almost all areas of my development. They said that I showed a 17-month increase in my social abilities in the space of 7 months! Most importantly I was very happy to be attending the day care. My parents were happy too. My father came one day and looked in the playground where I was playing. He saw many friends around me, interacting with me and talking to me. He was so pleased to see that I was a part of the group, he had tears in his eyes. (Logan)

The effectiveness of the IEI program in reaching its objectives (for the child, the family, and the day-care centers) is being monitored by a team of professionals from the RC in collaboration with researchers from the Université du Québec en Outaouais. A summary of results from children who completed the program between 2008 and 2011 (and for whom we have complete data) is presented here.

Child Development

Complete pre- and postprogram data are available for 21 children with a developmental delay or ID. IEI was offered to children up to 5 years of age, and the mean chronological age at entry in the program was 49 months. All children took part in IEI in a regular day-care environment for an average of 20 hours per week and an average duration of 16 months before entering kindergarten.

Child development was assessed with the Vineland Adaptive Behaviour Scales—Vineland-II (Sparrow, Cicchetti, & Balla, 2005) and the Assessment, Evaluation and Programming System for Infants and Children—AEPS (Bricker, 2006).

What did I learn during this special program? Now I know how to take turns when we play a game, and I can share my toys. But that's not all! I can say a lot more words and even combine a few words together. My parents like it when I say "Please" and "Thank you." And you know what else? I know a lot of colors, and I can count up to 10! (Emma)

The children's composite scores in adaptive behaviors averaged 49 when they entered the program (Table 1.1). But this tells us very little about the heterogeneity of the sample. When they joined the IEI program, Logan was 4 and a half and scored 37, whereas Emma, aged 2, scored 74. As a group, children in our sample finished the program with a mean composite score of 56.18 (see Table 1.1). Hence they gained 7.18 standard points in the 17.78 months between the pre- and post-IEI Vineland measures. The subscales with the most impressive gains were social and motor development.

Table 1.1. Mean Pre- and Postintensive Early Intervention Program Standard Scores on the Vineland II Adaptive Behavior Scales

Scales	Pre-IEI	Post-IEI	Difference
Communication	50.06	56.82	+6.76
Social development	51.65	57.12	+8.06
Daily living skills	56.53	64.59	+5.47
Motor development	46.53	55.65	+9.12
Composite	49	56.18	+7.18

Note: N = 21.

Table 1.2. Mean Percentage of Successful Items Pre- and Postintensive Early Intervention Program on the AEPS

Scales	Pre-IEI	Post-IEI	Difference
Fine motor	44.27	51.72	+7.45
Gross motor	50.45	62.53	+12.08
Adaptive	34.70	48.32	+13.62
Cognitive	28.98	37.30	+8.32
Communication	25.03	31.94	+6.91
Social	28.78	41.67	+12.89

Note: N = 20; AEPS = Assessment, Evaluation and Programming System (Bricker, 2006).

The percentage of successful items from the AEPS ranged from 25.03% on the communication subscale to 50.45% in gross motor development (see Table 1.2). Cognitive and social development was among the lowest scores at entry. At the end of the program, the areas with the highest gains were the social and adaptive behavior subscales.

Parent Satisfaction and Well-Being

Forty-seven parents whose children have taken part in IEI or IBI (intensive behavioral intervention—for children with ASD) programs were interviewed at the beginning and end of the program. An overwhelming majority (96%) were very satisfied with the IEI program. Some parents went as far as to say, "This program changed my life!" They felt reassured and were eager to take advantage of this opportunity to have their child included in a day-care environment.

It was very important for me to have access to this kind of individualized support. I didn't want my child to be on her own, because she could not express herself and needed help to be part of the group and follow the routines. Also, what really helped was that Pavillon du Parc [RC] visited the day-care every week. There was a very good follow-up on the goals and strategies. I really felt that we were all working together. This kind of collaboration is priceless (translated from parent interview). (Emma's mum)

Parents said their children's autonomy, social skills, and communication skills benefited the most from this program. "My child learned structure, routines and rules." This bodes well for the transition and adaptation to school. Parents also stated that they appreciated that everyone (rehabilitation center staff, day-care staff, and themselves) worked "with the same goals in mind." Parents named the following strengths of the IEI program:

1. the knowledge, support, and professionalism of the interdisciplinary team members;
2. regular and frequent follow-ups;
3. collaboration between different professionals and services;
4. child stimulation, behaviour modelling, accompaniment, and discipline in the day-care environment;
5. empathic listening, help in establishing routines, and support for parents at home; and
6. support and strategies in the transition to kindergarten.

Parents named the following challenges:

1. staff turnover;
2. gaps in communication; and
3. paperwork.

The ECEs hired for 20 hours per week often left for full-time employment and needed to be replaced during the IEI. This required parents, children, and staff to adjust, and in the parents' opinions, it may have slowed progress. It could also have fuelled what parents labelled as gaps in communication between ECEs (day-care staff versus IEI) and between ECEs and parents. The excessive paperwork for parents involved filling out forms for government subsidies, child evaluations, and the individualized intervention plan (revised every 3 months). Parents also reported that they would like to have even more hours of stimulation for their child, more help at home, and longer follow-up from the interdisciplinary IEI team after the child's transition to school. Due to this last comment, the RC's multidisciplinary team is now assigned to the case until the child reaches 7 years of age.

Impact on Day-Care Centers

Twenty-one day-care centers responded to our end-of-program questionnaire. The vast majority (86%) were very satisfied with the IEI program. Like parents, they stated that the collaboration, interdisciplinary teamwork, training and support, and regular visits provided by the rehabilitation center were the main strengths of the program. "It made inclusion possible." "The right support makes all the difference." The regular follow-up "allowed us to adjust [our interventions] rapidly."

In addition, day-care center staff appreciated the work plan, program, individualized objectives, and knowledge exchanges with psychoeducators. "It was a learning experience for us.... We learned a lot of good strategies." They also saw how IEI benefited both the target child's development and the other children's development, especially in terms of social skills. The IEI program helped raise disability awareness in all day-care staff, all other children at the day care, and their parents.

TRANSITION PRACTICES

The transition to school involves careful planning. This includes choosing which objectives to set in the IEI intervention plan for children while they are still in day care.

> When I was four years old, everybody started talking about school. They said we had to think ahead. When the team met for my intervention plan, they decided that I had to learn things so that I could be more 'independent.' That was hard! But they were right. Now I can put my coat and my shoes on all by myself! I eat with a fork like the other kids and drink from a glass without spilling. And of course, I can go to the bathroom on my own. (Emma)

> I feel that Emma progressed a lot in those three years. I think that because she learned to be more independent and socialize with other kids, she was better prepared for school. (Emma's mum)

The staff at the school was quick to identify the information and advice provided by the interdisciplinary team as a valuable asset. The school principal emphasized the fact that the intervention plan was very useful at the beginning of the year. 'This kind of collaboration, along with the passing on of information and skills, increased our confidence. It also contrib-uted to improving the staff's attitude towards inclusion.'

> It took a lot of meetings with my parents, the day care, my psychoeducator and my future school to help me to be ready for school—and to help the school to be ready for me and all my needs. In March, before I started school, they planned a list of activities to ease this transition. My future teacher, who was eager to meet me, came to visit at the day care. I was so happy to get to meet her. I heard my mum, who was also invited, my ECE, and my teacher go on and on and on about me. They shared information on how to communicate with me, how to understand my behaviour, and how to help me participate with the other children. (Logan)

Other transition practices have been put in place in order to ease the transition to school and to foster continuity amongst children's different environments. In the spring before the child starts school, the interdisci-plinary IEI program team meets with the future school to set the timeline for transition activities. They also identify the resources the child will need in this new setting. The future teacher and teacher's aide visit the child at day care during the spring before the child starts school. During this visit, they get acquainted with the child and observe him or her inter-acting with other children and adults. They also exchange strategies with the regular day-care center staff and the designated ECE. The children visit their future school and classroom and the school day care, and they meet their future school teacher again. Video or pictures can be taken for the children to look at during the summer to familiarize themselves fur-ther and refresh their memory of the visit.

Multiple meetings are scheduled for the different adults who know the child to share information before and after the start of the school year. Specialists from the RC (such as an occupational therapist) may visit the future classroom to suggest changes in the physical environment and in teaching or play resources in order to adapt them for the child's abilities. School transportation is arranged, and the child is encouraged to try it with somebody he or she knows before fall.

During the summer, the child is encouraged to play in the schoolyard so they can meet other children who will be in the same class. A preferred means of communication between school staff and parents (e.g., journal or e-mail) is identified. The day-care schedule can be gradually adjusted to fit the school schedule (e.g., nap time, lunch time). Parents and ECEs are encouraged to prepare a transition portfolio in which they present their child's abilities, special qualities, interests and preferences, and spe-cial needs. This creates yet another occasion for parents, the child, and school staff to meet, get to know each other, clarify expectations, and develop a trusting relationship.

Specialists from the RC remain involved in a variety of ways. They send their professional reports to the school. They meet with school staff to present the results of their evaluations and interventions in person in order to increase the understanding and feasibility of their suggestions in this new setting.

Not all of these practices are necessary for all children. This is why individualized planning is strongly recommended for children with special needs.

Before my first day at school (Mum says it's a "regular school"), I was a little bit anxious, though I had visited my class beforehand and met my teacher. How would it go with the new kids in class and with their parents? Would they accept me? Everything ended up going well. The other kids were curious and asked a lot of questions! Then they all wanted to try my wheelchair. It was fun. Also, I really like to take the school bus with my sister and my neighbor. When I get to my class, I'm so happy to see my friends! I give them a big hug. In the morning, I have a teacher's aide and she helps me learn new things. (Logan)

School Inclusion

The inclusion of children with special needs in a school environment can change classroom dynamics and even create a ripple effect throughout the entire school. A few strategies helped promote the inclusion of children like Logan: a letter explaining the purpose of inclusion, discussion between the principal and the parents on this topic, and an awareness activity with the children from the same class, their parents, and school staff. Results from the evaluation of transition practices and school inclusion for a sample of child graduates of our RC's IEI program suggest that preparing the transition to school is worthwhile. Shared knowledge about the children, awareness in school staff, and shared time and experiences with these children promote open mindedness about disability and difference. Some parents expressed how lucky their child without disabilities was to experience that proximity at such a young age. One parent wrote, "I find that these children have the right to attend a regular school as much as any other child." Another parent wrote, "My daughter talks about these children as if they were regular children—as her friends. I am pleased!"

The staff noticed that the school community was tolerant of the accommodations put in place. It was also a learning opportunity for the children (who asked a lot of questions), the teacher, and the rest of school staff. The principal said, "it had a ripple effect outside the classroom … it diminished prejudice; it lessened opposition. It facilitated school integration."

Some teachers expressed worries about school inclusion. Most of them are not trained to teach special needs students. They questioned whether the support from the RC and other stakeholders would always be sufficient. They worried that inclusion could be imposed on all teachers. They wanted to make sure that the resources required to fulfil the children's needs would be available. But overall they were pleased with the experience of inclusion at their school.

NEXT STEPS

Preliminary results from our small sample show promise for improving child development. However, many conditions, not just child stimulation, must be implemented in order for the program to successfully establish equal treatment for all children during their preschool years and encourage inclusion in school by providing transition strategies.

Government funding for universal day care in Quebec and grants for day-care centers that provide services to children classified as handicapped certainly set the stage for IEI to take place in a naturalistic setting for preschoolers with special needs. However, these measures are not enough to make this inclusion a reality. The RC and its partners must believe that is it not only possible but also in the child's and society's best interest for these children to be included in regular day care. Early childhood educators (and teachers) need to recognize that with the right training and support from an interdisciplinary team, they can gain the knowledge and experience to foster the optimal development and adaptation of children with special needs.

Although intervention plans need to have the flexibility to be individually tailored to children's abilities and support needs, family culture, and day-care functioning, the IEI program itself requires a clear structure and operating rules. The clinical process—from assessment to planning to intervention in the day care and home visits—must be respected to attain its objectives on all fronts (i.e., child development, parent well-being, day-care center inclusion). Yet for this structure to work, certain interactional processes need to be considered (Ruel, 2011). All partners involved need to feel guided and supported.

It comes as no surprise that a community's beliefs and attitudes are major barriers to the inclusion and social participation of children with ID or ASD. But awareness, training, and support are perceived by parents as the most useful tools for inclusion (Normand et al., 2011). Inclusion can be successful when all parties (parents, administrators, specialized service providers, and front-line workers) are dedicated to making it work and trust and respect each other's unique contributions.

Although our sample is currently very small, and there is no matched control group available to support the hypothesis that the gains in development we have witnessed are due not to the passage of time or a growth spurt, but to the IEI, the RC is still gathering data on all children taking part in IEI. We hope that as the sample size grows, so will the certainty of our conclusions. More research is needed to compare various models of early intervention of varying intensity, in different environments, and for children at various stages of development when entering the programs. Nevertheless, by implementing IEI in inclusive day-care environments, the Pavillon du Parc RC has demonstrated how combining research, policy, and practice can lead to positive outcomes for all parties concerned. It illustrates what difference an inclusive, intensive early intervention program can make, not only for children with an intellectual or developmental disability, but also for their families, friends, and caregivers. It helps build more accessible communities, fosters more equal access to health and social services, and makes it possible for complete inclusion in the school system when sufficient adapted support is provided. For Logan and Emma, it has meant that when they are out in their neighborhood, other school children and their parents will often stop to chat with them. They are recognized as being an integral part of their community, as they should be.

NOTE

1. Psychoeducators (sometimes called child and youth care workers as opposed to social workers) are university-educated professionals who work with children and adolescents in various therapeutic contexts. Psychoeducators are trained to conduct evaluations, design intervention plans, and lead group activities in a variety of settings for children and youth with or without behaviour or mental health problems. In Quebec, a master's degree is required to hold the title and to become a member of the *Ordre des psychoéducateurs et psychoéducatrices du Québec* [Professional Order of Psychoeducators].

REFERENCES

Berthelot, M., Camirand, J., Tremblay, R., & Cardin, J. F. (2006). *L'incapacité et les limitations d'activités au Québec, Un portrait statistique à partir des données de l'Enquête sur la participation et les limitations d'activités 2001 (EPLA)* [Disability and limitations to activities in Quebec: A statistical portrait from the 2001

Participation and Activity Limitation Survey (PALS)]. Quebec City, Quebec, Canada: Institut de la statistique du Québec.

Bricker, D. (2001). The natural environment: A useful construct? *Infants and Young Children, 13*(4), 12–31.

Bricker, D. (2006). *Programme d'évaluation, d'intervention et de suivi. Tome I: Guide d'utilisation et tests: 0 à 6 ans* [Assessment, evaluation and programming system] (C. Dionne, C.-A. Tavarès, & C. Rivest, Trans.) Traduction et adaptation auprès d'une clientèle québécoise. Montréal, Canada: Chenelière McGraw Hill.

Camirand, J., & Aubin, J. (2004). *L'incapacité dans les familles québécoises. Composition et conditions de vie des familles, santé et bien-être des proches* [Disability in Quebec families: Family composition and living conditions, health, and well-being of close family members]. Retrieved from http://www.stat.gouv.qc.ca/statistiques/sante/etat-sante/incapacite/incapacite-familles-quebec.pdf

Charman, T., & Howlin, P. (2003). Research into early intervention for children with autism and related disorders: Methodological and design issues. *Autism: The International Journal of Research & Practice, 7*(2), 217.

Childress, D. C. (2004). Special instruction and natural environments: Best practices in early intervention. *Infants and Young Children, 17*(2), 162–170.

Conseil de la famille et de l'enfance. (2007). *Tricoter avec amour: Étude sur la vie de famille avec un enfant handicapé* [Close-knit with love: A study of family life with a disabled child]. Quebec City, Quebec, Canada: Gouvernement du Québec.

Corsello, C. M. (2005). Early intervention in autism. *Infants & Young Children: An Interdisciplinary Journal of Special Care Practices, 18*(2), 74–85.

DeVore, S., & Russell, K. (2007). Early childhood education and care for children with disabilities: Facilitating inclusive practice. *Early Childhood Education Journal, 35*(2), 189–198.

Goldstein, H. (2002). Communication intervention for children with autism: A review of treatment efficacy. *Journal of Autism & Developmental Disorders, 32*(5), 373.

Guralnick, M. J. (2007). The system of early intervention for children with developmental disabilities. Current status and challenges for the future. In J. Jacobson, W. J. A. Mulick, & J. Rojahn (Eds.), *Handbook of intellectual and developmental disabilities* (pp. 465–480). New York, NY: Springer.

Guralnick, M. J., Neville, B., & Connor, R. T. (2008). Continuity and change from full-inclusive early childhood programs through the early elementary period. *Journal of Early Intervention, 30*, 237–250.

Irwin, S. H., Lero, D. S., & Brophy, K. (2004). *Highlights from inclusion: The next generation in childcare in Canada*. Retrieved from http://www.specialinkcanada.org/books/ING_highlights.pdf

Jourdan-Ionescu, C. (2003). L'intervention précoce et les programmes de prévention [Early intervention and prevention programs.] In M. J. Tassé & D. Morin (Eds.), *La déficience intellectuelle* (pp. 159–181). Boucherville, Quebec, Canada: Gaëtan Morin Éditeur.

Julien-Gauthier, F., Dionne, C., Lachance, J., & Lacharité, J. (2004). La socialisation des jeunes enfants dans les milieux de garde: préparer l'avenir [Socialization of young children in daycare: preparing the future]. *Revue francophone de la déficience intellectuelle*, *15*, 11–16.

Kaczmarek, L., & Groark, C. J. (2007). Early intervention practices for children with and at risk for delays. In C. J. Groark, K. E. Mehaffie, R. B. McCall, & M. T. Greenberg (Eds.), *Evidence-based practices and programs for early childhood care and education* (pp. 25–55). Thousand Oaks, CA: Corwin Press.

Kemp, C. (2003). Investigating the transition of young children with intellectual disabilities to mainstream classes: an Australian perspective. *International Journal of Disability, Development and Education, 50*, 403–433.

LoCasale-Crouch, J., Mashburn, A. J., Downer, J. T., & Pianta, R. C. (2008). Pre-kindergarten teachers' use of transition practices and children's adjustment to kindergarten. *Early Childhood Research Quarterly, 23*, 124–139.

Margetts, K. (2007). Understanding and supporting children: Shaping transition practices. In H. Fabian & A.-W. Dunlop (Eds.), *Informing transitions in the early years: Research, policy and practice* (pp. 107–119). Maidenhead, England: McGraw Hill.

Normand, C., Sallafranque-St-Louis, F., Ruel, J., Moreau, A. C., & Boyer, T. (2011). *Measuring barriers and accommodations to social inclusion and participation of children with an intellectual or developmental disability.* Paper presented at the Canadian Disability Studies Association Annual Conference, Fredericton, New Brunswick, Canada.

Odom, S. L., Buysse, V., & Soukakou, E. (2011). Inclusion for young children with disabilities: A quarter century of research perspectives. *Journal of Early Intervention, 33*(4), 344–356. doi:10.1177/1053815111430094

Odom, S. L., & Wolery, M. (2003). A unified theory of practice in early intervention/early childhood special education: Evidence-based practices. *The Journal of Special Education, 37*(3), 164–173.

Ouellet, S., & Poliquin, N. (2006). Créer une relation authentique: les aires de jeu en pédagogie.[Creating an authentic relationship: The role of play areas in pedagogy]. In J. Loiselle, L. Lafortune, & N. Rousseau (Eds.), *L'innovation en formation à l'enseignement: pistes de réflexion et d'action* [Innovation in teacher training: reflection and action plans] (pp. 169–180). Quebec, Canada: Presses de l'Université du Québec.

Pépin, G., Gascon, H., Beaupré, P., Tétreault, S., Dionne, C., Roy, S., & Ruel, J. (2006). *Les effets des programmes d'intervention pour les enfants de la naissance à sept ans présentant un retard global de développement et recevant des services d'un centre de réadaptation en déficience intellectuelle (CRDI)* [Effects of early intervention programs for children from birth to seven years of age with a developmental delay and receiving services from an intellectual disability rehabilitation centre]. Quebec City, Quebec, Canada: Laval University.

Pianta, R. C., Cox, M. J., Taylor, L., & Early, D. (1999). Kindergarten teachers' practices related to the transition to school: Results of a national survey. *The Elementary School Journal, 100*(1), 71–86.

Pianta, R. C., & Kraft-Sayre, M. (2003). *Successful kindergarten transition: Your guide to connecting children, families & schools.* Baltimore, MD: Paul H. Brookes.

Ramey, C. T., Ramey, S. L., & Lanzi, G. H. (2006). Children's health and educa-tion. In I. Sigel & A. Renninger (Eds.), *The handbook of child psychology* (pp. 864–892). Hoboken, NJ: Wiley & Sons.

Rogers, S. J., Reddy, L. A., Files-Hall, T. M., & Schaefer, C. E. (2005). Play inter-ventions for young children with autism spectrum disorders. In L. A. Reddy, T. M. Files-Hall, & C. E. Schaefer (Eds.), *Empirically based play interventions for children* (pp. 215–239). Washington, DC: American Psychological Association.

Rousseau, N., Dionne, C., Dugas, C., & Ouellet, S. (2010). *Enfants présentant des incapacités intellectuelles et inclusion en milieux de garde : vers l'établissement de stratégies et de modèles novateurs* [Children with intellectual disabilities and inclusion in day-care: Towards innovative models and strategies]. Research Report. Trois-Rivières, Quebec Ciy, Canada: Université du Québec à Trois-Rivières.

Ruel, J. (2011). *Travail en réseau, savoirs en partage et processus en jeu en contexte d'innovation: Une transition planifiée vers le préscolaire d'enfants ayant des besoins particuliers* [Networking, knowledge sharing and processes involved in the context of innovative practice: a planned preschool transition for children with special needs] (Unpublished doctoral dissertation). Université du Qué-bec en Outaouais, Gatineau, Quebec, Canada.

Ruel, J., Moreau, A. C., Normand, C., & Leclair Arvisais, L. (2010). Intervention précoce intensive en contexte inclusif pour les enfants de 2 à 5 ans présentant une déficience intellectuelle [Intensive early intervention in inclusive settings for children aged 2 to 5 with an intellectual disability]. *Revue francophone de la déficience intellectuelle, 21*, 90-100.

Ruel, J., Moreau, A. C., Bourdeau, L., & Lehoux, N. (2008). *Carte routière vers le préscolaire. Guide pour soutenir une transition de qualité des enfants ayant des besoins particuliers* [Roadmap to preschool: A guide to quality transition for children with special needs]. Retrieved from http://w3.uqo.ca/transition

Sandall, S., Hemmeter, M. L., Smith B. J., & McLean, M. E. (Eds.) (2005). *DEC recommended practices: A comprehensive guide for practical application in early inter-vention/early childhood special education*. Missoula, MT: Division for Early Child-hood.

Sandall, S., McLean, M. E., & Smith, B. J. (Eds.). (2000). *DEC recommended practices in early intervention/early childhood special education*. Longmont, CO: Sopris West.

Shonkoff, J. P., & Phillips, D. A. (Eds.) (2000). *From neurons to neighborhoods: the sci-ence of early childhood development*. Washington, DC: National Academy Press.

Sladeczek, I. E., & Amar, D. (2006). *A dynamic assessment of early intervention models in children with developmental delays: Creating a paradigm shift in early intervention policy and practice*. Retrieved from http://earlyinterventioncanada.com/home.html

Sparrow, S. S., Cicchetti, D. V., & Balla, D. A. (Eds.) (2005). Vineland Adaptive Behavior Scales, Second Edition (Vineland-II). Circle Pines, MN: American Guidance Services Publishing.

Tétreault, S., Beaupré, P., & Pelletier, M.-È. (2004). *Programme de préparation à l'inclusion et de soutien à la transition destiné à l'entourage des enfants d'âge présco-laire vivant des situations de handicap (PIST)* [Program to prepare inclusion and support transition for children with special needs.] Research report from the Centre interdisciplinaire de recherche en réadaptation et intégration sociale [Rehabilitation and Social Integration Interdisciplinary Research Centre]. Quebec City, Quebec, Canada: Université Laval, Université du Québec à Rimouski.

Tétreault, S., Beaupré, P., Pomerleau, A., Courchesne, A., & Pelletier, M.-È. (2006). Bien préparer l'arrivée de l'enfant ayant des besoins spéciaux à l'école. Proposition d'outils de communication [Preparing children with special needs to start school: Communication tools proposal.] In C. Dionne & N. Rousseau (Eds.), *Transformation des pratiques éducatives. La recherche sur l'inclusion scolaire* (pp. 181–209). Quebec City, Quebec, Canada: Presses de l'Université du Québec.

Therrien, J. (2008). Étude exploratoire sur l'entrée à l'école des enfants ayant un retard global de développement: pratiques et perceptions des éducatrices de centres de réadaptation en déficience intellectuelle [Exploratory study of children with a global developmental delay who are starting school: Practices and perceptions of educators from intellectual disability rehabilitation centres] (Unpublished doctoral essay in clinical psychology). Université du Québec à Montréal, Montreal, Quebec, Canada.

Therrien, J., & Goupil, G. (2009). Étude sur les pratiques et les perceptions d'éducatrices en centre de réadaptation en déficience intellectuelle concernant l'entrée à l'école [Study of practices and perceptions of starting school by educators from intellectual disability rehabilitation centres]. *Revue francophone de la déficience intellectuelle, 20*, 17–31.

CHAPTER 2

A CANADIAN PERSPECTIVE ON THE INCLUSION OF STUDENTS WITH INTELLECTUAL DISABILITIES IN HIGH SCHOOLS

Tiffany L. Gallagher and Sheila Bennett

This chapter provides an illustration from Ontario, Canada that aligns with the theme "effective education and psycho-educative intervention strategies for students with intellectual disabilities as a global priority." We begin with a review of the literature as it positions the state of inclusion for students with intellectual disabilities in Canadian schools (K–12) and the community. This is an incomplete picture as the education system has not been totally effective at preparing young adults with intellectual disabilities for the world into which they were supposed to enter—this represents the gap between the theory of inclusion and the practice of inclusion. Next, this chapter will assist in the contextualization of inclusive theory into practice. The reality is that high school students with intellectual disabilities need authentic, work placements that exemplify rights-based inclusion over charity-based inclusion. Ascribing to a long-standing model of inclusion, we will then provide an illustrative case of a school board that has attempted to provide a program for high school students with intellectual disabilities to assist them in transitioning successfully into the community workplace. This program is

Inclusive Education for Students with Intellectual Disabilities,
pp. 25–44

coordinated, collaborative, and belief driven on the part of high school teachers, job coaches, administrators, and community employers. It has enhanced the opportunities for successful community engagement beyond high school for students with intellectual disabilities. The students with intellectual disabilities also have social connectivity and are involved in environments where they can develop friendships and workplace networks. Accomplishment of social connectivity is the best example of belonging for an educational community.

INTRODUCTION

Consistent with basic human rights as outlined in The United Nations Convention on the Rights of Persons with Disabilities (CRDP) adopted in December, 2006 and ratified by Canada on March 11, 2010, individuals with disabilities are entitled, as are all citizens, to a system that facilitates full inclusion into the community. Full inclusion does not only encompass educational opportunities, but employment and community as well (United Nations, 2006). In Canada, education is administered under multiple provincial and territorial jurisdictional mandates (with one exception for aboriginal education which, in some cases is administered nationally). As a result, provinces and territories within Canada have complete control over the decisions and resulting practices that occur. Within the province of Ontario the interpretation of what full participation means can be ambiguous. Practices within educational contexts vary from school board to school board and are dependant, in a large part on their philosophical approach to the provision of services for students with exceptionalities. Regardless of their philosophical underpinnings, each school system struggles with finding an optimum way in which students can transition into productive and engaging work as adults (Neubert & Moon, 2006; Rogers, Lavin, Tran, Gantenbein, & Sharpe, 2008).

In Canada, the premise of inclusive education is that all learners are included in the regular classroom, in the neighborhood school with their same age peers. Educators foster the participation of all learners in socially valuing relationships and to the fullest possible development of all learners' human potential (Crawford, 2005). Accordingly, effective inclusive schools have four characteristics: a supportive environment, opportunities to participate, positive relationships, and promotion of feelings of competence (Specht, 2013). The school board and program that we offer as a case description herein, possesses these four characteristics of an effective inclusive school community. Moreover, as an example of an effective education program for students with intellectual disabilities, this case highlights a promising example of the focus of this monograph series.

THE STATE OF INCLUSION FOR STUDENTS
WITH INTELLECTUAL DISABILITIES

From a Canadian perspective, progress has been made but there is still gap between the theory of inclusion and the practice of inclusion. This continues to have an impact on the educational and social lives of students with intellectual disabilities. The education system has become complicit in the disconnection between protecting young adults with intellectual disabilities and preparing them for entry into the community and employment—this is the reality of the gap between the theory of inclusion and the practice of inclusion.

Education

Speaking to the practice of inclusion, the continuation of protectionist programming is still pervasive in many educational settings. This gap is particularly common as students enter high school settings. The widening gap in curriculum expectations becomes fodder for the rationalization and denial of curricular and experiential access for students with intellectual disabilities. Protectionism and our inability to program flexibly becomes a perfect storm for educational decisions that, on the surface seem well founded, but upon even the most superficial scrutiny fall apart. High school, for all students, should be a time of exploration, identity formation, and self-actualization (Maslow & Lowry, 1998). To prohibit participation in a broad range of curriculum as well as school related activities (e.g., choir, sports, dances) significantly curtails an individual's ability to grow and develop. Life skills programs, that often include, cooking, trips to the grocery store and menial tasks are not reflective of the experience of an average teenager. Hanging around the cafeteria, being in the school play, finding compatible interests, and developing relationships are reflective of the typical experiences of a teenager. Severe participation limitations placed on students with intellectual disabilities shines a glaring light on the blatant curtailing of fundamental rights for these students. As noted by Grover (2002, p. 259) in her review of the Canadian Supreme Court Decision in (*Eaton v. Brant County Board of Education* [1995]) a ruling which supported the school's right to segregate a student with multiple exceptionalities over her parents' wishes:

> No other group in a democratic society, save the disabled student, needs to meet a competency test of sorts in order to exercise a constitutionally guaranteed right to freedom of association where that group poses no risk to others.

In Canada, the inclusive schooling model for students with intellectual disabilities has been instituted to varying degrees of success. Some educational settings strive to create inclusive communities, but many do not fully practice within the context of the current human rights understandings. This is despite the fact that there is mounting evidence that the inclusion of students with intellectual disabilities may provide better lifelong opportunities for not just students with exceptionalities, but all students. The notion of protectionism through segregation flies in the face of the actuality that social capital and engagement in the broad community provide multiple safety mechanisms for each of us. Social connectivity is essential for full and meaningful participation in school and in society. Reluctance to broaden the experiences of students with intellectual disabilities within school settings sets them on a trajectory of isolation, loneliness and unrealized potential. Like all individuals, students with disabilities need networks and relationships to build on in order to transition into adulthood. Schools must provide opportunities for students to be involved in environments where they can learn in diverse curricular areas, develop friendships, and build social relationships. Accomplishment of social connectivity is the best example of belonging for an educational community.

Community and Employment

The juncture between late adolescence and early adulthood is marked by the need to further refine one's identity and participate in one's community. The ultimate accomplishment of belonging in a community is to be a fully participating member. Among many indicators, participation may encompass both social and vocational experiences. Salient work experiences and opportunities to explore potential career interests are needed for all young adults and this is especially true for young adults with intellectual disabilities. Yet, young adults with intellectual disabilities often face barriers in their pursuit to find meaningful, well-paying, and sustainable employment (Butcher & Wilton, 2008; Winn & Hay, 2009). How pronounced is this issue? In Canada, only 20% of young adults with intellectual disabilities are in paid employment and the remaining 80% are in unpaid jobs or unemployed (Galambos & Leo, 2010). There is a similar reality in other countries such as the United States where there is a 25% paid employment rate (3 to 5 years postgraduation) (Certo et al., 2008) and in Australia where research reports (Winn & Hay, 2009) cite pronounced unemployment for young adults with intellectual disabilities (three times the incidence of that for their nondisabled peers).

Ineffective transitioning from public education to opportunities within the community and employment is not a recent issue. For many years, school districts have been grappling with how to best facilitate the transition from student to employed and productive member of the adult community (Neubert & Moon, 2006; Rogers et al., 2008). In the Canadian provinces, contributing to this issue is the challenge of transitioning from one funding agency to another such as from a ministry/department of education to a ministry/department that is responsible for community and social services. Young adults with intellectual disabilities may fall through the gap of service provision between agencies.

Bridging the gap may be accomplished through providing supported school to employment transition programs for young adults with intellectual disabilities in the form of realistic work placements. It has been found (Rogers et al., 2008; Shandra & Hogan, 2008) that providing supportive employment opportunities during secondary school has contributed to sustainable employment for students. In particular, high school students with intellectual disabilities need programs in which they can learn functional work related skills and enhance their strengths and interests in the community. As they begin to consider potential work placements, an awareness of career options is essential to contribute to high self-efficacy in young adults with intellectual disabilities (Nota, Ginevra, & Carrieri, 2010). This chapter will espouse that high school students with intellectual disabilities need authentic work placements that exemplify rights-based inclusion over charity-based inclusion.

AN INCLUSION CASE STUDY

"Each Belongs" is a simple phrase; as a school board mission statement, it is also a profound declaration. In 1969, the Hamilton Wentworth Catholic District School Board adopted the vision that all elementary and secondary students should attend their neighborhood schools along with their siblings and peers. Given the era in education in the province of Ontario, Canada, this vision of integration was novel. It also suggested the notion of total inclusion of students with disabilities in their community schools which was a notion that was far ahead of its time. Over the course of 40 years, this school board has worked with families, teachers, and community agencies to include students with disabilities from their primary elementary grades through to secondary school graduation. They have consulted widely with advocates for inclusive education and developed relationships with community service providers, postsecondary institutions and international school districts.

A visiting scholar from the United Kingdom, who had come to see a model of inclusive practice posed the following question to school officials from Hamilton Wentworth Catholic District School Board, "Do you have any research data to show that this inclusion works or makes a difference for students by the time that they graduate?" The school board had decades of anecdotal accounts substantiating the benefits of espousing an inclusive model of education, but empirical research was absent. Consequently, researchers were approached by school board personnel to partner in a collaboratively developed and administered project that would allow the school board to examine the effectiveness of their inclusive model and ultimately how their students with disabilities transition from school to community.

As a function of their inclusive model, this school board has provided a long-standing exemplary model of a work experience program for students with disabilities (aged 16–21 years) who each has a job coach. This program is premised on the need to provide students with intellectual disabilities with meaningful work placements, support their job performance, and offer guidance for future vocational goals. Students receive a high school credit for their work in authentic jobs that are based on their interests (e.g., food preparation, retail, automotive maintenance, administrative data entry). The job coach acts as a liaison between the school and the workplace and provides on-site training and social skills development for the student in the workplace (half a day, five times per week). Gradually, the job coaches phase out their support and allow the student to work independently. This gradual release of responsibility fosters an interdependence and independence symbiosis. In this inclusive model, there is collaboration among teachers, job coaches, administrators, community employers, and parents.

METHODS

The overarching purpose of this research project was to evaluate whether the inclusionary practices in this school board were impactful. More specifically and as an exemplar of these inclusionary practices, the research sought to capture the relationship between inclusive schooling and the transition into the community based work. The operationalized research question was: Does an inclusive setting result in better transition for young adults with intellectual disabilities into the community work place? This question was addressed through both quantitative and qualitative research methods.

Participants

Consistent with an emancipatory research paradigm (Stone & Priestly, 1996) students with intellectual disabilities were the epicenter of this research. Their voices were privileged and not disadvantaged (McPhail & Freeman, 2005) as authentic informants and contributing to the research methodology rigor. Twenty-one high school students with intellectual disabilities (ages 16–21) were interviewed about a broad range of topics such as their school experiences, friends, family and work placements. These students ranged in terms of intellectual disability (mild to profound) and some were nonverbal and not ambulatory. Each student participant was supported to communicate a response in the manner that he/she was accustomed to (e.g., eye movements, smiles, "thumbs up," etc.)—the researchers accommodated to record the responses as communicated. Some of the students with intellectual disabilities did not have work placements ($n = 10$), while some were completing their first or second work term ($n = 11$).

The educators and community employers that support the students with intellectual disabilities were also integral participants. Data were collected from those individuals who were directly related to students' inclusionary education and employment experiences: teachers ($n = 91$); educational assistants ($n = 67$); job coaches ($n = 7$); administrator ($n = 1$); employers ($n = 20$). The majority of the teachers (55 female; 36 male) had 11–20 years of teaching experience. By contrast, the majority of the educational assistants (52 female; 15 male) had 6–10 years of experience. The administrator of special education was responsible for the supervision and evaluation of the job coaches. He met with them on a monthly basis to discuss their successes and challenges, and to intervene with employers, schools or parents if difficult situations arose. The community employers (18 female; 2 male; majority between the ages of 20–40 years) were the supervisors of the students with intellectual disabilities that hosted their student work placements in the community. Most of the employers ($n = 13$) had 3–10 years of experience in the workplace and prior experience hosting students ($n = 6$, less than 3 years; $n = 6$, 3–5 years; $n = 4$, 6–10 years; $n = 4$, 11–20+ years).

The peers (29 female; 14 male) without disabilities (ages 16–18) were randomly selected from among those classmates that attended classes with the students with intellectual disabilities. The peer group consisted of: 20 (Grade 9); 7 (Grade 10); 6 (Grade 11); and 10 (Grade 12). The majority of this peer group (i.e., $n = 33$) had been in inclusive classrooms in both elementary and high school. There were parents and guardians of students ($n = 22$) that also participated.

Data

There were two sources of data: interviews and surveys. The students with intellectual disabilities were interviewed about school, their classmates and friends, their family, and work. The administrator of special education was interviewed to gather his perspective on the students' experience in the job coaching program and their overall inclusion in the school and community.

There were six versions of the administered surveys. The survey that was given to students with intellectual disabilities asked them about school, their classmates and friends, their family and work. This survey was researcher designed and included questions such as, "I enjoy being at school," "My classmates are nice to me," "I like to spend time with my family," "I am good at my job." The survey for the teachers, educational assistants and job coach participants queried them about school climate, educators, students with disabilities and their colleagues. This survey was adapted from two instruments: Sprankle (2009) and Riegert (2006). Finally, the community employers' survey was comprised of questions related to interactions and experiences with inclusion (adapted from Gething, 1991). The parent participants responded to a survey that asked them about their child's disability, education, school climate and social interactions. This survey was adapted from a study done by Elkins, van Kraayenoord, and Jobling (2003). The peers of the students with intellectual disabilities responded to questions related to interactions and experiences with inclusion as well as friendships with students who are disabled (adapted from Aragon, 2007).

Data Analysis

Interview responses for the students with intellectual disabilities and the administrator were audio recorded and then transcribed. The transcriptions were independently reviewed and coded by the two researchers. Themes were identified according to the student participants' salient impressions of those directly involved in their work experiences: their employers and job coaches. Related to their work experience was a distinct theme that articulates their vocational self-efficacy. Finally, the student participants spoke to their social connectivity and peer relationships.

The survey data were quantitatively analyzed for each participant group. Survey responses were clustered into six areas of focus: placements, programming and instruction; attitudes and beliefs about inclusion; impact of inclusion of students with intellectual disabilities in the classroom and workplace; impact of inclusion on students *without* disabilities; support, socialization, and friendships of students with intellectual disabilities; confidence/comfort in teaching/work. Subscale means were calculated and these interval data were compared among groups using a one-way analysis of variance. The trends in the significant effects are discussed.

RESULTS

The results the students' interviews about their perceptions of their employers, coaches, vocational self-efficacy and social connectivity are presented first. Next, results of the surveys that relate to the clustered six areas of focus are presented. These results address the beliefs and attitudes about inclusion that the six groups of participants held and the analyses compare the different groups' responses to each other. Finally, there are recommendations for administrators based on the specific responses of the administrator of special education, the job coaches and employers.

Students' Perceptions of Their Employers and Job Coaches

Employers

The students with intellectual disabilities were asked to comment on their jobs and their employers. The questions prompted the students to evaluate their perceptions of inclusion in the workplace and the support that they receive from their employer/supervisor. The following student responses illustrate their positive regard for their work placements:

Do you like your employer?
Taylor: Yeah, they're nice there.
How does your employer help you?
Taylor: Well, um, if I have trouble, she will tell me, if I need any help. She's there for me to help me out.
Tell me about the person who helps you the most out work?
Jordan: At work? Well that would have to be my supervisor, J—.
What does she help you with?
Jordan: She helps me if I have a hard time with the residents. She helps me because some residents they don't talk and I don't know sign language so I don't understand what they say.
How does your supervisor help you?
Jordan: Um ... let's see well they help me find my way around and when I, when I first started there I was all confused. I was all mixed up but it's a big building right? So I was kind of like.... But that's okay that's why they're there. They are there to help right?

What more could your employer do for you to help you?
Jordan: ah … What more can they do to help me? Well if I need to push a wheelchair through they could hold the door for me.
What do you like about your job?
Jordan: Oh well everybody's really, really nice. Trust me if somebody was not nice I would not want to work there!

On the job, these students seem to assimilate into their roles. They viewed their supervisor or employer as helpful and coworkers as collegial.

Job Coaches

The students with intellectual disabilities acknowledged the support that their job coaches provided and offered specific examples of work-related tasks for which they have received guidance. Some of the students expressed a level of confidence with their work and their desire to be independent of their job coaches. This can be regarded as a success of the program as the workplace scaffolding could be scaled back and the student could be a fully functional employee. The excerpts below are a sample of these comments about the job coaches' support:

Who helps you the most at work?
Riley: um … like … Job coach … I am working at [name of discount store]
How do you get to your job?
Riley: I take a bus to going there… I [would] like to get a job [there in the future].

How does your job coach help you?
Dale: um … She helps me at [name of fitness club] … I'm good at cleaning, help the trainer, and they help me wipe down the equipment, and at [name of discount store] I stock the food and do my aisle checks … um … It's busy … I like chocolate … chocolate bars.

Who helps you the most at work?
Taylor: Well, I needed some at first but I don't need any more.
You no longer need your job coach?
Taylor: No I don't need them I'm doing it on my own now … I have two different jobs, one is on Tuesdays and Thursdays, and one of them I put movies away … another night on Thursdays, I work in an office, I work the [nonprofit organization's name].
What do you do there?
Taylor: I filed papers, I put them in the file and then put them away and I help out with anything else.

Do you have a job coach?
Reece: Yeah … I'm getting, I'm getting rid of her. I'll tell you, I don't really need her, because I can do it my own self … I've got it all in my head.

So you don't really need a job coach anymore?
Reece: No

The ultimate goal of scaffold use is to take it down. Workplace scaffolding for students with intellectual disabilities seemingly helped to establish work skills and routines. Then, the students were quick to exert their independence and express confidence in what they do.

Students' Vocational Self-Efficacy

The students with intellectual disabilities were placed in meaningful and authentic work placements. On the job, explicitly communicated tasks contributed to their perceptions of competence and tasks that were "easy to do" whereas, challenging tasks were those that were less well defined. The quotes below are a sampling of the students' responses with respect to their beliefs about their work self-efficacy:

What do you like about your job?
Taylor: I like one of them. One of them is my favorite ... the [name of not-for-profit organization], they've got nice people, they know me ... I'd like to work there.
And what did you find easy to do it your job?
Taylor: Well the easiest is when working with the papers and that's all they need me to do, it's not hard putting paper and files.
What do you find hard to do?
Taylor: Um, nothing really, there's nothing really hard there, it's so easy for me to learn.

Tell me about your job at the elementary school.
Sam: Well as soon as I walk into the school, I wash my hands and then I get a sticker and then I go to one of the classrooms that I help out with and as soon as I walk in the students, they'll recognize me right away and they'll run up to me and give me a hug. And that is [it] basically, I don't do anything else.
Do you help them with their work?
Sam: Yes
What do you find easy to doing your job?
Sam: Helping kids with their opening up their snacks.
What do you find hard to do at your job?
Sam: Cleaning the table, because sometimes I forget to clean off the table.
What do you think the teacher could do more of?
Sam: um, take care with help me some of the, help me figure out what the students would like to do

What do you do at your job?
Jordan: I help somebody. I transport the residents to mass. On Wednesdays I help somebody with a tea. Sometimes I help with the program, yeah something like that.
What do you like about your job?
Jordan: Oh well everybody's really, really nice. Trust me if somebody was not nice I would not want to work there.
What do you find easy to do at your job?
Jordan: Oh geez. Probably pushing wheelchairs.
What do you find hard to do your job?
Jordan: Um ... sometimes I have a hard time understanding the residents, sometimes.

Jessie: ah ... The job that I had was I helped, after school I helped coach basketball teams.
What did you like about the job?
Jessie: ah ... What I liked was because I actually got the chance to help younger kids learn the basics of basketball and was able to teach them some skills.
What did you find easy about the job?
Jessie: The explaining everything because I played basketball all the time so I already knew all the skills so it was easy to go you go this that that, it was easy to show the technique.
What did you find hard about the job?
Jessie: Trying to get them to pay attention [laughing]. When you work with Grades 4 to 6's they really don't want to pay attention [laughing]

Students described their workplace responsibilities with ease and articulated how well they performed their tasks. This was an important part of their vocational self-efficacy and developing identity.

Students' Perspectives on Their Social Connectivity

The students were forthcoming about offering their perspectives on the importance of friends and family. The latter were especially instrumental in the lives of these students. The interview questions elicited candor in the participants and they were positive in responding to prompts about their relationships.

Do you have a best friend?
Eric: Yes
Can you tell me about him?
Eric: He is nice.
Why is he nice?
Eric: He helps me.

What makes a good friend?
Eric: When they stick up for you
Is that what your friend does for you?
Eric: Yes.
Tell me about some of your other friends at school or at home? Do you have friends inside of school?
Eric: Yes.
Do they help you out a lot?
Eric: yes
What kind of things do you do together?
Eric: We hang out
What do you do?
Eric: Play on my PlayStation.

Do you live at home?
Hannah: Mhmm, pretty soon I'll move out, soon.
So at home do you do chores, do you help around the house?
Hannah: Not really.
No! Why not?
Hannah: Don't feel like it.
Your mom doesn't say, "Hannah, do the dishes?"
Hannah: That's my brother's job, not mine.
Oh, I see, so you do nothing at home?
Hannah: I'm a Princess, I do nothing.
You're a Princess!?
Hannah: Yeah, I do nothing.
I think I want to, I think I want come live at your house.
Hannah: Not going to happen.
Can I come live at your house?
Hannah: Maybe I'll give you chocolate milk and cookies.
Okay.
Hannah: What kind of cookies do you like? Chocolate?
Chocolate chip.
Hannah: Okay.

When you're done school what do you want to do?
Rachel: College.
What you want to go to college for?
Rachel: Acting.
I can see that, I think you'd be a good actor.
Rachel: Actress.
Actress, that's right, sorry.
Rachel: I'll be on TV and Hollywood.
So do you want to live on your own?
Rachel: Huh?
Do you want to have your own place?
Rachel: Yes.

Live by yourself?
Rachel: Sure.
Soon?
Rachel: Then I will get my license.

Noteworthy in the responses of the students with intellectual disabilities is their frankness about what makes a good friend, the importance of family, and their typical aspirations for the future.

Survey Results About Beliefs and Attitudes About Inclusion

Comparisons among the groups of participants for each of the six survey question subscales were made. The first subscale that included questions about appropriate placements, programming, and instruction for students with intellectual disabilities did not uncover statistically significant differences among participant groups. The lack of significant differences among the participants with respect to their beliefs about inclusive educational placements is not surprising given the inclusive practices that have been a reality in this school board for over three decades. Thus, participants hold similar values related to inclusion and the rights of students to appropriate educational program delivery.

For the other five subscales, there were statistically significant differences among participant groups and posthoc results provide specific data comparing each participant category. Overall, job coaches and parents held the most positive attitudes and beliefs about the inclusion of students with intellectual disabilities. Job coaches felt that the overall philosophy of the school board was well established and well supported and that having diversity in the workplace was beneficial. Parents, in particular, were more likely to agree with statements about the positive effects of inclusion for their children with ID in *both* the classroom and workplace. Parents also expressed confidence in their students' educational and work placement experiences. Complementing this was the perspective of the employers who were most likely to agree that students with intellectual disabilities are supported and interacting with others in the workplace. This is reasonable given the fact that the employers witness firsthand the engagement of the students with their coworkers. Employers expressed overwhelmingly positive attitudes about the inclusion of students in the workplace noting that as they get to know the students they simply notice the person and not the intellectual disability. Finally, looking at the classroom as a whole, teachers most often agreed that students *without* disabilities experienced positive effects as a function of inclusion. These classroom teachers have the benefit of perspective to see that all students thrive in an inclusive educational environment.

Perspective of and Recommendations From the Administrator of Special Education

Findings from the interview data with the administrator of special education speak to the principles that other administrators might bear in mind for school supported work placements for students with intellectual disabilities. These findings present as recommendations to inform administrators' decisions with respect to work experience program delivery and how it must be grounded in an inclusive foundation, foster student independence, workplace competence and social connectivity in the community.

Inclusive Foundation

A work experience program needs to be a practical extension of the school board's philosophy of inclusion and accordingly, the educators that support students need to genuinely believe in this inclusive mission.

> The school board's mission statement has always has been "Each Belongs" meaning that all students, regardless of ability, age attend their neighborhood schools along with their friends, and peers and siblings. Therefore whatever program supports a student requires will be delivered to whichever school they are at, as opposed to the student going to the program. All the life skills classes in the world have not prepared the young men and women who have disabilities to share in a community life. (Administrator of Special Education)

In keeping with this inclusive foundation, the administrator of special education also recommended that community employers need to be chosen for their humanistic qualities and authentic respect for an individual's contribution to the workplace.

Supporting Placements and Fostering Independence

An integral finding from research on this program was that the job coaches and employers felt that they were equipped to support students with intellectual disabilities in workplace settings. Overall, both job coaches and employers felt that they had the necessary training and skills needed to provide positive and meaningful placements for students. Job coaches need professional preparation to understand and respond to the work place context that their students will be immersed into. School environment accommodations may need to be adapted to these work place contexts. Employers may require preparation to receive student employees with intellectual disabilities and the scaffolded support from job coaches. These are the prerequisites to supporting placements and fostering independence.

> The work experience program was always about establishing community links and relationships or networks for students with intellectual disabilities. These are the links and networks that adolescents in general need as they approach their later high school years and they will need and value as they plan for postsecondary life ... I can think of no greater sense of satisfaction for the families of these young man and women, and for the individual themselves, when they are able to live and work in a community just as their friends and brothers and sisters do. (Administrator of Special Education)

Workplace Competence

When asked whether students with intellectual disabilities were competent and had the necessary skills to be successful in the workplace, job coaches expressed confidence in their ability to make these judgments as well as in the notion that employment opportunities were positive and worthwhile for students with intellectual disabilities. Employers were also positive noting that they were aware of the difficulties students in their workplace might have and they admired students' ability to adapt and cope. They also noted that while job coaches played an essential role, students with intellectual disabilities could work independently once their skills were established.

> Initially we introduced the work experience program in those secondary schools which demonstrated a strong commitment to and understanding of the inclusive process. These schools fully included students and did not simply timetable classes where it was "easier" to include all students. The job coaches had a good understanding that support meant just that, support and not something like a permanent shadow for the student. (Administrator of Special Education)

Employers indicated that they were aware of and prepared to support the needs of people with intellectual disabilities in the work environment. The goodness of fit between a student with an intellectual disability and their work placement contributes to a sense of competency. Together, an informed administrator, job coaches and employers support students with intellectual disabilities as they learn job-related tasks and execute them, however, workplace independence is the ultimate goal. Students with intellectual disabilities who achieve a degree of independence are confident and proud of their performance.

Social Connectivity in the Community

Within the complex workplace environment, positive interactions and dynamics among coworkers are important. While job coaches expressed the benefits of diversity in the workplace, they were unsure about the impact that students with intellectual disabilities would have on their coworkers. Sometimes, it is several years later that the impact of inclusion was realized.

> I met one young lady who was about 25 years old and had been out of secondary school for about 4 years. She was a charming and skilled young lady who had been identified as a student with an intellectual disability. She told me the story of how the most important feature of her school years was to be like her friends, to do things her friends did and to enjoy similar activities as her friends enjoyed. She said little or nothing about formal curriculum or life skills or any of those other aspects of school that as teachers and parents we falsely think are the most important features of school life. She said much about friends and hanging out with friends and going to the mall with friends and other activities which we really do not design curriculum for, but perhaps we should? (Administrator of Special Education)

Inclusion benefits everyone. Students with intellectual disabilities, students without disabilities, coworkers, employers and clients/customers should all be a part of a functional workplace dynamic. Each participant stands to benefit from inclusive interactions with other participants.

IMPLICATIONS FOR THEORY, RESEARCH, AND PRACTICE

The illustration profiled in this chapter has provided multiple perspectives from which to view and support work placements for students with intellectual disabilities. At the fore, are the perspectives of the students with intellectual disabilities. Their work placements proved to be satisfying, meaningful and enjoyable. Students felt supported and accepted in their placements. They expressed confidence in terms of not needing additional assistance once the necessary workplace skills had been learned and for the most part, found their work responsibilities well within their capabilities. Some of the students expressed a desire to retain their employment positions after graduation. Interestingly, our findings are contradictory to early research (Ochs & Roessler, 2001) that found that when compared to general education students, students with disabilities have significantly lower self-efficacy beliefs and expectations related to their future careers. Much has changed.

By providing insights from the students themselves, as well as their educators, job coaches, parents and employers, we garner a rich glimpse into the realities of students in employment settings. These realities might be mapped onto a set of principles that should be prerequisite for school supported work placements for students with intellectual disabilities. The importance of defined vision and strong leadership at the school board administration level should not be underestimated. The program profiled here is a function of coordinated, collaborative and belief-driven action on the part of high school principals and their senior administrator (Gallagher & Bennett, 2013). It is apparent that school leaders of inclusion ascribe to social justice, establish an inclusive school environment (Ryan, 2006), support teachers (Boscardin, 2005; Ryan, 2006) and espouse personal, inclusive beliefs (McInnis, 2013; Praisner, 2003).

Often there is a lack of transition planning from school into the community and into appropriate opportunities for young adults with intellectual disabilities. The transition juncture is demanding more attention, resources, and coordination among school boards, government, and employers. More importantly it requires us to reconceptualize how we look at school as a vehicle for preparing young people into adulthood. For many there still exists a distinguishing line between the experiences of "normal" students and those of students with intellectual disabilities. Successful transitions into adulthood occur when student experiences are diverse; when individuals are presented with wide curricular choices to develop their areas of interest; when students are exposed to diverse groups where compatibility, coping and the development of intimacy is learned and practiced, and; when students are given agency in their decisions that allow them to mature. Why, in some cases, do these circumstances only apply to "normal" students? This chapter has explored an inclusive environment where students with intellectual disabilities are given a broad experience of school and community.

There are some positive and encouraging signs on the educational landscape. In Ontario, large segregation embedded boards are examining their practice. The Toronto District School Board (2013) has recently released a report, *The Intersection of Disability, Achievement, and Equity: A System Review of Special Education in the TDSB* and it has identified the movement toward the inclusion of students with special needs as a critical piece of equity planning. Some school districts and boards are taking bold action with the disbanding of segregated classes and the direct provision of support to teachers in the form of inclusion coaches. Overall, the move toward authentic and meaningful inclusion is a positive prospect that allows us to see that we are moving in a direction that recognizes the full and vibrant life that each individual is entitled to.

Research documenting the work experience of students with intellectual disabilities is not common in the literature. It is critically important to honor their words and as educators and researchers to give voice to these students. Issues such as job satisfaction and work self-efficacy from the vantage point of students with intellectual disabilities, provides for us essential information with regard to the success (or lack of success) of transition endeavors. High school students with intellectual disabilities, just like all students, have dreams, ambitions, and a need to feel valued and supported as young adults. Continuing to collect their voices will add a much needed dimension to this important conversation on transitioning into community and employment.

REFERENCES

Aragon, L. (2007). *Inclusion of students with and without disabilities in two educational settings: The perceptions of the nondisabled students of this experience* (Doctoral dissertation). Available from ProQuest Dissertations and Theses database. (UMI No. 3361377)

Boscardin, M. L. (2005). The administrative role in transforming secondary schools to support inclusive evidence-based practice. *American Secondary Education, 33*(3), 21–33.

Butcher, S., & Wilton, R. (2008). Stuck in transition? Exploring the spaces of employment training for youth with intellectual disability. *Geoforum, 39,* 1079–1092.

Certo, N., Luecking, R., Murphy, S., Brown, L., Courey, S., & Belanger, D. (2008). Seamless transition and long-term support for individuals with severe intellectual disabilities. *Research & Practice for Persons with Severe Disabilities, 33*(3), 85–95.

Crawford, C. (2005). *Inclusive education in Canada—Key issues and directions for the future.* Retrieved from http://www.inclusiveeducation.ca/documents/ ROEHER-STATE-OF-2005.pdf

Elkins, J., VanKraayenoord, C., & Jobling, A. (2003). Parents' attitudes to inclusion of their children with special needs. *Journal of Research in Special Education Need, 3*(2), 122–129.

Galambos, L., & Leo, C. (2010, April). *Work experience transition program.* Paper presented at the Human Rights and Persons with Intellectual Disabilities Conference, Education and Employment Stream, Niagara Falls, Ontario, Canada.

Gallagher, T. L., & Bennett, S. (2013). School supported work placements for students with intellectual disabilities: Why inclusive principles/principals matter! *International Journal for Leadership in Learning, 1*(1), 1–25. Retrieved from http://ijll.journalhosting.ucalgary.ca/index.php/ijll/article/view/213/pdf

Gething, L. (1991). *Interaction with disabled persons scale: Manual and kit.* Sydney, Australia: University of Sydney.

Grover, S. (2002). Whatever happened to Canadian children's equality rights? A reconsideration of the Eaton special education case. *Education and the Law, 14,* 253–263.

Maslow, A., & Lowry, R. (1998). *Toward a psychology of being.* New York, NY: John Wiley & Sons.

McInnis, J. (2013). *Elementary school principals as leaders of inclusion for students with exceptionalities* *Unpublished master's thesis). Brock University, St. Catharines, Ontario, Canada.

McPhail, J. C., & Freeman, J. G. (2005). Beyond prejudice: Thinking toward genuine inclusion. *Learning Disabilities Research and Practice, 20*(4), 254–267.

Neubert, D., & Moon, S. (2006). Postsecondary settings and transition services for students with intellectual disabilities: Models and research. *Focus on Exceptional Children, 39*(4), 1–8.

Nota, L., Ginevra, M., & Carrieri, L. (2010). Career interests and self-efficacy beliefs among young adults with an intellectual disability. *Journal of Policy and Practice in Intellectual Disabilities, 7*(4), 250–260.

Ochs, L., & Roessler, R. (2001). Students with disabilities: How ready are they for the 21st century. *Rehabilitation Counseling Bulletin, 44*(3), 170–176.

Praisner, C. (2003). Attitudes of elementary school principals toward the inclusion of students with disabilities. *Exceptional Children, 69*(2), 135–145.

Riegert, J. (2006). *Teacher attitudes on the effects of inclusion on students without disabilities* (Master's thesis). University of Wisconsin-Stout, Menomonie, WI. Retrieved from www2.uwstout.edu/content/lib/thesis/2006/2006riegertj.pdf

Rogers, C., Lavin, D., Tran, T., Gantenbein, T., & Sharpe, M. (2008). Customized employment: Changing what it means to be qualified in the workforce for transition-aged youth and young adults. *Journal of Vocational Rehabilitation, 28*, 191–207.

Ryan, J. (2006). Inclusive leadership and social justice for schools. *Leadership and Policy in Schools, 5*(1), 3–17. doi:10.1080/15700760500483995

Shandra, C. L., & Hogan, D. (2008). School-to-work program participation and the post-high school employment of young adults with disabilities. *Journal of Vocational Rehabilitation, 29*, 117–130.

Specht, J. (2013). Inclusion (The Centre for Inclusive Education). Retrieved from http://www.edu.uwo.ca/inclusive_education/inclusion.asp

Sprankle, M. (2009). *Teachers' beliefs towards the inclusion of students with disabilities.* (Doctoral dissertation). Available from ProQuest Dissertations and Theses database. (UMI No. 3361933)

Stone, E., & Priestly, M. (1996). Parasites, prawns and partners: Disability research and the role of the non-disabled researchers. *British Journal of Sociology, 47*, 699–716.

Toronto District School Board. (2013). Retrieved from http://www.tdsb.on.ca/HighSchool/SpecialEducation/Programs.aspx

United Nations Convention on the Rights of Persons with Disabilities. (2006). Retrieved March 9, 2012, from http://www2.ohchr.org/english/law/crc.htm

Winn, S., & Hay, I. (2009). Transition from school for youths with a disability: Issues and challenges. *Disability & Society, 24*(1), 103–115.

CHAPTER 3

STARTING WITH THE END IN MIND

Inclusive Education Designed to Prepare Students for Adult Life

Kathryn Best, LaRon A. Scott, and Colleen A. Thoma

Universal design for transition (UDT; Thoma, Bartholomew, & Scott, 2009) is a relatively new term for the field of special education, designed to help teachers and educational planners link academic content to transition planning and individualized instruction and goals. UDT is designed to provide a framework for special education teachers, transition specialists, and administrators who want to revise instructional design and delivery so that they not only meet required academic standards, but also better prepare students with disabilities, including students with intellectual disability, for a successful transition to adult life. UDT was also designed to be useful for general education teachers who are looking for a way to teach academic standards in a manner that it is more functional and could link those standards with individualized goals and transition planning needs of students with and without disabilities who may learn in different ways. Universal design for transition builds upon the concept of universal design for learning (UDL; Center for Applied Special Technology, 1998), which is an instructional framework designed to meet the academic needs of all students.

Inclusive Education for Students with Intellectual Disabilities,
pp. 45–73

Recently we conducted a national survey to determine how secondary general educators, special educators, and transition specialists use elements of UDT in transition planning. The aim of this research is to investigate and disseminate findings from the survey to show the extent to which participants are using UDT components: (1) multiple transition domains, (2) multiple transition assessments, (3) self-determination, (4) and multiple resources/perspectives in their current practice to impact students with disabilities in preparing for their lives after high school. The UDT components are based on evidence-based practices to support the transition of students with disabilities (Test, Fowler, et al., 2009). We believe the premise of the UDT research is significant (linking academic and content and transition planning) to preparation of special education teachers and the academic performance of students with disabilities and their adult lives.

INTRODUCTION

This chapter will introduce you to a concept called "universal design for transition" (UDT; Thoma et al., 2009), first presented as a strategy to link transition education with academic instruction for youth with disabilities. As researchers focusing on the transition from school to adult life for youth with disabilities, we found that many special educators believed that inclusive educational opportunities came at the cost of more functional activities like employment, community living, recreation and leisure and using transportation. Students with disabilities most often learned these functional skills in the community, using very individualized instructional techniques, rather than in a classroom setting that focused on teaching academic content to a large group of diverse learners.

As a first year special education teacher, LaRon Scott struggled with that challenge. During his master's degree program he learned about universal design for learning (UDL), a research-based framework designed to guide teachers to plan, implement, and assess learning for a group of diverse learners. Grounded in cognitive neuroscience, UDL is based on three fundamental principles that address teaching and learning environments: provide multiple means of representation; provide multiple means of action and expression; provide multiple means of engagement (National Center on UDL, 2012a; Rose & Gravel, 2012; Rose & Meyer, 2002). Research from the National Center on Universal Design for Learning identified three primary brain networks involved as individuals receive and process information: (a) recognition networks, the "what" of learning; (b) strategic networks, the "how" of learning; and (c) affective networks, the "why" of learning. Each of these specialized areas of the brain helps account for individual differences, and no single educational approach will be ideal for every student (National Center on UDL, 2012a;

Rose & Gravel, 2012). UDL is built upon the idea that options and flexibility are important so that everyone has access to curriculum.

It made sense that a framework used to meet the learning needs of a diverse student population could serve as the starting point for linking academic and transition learning. Mr. Scott believed that all students are best prepared for adult life when they have a solid academic foundation and exit high school with an understanding of and plan for their lives in multiple areas or transition domains (Thoma et al., 2009). And so this new approach, UDT, was created. UDT applies the principles of UDL to the field of transition services for students with disabilities preparing to exit high school. UDT provides students with access to postsecondary life choices "through a process of self-determined planning, instruction, collaboration, and support services" (Thoma et al., 2009, p. 6).

Universal Design

UDL and UDT are part of a greater movement toward universal design, a term coined by architect and designer Ron Mace, which focuses on creating spaces, buildings, and tools that are accessible to individuals regardless of physical ability (Mace, Hardie, & Place, 1991). Examples of universal design include television captioning, entrance ramps, and automatic doors. While these features may have obvious advantages for individuals with physical disabilities, they have proven to be marketable and useful to people with diverse abilities as well (Mace et al., 1991; Rose & Gravel, 2012). For example, while ramps and automatic doors offer access to individuals in wheelchairs or with physical disabilities, they are also helpful to parents with strollers or with small children in tow, elderly pedestrians, or individuals carrying bags or pulling luggage. Similarly, closed captioning, another example of universal design in practice, makes television accessible to those with impaired hearing, but many also take advantage of this feature when watching television at the gym or in a noisy public place. Universal design seeks to identify and reduce barriers for everyone, rather than making customized adjustments for individuals.

Universal Design for Learning

UDL employs these concepts within the context of learning environments "to ensure that the means for learning, and their results, are accessible to all students" (Rose & Gravel, 2012). Defined by the Higher Education Opportunity Act of 2008, the term *universal design for learning* means:

a scientifically valid framework for guiding educational practice that—(A) provides flexibility in the ways information is presented, in the ways students respond or demonstrate knowledge and skills, and in the ways students are engaged; and (B) reduces barriers in instruction, provides appropriate accommodations, supports, and challenges, and maintains high achievement expectations for all students, including students with disabilities and students who are limited English proficient (20 U.S.C.§1003(24)).

Acknowledging individual variability, UDL provides a flexible framework of targeted goals, methods, materials, and assessments. Brain research reveals that the human brain is highly differentiated and specialized (National Center on UDL, 2012b; Rose & Gravel, 2012), debunking the myth of the "average learner." UDL looks at the ways individuals' brains perceive and understand information (recognition networks), communicate or organize information (strategic networks), and engage with information (affective networks). These primary brain networks become the basis not only for understanding learning but also for designing curriculum and learning environments (National Center on UDL, 2012b).

Inflexible curricula and one-size-fits-all methods raise unintentional barriers to learning for students. The UDL framework encourages flexible, customizable designs, which allow learners to master both academic content and the learning process (National Center on UDL, 2012b). Rather than retrofitting lesson plans that leave some learners behind, universally designed lessons strive to meet the needs of all learners by planning ahead for individuals' needs (Casper & Leuichovius, 2005; Rose & Gravel, 2012). When UDL principles serve as the foundation for educational practice, classrooms can become positive centers for inclusion and opportunity.

Universal Design for Transition

In addition to providing access to academic content, UDL has profound implications for the way that educators help students meet transition goals. UDT applies the principles of UDL to the transition of students from school to adult life (e.g., college, work, independent living) by including the key elements of multiple life domains, multiple means of assessment, student self-determination, and multiple resources and perspectives (Thoma et al., 2009). UDT's student-centered approach creates "an opportunity to develop a self-determined youth who is an expert in his/her own transition journey" (Smith & Karger, 2012, p. 36). Furthermore, UDT offers opportunities for students to express, explore, and demonstrate preferences, needs, strengths, capabilities, and goals (Smith,

Leconte, & Vitelle, 2012). By connecting transition planning and instruction to academic content, UDT can be incorporated successfully in secondary school programs as part of an integrated, barrier-free approach to preparing students for various aspects of life beyond school. Scott et al. (2011) examined the use of UDT and found that students with disabilities showed increased academic achievement and interest in a secondary exceptional education classroom. Students in the study reported greater engagement when a UDL/UDT approach to instruction was used in place of a more traditional instructional method. For example, a female student with an intellectual disability reported minimal engagement and had minimal academic achievement when a more traditional direct instructional approach was used in the classroom. When a UDT approach was introduced the student's engagement and academic performance increased, and she reported seeing a real-world connection between the lesson and her everyday life (Scott et al., 2011). The components of UDT are explained below, along with research findings to guide their implementation.

UDT and Multiple Life Domains

Based on the UDT understanding of transition, services and planning for students with disabilities extend to multiple life domains. As Thoma et al. (2009) asserted, this is a change from the previous focus of transition, which centered on preparing students with disabilities for the shift from school to work (Will, 1983). Research has shown that most current programs of study for students with disabilities do not always have both academic and transition types of goals (Thoma et al., 2009). Annual goals for students with significant disabilities are tied more directly to transition planning, while students with less intense support needs (i.e., those with high incidence disabilities such as learning disabilities, emotional disturbance, and/or communication disorders) are more likely to have annual goals focused on academic achievement. The requirements of the No Child Left Behind Act of 2001 and the Individuals With Disabilities Education Act of 2004 recognize that all students are best prepared for adult lives when they have a solid academic foundation and exit high school with an understanding of and plan for their lives in multiple domains. A UDT approach takes into account other factors of adult life such as transportation, community living and activity, leisure and recreation, and postsecondary education. Therefore, it is important that innovative curricula be designed to facilitate access to general education and include multiple-outcome measures and learning supports, combining both transition and academic standards (Kochhar-Bryant & Bassett, 2002).

50   K. BEST, L. A. SCOTT, and C. A. THOMA

Preparing students for successful transition from school to work, UDT incorporates information from varied assessments and perspectives, creating opportunities for students to explore and experience career options, set goals, and consider the use of technology in the workplace as well as the classroom. Research demonstrates that the transition to employment is more likely to occur when students have had employment experiences during high school. Such experiences can include paid employment as well as job shadowing, volunteer work experiences, and work-study programs (Fabian, 2007; Landmark, Ju, & Zhang, 2010; Test, Mazzotti, et al., 2009).

Transition services also need to prepare students for the demands of postsecondary educational settings. The number of students with learning disabilities (DeDeppo, 2009; Troiano et al., 2010) and intellectual disabilities (Kleinert, Jones, Sheppard-Jones, Harp, & Harrison, 2012; Martinez & Queener, 2010) attending college has increased steadily over recent years (DeDeppo, 2009; Troiano, Liefield, & Trachtenberg, 2010). A UDT approach to college planning involves the student in the decision-making process, stressing self-knowledge and self-advocacy. Furthermore, by incorporating multiple perspectives and resources, UDT provides opportunities for students to practice these skills beyond the classroom. Thoma et al. (2009) offered a list of ways for teachers to support students in the transition to postsecondary education:

- Arrange for students to meet with representatives from colleges and/or postsecondary institutions who are experts on topics ranging from academic supports to information about appropriate adult services for students with disabilities (including counselors from the campus office that serves students with disabilities and/or the academic advising center).
- Encourage students to research requirements for their desired school and be sure required documentation is in order.
- Prepare students for various kinds of assessments.
- Encourage students and their families to take college tours (pp. 130–131).

In addition to preparing students for employment and postsecondary education, UDT can be used to teach valuable skills for transition into community life. While these skills may seem more challenging to incorporate into the academic curriculum, Thoma et al. (2009) offer examples and UDT lesson plans that demonstrate functional math skills such as budgeting and bill paying, community resource mapping, and use of technology. Real-world examples and activities can prepare students for the various domains of life after high school, while reinforcing key academic skills. For example, authentic writing tasks may be used to teach grammar and vocabulary, while at the same time giving students skills for writing college essays, completing job applications, or writing business letters. Problem-solving skills for math and science may be applied to real-world situations such as gathering information to make a decision about employment or housing. In addition to teaching transition skills alongside academic content, evidence suggests that connecting learning to student interests and lives increases engagement and "helps the information stick" (Schwartz, 2013).

UDT and Self-Determination

Student self-determination, a concept reflecting the belief that all individuals have the right to direct their own lives (Bremer, Kachgal, & Schoeller, 2003), lies at the heart of quality transition planning. A position statement on self-determination (Field, Martin, Miller, Ward, & Wehmeyer, 1998) by the Council for Exceptional Children's Division on Career Development and Transition (n.d.) stated that a focus on self-determination is vital to help students "be more successful in education and transition to adult life" and "holds great potential to transform the way in which educational services are planned and delivered for students with and without disabilities" (p. 125). Research has shown the link between enhanced self-determination and positive outcomes in employment (Field & Hoffman, 1996; Field et al., 1998; Wehmeyer & Palmer, 2003; Wehmeyer & Schwartz, 1997), quality of adult life and community living (Wehmeyer & Palmer, 2003; Wehmeyer & Schwartz, 1997), and postsecondary education (Brinckerhoff, 1994; Field, Sarver, & Shaw, 2003; Greenbaum, Graham, & Scales, 1995). In a literature review conducted by the National Secondary Transition Technical Assistance Center, self-determination/self-advocacy was identified as 1 of 16 predictors empirically linked to postschool success for students with disabilities (Mazzotti, Test, & Mustian, 2012; Test, Mazzotti, et al., 2009).

Self-determination is a key component of intrinsic motivation, self-regulation, and personal responsibility, traits that are crucial for success in both education and society (Deci, Vallerand, Pelletier, & Ryan, 1991), and according to Halloran (1993) it is education's ultimate goal. Because UDL and UDT offer multiple means of representation, expression, and engagement, students play a more active role in creating their own learning experiences than they would in a more traditional program. UDL and UDT allow students to make and express choices based on their goals, learning styles, strengths and weaknesses, and preferences, fostering growth in understanding themselves and their own needs and predispositions.

According to the principles of UDT, transition and planning services are designed to give students multiple ways to be engaged in the process, beginning with setting goals and working in a "backward-planning process" (Thoma, Nathanson, Baker, & Tamura, 2002, p. 86) to identify the skills, resources, needs, or modifications necessary for students to achieve those goals. Benz, Lindstrom, and Yovanoff (2000) found positive correlations between completion of self-identified transition goals and competitive employment and enrollment in postsecondary education. There are many ways students can participate in this process, whether using a student-led or person-centered approach, depending on the student's "level of comfort and the availability of supports" (Thoma et al., 2002, p. 94). Self-determination involves the student's involvement in both the setting of goals and in the steps taken to achieve them (Landmark et al., 2010).

The self-determined learning model of instruction (Wehmeyer, Sands, Knowlton, & Kozleski, 2000) provides a framework to foster self-determination through a problem-solving approach. The SDLMI involves three phases of questions to help students set a learning goal, construct a learning plan, and adjust behaviors (Wehmeyer & Palmer, 2000). The self-determined learning model of instruction is an effective organizational tool that facilitates students' roles as "the causal agent in their transition planning" (Thoma et al., 2002, p. 36).

UDT and Multiple Means of Assessment

UDT incorporates a range of assessments, both formal and informal, to provide "a more accurate picture of a student's current functioning and support needs across multiple academic and transition domains" (Thoma et al., 2002, p. 63). These may include informal interviews or questionnaires and/or formal, norm-referenced measures. Assessment results drive the transition planning process by identifying the preferences and abilities of students and the skills needed for success in various areas (Mazzotti et al., 2009; Sitlington & Clark, 2007; Sitlington & Payne, 2004; Thoma et al., 2009). Using a variety of assessments facilitates transition planning and instruction by laying a foundation for developing goals, measuring growth, and targeting specific needs (Lowenthal & Bassett, 2012; Mazzotti et al., 2009). Gathering data on student performance also allows transition teachers to evaluate and improve instruction for all students, not only those with specific transition requirements (Batsche, Castillo, Dixon, & Ford, 2008; Test, Eddy, Neale, & Wood, 2004).

It is important that assessment measures are ongoing throughout the transition process so that changes in a student's preferences and skills are taken into account (National Secondary Transition Technical Assistance Center, 2007). Transition assessment is a key part of instruction planning (Lowenthal & Bassett, 2012; Test, Aspel, & Everson, 2006; Thoma et al., 2009), and a multitiered system provides opportunities to monitor instruction and progress, make adjustments, and focus interventions on a student's transition needs (Duffy, 2007; Lowenthal & Bassett, 2012).

UDT and Multiple Resources and Perspectives

UDT also integrates multiple resources and perspectives to inform goals and planning. Research identifies collaboration between schools and the community as a key element of effective secondary special education and transition services (Kohler, 1993; Stowitschek, Lovitt, & Rodriguez, 2001; Wehman, 1990). Collaboration allows for shared responsibility and pooled resources, which is ultimately more effective and beneficial (Thoma, Boyd, & Austin, 2013). This is more than just interagency collaboration; it requires identifying and including "the people who are most likely to contribute necessary information that would not otherwise be shared" (Thoma et al., 2009, p. 99). This might include the required participants for a student's transition Individualized Education Program planning process but could also expand to involve others who may also know the student, or those who have expertise in a specific career area who might not be typically part of the school-based planning process.

Collaborative partners are not limited to school personnel. Parents and other family members may play significant roles in coordinating and implementing community-based instruction (Tekin-Iftar, 2008), teaching self-determination (Rowe & Test, 2010), and process training (Crites & Dunn, 2004). Research has indicated a positive correlation between parent involvement in the transition process and improved postsecondary outcomes for students with disabilities (Fourqurean, Meisgeier, Swank, & Williams, 1991; Kraemer, McIntyre, & Blacher, 2003; Reiter & Palnizky, 1996; Rowe & Test, 2010; Schalock, Holl, Elliott, & Ross, 1992; Test, Mazzotti et al., 2009). Furthermore, the involvement of families and students in transition is a key element of self-determination, and it is crucial for goals and outcomes to reflect student and family preferences rather than just those of school personnel (Michaels & Ferrara, 2005; Wehman, Moon, Everson, Wood, & Barcus, 1988).

In addition to school and family resources, mentors may offer additional information and guidance for students with disabilities. Powers, Sowers, and Stevens (1995) suggested that contact with accomplished role models with disabilities may encourage successful educational and vocational obtainment. Mentors from outside the school community help students with disabilities explore academic and occupational opportunities and make more informed choices based on career requirements and availability (Thoma et al., 2009). These relationships may also facilitate the process of securing an internship or job (Daughtry, Gibson, & Abels, 2009). Mentoring has been associated with a variety of advantages for youth with disabilities, including better attitudes toward school, decreased likelihood of initiating drug or alcohol use, and improved academic performance (Daughtry et al., 2009), as well as improved relationships and social skills, and the development of career awareness (Campbell-Whatley, 2001; Rhodes, Grossman, & Resch, 2000; Sword & Hill, 2002).

Mentors play a valuable role on the transition team, but they are not limited to individuals in the community. Technology offers opportunities to connect students to mentors through e-mentoring, thus expanding the possibilities. Thoma et al. (2009) offered an overview of e-mentoring through programs such as EnvisionIT, and noted that these relationships can be an important component of UDT. In a systematic review of transition interventions and outcomes, Cobb and Alwell (2009) documented the key role of multiple resources and perspectives: "Many of the studies in our review highlight the need for flexibility in creating and providing individualized supports to youth with disabilities, rather than fitting them into existing service continuum options" (p. 79). A UDT approach embraces flexibility and multiple perspectives as information resources and guides.

Community transition teams, a model for creating connections and collaboration between education and adult services (Blalock & Benz, 1999), emerged during the 1990s. Research has indicated that interagency collaboration can foster positive transition experiences and post-school outcomes (Carter et al., 2009; Noonan, Morningstar, & Gaumer Erikson, 2008; Test, Mazzotti, et al., 2009). In a study examining the effectiveness of this model, Noonan, Gaumer Erickson, and Morningstar (2012) measured specific collaborative behaviors using a pre-post survey and found that transition collaboration skills improved as an outcome of community transition team development and training. This collaboration included coordinated transition services, shared vision in transition, improved productivity in transition meetings, and clarity of coworkers' jobs related to transition.

METHOD

Purpose of the Study

The Individuals With Disabilities Education Act of 2004 makes it clear that transition related support and services are required to ensure students with disabilities receive adequate preparation for their adult lives. The purpose of this study was to investigate the use of UDT themes in transition preparation for students with disabilities. The authors believe that UDT seeks to bridge the gap between academic and transition planning and is vital for stakeholders as they prepare instructional and transition plans to improve outcomes for students with and without disabilities. But do other teachers follow the concept of UDT by linking academic and transition goals? If so, are all of the UDT themes (e.g., life domains, assessments, self-determination, resources and perspectives) being addressed? And if so, what is working for teachers? What challenges do teachers face? The authors developed a descriptive survey study targeted to answer these questions about the use of UDT themes in transition planning and practice. The authors believe that obtaining this knowledge from stakeholders will be helpful in guiding transition practice and policy for the future.

Instrumentation

A survey was developed by the authors based on a review of literature about evidence-based practices for transition planning (Test, Fowler et al., 2009) and components of UDT (Thoma, Bartholomew, & Scott, 2009). The survey contained demographics, such as position, state in which the respondent was employed, academic content and disability category taught, and strengths and weaknesses around their ability to address students' transition needs. The components investigated in the survey and identified for analyses were assembled based on the UDT themes to include: linking academic and transition goals, multiple life domains, multiple means of assessment, self-determination, and multiple resources/perspective. The survey was presented to university faculty and preservice and in-service teachers in one of the authors' graduate level class for feedback ($n = 20$). The authors made revisions and eliminated any questions where negative feedback was provided. The final survey contained a total of 32 questions, whereas 14 of the 32 questions were used for this study. The 14 questions consisted of 12 quantitative (Likert-type) and 2 open-ended qualitative questions that were used to gather details on respondents' use of the UDT themes. The additional questions were not meaningful for the purpose of this study. Rating values for each survey question varied on a scale from 1 to 5, and lower scores indicated that respondents either "never" addressed the theme or found it "very difficult" to address the theme. Higher scores by the respondents indicated that the theme was addressed "frequently" or was "very easy" to address.

Participants

The survey was distributed using a snowball sampling method (Trochim, 2000) where the authors sent an e-mail request to contacts in school districts across the United States. The authors' requested that participants forward the survey to other secondary general educators, special educators, and transition specialists. The survey was sent via e-mail during the third week in June, 2013, using Research Electronic Data Capture, the university online survey system. The authors also sent a follow-up/ reminder e-mail after approximately 2 weeks, and again after 6 weeks. The snowball method resulted in 140 responses of which 49 (30.7%) were completed and used for this study. The remaining 91 surveys were started by respondents but not fully completed and therefore not usable for the study. The low response rate may be due to timing, as teachers and other stakeholders are often not working during the summer months, which is when the survey was disseminated. This may also account for the number of surveys that were incomplete; many participants started the survey but did not complete the questions. In all, a slight majority of the respondents were special education teachers ($n = 25$), with transition specialist ($n = 23$) and general education teachers ($n = 1$) rounding out the total. A majority of respondents indicated that they worked with students identified as having a high incidence disability [e.g., autism ($n = 38$); emotional disturbance ($n = 38$); intellectual disability ($n = 42$); specific learning disability ($n = 37$); and speech and language impairment ($n = 31$)]. Respondents were able to select more than one disability category; therefore, some response categories do not total 49. There were also questions regarding the core academic topics taught by respondents. While respondents were able to choose more than one category, a majority of respondents indicated that they held teaching responsibilities in math ($n = 18$), science ($n = 12$), English ($n = 21$), social studies ($n = 10$), and other academic subjects ($n = 33$) that were not identified. As a final demographic indicator, respondents assessed their ability to teach transition goals. A majority of respondents ($n = 18$) reported that they found teaching transition goals "somewhat difficult," ($n = 12$) indicated that it was "neither difficulty nor easy," ($n = 11$) "somewhat easy," ($n = 7$) "very easy," and ($n = 3$) found teaching transition goals "very difficult."

Data Analysis

Overarching components were formed based on the instrument and format of the survey. Specifically, the overarching components were aligned with the UDT themes. Descriptive statistics were calculated for each item in SPSS, and the raw scores of survey respondents are reported. Respondents had the option of selecting one or multiple choices within survey categories; therefore, in some instances totals will equal or be less than $n = 49$. The quantitative results were calculated and reported alongside the qualitative comments that were made by respondents. The comments respondents made on the two open ended questions were examined using recognized qualitative analysis techniques whereby data is broken down for distinct trends and patterns and reorganized into theme (Creswell, 2009). While the quantitative data produced some useful feedback about the use of the UDT themes, the qualitative data also generated some valuable information.

RESULTS

Linking Academic and Transition Goals

Respondents were asked to describe the message that they receive from their respective states, school districts, school administration, and colleagues with regards to linking academic and transition goals. When data was analyzed from this theme, answers were varied. Nevertheless, the majority of respondents indicated that the state ($n = 33$) and school district ($n = 23$) had an underlying focus on both academic and transition related goals. The results are presented in Table 3.1.

Despite the message from states and districts that the focus should be on both transition and academic instruction, several respondents indicated a lack of support and resources at the state and district level. Also noteworthy in the responses to this question is difference in focus at the school level compared to the district and state levels. The focus on "one area exclusively" is greater at the school level—administrators and colleagues—than at the district and state level.

Two follow up questions were asked in the survey, which highlighted respondents' ideas on what is working well and what challenges they face with linking academic and transition goals. Among the transition

Table 3.1.   Linking Academic and Transition Goals

Question:	Focus on One Area Exclusively (N)	Primarily Focus on One Area With Some Discussion (N)	No Focus on Either (N)	Instructing us to Focus on Both but Not Offering Real Support (N)	Focus on Both Areas and Provides Resources and Training (N)
How would you describe the message/support you receive about linking transition and academic instruction from your:					
1. State's depart. of education	20	9	5	20	13
2. District office	2	12	7	13	10
3. School admin	7	9	14	10	9
4. Colleagues (other teachers in your school)	7	15	12	9	6

Note: Numbers do not add up to total *n* because respondents were able to be in more than one category.

strengths listed, identifying goals and collaboration were the two most frequently noted. Several teachers listed "helping students set goals" as a strength, as well as "knowing students well," specifically their strengths, interests, and needs. Collaboration was expressed in terms such as "connecting students and families with adult service agencies," "bringing together teams including outside agencies," and "networking with a lot of other professionals in helping the student reach their goals." Several respondents also noted that professional development in transition was a "strength" in addressing their students' transition needs. One teacher wrote, "I've been taking masters classes that give me supports and resources for transition. I've been developing a transition toolkit, a live-binder with transition resources, and curriculum for transition." Another respondent wrote, "I have had the opportunity to participate in a college program which focused on transition. It gave me some great ideas for curriculum development," and others listed transition conferences and workshops as valuable sources of information.

Overall, respondents described challenges with having adequate time to coordinate the activities involved in linking academic and transition related goals. One participant's answer to the question "What do you find to be the most challenging about meeting both the academic and transition goals of your students?" was simply "Time—not enough hours in the day!!!!" Another teacher said that after funding, "the next most pressing issue is the time to complete the transition process. We have found ways to bring it into instruction of lessons, but finding time for assessments, either formal or informal, is a major problem as the rigor of classrooms has limited how often if ever we can pull a student from class of any kind. Even their elective courses now have state assessments tied to them, which could affect a teacher's employment, so they complain if we try to schedule testing during school hours." Respondents also described not having enough adequate resources (e.g., money, transportation, and supports within local communities) to create real-world experiences for students that would connect back to the academics. One teacher noted, "We live in a low income rural community, and it can be difficult to find businesses that are willing to work with the students. We have a very limited variety of businesses in our area." Another said, "With severe budget cuts it gets harder and harder at all levels to expose students to what they need. College trips to meet disability resource counselors have been all but eliminated unless parents take them, community-based instruction has been reduced to once a quarter, and community vocational instruction is hanging on by a thread." Finally, respondents described a lack of valid and reliable assessments that can be used for linking academics and transition related content. Teachers noted difficulty allotting "the time to do different transitional assessments," "finding more assessments and community resources," and "provid[ing] peer comparison as well as discrepancy when normed data is not readily available."

Multiple Life Domains

The next set of questions addressed the respondents' knowledge and use of the UDT theme, *multiple life domains*. In identifying the life domains that are regularly addressed for students, 100% of the respondents ($n = 49$) indicated that employment was the domain commonly addressed, followed by social skills ($n = 45$), self-determination ($n = 43$), and community living ($n = 39$). The results of this analysis are provided in Table 3.2.

The last question within this theme that respondents were asked to answer related to the difficulty in addressing each of the life domains. Respondents indicated that they had either a very difficult or somewhat difficult time with addressing transportation and mobility ($n = 20$), community integration ($n = 18$), community living ($n = 17$), recreation and leisure ($n = 15$) and social skills ($n = 15$). A significant number of respondents agreed that employment ($n = 32$), postsecondary education ($n = 32$), and self-determination ($n = 30$) were somewhat or very easy to address. The full results of this data have been included in Table 3.2.

Table 3.2.   Knowledge and Use of Multiple Transition Domains

Question:	Never (N)	Seldom (N)	Sometimes or Frequent (N)
How often do you address each of the following transition domains?			
1. Employment	0	0	49
2. Postsecondary education	1	10	38
3. Self-determination	2	4	43
4. Community integration	3	10	35
5. Community living	3	7	39
6. Recreation/leisure	3	13	33
7. Social skills	0	4	45
8. Transportation/mobility	4	12	33

Question:	Very Difficult or Somewhat Difficult	Neither Difficult nor Easy	Somewhat Easy or Very Easy
How difficult do you find it to address each of the following domains?			
1. Employment	8	9	32
2. Postsecondary education	11	6	32
3. Self-determination	12	7	30
4. Community integration	18	9	22
5. Community living	17	16	16
6. Recreation/leisure	15	8	26
7. Social skills	15	4	20
8. Transportation/mobility	20	11	18

Multiple Means of Assessments

In relation to the theme of *multiple means of assessment*, the respondents were asked to identify the forms of assessments they regularly addressed for students. Respondents indicated that informal assessments (e.g., surveys, checklists, observations, etc.) ($n = 43$), formal assessments (e.g., life skills measures) and curriculum based tests ($n = 36$) were most frequently used. While less than half of the respondents indicated performance based measures ($n = 21$) were used and formal self-determination assessments ($n = 11$) were used. Respondents were also asked the level of difficulty in addressing each form of self-determination assessment. Approximately a fifth of respondents indicated having either a very difficult time or somewhat of a difficult time with formal assessments ($n = 14$), curriculum based tests ($n = 9$), formal self-determination assessments ($n = 10$), and performance-based assessments ($n = 10$). Finally, respondents were asked how much the information collected from each assessment type informs transition goals. Respondents indicated that informal assess-

Table 3.3. Knowledge and Use of Multiple Means of Assessments

Question:	Very Difficult or Somewhat Difficult (N)	Neither Difficulty nor Easy (N)	Somewhat Easy or Very Easy (N)
How difficult do you find it to address each form of assessment?			
1. Formal assessments (life skills measures such as Brigance Life Skills Inventory, IQ tests, achievement tests)	14	13	21
2. Curriculum-based tests (both teacher-generated and state-generated/published curriculum tests)	9	13	22
3. Informal assessments (surveys and checklists, direct observation, interest inventories)	3	8	38
4. Formal self-determination assessments such as the Arc's Self-Determination Scale	10	13	18
5. Performance-based assessments (Portfolios and other holistic assessments of student abilities)	10	12	22

Question:	Not Applicable	Very Little or Somewhat	Strongly or Crucial
How much does the information collected from each of the following types of assessments inform your transition goals?			
1. Formal assessments (life skills measures such as Brigance Life Skills Inventory, IQ tests, achievement tests)	3	26	20
2. Curriculum-based tests (both teacher-generated and state-generated/published curriculum tests)	5	29	15
3. Informal assessments (surveys and checklists, direct observation, interest inventories)	1	10	38
4. Formal self-determination assessments such as the Arc's Self-Determination Scale	8	23	18
5. Performance-based assessments (portfolios and other holistic assessments of student abilities)	7	31	23

ments were either strongly informative or crucial in informing transition goals (*n* = 38); while less than half of the respondents indicated that this was the case for other forms of assessments. Table 3.3 provides a more

Table 3.4.   Knowledge and Use of Self-Determination

Question	Very Difficult or Somewhat Difficult (N)	Neither Difficulty nor Easy (N)	Somewhat Easy or Very Easy (N)
How difficult do you find it to address each form of self-determination?			
1. Choicemaker	7	0	5
2. Next S.T.E.P	7	0	4
3. Whose Future is it Anyway?	8	4	10
4. Steps	7	0	1
5. Self-determined learning model of instruction	6	1	6

comprehensive review of the data associated with multiple means of assessments.

Self-Determination

The next theme covered was the use and knowledge of *self-determination*. Respondents were asked to identify the types of curriculum and instructional strategies regularly used for self-determination. A majority of respondents indicated that they use curriculum and instructional strategies beyond the lists that was generated on the survey (n = 36). Lastly, when asked how difficult it is to address self-determination using the identified curriculum/instructional strategies, a majority of respondents indicated that this was not applicable since they used curriculum and strategies beyond what was indicated on the survey. Table 3.4 includes information about what curriculum/instructional strategies respondents were provided to choose from, as well as respondents' replies.

Multiple Resources and Perspectives

For the next theme, respondents were asked about their use and knowledge of having *multiple resources and perspectives* in transition planning and practice. Respondents indicated that meeting with students (n = 42), having a flexible schedule (n = 33), and having use of technology (n = 25) were resources used to solicit input or assure collaboration at Individualized Education Program meetings. Just under half of the respondents indicated that inviting an advocate or interpreter (n = 23) and meeting with the parent (n = 22) were resources used.

Table 3.5.   Knowledge and Use of Multiple Resources/Perspectives

Question	Very Difficult or Somewhat Difficult (N)	Neither Difficulty nor Easy (N)	Somewhat Easy or Very Easy (N)
How difficult do you find it to solicit input from others in addressing transition goals?			
1. General education teachers	22	8	15
2. Special education teachers	6	9	33
3. Guidance counselor	16	10	11
4. Transition coordinator	6	8	26
5. Adult service provider	26	9	9
6. Parent or guardian	7	17	24
7. Student	6	13	29
8. Administrator	15	16	13
9. Social worker	12	13	8
10. Vocational teacher/job coach	4	13	21

Question	Not Applicable	Very Little or Somewhat	Strongly or Crucial
How would you rate the importance of input of each of the following perspectives in the transition process?			
1. General education teachers	7	7	35
2. Special education teachers	0	3	45
3. Guidance counselor	9	10	29
4. Transition coordinator	7	2	40
5. Adult service provider	3	9	36
6. Parent or guardian	0	4	44
7. Student	0	2	47
8. Administrator	14	14	19
9. Social worker	16	11	21
10. Vocational teacher/job coach	4	4	41

When asked about input from others in addressing transition goals, about half indicated that they found it very difficult or somewhat difficult to solicit input from adult service providers ($n = 26$), general educators ($n = 22$), and guidance counselors ($n = 16$). Many respondents indicated that soliciting input from special education teachers ($n = 33$), transition coordinators ($n = 26$), parents or guardians ($n = 24$), and students ($n = 29$) was very or somewhat easy. Data on responses related to *multiple resources and perspectives* can be found in Table 3.5.

DISCUSSION

In reporting the results in the previous section, we detailed the UDT themes (e.g., life domains, assessments, self-determination, resources & perspectives) and sought to understand how teachers address the various components of implementing a UDT approach to instruction. In this section, we discuss what has been learned about teachers' implementation of UDT. As we indicated in our review, UDT may offer ways to enhance the approach to UDL by bridging the gap between academic and transition goals to meet the needs of diverse learners. What emerged from this descriptive study were teachers' use of UDT themes, including what is working for them and their challenges. In fact, almost half of the respondents indicated that they find it difficult (somewhat or very) to teach transition goals, evidence that training and resources may be needed to give teachers and transition specialists the tools they need. This is further supported by a perceived lack of support and resources at the state and district level, despite the message that the focus should be on both transition and academic instruction. Respondents' lists transition strengths such as individualized goal setting and collaborations, as well as challenges such as adequate time and resources.

Limitations

A survey was used to collect this information and therefore, the study has the typical limitations associated with this methodology (Visser, Krosnick, & Lavrakas, 2000). First, it only provides information about what these study participants believe they are doing; it does not determine how accurate those self-reports are, nor does it determine the quality of their practice. The accuracy of self-reported data is determined by how well the participants understand the questions, are able to reflect on what they are doing and how well it is working, and truthfully portray themselves (Carducci, 2009). The authors attempted to minimize this limitation to the study by conducting a pilot study of their survey and soliciting feedback from those participants about the wording used in questions and the survey directions to make it as clear as possible. Suggestions from that feedback were used to make some minor modifications before the survey was distributed through a national listserve.

A national sample of special education teachers, transition coordinators, and transition committee stakeholders was sought for this study. Despite a snow-ball sampling process, in which participants were asked to forward the survey link to others in the field, there was a small sample size. The small number of respondents coupled with the high percentage of respondents who did not complete the survey limits our ability to draw definitive conclusions from this study. Furthermore, the small sample size prohibited researchers from conducting psychometric analysis to determine the validity of the survey.

The list of potential respondents was obtained from the National Secondary Transition Technical Assistance Center and from contacts with states that had asked for the authors' help with improving their transition practices. Although National Secondary Transition Technical Assistance Center includes a diverse membership, it is possible that members of National Secondary Transition Technical Assistance Center may share common values, which would thus bias their responses. In future research, varied organizations should be contacted. Last, as mentioned earlier in the paper, the respondents were not asked to justify their ratings. To gain greater insight about their ratings it would have been useful to know why they thought a specific strategy or practice was important and why it deserved instructional attention. In addition, it would have been helpful to know if the challenges identified by respondents had to do with their own lack of knowledge or in the effectiveness of a specific strategy in addressing the needs of youth with disabilities.

IMPLICATIONS FOR FUTURE RESEARCH

Future research should first attempt to increase the participant pool, providing opportunities to collect information from a range of different transition and academic educational stakeholders including the youth themselves. The qualitative data collected in this study illuminated some of the challenges (time, resources, assessment, training) and strengths (professional development, goal setting, collaboration) of meeting both academic and transition goals.

Future qualitative investigations may address some of the following questions: What types of training do special educators and transition stakeholders find to be most effective? Do students learn academic content better when it is linked to real-world tasks they want to learn? Are youth with disabilities better prepared for their adult life when they have a solid academic preparation? And does using a UDT approach to teaching academic content improve transition outcomes for youth with and without disabilities?

The UDT approach has a relatively large number of core themes. Besides knowing whether transition stakeholders are implementing such an approach and whether it improves transition goal attainment, it will be also important for future research to determine what themes are having the desired results. Do they all need to be done in unison or is one or two most important?

Additional research about the training needs of transition personnel should also be done. Respondents noted challenges such as "educating employers and also administration "about the transition needs of students, cooperation between special education teachers and general education teachers, and "instructing teachers on how to do what I do when assessing [students with disabilities] for transition needs. To ensure optimal collaboration amongst stakeholders, transition training needs to extend beyond just transition specialists and special education teachers. Further research is needed in order to determine which personnel preparation practices have the best results, both in terms of the fidelity of implementation of these approaches and in practitioners' ability to self-reflect on their practices and seek additional supports when warranted. Lastly, future studies may determine whether training needs vary based on one's role within the transition planning process, or whether personnel preparation could be universal as well.

IMPLICATIONS FOR PRACTICE

Despite the limitations to this study, there are some conclusions we can draw from these findings. First, it is apparent that special educators and transition coordinators believe that it is important to address both academic and transition goals, and they perceive that they are required to do that by their school, district, and state administrators. They do not, however, feel that they are being given much direction about how to do that, and they find that they are struggling to accomplish it all. Nevertheless, there are a few aspects of transition planning that they perceive to be easier to address than others. For example, employment was the aspect of transition planning that participants identified as easy to address, and all respondents indicated that they addressed employment in the student's transition planning process.

Despite the fact that it can be difficult to teach academic content while still addressing transition goals, these findings provide hope for the future. Respondents indicated that they addressed a range of transition domains, even when they found it difficult to do so. For example, respondents were most likely to indicate that it was difficult to address the transportation domain of transition planning, yet 67% of respondents indicated that they did so. Teaching someone to use transportation can be difficult to do in an inclusive classroom setting, especially as the time necessary to learn to take a bus or drive a car can detract from time available to learn academic content. However, more than two thirds of the participants in this study reported that they found creative ways to do just that.

Creativity was the skill that helped Mr. Scott as he faced the challenges in his first classroom. It can also help special educators and transition coordinators develop strategies to overcome challenges they currently face in implementing a UDT approach. For example, in terms of using multiple means of assessment, respondents reported that informal transition assessments were more likely to yield useful information to inform transition goals, but they did not know of useful informal assessments that addressed all aspects of transition planning. The field needs to develop transition assessment tools that can be used for this purpose, and provide opportunities for sharing new assessment tools that teachers develop.

The UDT theme of multiple sources of information is the one that teachers and transition stakeholders reported to be least likely to use and most difficult to implement. However, in terms of an impact on delivering transition education in inclusive settings, an interdisciplinary team working together is critical to success. Not only does the general education teacher need to play a role, but the entire transition team needs to be able to work together and think collaboratively about ways to address students' transition goals and link them to academic content. It is helpful to solicit input from people outside the typical members of the transition team who can provide specific information about academic content needed to be successful in specific occupations and settings. And, of course, it is important to be sure to include students and parents in these planning activities in ways that are meaningful and supportive.

The role of the student in the transition planning process was reported to be very important by more than 90% of the participants in this study. The findings of this study also indicated that they found ways to increase student self-determination in the process by using one or more self-determination curriculum, assessment, or instructional method. Given the impact that self-determination can have on improved postschool outcomes such as employment, perceived quality of life, and postsecondary education, this is a very positive finding. However, most reported that they used a strategy other than one of the research-based curricula, and only 12.9% reported that they found the self-determined learning model of instruction to be easy for them to implement. This is particularly troubling since this is the one self-determination approach that has been shown to be flexible enough to be useful in inclusive educational settings (Wehmeyer, 2000).

There is still much to be learned about how to prepare students with disabilities for a successful transition from school to adult life within an inclusive secondary educational experience. The UDT model provides a theoretical framework for instructional planning and implementation that addresses academic content as well as functional goal attainment. There is evidence from a study conducted by Scott et al. (2011) that this approach can have a positive impact on student engagement and goal attainment. In addition, it is apparent from the findings of this study that many of the components of this approach are being used to guide the practice of special educators and transition coordinators, and despite the challenge of implementing this approach, creative practitioners like Mr. Scott are successfully linking academic instruction and transition practices.

REFERENCES

Batsche, G. M., Castillo, J. M., Dixon, D. N., & Forde, S. (2008). Best practices in designing, implementing, and evaluating quality interventions. In A. Thomas & J. Grimes (Eds.), *Best practices in school psychology V* (pp. 177-193). Bethesda, MD: National Association of School Psychologists.

Benz, M. R., Lindstrom, L., & Yovanoff, P. (2000). Improving graduation and employment outcomes of students with disabilities: Predictive factors and student perspectives. *Exceptional Children*, *66*, 509–529.

Blalock, G., & Benz, M. R. (1999). *Using community transition teams to improve transition services*. Austin, TX: PRO-ED.

Bremer, C., Kachgal, M., & Schoeller, K. (2003). Self-determination: Supporting successful transition (National Center on Secondary Education and Transition Research to Practice Brief). *Improving Secondary Education and Transition Services through Research*, *2*(1), 1–6.

Brinckerhoff, L. C. (1994). Developing effective self-advocacy skills in college-bound students with learning disabilities. *Intervention in School and Clinic*, *29*(4), 229–237.

Campbell-Whatley, G. (2001). Mentoring students with mild disabilities: The "nuts and bolts" of program development. *Intervention in School and Clinic*, *36*, 211–216.

Carducci, B. J. (2009). *The psychology of personality: Viewpoints, research, and applications*. Malden, MA: Wiley-Blackwell.

Carter, E. W., Trainor, A. A., Cakiroglu, O., Cole, O., Swedeen, B., Ditchman, N., & Owens, L. (2009). Exploring school-employer partnerships to expand career development and early work experiences for youth with disabilities. *Career Development for Exceptional Individuals*, *32*, 145-149.

Casper, B., & Leuichovius, D. (2005). *Universal design for learning and the transition to a more challenging academic curriculum: Making it in middle school and beyond* (NCSET Report). Retrieved from http://www.eric.ed.gov/ERICWebPortal/detail?accno=ED495873

Center for Applied Special Education Technology. (1998). What is universal design for learning? Retrieved July 31, 2013, from http://www.cast.org/research/udl/index.html.Individuals

Cobb, B., & Alwell, M. (2009). Transition planning/coordinating interventions for youth with disabilities: A systematic review. *Career Development for Exceptional Individuals*, *32* (2), 70–81.

Creswell, J. W. (2009). *Research design: Qualitative, quantitative, and mixed methods approaches* (3rd ed.). Los Angeles, CA: SAGE.

Crites, S., & Dunn, C. (2004). Teaching social problem solving to individuals with mental retardation. *Education and Training in Developmental Disabilities, 39*(4), 301–310.

Daughtry, D., Gibson, J., & Abels, A. (2009). Mentoring students and professionals with disabilities. *Professional Psychology: Research and Practice, 40*(2), 201–205. doi:10.1037/a0012400

Deci, E. L., Vallerand, R. J., Pelletier, L. G., & Ryan, R. M. (1991). Motivation and education: The self-determination perspective. *Educational Psychologist, 26*(3&4), 325–346.

DeDeppo, L. M. W. (2009). Integration factors related to the academic success and intent to persist of college students with learning disabilities. *Learning Disabilities Research & Practice, 24*(3), 122–131.

Division on Career Development and Transition (n.d.). *Age appropriate transition assessment: Fact sheet.* Retrieved from http://www.dcdt.org/wp-content/uploads/2011/09/DCDT_Fact_Sheet_age_appropriate_Transition_Assessment.pdf

Duffy, H. (2007, August). *Meeting the needs of significantly struggling learners in high school: A look at approaches to tiered intervention.* Washington, DC: National High School Center at the American Institutes for Research. Retrieved from http://www.betterhighschools.org/pubs/usergd_stlr.asp

Fabian, E. (2007). Urban youth with disabilities: Factors affecting transition employment. *Rehabilitation Counseling Bulletin, 50*(3), 130–138.

Field, S., & Hoffman, A. (1996). Increasing the ability of educators to support youth self-determination. In L. E. Powers, G. H. S. Singer, & J. Sowers (Eds.), *Promoting self competence in children and youth with disabilities: On the road to autonomy* (pp. 171–187). Baltimore, MD: Brookes.

Field, S., Martin, J., Miller, R., Ward, M., & Wehmeyer, M. (1998). Self-determination in career and transition programming: A position statement of the Council for Exceptional Children. *Career Development for Exceptional Individuals, 21*, 113–128.

Field, S., Sarver, M. D., & Shaw, S. F. (2003). Self-determination: A key to success in postsecondary education for students with learning disabilities. *Remedial and Special Education, 24*(1), 339–349.

Fourqurean, J. M., Meisgeier, C., Swank, P. R., & Williams, R. E. (1991). Correlates of postsecondary employment outcomes for young adults with learning disabilities. *Journal of Learning Disabilities, 24*, 400–405.

Greenbaum, B., Graham, S., & Scales, W. (1995). Adults with learning disabilities: Educational and social experiences during college. *Exceptional Children, 61*, 460–471.

Halloran, W. D. (1993). Transition services requirement: Issues, implications, challenge. In R. C. Eaves & P. J. McLaughlin (Eds.), *Recent advances in special education and rehabilitation* (pp. 210-224). Boston, MA: Andover Medical.

The Higher Education Opportunity Act. (2008). PL 110-315, 122 § 3078.

Individuals With Disabilities Education Act (IDEA) of 2004, PL 108-446, 20 U.S.C. § 1400 *et seq.*

Kleinert, H. L., Jones, M. M., Sheppard-Jones, K., Harp, B., & Harrison, E. M. (2012). Students with intellectual disabilities going to college? Absolutely! *Teaching Exceptional Children, 44*(5), 26–35.

Kochhar-Bryant, C. A., & Bassett, D. S. (2002). *Aligning transition and standards-based education: Issues and strategies.* Arlington, VA: Council for Exceptional Children.

Kohler, P. (1993). Best practices in transition: Substantiated or implied? *Career Development for Exceptional Individuals, 16*, 107–121.

Kraemer, B. R., Mcntyre, L. L., & Blacher, J. (2003). Quality of life for young adults with mental retardation during transition. *Mental Retardation, 41*, 250–262.

Landmark, L., Ju, S., & Zhang, D. (2010). Substantiated best practices in transition: Fifteen plus years later. *Career Development for Exceptional Individuals, 33*(3), 165–176.

Lowenthal, A., & Bassett, D. (2012). Transition assessment: Using gap analysis to enhance effective transition planning. *Intervention in School and Clinic, 48*(1), 30–37.

Mace, R., Hardie, G., & Place, J. (1991). Accessible environments: Toward universal design. In W. E. Preiser, J. C. Vischer, & E. T. White (Eds.), *Design intervention: Toward a more humane architecture* (pp. 155–176). New York, NY: Van Nostrand Reinhold.

Martinez, D. C., & Queener, J. (2010). Postsecondary education for students with intellectual disabilities. Retrieved from http://www.heath.gwu.edu/publications/postsecondary-education-for-students-with-intellectual-disabilities/

Mazzotti, V., Rowe, D., Kelley, K. R., Test, D. W., Fowler, C., Kohler, P., & Kortering, L. (2009). Linking transition assessment and postsecondary goals: Key elements in the secondary transition planning process. *Teaching Exceptional Children, 42*(2), 44–51.

Mazzotti, V., Test, D., & Mustian, A. (2012). Secondary transition evidence-based practices and predictors: Implications for policymakers. *Journal of Disability Policy Studies.* doi:1044207312460888

Michaels, C., & Ferrara, D. (2005). Promoting post-school success for all: The role of collaboration in person-centered transition planning. *Journal of Educational and Psychological Consultation, 16*(4), 287–313.

National Center on UDL. (2012a). *UDL guidelines, Version 2.0.* Retrieved from http://www.udlcenter.org/aboutudl/udlguidelines

National Center on UDL. (2012b). *What is UDL?* Retrieved from http://www.udlcenter.org/aboutudl/whatisudl

National Secondary Transition Technical Assistance Center. (2007). *Age appropriate transition assessment toolkit* (3rd ed.). Charlotte, NC: Author.

Noonan, P., Gaumer Erickson, A., & Morningstar, M. E. (2012). Effects of community transition teams on interagency collaboration for school and adult agency staff. *Career Development and Transition for Exceptional Individuals, 36*(2), 96–104.

Noonan, P., Morningstar, M. E., & Gaumer Erickson, A. (2008). Improving interagency collaboration: Effective strategies used by high-performing local districts and communities. *Career Development and Transition for Exceptional Individuals, 31*, 132–143.

Powers, L. E., Sowers, J., & Stevens, T. (1995). An exploratory, randomized study of the impact of mentoring on the self-efficacy and community-based knowledge of adolescents with severe physical challenges. *Journal of Rehabilitation, 61*, 33–41.

Reiter, S., & Palnizky, A. (1996). Transition from school to work of parents with developmental disabilities and mental retardation: An Israeli perspective. *International Journal of Rehabilitation Research, 19*, 27–38.

Rhodes, J. E., Grossman, J. B., & Resch, N. L. (2000). Agents of change: Pathways through which mentoring relationships influence adolescents' academic adjustment. *Child Development, 71*, 1662–1671.

Rose, D., & Gravel, J. (2012). *Curricular opportunities in the digital age.* Retrieved from http://www.studentsatthecenter.org/papers/curricular-opportunities-digital-age

Rose, D. H., & Meyer, A. (2002). *Teaching every student in the digital age: Universal design for learning.* Alexandria, VA: Association for Supervision and Curriculum Development.

Rowe, D. A., & Test, D. W. (2010). The effects of computer-based instruction on the transition planning process knowledge of parents of students with disabilities. *Research and Practice for Persons with Severe Disabilities, 35*(3–4), 1–14.

Schalock, R. L., Holl, C., Elliott, B., & Ross, I. (1992). A longitudinal follow-up of graduates from a rural special education program. *Learning Disability Quarterly, 15*, 29–38.

Schwartz, K. (2013, December 9). In teaching algebra, the not-so-secret way to students' hearts (web log). Retrieved from http://blogs.kqed.org/mindshift/author/katrinaschwartz/

Scott, L., Saddler, S., Thoma, C., Bartholomew, C., Adler, N., & Tamura, R. (2011). Universal design for transition: A single subject research study on the impact of UDT on student achievement, engagement and interest. *Journal on Educational Psychology, 4*(4), 21–31

Sitlington, P., & Clark, G. (2007). The transition assessment process and IDEIA 2004. *Assessment for Effective Intervention, 32*, 133–142.

Sitlington, P., & Payne, E. (2004). Information needed by postsecondary education. Can we provide it as part of the transition assessment process? *Learning Disabilities: A Contemporary Journal, 2*(2), 1–14.

Smith, F. G., & Karger, J. (2012, October). *Universal design for learning (UDL) and the transition journey: Better transition planning by design.* Paper presented at Arizona's Twelfth Annual Transition Conference, Scottsdale, AZ.

Smith, F. G., Leconte, P., & Vitelle, E. (2012). The VECAP position paper on universal design for learning for career assessment and vocational evaluation. *Vocational Evaluation and Career Assessment Journal, 8*(1), 13–26.

Stowitschek, J. J., Lovitt, T. C., & Rodriguez, J. A. (2001). Patterns of collaboration in secondary education for youth with special needs: Profiles of three high schools. *Urban Education, 36*, 93–128.

Sword, H., & Hill, K. (2002, December). *Creating mentoring opportunities for youth with disabilities: Issues and suggested strategies.* Retrieved from http://www.ncset.org/publications/viewdesc.asp?id=704

Tekin-Iftar, E. (2008). Parent-delivered community-based instruction with simultaneous prompting for teaching community skills to children with developmental disabilities. *Education and Training in Developmental Disabilities, 43*(2), 249–265.

Test, D., Aspel, N. P., & Everson, J. M. (2006). *Transition methods for youth with disabilities.* Upper Saddle River, NJ: Pearson Merrill Prentice Hall.

Test, D., Eddy, S., Neale, M., & Wood, W. (2004). A survey of the types of data collected by transition teachers. *Career Development for Exceptional Individuals, 27*(1), 87–100.

Test, D., Fowler, C. H., Richter, S. M., White, J., Mazzotti, V., Walker, A. R., … Kortering, L. (2009). Evidence-based practices in secondary transition. *Career Development for Exceptional Individuals, 32,* 115–128.

Test, D., Mazzotti, V., Mustian, A., Fowler, C., Kortering, L., & Kohler, P. H. (2009). Evidence-based secondary transition predictors for improving post-school outcomes for students with disabilities. *Career Development for Exceptional Individuals, 32,* 160–181.

Thoma, C. A., Bartholomew, C. C., & Scott, L. A. (2009) *Universal design for transition: A roadmap for planning and instruction.* Baltimore, MD: Paul H. Brookes.

Thoma, C. A., Boyd, K., & Austin, K. (2013). Assessment and teaching for transition. In P. Wehman (Ed.), *Life beyond the classroom* (5th ed., pp. 235–260). Baltimore, MD: Brookes.

Thoma, C. A., Nathanson, R., Baker, S. R., & Tamura, R. (2002). Self-determination. *Remedial & Special Education, 23*(4), 242.

Troiano, P. F., Liefield, J. A., & Trachtenberg, J. V. (2010). Academic support and college success for postsecondary students with learning disabilities. *Journal of College Reading and Learning, 40*(2), 35–44.

Trochim, W. (2000). *The research methods knowledge base* (2nd ed.). Cincinnati, OH: Atomic Dog.

Visser, P. S., Krosnick, J. A., & Lavrakas, P. J. (2000). Survey research. In H. T. Reis & C. M. Judd (Ed.), *Handbook of research methods in social psychology* (pp. 223–252). New York, NY: Cambridge University Press.

Wehman, P. (1990). School to work: Elements of successful programs. *Teaching Exceptional Children, 23,* 40–43.

Wehman, P., Moon, M. S., Everson, J. M., Wood, W., & Barcus, J. M. (1988). *Transition from school to work.* Baltimore, MD: Paul H. Brookes.

Wehmeyer, M. L. (2000). Assessment of self determination: Negotiating the mine field. *Focus on Autism and Other Developmental Disabilities, 15,* 157–158.

Wehmeyer, M. L., & Palmer, S. B. (2000). Promoting causal agency: The self-determined learning model of instruction. *Exceptional Children, 66*(4), 439.

Wehmeyer, M. L., & Palmer, S. B. (2003). Adult outcomes for students with cognitive disabilities three years after high school: The impact of self-determination. *Education and Training in Developmental Disabilities, 38,* 131–144.

Wehmeyer, M. L., Sands, D. J., Knowlton, H. E., & Kozleski, E. B. (2002). *Teaching students with mental retardation: Providing access to the general curriculum.* Baltimore, MD: Paul H. Brookes.

Wehmeyer, M. L., & Schwartz, M. (1997). Self-determination and positive adult outcomes: A follow-up study of youth with mental retardation or learning disabilities. *Exceptional Children, 63*, 245–255.

Will, M. (1983). *OSERS programming for the transition of youth with disabilities: Bridges from school to working life.* Washington, DC: Office of Special Education and Rehabilitative Services.

CHAPTER 4

ENHANCING THE POSTSCHOOL OUTCOMES OF STUDENTS WITH INTELLECTUAL DISABILITIES IN SINGAPORE

An Illustrative Example of Developing a Transition Program

Mee Choo Soh and Levan Lim

Transition planning provides the necessary supports and services while students are still at school to equip them with the relevant values, knowledge, and skills for their postschool lives, with particular emphasis to their readiness to secure, engage in, and maintain meaningful employment. Transition planning, however, has not been a formal and compulsory part of the special school experience for many students with disabilities in Singapore; and therefore, there exists the need to develop prototype transition programs that can serve as school-to-work pathways for students with disabilities as well as provide field-tested transition models for special schools in Singapore and elsewhere. This case study provides, through a retrospective account using an action learning and research framework, an illustrative

Inclusive Education for Students with Intellectual Disabilities, pp. 73–93
Copyright © 2015 by Information Age Publishing

example of developing a transition program at a special school in Singapore with key insights into the relevant processes and practices that contributed to its chronological development over a 3-year period. This illustrative case study example contributes toward the understanding of the development work involved in setting up transition programs, which is an area of study that is sorely lacking in the international research literature.

INTRODUCTION

For all students, including students with disabilities, the question of "what do I do after school?" inevitably arrives at the critical juncture of leaving or graduating from the uppermost level of schooling and entering postschool environments. This process of moving from school to postschool life is known as transition and its success in terms of students achieving quality of life postschool outcomes, such as securing employment, depends on planning efforts and steps to help students achieve such outcomes (Dietrich, Parker, & Salmela-Aro, 2012). Transition planning therefore refers to the planning efforts and steps taken to facilitate the movement from school to postschool life (Flexer, Simmons, Luft, & Baer, 2005).

Transition planning is especially crucial for students with disabilities as it provides the necessary opportunities, supports and services while students are still at school to equip them with the relevant values, knowledge and skills for their postschool lives, with particular attention to their readiness to secure, engage in and maintain meaningful employment. In Singapore, where the transition of students with disabilities, including those with intellectual disabilities, moving from school to postschool environments is not a formal and compulsory part of the special educational school experience. Thus, the potential of these students to lead productive and fulfilling lives after leaving school can be heavily compromised through inadequate pathways to support their transition into employment opportunities and community inclusion.

This illustrative case study example describes, through a retrospective account using an action research framework, the key processes and practices that contributed to the chronological development of a transition program at a special school in Singapore over a 3-year period across three cyclical phases from its beginnings when there was no evidence of any structure nor formal programs to facilitate students' transition into postschool life and when transition planning was done on an ad-hoc basis by individual teachers and/or school professionals, to when the program was developed to the extent that it became central to facilitating students to transition from school to work. This framework consisted of action learning cycles over this period where the key processes and practices involved in the planning, development, implementation and evaluation of the transition program are described in retrospect. The significance and contribution of this study lies in its descriptive evolution of and key insights into significant developments of a prototype field-tested transition program for students with mild intellectual disabilities in Singapore, which is an area of study that is sorely lacking in the international research literature on the development work of transition programs.

Background of the Study

The development of the transition program at a special school is nested within an associationwide curriculum reform chaired by the second author at an organization operating a few special schools for students with mild intellectual disabilities in Singapore. This organization, the Association for Persons with Special Needs (APSN), is one of the largest voluntary welfare organizations in Singapore serving the needs of children, adolescents and young adults with mild intellectual disabilities. The APSN is supported by the National Council of Social Service, the Ministry of Education, and the Ministry of Social and Family Development (formerly known as the Ministry of Community Development, Youth and Sports).

The APSN exists with the mission to equip persons with mild intellectual disabilities through best practices in education, training and support services, for open employment and life-long learning in partnership with stakeholders and the community. It envisions itself to be the premier organization that develops individuals with mild intellectual disabilities to their fullest potential so that they can lead dignified, fulfilling and independent lives as integral members of society.

The APSN currently runs four special schools—Chaoyang School, Katong School, Tanglin School and Delta Senior School, as well as a center for young adults who are 18 years old and above, known as the Centre for Adults. The four schools and the center for young adults serve a total population of about 1,200 individuals. Chaoyang School is a junior primary school for students aged 7 to 12 years old, while Tanglin School serves adolescents aged 13 to 16 years old at the secondary level. Katong School caters to students ranging from the primary to secondary years (7 to 16 years of age). Upon completion of secondary education at Tanglin School and Katong School, students enter the postsecondary or transition program at Delta Senior School where they stay for 2-years in preparation for transitioning from school to postschool work and adult life in the community. Students who are not yet ready for employment proceed on to the Centre for Adults for further training.

If we can identify the pivotal question that began the curriculum reform at the APSN, it would be "How has the school years prepared our students for life after school?" This question is indeed significant as post-school outcomes are a litmus test of how well schools have prepared students for life beyond the school years, and therefore are indicative of the effectiveness and quality of curriculum and its delivery. The analysis of postschool outcomes can, in turn, inform the development of appropriate learning experiences and activities which can then be incorporated into the curriculum to improve its relevance and usefulness to the postschool lives of students. In other words, curriculum can be made more relevant by referencing the demands of postschool environments to what students can learn in the secondary and transition years of schooling before they graduate.

This "backward" design model of curriculum design and development (Wiggins & McTighe, 2005) begins with an assessment of how students are performing and functioning in postschool environments (e.g., employment settings) and then uses this assessment information for curriculum development purposes. Initial efforts at the APSN in assessing the postschool outcomes consisted of curriculum reviews that yielded significant findings which then provided the impetus for reforming the existing curriculum. These curriculum reviews consisted of assessments of graduated students' actual performance and functioning in postschool environments as well of evaluation of current curriculum practices. Assessments (e.g., observations) and employers' feedback of these students revealed that many lacked adequate and appropriate skills and behaviors to function effectively in work environments. For example, there were found evidence of poor work attitude, slow work rate, inability to cope with job demands, inappropriate social skills, and poor personal hygiene and grooming.

In-house school evaluations of curriculum practices exposed a similarly dismal scene. They revealed that school processes and practices related to the existing curriculum and its delivery were inadequate to ensuring a smooth and continuous educational experience throughout the school years and the students' transition into the community. There were many content-based curriculum materials; however, they were disintegrated without a common, integrated focus. There were many educational programs within and across grade levels but no overarching and interlinking framework that guided how these programs would contribute toward the mission and vision of the APSN for students to achieve dignified and fulfilling postschool lives. What was clearly missing was a formalized transition program for students in the senior school years to consolidate prior education and link with relevant learning opportunities and experiences in transitioning from school to work life.

Transition

Transition has been described as the life changes and adjustments that occur in the lives of young adults when they move from school to new roles within work and community settings (Wehman, 2001). Definitions of transition can be found in the international literature, most notably the American Individual with Disabilities Education Act (IDEA; PL 101-476) which requires transition services for all children with disabilities. The IDEA refers to transition services as a coordinated set of activities, based on individual needs, to promote the movement from school to postschool activities such as postsecondary education, vocational training and supported employment (IDEA; PL 101-476).

Another definition of transition, by the Council for Exceptional Children's Division on Career Development and Transition, describes it as a change in status from being a student to assuming roles associated with adults living and working in the community (Halpern, 1994). Besides emphasizing the participation and coordination of school programs with adult services and natural supports within the community, this council's definition also notes the importance of laying down the foundations for transition in the earlier years of school and states that transition planning should begin no later than age 14.

Numerous research have shown that many students with special needs leave school unprepared for demands of adulthood and employment (e.g., Burnham & Houseley, 1992; Hasazi, Gordon, & Roe, 1985). The lack of preparation in terms of inadequate transition planning impacts greatly on the postschool outcomes of persons with disabilities. For instance, the unemployment rate for people with disabilities in 2000 in the United States has been reported to be as high as between 50% to 75% (Wehman, 2001). The less than desirable postschool outcomes urgently point at the dire need for quality transition programs and pathways to be in place to prepare students with disabilities for positive and inclusive futures.

Research has shown that transition planning is integral to improving the postschool outcomes of students with disabilities because it provides a pathway to smoothen the change from school to postschool life (e.g., Cooney, 2002; Kober & Eggleton, 2005; Wehman, 2001). The tenet behind providing transition planning revolves around preparing students with disabilities to live dignified quality life as contributing members of society. Seven common transitions faced by youth include: employment,

living arrangements, getting around the community, financial independence, making friends, sexuality and self-esteem and having fun
(Wehman, 2001). Successful transition from school to adult life therefore
requires coordinated efforts between the students themselves, families,
school and the community (Noyes & Sax, 2004). Increasingly, students
with disabilities are empowered to make decisions and choices in person-
centered transition planning. Positive outcomes have been observed in
students equipped to make self-directed goals (Johnson, Agran, Sitlington, Cavin, & Wehmeyer, 2003).

Transition planning means providing school experience to equip students with special needs with skills relevant to their adult lives, in particular, readiness for meaningful employment. Though quality of life
encompasses more than being employed, employment was perceived as
providing challenge and helping persons with disabilities to become
adults. Many studies have highlighted the positive outcomes in youths
with disabilities purposefully engaged in employment (e.g., Cinamon &
Gifish, 2004; Cooney, 2002). In addition, employment provides a natural
avenue for the inclusion for young people with disabilities within society
(Lim & Sim, 2000). Hence, the underlying principle in transition planning focuses on preparing transition-age students with disabilities for
employment.

Transition in Singapore

In Singapore where there is no legislation advocating for and safe-
guarding employment opportunities for people with disabilities, they are
expected to compete in the open market for jobs and undergo continuous
upgrading to remain relevant. Moreover, unlike the United States where
transition planning is a mandated requirement for students with disabilities, the situation in Singapore is such that transition planning has traditionally not been a required and formal part of the school experience for
students with disabilities (Lim & Nam, 2000), and remains so till today.

Unlike other countries, such as the United States, where a large body of
research evidence has highlighted the less than desirable postschool outcomes of the lives of individuals with disabilities (which, in turn, has
helped promote the channeling of funds into transition services and
informed the development of transition guidelines, policies and practices
over the past few decades), there is a scarcity of published research on the
postschool outcomes of exstudents with disabilities in Singapore and
therefore little is known of the lives of students with disabilities after they
leave school.

This dearth of research on the postschool outcomes of students with disabilities, including students with intellectual disabilities and the lack of formal transition services to prepare youth in special schools for post-school life, reveal that transition planning has long not been a key priority in the special education system in Singapore. This situation can be said to be an effect of a larger long-standing issue—the relative lack of discourse and awareness of disability and inclusion as prominent social issues within Singaporean society until recently (Lim, Thaver, & Slee, 2008).

The driving force in Singapore behind the changing landscape regarding people with disabilities and the field of special education can be attributed to the first official announcement of the vision of Singapore as an inclusive society by Prime Minister Lee Hsien Loong in 2004. In 2004, PM Lee proclaimed in his inauguration speech, the vision of a "Government that will be inclusive in its approach toward all Singaporeans, young and old, disabled and able-bodied" (Ibrahim, 2004). A month after his inauguration speech, he announced that $220 million ($55 million over the next 4 years) would be set aside to implement initiatives to improve the quality of education for students with disabilities (Teo, 2004).

In 2007, the most thorough and wide-ranging plan for people with disabilities the nation has ever seen, the Enabling Masterplan, 2007–2011, built upon the premises of the Prime Minister's vision of an inclusive society for people with disabilities, was released. This Enabling Masterplan consists of a slew of proposals to address services and supports in key areas, over a period of 5 years (2007–2011) with the aim to achieve the vision of Singapore as an inclusive society where people with disabilities are to be given the opportunity to receive effective intervention and education services, equal opportunity in employment to become equal, integral and contributing members of society, achieving self-reliance through work, and living life with dignity in the community. A collaborative approach was adopted through the "Many Helping Hands" approach involving the public, and private sectors working together with people with disabilities and their families to achieve the vision of an inclusive society (Ministry of Community Development, Youth & Sports, 2007).

The Enabling Masterplan 2007–2011 and its successive Enabling Masterplan 2012–2016 (Ministry of Social and Family Development, 2012) provide a blueprint that outlines clearly Singapore's approach with key recommendations on how people with disabilities should be supported to reach their full potential and be included as part of society. One of their key recommendations is about transition management and funding of enabling services in which people with disabilities are to be given optimal opportunities to be prepared and trained for sustainable employment. The importance to prepare students with special needs to transition from school into employment or further studies was strongly advocated. The critical success factor identified is about providing a planned transition. Although the Enabling Masterplans make no provision to mandate the requirements of transition programming in the formal schooling experience of students with special needs, it is timely for special schools in Singapore to begin to formalize transition planning as part of their school's educational experience for all students with disabilities through the development of transition programs.

Developing a Local Transition Model— The Delta Senior School Experience

A review of the international literature on transition for students with disabilities found many research studies on the development and efficacy of various transition practices (e.g., the provision of carefully planned and structured work opportunities and experiences; promoting students' engagement with work that builds on individual needs, strengths and preferences; support of self-determination skills; involvement of community partners), but did not yield any published research describing nor documenting the process of developing a transition program over a length of time. Most intervention-based research in the transition literature focused on the development and efficacy of transition practices as opposed to the development and efficacy of transition programs.

The difference between the two is salient. Research that reports on certain transition practices and its evaluation assesses the specific components of transition programs (e.g., self-determination or person-centered approaches), while, in contrast, descriptive research on the chronological evolution of the key processes and practices leading to the development of a field-tested transition program is nonexistent. This is perhaps due to the fact that such studies would be longitudinal in scope with regards to developmental processes and complex in nature in terms of the dynamics of working with multiple layers of operations and stakeholders. Nevertheless, such studies are important to educators and practitioners who are interested in understanding the development work of setting up a transition program and appropriate methodologies to frame, guide and describe complex developmental work. This descriptive study illustrating key processes and insights of the development of a transition program for students with mild intellectual disabilities in Singapore is particularly significant as it constitutes a field-tested prototype for other special schools in Singapore and elsewhere interested in what such development work entails.

METHOD

This study sought to describe, through a retrospective account using an action learning and research framework, the key processes and practices that contributed to the development of the transition program at Delta Senior School. Retrospective studies intentionally investigate a phenomenon, problem or situation referenced to a time frame in the past (Kumar, 1996), and can involve descriptive accounts or reviews of evolutionary changes toward quality improvement in diverse fields (e.g., Richardson & Cooper, 2003; Sobiechowska & Maisch, 2006) or personal narratives of change management (e.g., Margolin, 2007).

The action learning and research framework was selected because of its methodological fluidity in facilitating, informing and monitoring change. Action research or participatory action research methodology applies fact-finding to a practical problem or issue for the aim of enabling relevant stakeholders/participants to improve the quality of action or practice within it. Action research constitutes a process in which a problem situation is examined, appropriate action planned and implemented, and its impact or effects monitored, for future improvements to be carried out (McTaggart, 1997).

The major components of the action research framework, unlike certain research methodologies, are not strictly linear, but, in fact, are cyclical or spiral in nature since planning is followed by implementation which is monitored by evaluative feedback that feeds or loops back into planning for further action. This framework for change was especially appealing to use in guiding the method of describing the development of the critical events of the transition program which involved the participation of relevant stakeholders (such as staff, students, families and/or employers) in continually examining and revising their understandings and actions based on cyclical and reflective processes.

The action research framework consisted of action learning cycles where the key processes and practices involved in the planning, development, implementation and evaluation of the transition are described in retrospect. This retrospective account of processes, practices and actions leading to the development of the transition program comprises a systematic method to not only describe the program's evolution but also to help understand and document how this approach, utilizing relevant evidence, served to inform decisions and actions within the learning cycles. The first author, as the former principal of the school and leader of the development work, provided the retrospective account of the action research phases and events by explicating the key processes and practices which were implemented within the cycles of action learning and research.

Evidence used to inform the action learning and research cycles was drawn from data collected from a variety of sources (upon which decisions for further action were made) such as naturalistic observations of students' performance in work environments, interviews with employers, and staff review and feedback. Such evidence pertaining to processes and the development of practices also helped triangulate and provided support for the author's retrospective account of the significant phases and events of the development work.

Given the breadth and depth of Delta Senior School's transition development work, the next section on results highlights key insights into the significant processes and practices to illustrate the unfolding of the development work over three cyclical action learning phases across a 3-year period.

RESULTS

Phase 1

When the first author took over the leadership of Delta Senior School, there was no evidence of structured and formal programs to facilitate the students' transition into their postschool lives in open employment. While some of the students applied to continue in the APSN at the Centre for Adults, some students left the APSN altogether in search of jobs while others stayed at home.

Clarify Vision and Mission through Strategic Envisioning

The development of a transition program to enhance the postschool outcomes of the students posed a massive undertaking especially when there existed a particular work culture that was maintained by the previous status quo of how the school operated. It is essential that school leaders who are about to embark upon such reform work to possess a clarity of the vision and mission of what they would like to achieve and the fortitude to translate the vision and mission into reality. Clarity of vision is vital for school leaders to set strategic directions and engage staff to co-own the vision and mission.

To galvanize staff toward a clear direction for their work, the first author began to facilitate a series of envisioning exercises to revisit and operationalize the vision and mission of the APSN for the whole school community. This envisioning work is the first critical step taken with the intent to establish a collective understanding as well as to forge a common direction among all staff members in preparation for the long intensive work ahead. In these exercises, the staff at Delta Senior School were clustered in cross functional groups to unpack and jointly define the key words and phrases in the vision and mission statements of the APSN.

The collective importance, as mentioned above, of this initial envisioning work and its significance for staff members cannot be understated. The collective unpacking of the vision and mission of the school and the confrontation of uncomfortable evidence, such as the poor performance of the graduates in work environments and the inadequacy of school-to-work pathways, brought about a greater consciousness on the part of the staff of the purpose and meaning of what their work entailed.

Identify Desired Student Outcomes and Define Key Performance Indicators

During the envisioning work, staff were also asked to identify significant student outcomes to provide strategic direction for the work ahead. This exercise was crucial to operationalizing and concretizing the desired student outcomes with reference to the school vision. Once the desired future of Delta Senior School and desired student outcomes were clarified, the staff were then tasked and guided to evaluate the current reality at Delta Senior School through the use of a SWOT analysis (strengths, weaknesses, opportunities and threats).

The evaluation through this SWOT analysis marked the beginning of the formalization of an annual evidence-based cycle of practices involving action planning, implementation and evaluation/reflection. The SWOT analysis enabled the staff to identify that the school (1) lacked a student management system; (2) lacked an integrated outcome-based curriculum to prepare the students for postschool life; (3) did not have a coherent assessment system to assess student learning; and (4) had little or no collaboration between professional and teaching staff.

Having determined the desired outcomes of students and identified the areas of concern, the school had to then define the key performance indicators of those desired outcomes, set targets and design action plans that can concurrently achieve those outcomes as well as organize and align various school subsystems such as the student management system, staff performance system, and the assessment and reporting system.

Implementing a Structured Job Placement Program

It was in this first phase that the key goal of developing and implementing a structured job placement program was selected by staff. This goal provided a focal point to align desired outcomes and key performance indicators for action planning. The action planning work to achieve this goal formed the initial part of the spiral of action learning activities of planning, implementation, evaluation and reflection at Delta Senior School. Review was done once every two months which then culminated in the midyear review and eventually in the year-end review. The learning points that emerged at each review point were used to inform on practice, with the learning points of the final year-end review used for strategic planning for the following year.

The action plans related to this key goal had clear goal owners as well as specific staff and timelines for implementation. All staff were involved in the collaborative implementation of the action plans to achieve the targets set. As staff were required to work in collaborative teams to prepare students for post-school life, a session of values clarification was conducted to craft a set of shared school values as the cornerstone for supporting the individual and collective efforts of staff.

Enhance Supporting Structures

Many supporting structures such as a calendar of events, a manual of procedures and other work schedules, were also simultaneously put in place to help staff to organize their time and their work more efficiently and effectively to achieve some quick successes. A data collection system with monitoring and review schedule was also built into the action plans to ensure effective implementation and documentation of the action plans. The initiation of data-based practices grounded on objective indicators of performance and accountability also impacted on the performance management process at Delta Senior School. For the first time, the performances of the staff at Delta Senior School were directly linked to the key performance measures and targets of the school.

Every staff member now had to set personal targets, which were aligned to the school targets, with respect to the roles that they played. New reporting structures were also set up to facilitate the annual performance management process which included start-of-year performance planning, midyear review and year-end performance appraisal. The annual performance appraisal served a dual purpose of staff performance evaluation as well as personal and professional development of staff and their reporting officers. This performance management cycle for staff development, evaluation and deployment, which also constitutes a system of continuous learning in staff, ran parallel with the school strategic planning process to support continual school improvement.

Supporting the Development Work Through a Whole School Approach

In Phase 1 (the first year), Delta Senior School had managed to formalize, through the development of a job placement manual, a more structured job placement/ open employment program. Delta Senior School had also managed to establish nine community partners for students to enter as trainees. By the end of the year, Delta Senior School had managed to achieve its target of either securing job attachment or open employment for 32 students.

The initial success at Delta Senior School, though modest, injected confidence in the school that it was moving in the right direction. However, this success cannot be solely attributed to the formalization of the job placement/open employment program at Delta Senior School. The success has to be seen within a more holistic school context where other school processes and practices had played an equally important role. More importantly these school processes and practices that were also initiated across other school subsystems (e.g., student well-being and curriculum review), laid the initial groundwork for future phases.

Phase 2

In this next cycle of action learning at Delta Senior School, staff were brought together to reaffirm their shared understanding of the vision and mission of the school as well as the desired outcomes of students, and also review the efforts in Phase 1. In addition, a SWOT analysis was performed again, this time with evidence derived from the respective action plans to address the concerns and desired outcomes across the relevant school subsystems identified in the first phase.

Expanding Organizational Capacity for Job Placement

The key thrust of developing a job structured program (from Phase 1) was reviewed with the goal to further systematize the program. Three other goals supportive of this key thrust were developed: (1) providing enabling experiences to promote the well-being and self-respect of students; (2) improving the quality of teaching and learning; and (3) building sustainable and synergistic partnerships with relevant stakeholders (e.g., parents, employers).

The modest success achieved in securing job attachments or open employment with a number of community partners in the first phase provided the basis and incentive to further strategize for expansion. In this second phase, Delta Senior School together with the Centre for Adults managed to seize an opportunity to secure a 2-year funding scheme to pilot a training and employment project. Delta Senior School used part of this fund to recruit two job placement officers to support its efforts to train and place students for open employment. These two job placement officers were responsible for implementing transition planning for students, the sourcing of employers, the restructuring and systematization of the program, the provision of support for students and their parents, and the management of information.

Enhancing Home, School, and Community Partnerships

To enhance home-school partnerships, Delta Senior School developed a guide for parents to help them understand the job placement process. Steps were taken to involve parents in the job placement process by openly sharing information with them, engaging them to discuss their apprehensions, clarifying financial concerns, and facilitating joint decision making before a student was placed out. The school also continued to engage the families through the Individual Education Plan (IEP) process which also involved teachers and related professional staff (e.g., psychologist, occupational therapist, social worker) working together to address issues of job readiness with students in order to prepare them for open employment. For instance, the occupational therapist was assigned to work more closely with teachers in assisting students to build physical endurance and practice effective body movements within their school and work routines.

In terms of community partnerships, Delta Senior School established links with 13 community partners, up by 44% in the previous phase. An employer's handbook was developed to clear directions for the employers involved in the job placement process. It was very important to develop closer and supportive relationships between existing community partners, such as the Holiday Inn Park View Hotel which broadened their provision of on-site job training and attachment opportunities from laundry work to include housekeeping work as well.

At the same time, Delta Senior School also managed to secure new community partnerships for more opportunities in on-site training, job attachment and employment placement for its students. The community partners provided invaluable community-based learning experiences for students to successfully make the transition from school to work. In this second phase of the development work, 40% of the total number of 59 graduating students experienced and completed at least 4 hours of on-site community-based training.

In view of the teachers' lack of industry knowledge and skills to provide effective vocational training to students (e.g., in baking)—a weakness which was highlighted in the SWOT analysis, Delta Senior School, in response, began to leverage on school-employer partnerships by arranging for staff to develop a greater awareness of industry standards and learn specific industry skills as they accompany students for on-site training. Since the teachers still lacked the expertise to provide vocational training for certification purposes, the school continued to depend on external community partners to provide such training for students. For example, during this phase, Delta Senior School linked up with the Baking Industry Training Centre to provide training in baking. This training, together with the additional support received from teachers, enabled 10 students to obtain the National Institute of Technical Education Certificate in the Intermediate Cake module.

Phase 3

Having paved the structures for a reflective action learning culture at Delta Senior School and with the shared vision, mission and values of the school established, the strategic planning cycle continued into its third phase with an additional focus on widening efforts to reinforce relevant skills for greater success and sustainability at employment sites, enhancing supports at these placement sites, and strengthening home and community partnerships.

Reinforcing Relevant Skills and Sustainability for Employment

To initiate this third phase, Delta Senior School conducted the action planning exercise jointly with Tanglin School—the secondary school which students attend prior to coming to Delta Senior School. In the course of the last phase, staff had noted the students' lack of soft skills, which was a major stumbling block to successful employment. Moreover, it was also noted that poor literacy and numeracy skills had prevented many students from being selected for training in vocational certification. Staff at Delta Senior School felt that these skills could be more explicitly taught at Tanglin School. As such, Delta Senior School initiated the joint action planning exercise with its sister school.

Community-based training within authentic work sites was also increased for both students and teachers to reinforce relevant employment skills. The professional development of staff in community-based vocational training was promoted through site visits and attachments. A total of 11 staff members, with at least one teacher representative from each vocational area, were given the opportunity to visit job sites where the students were working. Arrangements were made for three staff members to accompany students on community-based vocational training so that the staff could pick up the necessary vocational skills for training. In this third phase, the percentage of graduating students who had experienced and completed at least 40 hours of on-site community-based training had risen to 46%, with a total number of 87 graduating students, as compared to 40% in Phase 2, with a total number of 59 graduating students.

Delta Senior School continued to pursue its strategic thrust of developing its job placement program, with its related supportive goals, by highlighting the element of sustainability as another criterion for successful job placement. Thus, job sustainability would be another indicator of the overall effectiveness of the transition program at Delta Senior School. The 14 students who were successfully placed out in open employment in the second phase and the subsequent students were tracked to determine whether they would be able to sustain in their jobs for at least a year.

Enhancing Supports for Students at Job Placements

In order for Delta Senior School to achieve this end, the school set out to enhance the structures and processes for supporting students who had either been placed on job attachment or who had obtained a job in open employment. Throughout this third phase, the school ran a total of five structured support group sessions involving 53 students who were either on job attachment or in open employment. These group work sessions for students, with each group of about 10 students, were facilitated by the social worker and job placement officers on a weekly basis in which students were encouraged to share their experiences, problems and successes while on their jobs. The job placement officers, teachers and professional staff continued to provide ongoing support for students to help them address work-related issues and concerns.

Strengthening and Expanding Home and Community Partnerships

In the home front, Delta Senior School continued to strengthen partnerships with parents, families and caregivers. A preemployment parental conference was put in place to allow job placement officers to address parental concerns as well as explain the job requirements to the families. Parents were also required to sign a letter undertaking to share the responsibilities for supporting the students' job attachment. The job placement officers would then provide intensive support for both the students and their families during the initial phase of the job placement process in order to ensure a smooth transition of the student from the school to the work place. The IEP continued to provide the established structure and platform for the staff to continually engage with parents as well as among staff by linking the processes of IEP planning with case referral and transition planning processes. Hence the IEP was enhanced by aligning it to the work context where teachers were required to identify and plan one aspect of developmental needs related to job readiness as an IEP goal for each student.

Delta Senior School managed to forge new collaborative partnerships with agencies and industries in the community in this third phase to open up more opportunities to place out students with different levels of capabilities and abilities across various vocational areas. A majority of the new employer contacts made were followed up by either a formal or informal employer education briefing. The principal or job placement officers at

Delta Senior School conducted employer education briefings for 10 companies over the course of the year. By the end of the year, a total of 12 new partnerships, excluding seven McDonald's branches, were formed, such as, with the Grand Hyatt Hotel, a nursery and a laundry service.

Accomplishments Toward the End of Phase 3

The results from the feedback forms sent out to employers had shown that 100% of the employers in partnership with Delta Senior School had indicated that they were satisfied with the support provided by the job placement officers and instructors. By the end of the third phase, 31 students were able to complete their job attachments. Of these, 26 students had gained or were offered jobs in the open employment. Of the 14 students placed out into open employment in previous phase, 11 students were able to sustain their job for at least 1 year.

DISCUSSION

This study describes, through a retrospective account using an action learning and research framework, the key processes and practices that contributed to the development of a transition program at a special school in Singapore across its initial 3 years. In retrospect, the formalization of the action learning and research cycles with an evidence-based emphasis to inform planning and action facilitated the continuous development and implementation of the transition program from its beginnings to when it became central to the school's role in transitioning its students from school to work.

The transition development work at Delta Senior School proved to be very significant and meaningful to the postschool lives of its students as this program created the pathways and supports for them to access opportunities for work experience and employment success in the community. As mentioned, such a system of structured inroads into work opportunities for the students was virtually nonexistent when the first author assumed her leadership of the school 3 years prior. This descriptive retrospective account of transition development work at Delta Senior School serves to validate its transition program as a prototype fieldtested model for the Singapore context as well as internationally where there are virtually no published case studies in the school-to-work transition literature that illustrates the key processes and practices in developing a transition program for students with intellectual disabilities.

The cumulative charting of this program's evolution from the beginning to its achievements at the end of three cyclical phases was invaluable to documenting the evolution of the program in a systematic, evidence-based manner. This approach of couching the work within action learning cycles has been the basis for decision making and for sustaining its continuing development during and beyond the three cyclical phases. The ongoing development and continuous quality improvement were made possible through the planning, development, implementation and evaluation efforts of multiple stakeholders who participated in the various phases of the work. Many decisions made during the various development phases were based on the evaluation of relevant evidence through multiple sources (e.g., surveys, interviews, meetings, outcomes) and stakeholders (e.g., students, parents, teachers, employers).

Thus, a strong feature of the development work refers to its methodological framework. As noted in various studies in the area of transition of students with special needs (e.g., Cooney, 2002, Grigal, Test, Beattie, Wood, 1997; Johnson et al., 2003; Kober & Eggleton, 2005; Ward, Mallett, Heslop, & Simons, 2003), the recognition and involvement of key stakeholders in planning for transition through soliciting their participation and/or perspectives provides a more comprehensive base upon which to evaluate the quality of processes and practices so as to better inform future action. The encasement of this development work within an action learning/research framework, which involved a participatory element and ethos to include relevant stakeholders, lent itself well to the inclusion of various stakeholders during the phases of the work.

Limitations of the Study

The in-depth description of the transition development program work is solely based on development work in one special school in Singapore. In addition, this special school caters specifically for students with mild intellectual disabilities. Hence, a key limitation of the study refers to the generalizability of some of its field-tested outcomes and the relevant processes and practices facilitating such outcomes to other special schools where the student population may not be as homogeneous in terms of age range and ability level.

Besides the external validity of extrapolating the processes and practices at Delta Senior School to other special schools, another limitation of the study refers to the method for its description which was done retrospectively. As the author of the study as well as the leader in charge of the development of the transition program, it is inevitable that the retrospective account involved a certain degree of personal subjectivity that can color its reporting. This subjectivity in retrospective reporting is a limitation in itself and was addressed through the corroboration of another key staff member with intimate knowledge of the entire development of the transition program. To review the accuracy of the reporting, this person was asked to validate the relevant documents and evidences corresponding to the chronological phases of the development process reported in this study.

CONCLUSION

A powerful lesson from this development work is that students with intellectual disabilities, like those at Delta Senior School, are more capable than first believed. School expectations and supports can play an extremely important part in influencing the self-belief and achievements of students and their significant others (e.g., parents and teachers). With higher expectations and greater supports of its students for life beyond school, the school community were able to open up and explore unprecedented opportunities in and out of school to experience success in training and open employment. Success breeds success as the adage goes, and the increasing numbers of students across cohorts in successful real-life training and employment arrangements gradually built a thriving school culture and community that continuously sought to generate self-improvement and innovation in order to chart a brighter future for its students.

REFERENCES

Burnham, S. C., & Housley, W. F. (1992). Pride in work: Perceptions of employers, service providers and students who are mentally retarded and learning disabled. *Career Development Exceptional Individuals*, *15*, 101–108.

Cinamon, R. G., & Gifish, L. (2004). Conceptions of work among adolescents and young adults with mental retardation. *The Career Development Quarterly*, *52*(3), 212–223.

Cooney, B. F. (2002). Exploring perspectives on transition of youth with disabilities: Voices of young adults, parents, and professionals. *Mental Retardation, 40*, 425–435.

Dietrich, J., Parker, P., & Salmela-Aro, K. (2012). Phase-adequate engagement at the post-school transition. *Developmental Psychology, 48*, 1575–1593.

Flexer, R. W., Simmons, T. L., Luft, P., & Baer, R. M.(2005). *Transition planning for secondary students with disabilities* (2nd ed). Columbus, OH: Pearson Merrill Prentice Hall.

Halpern, A. S. (1994). The transition of youth with disabilities to adult life: A position statement of the Division of Career Development and Transition. *Career Development for Exceptional Individuals*, *17*, 115–124.

Hasazi, S., Gordon, L., & Roe, C. (1985). Factors associated with the employment status of handicapped youth exiting high school from 1979 to 1983. *Exceptional Children, 51*(6), 455–469.

Grigal, M., Test, D. W., Beattie, J., & Wood, W. M. (1997). An evaluation of transition components of Individualised Education Programs. *Exceptional Children, 63*(3), 357–372.

Ibrahim, Z. (2004, August 13). Let's shape our future together. *The Times*, p. 10.

Individuals with Disabilities Education Act, PL101-476 (1990, Oct.30).

Johnson, J. M., Agran, M., Sitlington, P., Cavin, M., & Wehmeyer, M. (2003). Enhancing the job performance of youth with moderate to severe cognitive disabilities using the Self-Determined Learning Model of Instruction (SDLMI). *Research & Practice for Persons with Severe Disabilities, 28*(4), 194–204.

Kober, R., & Eggleton, I. R. C. (2005). The effect of different types of employment on quality of life. *Journal of Intellectual Disability Research, 49*(10), 756–760.

Kumar, R. (1996). *Research methodology: A step-by-step guide for beginners*. Melbourne, Australia: Addison Wesley Longman Australia.

Lim, L., & Nam, S. S. (2000). Special education in Singapore. *Journal of Special Education, 39*(2), 104–109.

Lim, L., & Sim, J. (2000). Enhancing quality of life through work: The conversion of a vocational rehabilitation program for adults with disabilities in Singapore. *Saudi Journal of Disability and Rehabilitation, 6*(4), 276–282.

Lim, L., Thaver, T., & Slee, R. (2008). *Exploring disability in Singapore: A personal learning journey*. Singapore: McGraw-Hill

Margolin, I. (2007). Shaping a new professional identity by building a new personal concept of leadership through action research. *Education Action Research, 15*(4), 519–543.

McTaggart, R. (Ed.). (1997). *Participatory action research: International contexts and consequences*. Albany, NY: State University of New York Press.

Ministry of Community Development, Youth & Sports. (2007). *Enabling Masterplan 2007–2011*. Retrieved from http://www.mcys.gov.sg/enabling masterplan/mainreport.html

Ministry of Social and Family Development. (2012). *Enabling Masterplan 2012-2016*. Retrieved from http://app.msf.gov.sg/Policies/PersonswithDisabilities/EnablingMasterplan20122016.aspx

Noyes, D. A., & Sax, C.L. (2004). Changing systems for transition: students, families, and professionals working together. *Education and Training in Developmental Disabilities, 39*(1), 35–44.

Richardson, B., & Cooper, N. (2003). Developing a virtual interdisciplinary research community in higher education. *Journal of Interprofessional Care, 17*(2), 173–182.

Sobiechowska, P., & Maisch, M. (2006). Work-based learning: In search of an effective model. *Educational Action Research, 14*(2), 267–286.

Teo, L. (2004, September 19). $220m school aid for disabled kids. *The Straits Times*, p. 1.

Ward, L., Mallett, R., Heslop, P., & Simons, K. (2003). Transition planning: How well does it work for young people with disabilities and their families? *British Journal of Special Education, 30*(3), 132–137.

Wehman, P. H. (2001). *Life beyond the classroom: Transition strategies for young people with disabilities* (3rd ed.). Baltimore, MD: Paul H. Brookes.
Wiggins, G., & McTighe, J. (2005). Understanding by design. Virginia: ASCD.

PART II

PEDAGOGY AND LEARNING ENVIRONMENTS THAT ENHANCE SOCIAL JUSTICE AND EDUCATIONAL OUTCOMES

CHAPTER 5

LOOKING BACK ON THE INCLUSIVE EDUCATION CAREER OF THREE YOUNG ADULTS WITH INTELLECTUAL DISABILITIES IN THE FLEMISH SPEAKING PART OF BELGIUM

Becoming and Belonging

Geert Van Hove, Elisabeth De Schauwer, and Inge Van de Putte

In this chapter we take you on a journey based on "key incidents"—detailed data with observations made by the authors—and "narrative snapshots"— these can be situated within the philosophy of informal qualitative inter- viewing—about the lives of 3 young adults with an intellectual disability in the Flemish speaking part of Belgium. The three of them followed an inclu- sive trajectory within their school career. We will build up this chapter around the question: What did Nathalie, Walter and Nicolas teach us about participation and belonging throughout their inclusive trajectory?

Within the chapter we will discuss how:

- looking at people as "continuously becoming" instead of "static fixed disabled human beings";

Inclusive Education for Students with Intellectual Disabilities,
pp. 97–115

- presuming competence instead of a "defectological point of view"; and
- education as a healthy mixture of qualification, socialization and subjectivation instead of a tool "to fix children"

can become important elements to inspire teachers to work with children and to open up possibilities for belonging and inclusion now and in the future.

What the stories of the youngsters teach us is that the competences they show are not the competences we can find in standardized lists of educational outcomes. It will be important to use a broad framework to inclusive education that opens up opportunities for multiple talents to assure that persons with intellectual disabilities get the time and opportunities to become respected citizens. This is a complex and time consuming process where no simple answers or linear solutions can be found.

INTRODUCTION

In this chapter we take you on a journey based on "key incidents" (Emerson, 2004) and "narrative snapshots" (Van Hove et al., 2012) about the lives of three young adults with an intellectual disability in the Flemish speaking part of Belgium. Nathalie, Walter and Nicolas (we have given them a fictitious name to ensure the anonymity) followed a path of Inclusive Education. Together with L. Jackson, Ryndak, and Wehmeyer (2008–2009), we believe it is within the contexts where all children of a particular age participate that developmental growth—including academic, social and interpersonal behaviors—is most likely to occur. But for Nathalie, Walter and Nicolas it is not enough to be present. They want to participate in everyday life. We see participation as complex: it is about belonging and being actively involved in whatever is going on (Biklen, 1992). It makes us listen very carefully to what people want and how they want to participate in it. It makes us think about ways we can/should support people to enhance their participation and opportunities to participate. In 1994, on the World Conference on Special Needs in Education, the Salamanca Statement (UNESCO, 1994, p. 11) said: "Inclusion and participation are essential to human dignity and to the enjoyment and exercise of strategies that seek to bring about a genuine equalization of opportunity." In addition, we are interested in the barriers which people face and which prevent them to participate. We will build up this chapter around the question: What did Nathalie, Walter and Nicolas teach us about participation and belonging throughout their inclusive trajectory?

METHODOLOGY FOR THIS CHAPTER

The research material for this chapter was sourced from an action research project in which the three authors have been closely involved for the last 15 years. Parents for Inclusion—a family project in the Flemish speaking part of Belgium—has a structural relationship with our University Department. Within this structural partnership university students can give support to children and youngsters with disabilities who are attending regular schools. The parents movement is also seen as a very important partner in several little research projects in a continuing stream of a larger action research program about inclusive education. Parents for Inclusion is a parents group project that advocates for families who decide for their children with a label of (intellectual) disability to be educated in mainstream facilities (and this decision is often against professional advice). Within this long-term research relationship a lot of informal (e.g., visits at home, sharing family activities and school team meetings) and formal research moments (e.g., [focus] group discussions, interviews, collection of narratives) took place. For this chapter we worked with the "key incident method" (Emerson, 2004). This method is situated within the tradition of naturalistic ethnography. We will use detailed data with observations made by the authors (they will appear in italics throughout our chapter) and with narrative snapshots (these can be situated within the philosophy of informal qualitative interviewing). The quotes will be presented in italics, with the addition of speech marks.

Within this chapter we will introduce quotes and observations linked to three young adults and their inclusive education career:

- Walter is in his early twenties. He is diagnosed with Down syndrome. He has just finished secondary school after a full inclusive school career. He lives now with his father and mother; he has five sisters who all left home already. He works part time in a project where they take care for "retired horses." Walter is a street dancer, a guitarist and a basketball player.
- Nathalie is in her twenties. She received labels like "intellectually disabled," "slow learner," "developmentally delayed." She lives with her parents and her brother. She works as a volunteer as a part-time classroom assistant and as an office assistant to the coordinator of a nongovernment organization that gives support to families with children with disabilities.
- Nicolas is in his early twenties and lives with his brother and parents on a large farm. He has a full inclusive educational career. Being in his last year of secondary school his parents dream about a

future job combination of bed and breakfast owner on the farm with working in a little farm shop.

The three young adults and their families have been known to the researchers since they were pupils in regular primary school settings.

Within the chapter we share our insights about the most important things we learned from our long term action research project with Parents for Inclusion. We will discuss how:

- looking at people as "continuously becoming" instead of "static fixed disabled human beings";
- presuming competence instead of a "defectological point of view";
- education as a healthy mixture of qualification, socialization and subjectivation instead of a tool "to fix children"

can become important elements to inspire teachers to work with children with special educational needs and to open up possibilities for belonging and inclusion now and in the future.

LOOKING AT PEOPLE AS CONTINUOUSLY BECOMING

Walter August 2013, observation by Geert

I am taking my bike to go to our office, I run into heavy traffic, it is clear that holidays are finished. At one of the bus stops I see an "old acquaintance" of the Parents for Inclusion network: cool young guy, wearing Abercrombie and Fitch, sky blue hoody, fashionable glasses, waiting for the bus, relaxed,... Walter finished his secondary school not that long ago. Has been in inclusive classes for his whole school career, has done his student trainee work placement in a riding school. Walter is the son of great parents, brother of a bunch of sisters, street dancer and basketball lover, born with Down Syndrome.

While observing him I am wondering where he is going to... Five minutes later I meet Walter again at the rail way station crossing the street to catch a train....

Walter has a completely different lifestyle and life than a lot of his "cocitizens with intellectual disabilities." They are driven with a van of a nongovernmental organization to their day care center where they work together with other "colleagues with intellectual disabilities." A lot of them can't live with their family, a lot of them don't have the opportunity to play ball or to go to a street dance course. They live in groups, they can go to weekend activities organized once a month for citizens with intellectual disabilities.

Nathalie September 2013, narrative snapshot by Inge

Nathalie takes her agenda. Each day she planned an activity:

Monday I work in preschool. Tuesday I have to go to my physiotherapist and in the afternoon I go with my cousin to the shopping mall. On Wednesday I work at the office and on Thursday I paint with Caroline and cook a dinner for my family. Friday I work again in preschool. No, we can't meet on weekdays. Perhaps in the weekend but not too early I want to have a good and long sleep. We could meet at the sailing club. If you come at four a clock I have already sailed. And then we could drink something together.

Her brother comes along and says: *"Definitely a glass of beer. Or two...."* Nathalie smiles and writes in her diary when we meet.

Each of the authors has a lot of stories in his memory. In all of these stories we learned to know youngsters who participate in the community. It strikes us how "common" and recognizable their stories are ... waiting for the bus, having an agenda. Yet for a lot of people with an (intellectual) disability in our society this is not the case. They often find themselves in situations where they have no place or they can be found in the margins. They live in a kind of parallel world within special facilities, with experts helping them, going to special clubs and working in special workshops.

Within inclusive practices we abandon the idea that people with a disability have to become "normal" in order to contribute to the world. Together with Kunc (1992) we search for and nourish the gifts that are inherent in all people. We begin to look beyond typical ways of becoming valued members of the community, and in doing so, begin to realize the achievable goal of providing all children with an authentic sense of belonging.

Walter, Nathalie and Nicolas have the right, regardless of their label of "intellectual disability," to choose what they like to do and/or have the talent for. Their strengths and the development of those strengths are important parameters in the way their weekly schedule is built up. And because these activities are in the society, possibilities are created to connect with other people. In this way, Nathalie, Walter and Nicolas have a place where they belong.

The desire to be an individual is echoed in the stories of these young people and their families. They are not reduced to their label. They are like all of us continuously becoming, ... becoming a student, becoming a young adult, becoming an employee, becoming a sister, becoming a daughter. "Becoming explodes the ideas about what we are and what we can be beyond the categories that seem to constrain us" (Sotirin, 2005, p. 99).

Many youngsters with an intellectual disability in inclusive education have a (long) personal history of persisting and surviving, sometimes going through several segregated and regular education and health systems.

Nathalie, Process Follow-Up by Inge

Nathalie for example, has been to a special school in the first years of her life. The parents of Nathalie felt that they had to constantly show the teachers what Nathalie's potential was. As Nathalie now talks about her life, she still refers to that period and moments where they have to stand up for who she is and what she can do.

Nathalie, Narrative Snapshot by Inge

They did not believe I could read. Whenever I had a book with me, the teachers thought that I had memorized the book. But also Els (a colleague from her work) doesn't believe I can read. I'm reading a novel of a TV series and she thinks I remember the content of the book because I have seen it on TV.

Nathalie, Walter and Nicolas are talking about themselves, their abilities, their difficulties and daily lived experiences. They are blurring and breaching boundaries in a constant stream of playing with certain social expectations and they live in between the "regular" and the "special" world.

It is important to view and experience students as potentials—as virtual spaces that have the possibility for actualization. A person according to Deleuze and Guattari (cited in Williams, 2003) is a continuous becoming not defined by static concepts and categorizations such as disabled/able-bodied, male/female, homosexual/heterosexual or even person/thing. Subjects, bodies, minds and rhizomes are connected, constantly produced, shifting and changing. Within these multiple, heterogeneous and rhizomatic processes of transformation of self and others, we are able to understand "disability" as a new, unstable and uncertain flux of self. If we see disability as a fluid category than we can all move in and out (Gibson, 2006). If we look at disability in this way somebody is more than a category.

When somebody called Nathalie "an idiot," she replied: *"It's not because my brain is slower that I can't think"* (narrative snapshot by Inge).

Youngsters themselves recognize that they are different but as they make clear, this difference only becomes relevant at certain times in particular contexts.

When education can tune in to this fluidity, teachers rethink their representations of youngsters with an intellectual disability and the opportunities youngsters present them. You have to learn to see with "new eyes": carefully observe what youngsters can do, expect evolution (even little steps) in their learning and practice positive language to talk and write about this. Rinaldi (2006, p. 131) compares learning to a bowl of spaghetti: "Learning does not proceed in a linear way, determined and deterministic, by progressive and predictable stages, but rather is constructed through contemporaneous advances, standstills and retreats that take many directions." This is not easy, it needs a lot of practicing and goes together with many insecurities. Uncertainties and insecurities arise because the "standard path" is not followed. So teachers in inclusive education have to leave their safe and familiar situation and make place for what they don't know.

Nathalie, Process Follow-Up by Inge

Nathalie is not seen as a person with a disability. She is now a woman that has a full, busy life and can do the things in life she likes. Throughout her journey she is seen in the first place as a girl/woman who had dreams. Like her mother expressed in a dialogue about the transition from secondary education to work: "I hope she is tired at the end of the day. I hope she can have a meaningful life. It doesn't mean that she should do the same things as everyone else and should work at 'the tips of her toes." But we dream she can do what she wants to do and experience success in that." From the beginning it became clear Nathalie liked to work with children. So it was an evident, logical choice to visit a school where she could follow a childcare course. A lot of her teachers learned to know her as a girl with a "passion for children." Not all teachers were able to see this, but many teachers had expectations for Nathalie to make this dream possible and searched how she could participate. For example Nathalie has the ability to change a diaper of a child but she doesn't see that you can't leave a baby unattended. So the teachers sought solutions by making the arrangement that Nathalie can take care of a baby when a colleague works beside her. These great teachers were looking at her possibilities rather than her deficits. For them Nathalie does not have to meet all the standards.

We can see that Nathalie, Walter and Nicolas met teachers on their inclusive pathway who built a relationship with them. Through this relationship it becomes possible for the teachers to discover the possibilities, dreams, and opportunities of the youngsters. In this way it is possible for the youngsters to become a "student" and for the teacher to become a "teacher." It is in the interaction that becoming becomes possible, here becoming can be seen as a continuous process.

PRESUMING COMPETENCE OF THE LEARNER

From Biklen (1999) we take the suggestion that adopting the concept of "presuming competence" places an onus of responsibility on educators and researchers to figure out how the person can better demonstrate ability.

By presuming the competence of children who do not always demonstrate it in traditional or expected ways, the teacher is then freed to approach the learner with thoughts and practices that would lead her/him to engage the student in meaningful academic opportunities and allow for the person with a disability to make contributions to the (class) community.

Concerns for both the inappropriate denial of access to the learning opportunities provided to other students in schools and changing definitions of disability compel us to take a presumption of competence perspective when considering what constitutes an appropriate educational program for students with extensive support needs. This perspective requires that we start with a premise that a student can meet expectations associated with the education of peers without disabilities rather than using the more prevalent starting point that their disability makes such an expectation inherently unrealistic (Jackson et al., 2008–2009).

Nathalie 2009, Observation by Inge

Nathalie is not seen as "uneducable." Along the way she met people who believed that she can develop and can make a positive evolution. Like her principal of secondary school said: "In the first year she didn't talk to me. Every time I saw her, I greeted her as I do with the other students. The second year I stopped and waited, then she said a very silent "hello." Now she comes to my office, knocks on the door, greets me and gives the message of the teacher. Sometimes she even tells me something about her classroom or her internship. So it is important to believe she can learn. Because if you don't expect she can learn she will not learn" (narrative snapshot by Inge).

When we talk to Nathalie, Walter and Nicolas about how they look at themselves, they talk about what they are good at and able to do. This is not always related to their intellectual abilities. Their interests and talents can become points of contact in their inclusive pathway and can help to make choices, add content to subjects at school, and give direction to their field of study, of work and leisure time. For teachers this means they can make use of interests and talents in building up their weekly program and curriculum. As with Nathalie her fascination for working with small children has determined her way in secondary education and further life. With Kittay (2001) we can say that if people give an exclusive focus on Nathalie, Walter and Nicolas' limitations, this would set them outside neoliberal definitions of "members of the society." In this neoliberal perspective you can only become a member if you are "independent" and "competent."

As an alternative for the neoliberal option someone can learn to think in terms of desire, which gives different options. "Desire is about production. Desire's production is active, becoming, transformative. Desire is not linked to "lack"—something that we do not have—" (Jackson & Mazzeï, 2012, p. 91) "but to the forces and action that are actively becoming" (p. 92). If desire is productive then students (with disabilities) are always considered productive. Allan (1999, p. 116) assigns teachers a significant role in this struggle between desires and needs: "Teachers might help pupils to explore their sense of self—expressed as desires rather than needs—and to analyze the constraining and enabling factors, but should avoid passing judgments on them." This contains a plead for a more rhizomatic making sense of becoming-human that helps teachers and parents search how they can best support the youngster's learning and growth. It is important that teachers do not assume they know everything about the student and his/her future. By asking teachers to look at desire instead of needs, we challenge them to keep an open mind, to go for a constant quest in confrontation with the question: "Who is Nathalie, Walter and Nicolas?" This is only possible if teachers build relationships with their students: inclusion asks for close encounters. Inclusive education is not about learning at the same pace; it is not about adapting the child to the school but adapting the education to the child. Child-centered learning (versus teacher-centered learning) became the focus in the educational processes of Walter, Nathalie and Nicolas.

It is very clear: by bringing the focus in our education system on independence we risk losing connectivity and interdependence as core values of inclusive education. Teachers work very actively with the diversity in the classroom through cooperative learning strategies (let them work together in pairs or small groups, set up buddy systems, etc). Independence limits desire and the appreciation of connectivity. Teachers can follow Gibson when she states "there are possibilities in experimenting with various forms of dependency, giving and receiving, expecting nothing and everything" (Gibson, 2006, p. 190).

A focus on desire instead of needs and limitations provides a serious task for education in our society. It is from the work of Kittay, Jennings, and Wasunna (2005) that we get inspiration to work with the ideas of an ethic of care that takes dependence as a central feature of human life and focuses on interdependency rather than independence as a goal of human development. The interplay between youngsters and environment is very important to have a more clear view on the capacities and desires. Youngsters "do not perform their agency, alternating sameness and difference and performing hybrid, nomadic identities in a vacuum. It is the welcoming ability of the teachers that creates the context in which this agency or this relational citizenship takes form" (Vandenbroeck, Roets, & Snoeck, 2009, p. 213). This works in multiple directions and connections with the environment and other human beings play an important role. This implies that a teacher needs to investigate how all students can communicate and interact in the classroom, how all students can build up relationships, make friends and solve conflicts, how all students can get involved in the learning process. It is a never ending research process that requires time and asks for a shift in focus from performance to involvement of all students. At this moment, the desires, plans, dreams and capacities of youngsters with an intellectual disability are most of the time irrelevant for the care and support they receive. It is acceptable as part of "the intake procedure," but never becomes a substantial part of a "traditional individualized trajectory." Olsson (2009) highlights desire from a historical perspective (p. 145):

> by proposing that desire is production of real, lack or need can be positioned not as a cause but rather as an effect. Within the logic of desire as lack, mad people and children become "needy" since institutions never capture their desires as production of real, but reduce them, tame them and adapt them as signs of need and lack.

This is often an ongoing struggle in the lives of people with an intellectual disability since they were very young.

Nicolas 2009, Narrative Snapshot From his Mother by Elisabeth

In the case of Nicolas we never noticed something special, we always went along with what he demonstrated to us. It began in the third year of preschool. There were tests to see if he was ready for primary education. The school psychologist was not pleased with the results, they used for the first time the word "mild mental retardation." We never talked about him in those terms, even not now. We realize that he needs support but it is not dramatic. (mother of Nicolas)

QUALIFICATION, SOCIALIZATION, AND SUBJECTIFICATION OF EDUCATION

In an attempt to find answers to the question what kind of education makes it possible for young people to build an inclusive life, we also rely on Biesta (2009) when he presents a conceptual framework based on a distinction between the qualification, socialization and subjectification as possible functions of education. This might help us to ask better and more precise questions about the aims and outcomes of education. All these functions are related to each other.

Qualification

In our society a lot of attention is given to qualification of children, young people and adults. It is all about the curriculum and achieving the (standards) goals. It is about preparing students to enter the workforce and make them workplace ready. Education is strongly connected with the—neoliberal—economic system to deliver competent people who are prepared to work. The qualification function cannot stand alone. Providing students with knowledge and skills is also important for other aspects of their life and their participation as citizens in the society. Masschelein and Quaghebeur are (from a critical perspective) introducing the concept of the active citizen:

> a citizen able to speak up for his/her own interest, a responsible citizen who has no rights without duties, cherishing the values of "free choice" and taking responsibility over his/her life as a personal entrepreneur and therefore actively participating in the democratic fora that are made available to him (Masschelein & Quaghebeur, 2005, as cited in Vandenbroeck, Roets, & Snoeck, 2009, p. 212).

Nathalie 2012, Observation and Narrative Snapshot by Inge

In Nathalie's secondary school a lot of attention was given to job related skills: time management, wearing the appropriate outfit.... Now when Nathalie is working we observe that she is a real role model and is very motivated to work. She enjoys and wants to achieve her tasks. This is possible within a framework of a positive and disciplined attitude, this means e.g., going to sleep in time to find enough energy for the next day.

Eline (one of the support staff members of Nathalie) is blocked in a traffic jam and gets a lot of text messages from Nathalie: Eline where are you? My colleagues rely on me.

Nathalie's job is also about achieving goals. She works with toddlers in kindergarten. She shares a lot of tasks with the preschool teacher. For every task a balance is sought between Nathalie's talents, the things she really likes to do and little moments of challenge. Taking the strengths of Nathalie as starting point is quintessential. Nathalie gets a lot of opportunities to feel competent, to get little moments of success and satisfaction. Nathalie: I teach children to use a computer and at the end of the school year every toddler was able to handle a mouse.

Within the whole process support seems to be central. Support has to be seen as something broad: from technical tools (mobile phone with alarm system to warn for the beginning of a new task like going to supervise on the playground) to a one-to-one assistant who gives help to participate. Nathalie is not fully dependent on the support staff. She can decide when (and when not) she needs some help.

The learning of children and youngsters with an intellectual disability is situated in a sociocultural context that takes place in interrelationships, requiring the construction of an environment that allows for maximum movement, interdependence and interaction (Rinaldi, 2006). Youngsters should get opportunities to grow up with the idea that the other is necessary for their own identity and existence (Rinaldi, 2006). Every subject is considered as a construction, "both self-constructed and socially constructed within a context and a culture" (Rinaldi, 2006, p. 138). When youngsters with a disability talk about "who" they are, they talk about what they share with peers to explain their own interests. The feeling of connectedness is very important in going to school.

If we talk with Nathalie, Walter and Nicolas about their inclusive school they talk about field trips, school treats, and what happens at the playground and during lunchtime.

Nathalie, Walter and Nicolas show how hard they—and their allies—try to create a sense of belonging.

Nathalie 2006, Observation by Inge

When Nathalie signs her letters with her name and the abbreviation for her class group (Nathalie Deschamps, 4BKb), she shows to be proud of being part of that group. It is part of who she is.

We want to invest in pedagogical relations where knowledge is seen as a consequence of a process of meaning making in continuous encounters with others and the world. Children, youngsters and their teachers are understood as coconstructors of knowledge and culture (Rinaldi, 2006). Teachers and support givers in an inclusive situation talk a lot about what they learn from pupils and how a positive and friendly relation with them is essential in order to learn. Learning is seen in a very broad sense: it is not only about content, but also about learning to live together. Learning happens in multidirectional ways: youngsters learn from each other, a teacher learns from the pupils, a support worker learns from a teacher. The class environment and atmosphere is very crucial in welcoming and inviting learning. A classroom is a web of connections that come and go, that change over time and in intensity.

Socialization

The second major function of education is the socialization function. It has to do with becoming a participant. Mostly socialization is not the explicit aim of educational programs; it is part of the so called "hidden curriculum" (Biesta, 2009). It is not explicitly taught how you communicate and interact with others, how you develop friendships, how you solve conflicts. Deleuze and Guattari (1987) present us with the provocative possibility that desire does not have to be about what a personal self wants, but could be about connecting with the world, making things happen and experiencing what happens in ways that defy subject/object and self/other dichotomies. In this sense, desire can create for youngsters with disabilities belonging in constant movement (Diedrich, 2005). Together with Lorraine (2008) we see how desire becomes productive, it connects, makes things happen and extends someone's capacities to affect and to be affected.

The reciprocity between the individual and the surrounding environment is the focus of attention for teachers. They are part of the assemblages and use these connections to support the desire. Such a pedagogy of desire opens up a source of natural solidarity, and an enormous amount of possibilities to learn in connection with professionals and peers. It is about "us" (Bogdan & Taylor, 1989). Desire has "to do with cultivating and facilitating productive encounters, which sustain processes of self-transformation or self-fashioning in the direction of affirming positivity" (Braidotti, 2006, p. 3).

Nathalie, Follow-Up of Process by Inge

Within the educational trajectory of Nathalie a lot of attention is given to communication and interaction, how do I start a conversation, how do I handle keeping distance/coming into the inner circle of people, … how can I "read" somebodies behavior, how do I handle the idea that some people say something they don't mean…. Within this process Nathalie needed a lot of practice and support. In former days Nathalie could get really upset when someone was too directive or not clear enough in the communication…. But she learned how to handle these very precious moments of interaction and became "a strong communicator." This is illustrated in following narrative snapshot.

Nathalie: "You should come with me to the kindergarten Inge, one of the teachers there is really a complex person. Best is to answer her questions with a straight yes or no, she needs short answers and a lot of confirmation."

Socialization was not the easy chapter within Nathalie's curriculum. It looks like school has not given enough attention to this topic. As a consequence she has to build a new network of friends after her school career; there is only one good friend left from her class group.

Belonging does not happen everywhere and automatically. It needs to be facilitated by the person with a disability, his/her peers, the surrounding context. Here teachers can play an important facilitating role in a classroom reality that can be seen as a "social laboratory." We cannot look at belonging as a permanent state of being, but as a process with ups and downs. As supporting networks, we need to have high expectations, provide necessary support, create connections, solve barriers and make sure the successful moments are visible.

Nicolas 2013, Observation by Elisabeth

In Nicolas' case, socialization—especially in secondary education—confronted him with a lot of vulnerability. He missed the nice places and his safe environment from primary school. He had to let go a lot of rituals and people he could trust. In his new school he had to learn a lot of things all over again, he had to find new teachers that he could confine in. This asks much more time and Nicolas had not a lot of strategies to solve these problems. On top of that, he ended up in a difficult class group with a lot of classmates with personal problems. Bullying Nicolas was taking big proportions. Nicolas was hit at constantly, verbally and emotionally. He could not stop or avoid it. Often in moment of powerlessness, he began to defend himself physically. It made him very nervous, fearful and even suspicious. Sometimes he came home after school and just went to bed, crying. His parents tried to listen to him and kept him home once in a while. They find it important that school is interesting and fun, … it needs to augment your interest to learn in a positive way. A good atmosphere is important in order to work on your intellectual development … is their credo.

Within socialization we see an ambiguous relationship between "strengths" and "vulnerabilities." Most youngsters are vulnerable: their control is—from their perspective—blown away. A complex social life brings a lot of unsteadiness and questions. They have to look for connections and alliances while they are confronted with upsetting feelings nobody can fully explain or understand. Encounters with bullies or negative social interactions are influencing youngsters with an intellectual disability deeply for the rest of their lives. At the same time becoming-adult opens up a strength not many youngsters knew they could develop. They show more patience, assertiveness, are less touched by authorities and social codes. They gather situated knowledge around themselves and their social contacts with peers. They have to "lodge [them]self on a stratum, experiment with the opportunities it offers, find an advantageous place on it, find potential movements of deterritorialization, possible lines of flight, experience them, … experiment, living-in-itself, connect, conjugate and continue" (Deleuze & Guattari, 1987, p. 161).

Support of social networks who are professionally involved like teachers, family and friends play a very important role in that process. Being able to say what support you need and managing that support is part of becoming for youngsters (and adults) with a disability. Often youngsters tell us about the big anxiety of their parents, the overprotecting teachers, the support workers that hinder contacts with peers and teachers. We learned from Kittay et al. (2005) that we only should provide care when care is required, we do not have to eliminate all dependency, but just those dependencies that undermine or interfere with the freedom to exercise whatever capacities one has or can develop.

Youngsters with disabilities spend a large amount of their time in the company of adults and in social spaces where adults are actively present. Most of the children think very positively about support that is related to positive consequences: they do more work and it is easier to participate in the activities just like peers. Youngsters are also explicit about doing things on their own. They want to do things independently as much as possible. As a professional we need to be aware of our role and our influence on the person we support. This is an important branch of becoming-professional. Connecting to Walter, Nicolas or Nathalie, his/her story and his/her parents teach the professionals to constantly monitor and change our position; we have to be able to leave our own goals and tasks. We have to step into the "shoes" of the person we are supporting. We are not only professionals but also human beings AND women/men AND mothers/fathers etc. We have to admit that we do not know sometimes. Professionals can only give support if we are willing to leave our known expert territory and go into dialogue with pupils and parents.

Subjectivation

Education also impacts on what we might refer to as processes of individuation or the processes of subjectification—"of becoming a subject, ways of being in which the individual is not simply a 'specimen' of a more encompassing order" (Biesta, 2009, p. 40). Nathalie, Nicolas and Walter are "traveling," are on a "long journey" and take unexpected steps in their personal lives. We see them as "nomads" (Braidotti, 1994, in Roets, 2009) with their self in a process of constant transformation. They built opportunities to reinvent multiple selves instead of static identities. Becoming (Nashef, 2010) is in such a perspective a source of creativity, opening up possibilities for a new beginning.

Walter 2011, Observation by Geert
One day Walter told me that he wanted to change his name from Walter to Michael. In a playful dialogue I tried to find out why this name change and why Michael. Because we are both basketball freaks we came to the idea that in our dreams a lot of us wanted to become Michael Jordan… But Walter was also thinking about who he wanted to become: get rid of the Walter-the-nice-adolescent role and moving to Michael-the-cool-young-adult position… (new name, tattoo????) I can tell you he promised me to wave at me in the street if I would call him Walter (knowing that we were playing as if).

Becoming is strictly a matter of deterritorialization (Deleuze & Guattari, 1987). Youngsters with an intellectual disability move, in Deleuzian terms, from the center to the periphery and to the limits. Their confrontation with the otherness has imposed a becoming and challenges the preexisting order of giving birth to "healthy," "normal" and "fully active" youngsters. They are confronted with life in-between, life at the "borderland." Such borderlands (Estrada & McClaren, 1993) are places where cultures collide creatively such that the identities of those who "cross over" are enriched and challenged.

Nathalie 2008, Observation by Inge

When Nathalie made the transition to secondary education, no school in her neighborhood was willing to give her access. This means that her classmates came from a different part of town, she had to take her internships far from her home. When she graduated Nathalie wanted to have a job just like her brother and her cousin. In the beginning she continued to work as a volunteer in the places where she had done her internship. Later, workplaces were found closer to her home address. More and more independence became an important asset for Nathalie.

"You know what I like about working in that kindergarten, I can go by myself, with my bicycle."

Walter 2012, Observation by Geert

Walter comes into the University building with a big smile. Today we evaluate "his student." For the last six months Willy has been with Walter for more than 15 hours a week. They were working toward Walter's first steps into his practice period in the riding school. Willy, Walter's parents and Walter himself were convinced that the evaluation process of Willy couldn't get an end without Walter being present at the official evaluation ritual. Walter was invited just as the other official student's practice mentors of Willy's study group. It was good to see that Walter and his parents prepared this official moment by organizing a short evaluation questionnaire where Walter got very concrete questions about Willy's activities (e.g. questions about the competencies of Willy to build contact with Walter—questions about Willy's capabilities to work together—questions about the clarity of communication and punctuality of Willy). The most exciting step in the process for Walter was connected with giving a grade to Willy.

CONCLUSIONS

Drawing on a qualitative approach, this study aimed to explore what we can learn from former students with a label of intellectual disability who were following an inclusive schooling trajectory. By following those youngsters we learned from the way the families of Walter, Nicolas and Nathalie have given opportunities and roles to their children with intellectual disability, who—when individualized, responsive, comprehensive and especially designed support are put into place—can live an enviable life (Turnbull, 2010).

These stories provide also valuable insights about what we ask from teachers in inclusive trajectories. Their task is to assure that inclusive education is all about becoming and belonging. In our analysis it becomes clear that the way the teacher looks at the child with a disability is crucial. Because how we think about and look at children determines the ways in which we deal with them. It is in the encounter that teachers get to "know" the child. It is about creating and supporting opportunities for children to participate in the classroom. The stories of Walter, Nathalie and Nicolas teach us that barriers will come up in achieving the involvement of the child with a disability. These barriers can be seen as challenges and a quest for answers. Teachers must relinquish standard pathways and what we take for granted. It requires of a teacher to become "a listener" and "follower," to discover and focus on the desire of the child with a disability. When teachers and education can tune into this "fluidity," students with a disability can become more than the category that constrains them.

Over the past decades there is remarkable interest in measuring educational outcomes. What the stories of the youngsters teach us is that the competences these youngsters show are not the competences we can find in standardized lists of educational outcomes. It will be important to use a broad framework to inclusive education that opens up opportunities for multiple talents (Callahan, Tomlinson, Moon, Tomchin & Plucher, 1995) to assure that persons with intellectual disabilities get the time and opportunities to become respected citizens. This is a complex and time consuming process where no simple answers or linear solutions can be found.

We end this chapter with the parents of Nicolas talking about his future:

> We want him to live as independently as possible, he can do whatever he wants. Make his own choices and feel control over his life. Sometimes people think we ask too much of him, we never had the feeling we did that. We always had to fight to not underestimate him. There is a difference between demanding the impossible and asking for the maximum. Now Nicolas helps us to make decisions, we can talk with him and often see from his body language how he feels about it. He doesn't mind big efforts, but he also needs the feeling of succeeding. He can feel very proud of himself and what he already reached in life.

REFERENCES

Allan, J. (1999). *Actively seeking inclusion: Pupils with special needs in mainstream schools.* London, England: Falmer Press.

Biesta, G. (2009). Good education in an age of measurement: On the need to reconnect with the question of purpose in education. *Educational Assessment, Evaluation and Accountability, 21,* 33–46.

Biklen, D. (1992). *Schooling without labels: Parents, educators and inclusive education.* Philadelphia, PA: Temple University Press.

Biklen, D. (1999). The metaphor of mental retardation: rethinking ability and disability. In H. Bersani, Jr. (Ed.), *Responding to the challenge: Current trends and international issues in developmental disabilities: Essays in honor of Gunnar Dybwad* (pp. 35–52.) Cambridge, MA: Brookline.

Bogdan, R., & Taylor, S. J. (1989). Relationships with severely disabled people: The social construction of humanness. *Social Problems, 36*(2), 135–148.

Braidotti, R. (2006). Affirmation versus vulnerability: On contemporary ethical debates. *Special Issue of Symposium: Canadian Journal of Continental Philosophy, 10*(1), 235–254.

Callahan, C., Tomlinson, C., Moon, T., Tomchin, E., & Plucker, J. (1995). *Project START: Using a multiple intelligences model in identifying and promoting talent in high-risk students* (Research monograph 95136). Storrs, CT: The National Research Center on the Gifted and Talented, University of Connecticut.

Deleuze, G., & Guattari, F. (1987). *A thousand plateaus: Capitalism and schizophrenia* (B. Massumi, Trans). Minneapolis, MN: University of Minnesota Press.

Diedrich, L. (2005). Aids and its treatments: Two doctors' narratives of healing, desire and belonging. *Journal of Medical Humanities, 26*(4), 237–257.

Emerson, R. (2004). Working with 'key incidents.' In C. Seal, G. Gobo, J. Gubrium, & D. Silverman (Eds.), *Qualitative Research Practice* (pp. 457–472). London, England: SAGE.

Estrada, K., & McClaren, P. (1993). A dialogue on multiculturalism and democratic culture. *Educational researcher, 22*(3), 27–33.

Gibson, B. E. (2006). Disability, connectivity and transgressing the autonomous body. *Journal of Medical Humanities, 2*, 187-196.

Jackson, A., & Mazzeï, L. (2012). *Thinking with theory in qualitative research: Viewing data across multiple perspectives.* Milton Park, Abingdon, United Kingdom: Routledge.

Jackson, L., Ryndak, D., & Wehmeyer, M. (2008-2009). The dynamic relationship between context, curriculum and student learning: A case for inclusive education as a research based practice. *Research and Practice for Persons with Severe Disabilities, 33–4*(4-1), 175–195.

Kittay, E. (2001). When care is just and justice is caring: Justice and mental retardation. *Public Culture, 13*(3), 557–579.

Kittay, E., Jennings, B., & Wasunna, A. (2005). Dependency, difference and the global ethic of long term care. *The Journal of Political Philosophy, 13*(4), 443–469.

Kunc, N. (1992). The need to belong: Restructuring Maslow's hierarchy of needs. In R. A. Villa, J. S. Thousand, W. Stainback, & S. Stainback (Eds.), *Restructuring for caring and effective education: Administrative guide to creating heterogeneous schools* (pp. 25–39). Baltimore, MD: Paul H. Brookes.

Lorraine, T. (2008). Feminist lines of flight from the majoritarian subject. *Deleuze Studies, 2*, 60–82.

Nashef, H. (2010). Becomings in J.M. Coetzee's Waiting for the Barbarians and Jose Saramago's Blindness. *Comparative Literature Studies, 47*, 1, 21–41.

Olsson, L. (2009). *Movement and experimentation in young children's learning: Deleuze and Guattari in early childhood education.* London, England: Routledge Falmer.

Rinaldi, C. (2006). *In dialogue with Reggio Emilia. Listening, researching and learning.* London, England: Routledge Falmer.

Roets, G. (2009). Unravelling Mr. President's Nomad Lands: Travelling to inter-disciplinary frontiers of knowledge in Disability Studies. *Disability and Society, 24*(6), 689–701.

Sotirin, P. (2005). Becoming-woman. In C. J. Stivale (Ed.), *Gilles Deleuze: Key concepts* (pp. 98–109). Stocksfield, United Kingdom: Acumen.

Turnbull, A. (2010). *Transitioning to enviable lives for adults with autism*. Lecture to the Geneva Centre International Symposium on Autism, Toronto, Canada.

UNESCO. (1994). *The Salamanca statement and framework for action on special needs education adopted by the World Conference on Special Needs Education: Access and quality*. Paris, France: Author.

Vandenbroeck, M., Roets, G., & Snoeck, A. (2009). Immigrant mothers crossing borders: Nomadic identities and multiple belongings in early childhood education. *European Early Childhood Education Research Journal, 17*(2), 203–216.

Van Hove, G., Gabel, S., De Schauwer, E., Mortier, K., Van Loon, J., Loots, G., Devlieger, P., Roets, G., & Claes, L. (2012). Resistance and resilience in a life full of professionals and labels: Narrative snapshots of Chris. *Intellectual and Developmental Disabilities, 50*(5), 426–435.

Williams, J. (2003). *Gilles Deleuze's difference and repetition. A critical introduction and guide*. Edinburgh, Scotland: Edinburg University Press.

CHAPTER 6

INCLUSIVE RESEARCH AND LEARNING ENVIRONMENTS

Ideas and Suggestions for Inclusive Research and the Development of Supportive Learning Environments for Children With Autism and Intellectual Disabilities

Eija Kärnä

In the mid-1990s, the Salamanca Statement (UNESCO, 1994) focused the majority of Western countries on the need to include children with special educational needs in regular education. Today, more than 2 decades later, ensuring high quality education for all children is still a challenge. Inclusive education involves much more than placing children with special educational needs in regular classrooms. Thus, what happens in classrooms is critical for achieving genuine inclusive education. In recent years, the discourse around inclusive education has moved from justifying why the approach should be adopted, to figuring out how to build effective inclusive learning environments. This chapter will introduce the idea of a supportive technology-enhanced learning environment that emphasizes the emergence of the strengths and creativity of children with autism spectrum disorder (ASD) and intellectual disabilities. The environment is developed in the ongoing interdisciplinary research project, Children with Autism Spectrum Disorders

Inclusive Education for Students with Intellectual Disabilities,
pp. 117–138

as Creative Actors in a Strength-Based Technology-Enhanced Learning Environment (CASCATE) that aims to investigate the actions of children with ASD in a strength-based multiple-technology learning environment. The environment is developed to be adaptable and transferrable and thus, it could be used in the future to support learning and inclusion of children with special educational needs in different educational contexts. The chapter will utilize the results of a midevaluation study of the project and include discussion on the participating teachers' and assistants' views on the adaptivity and transferability of the learning environment and on participants' inclusion in the project.

INTRODUCTION

Inclusive education is an approach that provides education to children with special educational needs in regular classrooms. Inclusion provides the necessary support services in the same classroom with other children of the same age on a full-time or part-time basis (e.g., Ferguson, 2008; Miles & Signal, 2010). The inclusion movement began primarily in the United States and Europe as a special education initiative on behalf of children with disabilities in the 1980s. In the mid-1990s, the Salamanca Statement (UNESCO, 1994) focused the majority of Western countries on the need to include children with special educational needs in regular education. Today, more than 2 decades later, including children with special educational needs in mainstream schools is still a global issue as countries are attempting to implement inclusive education reforms. Even though diversity is seen as a value that ensures the highest quality education for all children, implementation is still a challenge (European Agency for Development in Special Needs Education, 2011; Ferguson, 2008).

The motivation for writing this chapter originates from the midevaluation findings of an ongoing project called Children with Autism Spectrum Disorders as Creative Actors in a Strength-Based Technology-Enhanced Learning Environment (CASCATE). CASCATE is an interdisciplinary research project that investigates the actions (mainly attention, communication, interaction and creativity) of children with autism spectrum disorders (ASD) in a strength-based multiple-technology learning environment (Vellonen, Kärnä, & Virnes, 2013; Voutilainen, Vellonen, & Kärnä, 2011). The findings of the project indicate that the learning environment matters for the emergence of potential skills of children with ASD (Vellonen, Kärnä, & Virnes, 2012, 2013). The findings also show that it is important to include both children with special educational needs and adults working with them in the design and development of the learning environment. The participants' involvement facilitates the construction of a supportive environment that fits the needs of a variety of learners in different educational settings. Consequently, a learning environment that is usable and transferrable to any educational setting facilitates the inclusion of children with special educational needs in regular education.

The structure of this chapter is fourfold. First, the chapter introduces the current state of inclusion in comprehensive education. A special focus is placed on the development of inclusive education in the Finnish educational system. Second, the chapter discusses the possibilities for learning environment and technology to facilitate the inclusion of children with special educational needs, particularly children with ASD and intellectual disabilities. Third, the chapter introduces the CASCATE project and its midevaluation findings, which show how the learning environment and inclusion in development and research is successful from the point of view of the adults who participated in the project. Finally, the chapter will discuss the possibilities and pitfalls of inclusive development and research on the supportive learning environment for children with special educational needs.

TOWARD INCLUSIVE EDUCATION

While there is universality to the underlying view that inclusive education is a fundamental way of realizing quality education for all, there are clear differences in national policies for transformation of the school system (Savolainen, Engelbrecht, Nel, & Malinen, 2012). This is because the definitions of inclusion and inclusive education vary greatly within countries and the implementation of inclusive education is influenced by a range of social, cultural, historical and political issues. In addition, inclusive education is not a static phenomenon; rather, conceptions of, policies for, and practices in inclusive education are constantly changing. Therefore, any examination of inclusive education and "current" practices must be considered within the context of the wider educational reforms occurring in a specific country (European Agency for Development in Special Needs Education, 2010).

In Europe as well as in other parts of the world, many countries have already instituted the laws and policies that make children with disabilities no different than any other child—the general education classroom is meant for all, or nearly all, children. For example, according to the 2012 country data collected by the European Agency for Special Educational Needs, Sweden, Italy, and Iceland are examples of countries where support for children with special educational needs in compulsory education is organized mainly in inclusive settings. However, some countries have retained parallel systems for general and special education and some countries are somewhere in the middle, with parallel systems that are gradually transforming into various partnerships and collaborations with the general education system offering a range of options for children with special educational needs. In France and Germany, for example, approximately 70% of children with special educational needs study in noninclusive settings and only about 30% study in inclusive settings (European Agency for Development in Special Needs Education, 2012). Regardless of the efforts to provide inclusive education for all children, in most countries, some children are still excluded from mainstream education, do not meaningfully participate in school or have little to show for their time in school (e.g., European Agency for Development in Special Needs Education, 2012; Ferguson, 2008; Savolainen et al., 2012).

In the Finnish education system, the need for special education started to expand when comprehensive school was introduced in the 1970s. This reform combined the dual system (i.e., grammar school and civic school) into a single 9-year comprehensive school. As a result, the children's heterogeneity in the classroom increased and part-time special education was introduced as a means to support the education of children with special educational needs. The need for support continued to expand until 2010. During that year, approximately 22% of children received part-time special education and more than 8% were identified as having special educational needs (Official Statistics of Finland, 2009). However, the number of children receiving special education included children who received special support without an official diagnosis, which should be taken into account when comparing data from different countries.

Over the last few years, there have been major attempts in Finland to reform special needs education services to be more inclusive. The new Special Education Strategy (Ministry of Education of Finland, 2007), the related additions to the Basic Education Act (Finnish Law 642/2010; National Board of Education, 2010) and the Curriculum guidelines (National Board of Education, 2010) have contributed to a change that has affected the provision of services. Before these changes in legislation, special education services were divided into part-time special education and special education. From 2011 onwards, the support given to comprehensive school children became tripartite. Support for learning and school attendance was divided into general, intensified and special support, depending on the duration and extent of the support. If general support is not enough, intensified support can be provided. If intensified support is not sufficient, children can receive special support (Finnish Law 642/2010).

In autumn 2012, intensified or special support was given to 12.7% of children in comprehensive school, which was one percentage point higher than in 2011. On one hand, the number requiring special support has decreased since the legislative change, but the number of children requiring intensified support has slightly increased. The same phenomenon can be observed when looking at the numbers that indicate the places where children receiving special support were taught. The number of children receiving special support who had been fully integrated into general education groups was 21% in 2011 and 19% in 2012. However, the share of recipients of all teaching in a special group was 42% in 2011 and 41% in 2012. Among the children of special support, 37% received part of their education in a general education group and part in a special education group in 2011; in 2012, that number was 40% (Official Statistics of Finland, 2011, 2012). Thus, the change toward inclusion in Finnish school system seems to be very slow and the long-term effect of the legislative changes can only be seen after several years when the system has adjusted its activities according to reforms.

SUPPORTIVE LEARNING ENVIRONMENTS, A KEY TO INCLUSIVE EDUCATION?

However, the numbers only tell a small part of the inclusion story. It remains troubling that the rhetoric of inclusive education for children with special educational needs is not matched by reality. The numbers show how many children have access to inclusive education in general education classrooms and schools, but they say nothing about what happens to children in those environments. This may mean that children are in regular schools, but are spending most of their time in separate classes within those schools. In addition, children can be in a class, but not be part of it in terms of social and learning membership. What happens in the classrooms, thus, is critical to achieving genuine inclusive education (Ferguson, 2008). The discourse around inclusive education is slowly moving from a justification of why the approach should be adopted, to how it can be successfully implemented (Loreman, 2007).

It is challenging to implement inclusive education. Teachers often can have fears related to educating and managing diverse student groups. For example, teachers have concerns about including children with autism and intellectual disabilities because it may force them to change their teaching format and implement practices that are unique and complicated (Niles, 2005). In addition teachers are reported to believe that they are insufficiently prepared to teach students with special educational needs (Cook, 2002). However, the provision of a supportive learning environment that effectively meets the needs of all children could facilitate the implementation of an inclusive classroom. A supportive learning environment and children's engagement with a variety of abilities in effective learning means teaching practices must extend beyond teaching the content of a subject (Jiménez, Graf, & Rose, 2007; Loreman, 2007; Watkins, 2005). The practical question that teachers must address is how to build an effective supportive learning environment. Problems of children with special educational needs are commonly used as the main starting point for the development of pedagogical practices. However, it can be asked whether the unheeded strengths and creativity of children with special educational needs would be a more efficient and inclusive basis for the construction of supportive learning environments and the implementation of inclusive education? Research supporting the strength-based approach already exists (e.g., Cosden, Kern, Koegel, Koegel, Greenwell, & Klein, 2006; Craig & Baron-Cohen, 1999; Yechiam, Arshavsky, Shamay-Tsoory, Yaniv, & Aharon, 2010). It can be further speculated whether children with special needs can be included in the development of a supportive learning environment and if so, how.

Elements of a Supportive Learning Environment

The "learning environment" is a term used to describe a range of specific areas of education and to convey broad ideas about learning. Nevertheless, a learning environment's characteristics (e.g., class arrangements, computers, laboratory experiment kits, teaching methods, learning styles and assessment methods) influence a learner's academic achievements and other learning outcomes in cognitive and affective domains (Doppelt, 2004, 2006; Doppelt & Schunn, 2008). The impact is even more remarkable when learners have intellectual disabilities and ASD (Sze, 2009; Verdonschot, de Witte, Reichrath, Buntinx, & Curfs, 2009; Williams, 2008; Williams, Petersson, & Brooks, 2006). A growing number of studies suggest that interactive causal multisensory environments are stimulating for people with disabilities (Williams, 2008; Williams et al., 2006). In addition, recent research indicates that children with ASD benefit from environments that provide structure while allowing them to express their personalities in the learning choices they make (Sze, 2009). In other words, if the structure and the visual supports of these environments provide sufficient guidance and assistance for children with ASD the environments also facilitate children with ASD to focus on social understanding and communication (Guldberg, 2010; Parsons et al., 2009, 2011).

Technology can also be an important element for developing a supportive learning environment. Recent research addresses the advantages of technology for the learning, full participation and inclusion of individuals with special educational needs (Baker, Lang, & O'Reilly 2009; Kelly, 2009; Kozima, Nakagawa, & Yasuda, 2005; Mechling, Gast, & Krupa,

2007; Mechling, Gast, & Seid, 2009; Myers, 2007; Olive et al., 2007; Olive, Lang, & Davis, 2008; Passerino & Santarosa, 2008; Robins, Dautenhahn, te Boekhorst, & Billard, 2005; P. Williams, 2006). However, the benefits of technology inclusion of children with special educational needs are often abandoned for many reasons (P. Williams, 2006). Technology might not be considered as a relevant means to enhance children's learning or to include them into society because teachers are not aware of or familiar with the latest developments in educational technology. Sometimes technology fails to match the child's desires and/or needs, or the child outgrows the capacities of a particular device. Technology might also be considered too costly compared to its usability and benefits for learning and teaching. Therefore, in order to increase the transferability, availability and beneficial use of technology for children with special educational needs, the development of and research on technology must be conducted inclusively in natural settings.

In order to foster the optimal use of technology, there is also a need for greater awareness of the usability of modern technology for children with special educational needs. The obstacles for the use of technology can be removed if an individual user is placed at the center of the development and assessment process (Williams, 2006). This is a particularly important issue when researching and developing technology for children with special educational needs. The development of and research on technology is often based on professionals' views of children's disabilities or special educational needs, which prevents or makes their learning or inclusion into society difficult. In addition, if a child with special educational needs is rarely viewed as an active and creative developer of technology, it can hinder the development of a piece of technology, which could provide a full scale of educational and inclusive opportunities for a child with special educational needs. In the case of children who need personal assistance, the inclusion of the personnel working with them in the development and research process is crucial.

It is also important to consider a number of other dimensions, such as teaching practices, learning contexts and child characteristics when building a supportive and activating learning environment for children with ASD and intellectual disabilities. Overall, assessment is a crucial component in the development of a supportive learning environment. It gives a firm basis for a systematic preparation and development of effective pedagogical interventions. Assessment, planning and facilitation need to focus on helping children with ASD and intellectual disabilities develop the understanding and skills that will enable them to access the curriculum, engage in learning and experience true inclusion. While a diagnosis might give a signpost to the needs of a child or a young person with disabilities, identification of those needs can only arise from an understanding of how the condition affects the individual at a particular time and in a particular learning environment (Parsons et al., 2009, 2011).

DEVELOPMENT OF A SUPPORTIVE TECHNOLOGY-ENHANCED LEARNING ENVIRONMENT VIA INCLUSIVE RESEARCH— A CASE OF THE CASCATE PROJECT

The assessment of children with special educational needs is often a bureaucratic professional-driven process where it is difficult for the voices of all participants to be heard (Farrell, 2001). In order to increase the quality of the participants' inclusion in the assessment process, it is important to include all participants in every step of the process. This is also important when designing and implementing a supportive learning environment for children with special educational needs. The design and development of the environment should be implemented in close collaboration with children, teachers and other adults working in an educational setting. The evaluation of the implementation process could be carried out using participatory and inclusive research methods.

In research, inclusion refers to a range of research approaches that have traditionally been termed "participatory" or "emancipatory." The approaches have been developed as a response to the criticism of the objectification of respondents in traditional research processes. In a participatory or emancipatory research process the power imbalance between participants and researchers is acknowledged and the aim is to empower respondents through research. Research that includes people with learning difficulties as active participants is now fairly common and has been fostered by ideologies such as normalization and the social model of disability. It has also been influenced by arguments for qualitative research methods in social science and stimulated by the critiques of traditional research relationships made by supporters of self advocacy (Aspis, 1997; Walmsley, 2001).

CASCATE Project

In this chapter, inclusive research refers to the arrangement of activities and research in the CASCATE project. The 4-year (2011–2014) CASCATE project investigates the actions of children with ASD and intellectual disabilities in a technology-enhanced environment and develops technologies and a supportive learning environment in close collaboration with teachers, assistants and children. Moreover, as these participants have very limited speech, they are often excluded from research because studies usually focus on individuals with developed verbal skills or "high-functioning" ASD (Boucher, 2012; Crosland, Clarke, & Dunlap, 2012).

The project is carried out as an inclusive research project. In the CASCATE project, inclusion refers to the active involvement of the participating children with ASD and the adults working with them. The CASCATE project research participants include four children with ASD at one comprehensive school. Two children are 10- and 12-year-old boys, and two are 8- and 13-year-old girls. The instruction of all children is based on their individual educational plan. The children face many challenges in their actions and learning, yet have multiple strengths, such as good visual or auditory skills, and a variety of skills to use technology (e.g. to play computer games). All the children have limited verbal language skills and use augmentative and alternative communication (AAC) methods, particularly picture symbols, in their daily communication. The children's teachers and school assistants also participate in the research project by giving valuable information about the children's interests and needs, knowledge about their actions in their respective classrooms, and feedback about the learning environment.

Four Principles of a Supportive Learning Environment in CASCATE Project

The CASCATE project uses four main principles as the basis for the establishment and development of a supportive technology-enhanced learning environment: (1) fostering children's active role and creativity; (2) fostering their strengths; (3) utilizing technology solutions that are modifiable to enable children's roles as developers; and (4) utilizing technology solutions that are transformable so as to render them applicable in the school context (Vellonen et al., 2013; Voutilainen et al., 2011).

The first principle—children's creativity and active roles as actors and developers in a learning environment—is based on the idea that children with ADS and intellectual disabilities have potential skills that are often hidden and are, therefore, much less researched compared to more typical features of ASD, such as repetitive and invariant behavior (Napolitano, Smith, Zarcone, Goodkin, & McAdam, 2010). The CASCATE project implements the children's active role by letting them interact with many different kinds of technology in the learning environment. The available technologies are designed to be used in multiple ways through different kinds of user interfaces (e.g., mouse, touch screen, tiles and motion-based interfaces). In addition, the variety of the contents (e.g., games, tasks, creation of stories, and building models) are designed to nurture the children's creativity.

The second principle—comprehensive support for the emergence of children's strengths—stems from the finding that the majority of research on children with ASD and technology attempts to find solutions to problems connected to ASD (e.g., Austin, Abbott, & Carbis, 2008; Bernard-Opitz, Sriram, & Nakhoda-Sapuan, 2001). The CASCATE project supports the emergence of children's strengths via the use of multimodal interactions, the utilization of different senses and the individual modifiability of technical solutions. In addition, the clarity and openness of the learning environment with minimal external stimuli, group session routines, and the multiple use of augmentative and alternative communication (AAC) methods support children's concentration on activities and enhance the clarity of the learning environment.

The third principle—modifiability of technology—emphasizes the children's active role and creative actions in the learning environment. The principle also challenges the typical design and development process of technical applications for educational purposes. The processes often include a selected group of test persons and exclude participants that might be challenging to be involved. In addition, the content and the usability of the application can be narrow covering, for example, only a few skills (e.g. social skills) that can be practiced with the application. There are plenty of examples of state-of-the-art technology solutions with predefined purposes for children with ASD and intellectual disabilities. These technologies include mobile devices to improve communication skills (De Leo & Leroy, 2008) and scheduling (Hayes, Patterson, Monibi, & Kaufman, 2008), virtual learning environments and computer games for developing social skills (Battocchi et al., 2009; Cheng, Chiang, Ye, & Cheng, 2010) and encouraging exercise (Finkelstein, Nickel, Barnes, & Suma, 2010), and robotics for improving imitation skills (Fujimoto, Matsumoto, De Silva, Kobayashi, & Higashi, 2010). Although technology is often useful for acquiring specific skills, modifiability is often limited and it cannot be customized to support the learning of children with special educational needs in an inclusive environment.

The CASCATE project involves children and the adults working with them in the physical and content modification of the applications. For example, children and adults can reconstruct the tiles used in one workstation or produce content for all of the applications. Modification choices are based on the children's interests and iterative feedback after participation at the workstations. Thus, the children have an untraditional and unique role in the study because they operate as innovative and active research partners (Druin, 2002; Marti & Bannon, 2009; Olkin, 2004) rather than as objects of inquiry. The teachers' and school assistants' roles are also important in the development of the technologies because they know the children's individual pedagogical goals.

The fourth principle, the transformability of technology solutions to everyday life, in CASCATE project is crucial for two reasons. First, commercially available technologies such as robotics are often too expensive to use in education (Bryant, Bryant, Shih, & Seok, 2010). Second, technologies are often difficult to use and time-consuming to learn how to use them (Copley & Ziviani, 2004). Nevertheless, research on advanced technologies confirms that children with ASD and intellectual disabilities benefit from various technologies (e.g., Finkelstein et al., 2010; Williams et al., 2006; Williams, Wright, Callaghan, & Coughlan, 2002); therefore, applying technology in supportive learning environments could enhance inclusive education. Thus, it is important that applications are easy to use and modifiable without external technical support.

These four principles were selected as the core elements of the supportive learning environment in the CASCATE project for many reasons. First, the focus of the interventions and technical solutions for children with special educational needs, particularly with intellectual disabilities and ASD, is often on their problems and difficulties rather than their strengths, creativity, and potential abilities and skills. This emphasis on strengths and creativity is important because these aspects in relation to ASD are less researched and understood (Happé & Frith, 2009). Second, research indicates that children with special educational needs are often seen as users rather than as active players and developers of technologies; thus, technical applications have not been able to provide a full scale of educational opportunities for children with special educational needs (LeGoff & Sherman, 2006; Virnes, Sutinen, & Kärnä-Lin, 2008). Third, previous research suggests that flexible, choice-based and tangible technology in cooperation with appropriate and inspiring pedagogical content can compensate for learning challenges and facilitate the child's role in becoming active actors and creators of their learning environment (Robins et al., 2005).

Technologies and Activities in CASCATE Project

A supportive learning environment includes four technology-based action stations, that is, symbol matching, LEGO building, storytelling and playing. At the symbol matching action station, the children have the task of matching a symbol from the computer application with the corresponding symbol or the theme on one of six tiles. At the LEGO building action station, the children make a LEGO Duplo or LEGO construction from the model on the computer application. At the storytelling action station, the children create a story by using a picture-based computer application and a touch screen. At the playing action station, the children play short games by Kinect, a motion-sensing input device.

The CASCATE project runs weekly 1-hour group sessions nine times each semester. A technology-enhanced learning environment is set up in the school's lunchroom. At the beginning of the session, there is a short warm-up and researchers give the children a pictured map of the workstations to guide them from one station to another. The children work individually with their teachers or school assistants at each station for 10 to 15 minutes. The children can choose a variety of tasks or games to work with at each workstation. During the session, the children are encouraged to work actively and to give immediate feedback about the activities at each workstation for every session. For this purpose, an easy-to-use feedback system was developed. The system consists of three feedback cards with pictures of facial expressions: very happy face, neutral face and sad face. The faces are selected from Picture Communication Symbols (PCS) using Boardmaker 5.1 software by Mayer and Johnson and the scale is similar to one used with children in various technology development projects that apply a participatory design model (Nissinen, Korhonen, Vellonen, Kärnä, & Tukiainen, 2012; Read & MacFarlane, 2006; Read, MacFarlane, & Casey, 2002). The children's feedback is considered when developing the environment during the project. For example the children's positive feedback after changes in the content of an application is taken into account when developing the application further.

HOW HAS THE DEVELOPMENT OF THE SUPPORTIVE LEARNING ENVIRONMENT AND INCLUSION IN THE PROJECT SUCCEEDED IN CASCATE?

The findings of this chapter are based on a midevaluation study (Kärnä, Parkkonen, Voutilainen, & Tuononen, 2013) that examined the views and thoughts on inclusion of the participating special education teachers and the special needs assistants in the CASCATE project. The chapter focuses on the following issues: how teachers and assistants described the supportiveness of the learning environment of the action group sessions for the participating children and adults; how teachers and assistants experienced the inclusion of the CASCATE project in the school environment; and how teachers and assistants felt about the inclusiveness of the research conducted in the CASCATE project. The children are also involved in the development of the learning environment by giving feedback in each workstation during every group session. However, their feedback is not included in this chapter due to time constrains. Their feedback will be included to the final evaluation report of the project.

Participants and Data Collection

The participants of the evaluation study were eight special education teachers and special needs assistants who had been involved in the CAS-CATE project in 2011 and the spring of 2012. The study was carried out using qualitative research methods. Seven structured interviews were conducted at a school and one at a nearby university in April and May 2012. The structured interview outline consisted of five themes:

1. interviewees' experience and background in relation to education of children with ASD,
2. teachers' and assistants', views on children's experiences of the activities and technologies used in the project and on the impact of the activities on children's behavior and actions in the classrooms,
3. teachers' and assistants experiences on their own participation to the activities of the action groups,
4. teachers' and assistants' evaluation of the adaptiveness and inclusiveness of the technology-enhanced learning environments for children with ASD,
5. the transferability of the learning environment to interviewees' own school environment and to other educational contexts.

Each interview took approximately 10 to 30 minutes. During the interviews the teachers and assistants were asked to evaluate the adaptiveness and inclusiveness of the learning environment from their own and children's point of view. In addition, the interviewees were encouraged to reveal their real experiences of the project and research conducted in it. For example, at the beginning of the project the teachers and assistants had been concerned about the videotaping that was used to collect data from children during their activities in the work stations. As the interviewees worked with children, their activities in the workstation were videotaped as well even though some of them found it a bit uncomfortable. However, the participants were aware of the situation and those staff members who did not like to be videotaped were not participating in the study. In the midevaluation phase it was important to know whether concerns such as the videotaping were still evident. The transcripts were then carefully read and notes were written. The data were analyzed using qualitative content analysis by coding the data and identifying different themes based on the five themes of the interview outline. As the interview was clearly structured and the interviews were implemented by one researcher who followed the order and the content of the themes in the outline, the coding of the data was easy to carry out. The researcher who had conducted the interviews coded the data based on the themes of the interview outline. Later the coded data was crosschecked and verified by another researcher.

Results

Overall, the interviewees said the action stations were environments that worked well for the children: the children were able to act in the action group sessions well, and the sessions enhanced many of the children's skills. Moreover, the children were motivated to participate in the action group and often looked forward to the sessions.   The interviewees found all the technologies of the action group to be useful. The most common positive comments on the technologies were related to the versatility, adaptivity and functionality of the devices. The devices and software applications were easy to use and they supported well the children's active participation. In addition, the adults found the technologies to be motivating, appropriate and successful, based on their own and children's feedback.

Nevertheless, the school personnel also gave negative feedback on the technologies. They wanted more variety in the contents and a wider selection of options for the children. In addition, the technologies were criticized for not supporting the social interaction of the children. Overall, the interviewees were mostly satisfied and found that the technologies adequately supported the inclusion of all the children as active participants in the action group. In addition, the positive impact of the action group participation was considered to be evident also in other settings besides that of the action group.

The arrangements of the action group were seen as helpful to the children. The structure and the continuity of the environment were mainly seen as positive and successful elements of the environment and crucial in terms of inclusion. The flexibility of the arrangements in the action group and the adaptability of the technology solutions were also seen to make the environment more supportive for learners. The interviewees noted that by participating in the action group, the teachers and the assistants were able to better perceive the children's abilities and identify their strengths and abilities. In addition, even though the children sometimes became overly focused and anxious and stereotypical characteristics of their behaviors increased, the structure and flexibility of the action group were seen as helpful for overcoming these challenges.

The evaluation of the effect that the action group had on the adults' and children's school routines varied among the interviewees. On one hand, the action group was considered to bring a nice variety to their normal school routine. On the other hand, the action group caused extra work for the teachers. Moreover, the adults participating in the action group with the children tended to change every week, which confused the children and the adults. Thus, the integration of the action group activities into school routines was not always regarded as smooth and many of the challenges mentioned were related to the action group's detachment from the other school routines. Indeed, the school personnel suggested that the activities of the action group could be extended so that even more children would have the opportunity to benefit from the supportive environment and the transferability of the environment as an integral part of the school routines should be better actualized.

In terms of the children's inclusion in the research process, the interviewees' opinions were not all positive. Even though efforts were made to include children in the development and research in the project through the feedback cards the system, it was not considered a completely functional means of including children in the research process. This was based on the teachers' and assistants' notions that often children's feedback was different from the adults' understanding and evaluation about the situation. In addition, it was not always clear what the children meant when they gave feedback by using cards. Therefore, according to the interviewees, the feedback system should be developed further so that the variety of children's skills and needs would be better taken into account and their possibilities to truly participate in the development of the environment could be guaranteed.

In terms of the staff members' inclusion in the research, all of the interviewees were satisfied with the flow of information between the researchers and themselves. The negative experiences in relation to the research in the CASCATE project were connected to the method of data collection during the action group sessions. Since all the sessions were videotaped, the teachers' and assistants' actions were also recorded. This method of data collection caused discomfort and reluctance and reduced the inclusiveness of the research for the adults.

Discussion and Recommendations

The process of developing inclusive education and supportive learning environments has been slow in Finland, as well as in other parts of the world. One central element preventing the progress of inclusive education has been teachers' attitudes and fears toward diverse learners. This fear is understandable as teachers feel they are lacking the necessary skills to teach children with special educational needs. However, the role of teachers in developing schools for all types of learners is crucial and they should receive all the encouragement and support they need to implement inclusive education. Thus, instead of focusing on teachers' skills, more attention should be given to the development of supportive learning environments for all learners; specifically to the use of technology as a means to enhance the inclusiveness of learning environments.

The midevaluation results of the CASCACATE project suggest that efforts to develop supportive learning environments are worthwhile and the inclusion of all participants in the development proccss could facilitate the successful development of an inclusive learning environment. For example, the teachers and assistants participating in the CASCATE project found the activities and technologies in the action group session appropriate and suitable for the children. Moreover, the arrangement of the environment and the structure of the action group were appreciated. Therefore, the recommendations in relation to the action group were mostly minor.

The results of the midevaluation study in CASCATE project also indicate that the applicability of devices and software application seem to facilitate the inclusion of children with ASD as active participants of a learning environment. However, it can be further suggested that in order to take full advantage of the technologies for building supportive learning environments, development and research should be conducted in real classroom contexts, not in a separate learning environment. It would guarantee that the transferability of the environment as an integral part of the school context could be actualized. Similar results can be found in previous research on this topic (e.g., Mechling et al., 2007; Mechling et al., 2009; Myers, 2007; Olive et al., 2007; Olive et al., 2008; Passerino & Santarosa, 2008).

The findings also suggest that it is possible to include children with ASD and intellectual disabilities in the research on and development of learning environments even though the inclusion is very challenging. The findings are parallel to the previous studies conducted on the inclusion of children with special educational needs in the research and development of technologies (Nissinen et al., 2012; Read et al., 2002; Read & MacFarlane, 2006). Yet, as the results of midevaluation study also suggest, the means to include children with special educational needs in the development of their own learning environments are still too few and underdeveloped and the true participation does not occur easily.

In terms of inclusion in the research activities, the interviewees expressed a desire for the activities to be continued without time limits.

This would allow for further development of the activities and technologies, and for the development to be driven from the point of view of the school and its staff members. This indicates that to some extent, the school personnel perceived the project to be more researcher driven than based on the wishes and ideas of the school personnel. Thus, it can be further concluded that the implementation of the inclusive development project for supportive learning environments requires continuous dynamic evaluation of the process and the use of participatory research methods.

With regards to the implementation of inclusive research, the most sensitive activity seems to be data collection. In the CASCATE project, the personnel felt considerably distressed about being videotaped and the results indicate that rather than being inclusive, the data collection method objectified the adult participants. Since the arrangement had a negative effect on the adults' feelings toward the project, it most likely had an impact on the adults' activities with the children during the action group sessions. Therefore, it is necessary to consider how the participants could be truly included in the data collection in order to increase the inclusiveness and quality of the data collected (i.e., Walmsley, 2001).

A solution to this problem could be the use of an optional data collection method that would merge with the learning environment. More preparatory work as well as collaboration with the participants is also needed to allow the research to merge with the lives of the participants. The data collection method should be seen as a natural process. It would also be useful to consider how the analysis and interpretation of the videos could be done jointly so that the feeling of being an object rather than a subject of the research could be eliminated. Participatory videotaping, which has been increasingly used, particularly in community development and anthropological research, is an example of a collaborative or participatory methodology that seeks to reduce the distance between the researcher(s) and research participants by using video as an empowering, democratizing method that challenges the hierarchical researcher/researched relationship (Pink, 2001). Such an approach could be a solution to balance the power relationships between the participants and the researchers and to make the development of supportive learning environments more inclusive.

ACKNOWLEDGMENTS

I acknowledge with thanks the financial support of the Children with Autism Spectrum Disorders as Creative Actors in a Strength-based Technology-enhanced Learning Environment Project from Academy of Finland, 2011-2014.

REFERENCES

Aspis, S. (1997). Self-advocacy for people with learning difficulties: Does it have a future? *Disability and Society*, *12*(4), 647–654.

Austin, D. W., Abbott, J. M., & Carbis, C. (2008). The use of virtual reality hypnosis with two cases of autism spectrum disorder: A feasibility study. *Contemporary Hypnosis*, *25*(2), 102–109.

Baker, S. D., Lang, R., & O'Reilly, M. (2009). Review of video modelling with students with emotional and behavioural disorders. *Education and Treatment of Children*, 32(3), 403–320.

Battocchi, A., Pianesi, F., Tomasini, D., Zancanaro, M., Esposito, G., Venuti, P., Ben Sasson, A., Gal, E., & Weiss, P. L. (2009). Collaborative puzzle game: A tabletop interactive game for fostering collaboration in children with autism spectrum disorders (ASD). *Proceedings of the ACM International Conference on Interactive Tabletops and Surfaces* (pp. 197–204). New York, NY: ACM.

Bernard-Opitz, V., Sriram, N., & Nakhoda-Sapuan, S. (2001). Enhancing social problem solving in children with autism and normal children through computer-assisted instruction. *Journal of Autism & Developmental Disorders*, *31*(4), 377–384.

Boucher, J. (2012). Review: Structural language in autistic spectrum disorder—chaRacteristics and causes. *The Journal of Child Psychology and Psychiatry*, *53*(3), 219–233.

Bryant, B. R., Bryant, D. P., Shih, M., & Seok, S. (2010). Assistive technology and supports provision: A selective review of the literature and proposed areas of application. *Exceptionality*, *18*(4), 203–213.

Cheng, Y., Chiang, H., Ye, J., & Cheng, L. (2010). Enhancing empathy instruction using a collaborative virtual learning environment for children with autistic spectrum conditions. *Computers & Education*, *55*(4), 1449–1458.

Cook, B. G. (2002). Inclusive attitudes, strengths, and weaknesses of pre-service general educators enrolled in a curriculum infusion teacher preparation program. *Teacher Education and Special* Education, *25*, 262–277.

Copley, J., & Ziviani, J. (2004). Barriers to the use of assistive technology for children with multiple disabilities. *Occupational Therapy International*, *11*(4), 229–243.

Cosden, M., Kern Koegel, L., Koegel, R. L., Greenwell, A., & Klein, E. (2006). Strength-based assessment for children with autism spectrum disorders. *Research & Practice for Persons with Severe Disabilities*, *31*(2), 134–143.

Craig, J., & Baron-Cohen, S. (1999) Creativity and imagination in autism and asperger syndrome. *Journal of Autism and Developmental Disorders*, *29*(4), 319–326.

Crosland, K., Clarke, S., & Dunlap, G. (2012). A trend analysis of participant and setting characteristics in autism intervention research. *Focus on Autism and Other Developmental Disorders*, *28*(3), 159–165.

De Leo, G., & Leroy, G. (2008). Smartphones to facilitate communication and improve social skills of children with severe autism spectrum disorder: Special education teachers as proxies. *Proceedings of the 7th International Conference on Interaction Design and Children* (pp. 45–48). New York, NY: ACM.

Doppelt, Y. (2004). Impact of science-technology learning environment characteristics on learning outcomes: Pupils' perceptions and gender differences. *Learning Environments Research, 7*(3), 271–293.

Doppelt, Y. (2006). Science-technology learning environment: Teachers and pupils' perceptions. *Learning Environments Research, 9*(2), 163–178.

Doppelt, Y., & Schunn, C. D. (2008). Identifying students' perceptions of the important classroom features affecting learning aspects of a design-based learning environment. *Learning Environments Research, 11*(3), 195–209.

Druin, A. (2002). A role of children in the design of new technology. *Behaviour and Information Technology, 21*(1), 1–25.

European Agency for Development in Special Needs Education. (2010). *Inclusive education in action—Project framework and rationale.* Odense, Denmark: Author.

European Agency for Development in Special Needs Education. (2011). *Participation in inclusive education—A framework for developing indicators.* Odense, Denmark: Author.

European Agency for Development in Special Needs Education. (2012). *Special needs education country data 2012.* Odense, Denmark: Author.

Farrell, P. (2001). Special education in last twenty years: Have things really got better? *British Journal of Special Education, 28*(1), 1–9.

Ferguson, D. (2008). International trends in inclusive education: The continuing challenge to teach each one and everyone. *European Journal of Special Needs Education, 23*(2), 109–120.

Finkelstein, S., Nickel, A., Barnes, T., & Suma, E. A. (2010). Astrojumper: Motivating children with autism to exercise using a VR game. *Proceedings of the 28th of the International Conference Extended Abstracts on Human Factors in Computing Systems* (pp. 4189–4194). New York, NY: ACM.

Finnish Law 642/2010; http://www.finlex.fi/fi/laki/alkup/2010/20100642

Fujimoto, I., Matsumoto, T., De Silva, P. R. S., Kobayashi, M., & Higashi, M. (2010). Study on an assistive robot for improving imitation skill of children with autism. *Proceedings of the second International Conference on Social Robotics* (pp. 232–242). Berlin, Germany: Springer-Verlag.

Guldberg, K. (2010). Educating children on the autism spectrum: Preconditions for inclusion and notions of 'best autism practice' in the early years. *British Journal of Special Education, 37*(4), 168–174.

Happé, F., & Frith, U. (2009). The beautiful otherness of the autistic mind. *Philosophical Transactions of the Royal Society, 364*, 1345–1350.

Hayes, G. R., Patterson, D. J., Monibi, M., & Kaufman, S. J. (2008). Interactive and intelligent visual communication systems. *Proceedings of the 7th International Conference on Interaction Design and Children* (pp. 65–68). New York, NY: ACM.

Jiménez, T. C., Graf, V. L., & Rose, E. (2007). Gaining access to general education: The promise of universal design for learning. *Issues in Teacher Education, 16*(2), 41–54.

Kärnä, E., Parkkonen, A., Voutilainen, M., & Tuononen, K. (2013). Teachers' and assistants' views on an action research project with children with autism spectrum disorders: The positive outcomes and pitfalls of inclusion. *Pedagogia Oggi, 1*, 115–130.

Kelly, S. M. (2009). Use of assistive technology by students with visual impairments: Findings from a national survey. *Journal of Visual Impairment and Blindness, 103*(8), 470–480.

Kozima, H., Nakagawa, C., & Yasuda, Y. (2005). Interactive robots for communication-care: A case study in autism therapy. *The proceedings of the IEEE International Workshop on Robots and Human Interactive Communication* (pp. 341–346). Piscataway, NJ: IEEE Press.

LeGoff, D., & Sherman, M. (2006). Long-term outcome of social skills intervention based on interactive LEGO play. *Autism, 10*(4), 317–329.

Loreman, T. (2007). Seven pillars of support for inclusive education. Moving from "why?" To "how?" *International Journal of Whole Schooling, 3*(2), 22–38.

Marti, P., & Bannon, L. (2009). Exploring user-centred design in practice: Some caveats. *Knowledge Technology & Policy, 22*(1), 7–15.

Mechling, L. C., Gast, D. L., & Krupa, K. (2007). Impact of SMART Board Technology: An Investigation of Sight Word Reading and Observational Learning. *Journal of Autism Developmental Disorder, 37*(10), 1869–1882.

Mechling, L. C., Gast, D. L., & Seid, N. H. (2009). Using a personal digital assistant to increase independent task completion by students with autism spectrum disorder. *Journal of Autism and Developmental Disorders, 39*(10), 1420–1434.

Miles, S., & Signal, N. (2010). The education for all and inclusive education debate: Conflict, contradiction or opportunity? *International Journal of Inclusive Education, 14*(1), 1–15.

Ministry of Education of Finland. (2007). *Special education strategy* (Reports of the Ministry of Education, Finland, No. 47). Helsinki, Finland: Author.

Myers, C. (2007). "Please listen, it's my turn": Instructional approaches, curricula and contexts for supporting communication and increasing access to inclusion. *Journal of Intellectual & Developmental Disability, 32*(4), 263–278.

Napolitano, D. A., Smith, T., Zarcone, J. R., Goodkin, K., & McAdam, D. B. (2010). Increasing response diversity in children with autism. *Journal of Applied Behavior Analysis, 43*, 265–271.

National Board of Education. (2010). Perusopetuslaki [Basic Education Act]. Helsinki, Finland: Author.

Niles, W. J. (2005). Building a classroom management plan for inclusive environments: From fear to F.E.A.R. *Teaching Exceptional Children Plus, 2*(1), 1–12.

Nissinen, E., Korhonen, P., Vellonen, V., Kärnä, E., & Tukiainen, M. (2012). Children with special needs as evaluators of technologies. *Proceedings of World Conference on Educational Multimedia, Hypermedia and Telecommunications 2012* (pp. 1356–1365). Chesapeake, VA: AACE.

Official Statistics of Finland. (2009). Erityisopetus [Special education]. *Statistics Finland*. Retrieved from https://www.tilastokeskus.fi/til/erop/2009/erop_2009_2010-06-11_tie_001_en.html

Official Statistics of Finland. (2011). Erityisopetus [Special education]. *Statistics Finland*. Retrieved from https://www.tilastokeskus.fi/til/erop/2011/erop_2011_2012-06-12_tie_001_en.html

Official Statistics of Finland. (2012). Erityisopetus [Special education]. *Statistics Finland*. Retrieved from https://www.tilastokeskus.fi/til/erop/2012/erop_2012_2013-06-12_tie_001_en.html.

Olive, M. L., de la Cruz, B., Davis, T. N., Chan, J. M., Lang, R. B., O'Reilly, M. F., & Dickson, S. M. (2007). The effects of enhanced milieu teaching and a voice output communication aid on the requesting of three children with autism. *Journal of Autism and Developmental Disorders, 37*, 1505–1513.

Olive, M. L., Lang, R. B., & Davis, T. N. (2008). An analysis of the effects of functional communication and a voice output communication aid for a child with autism spectrum disorder. *Research in Autism Spectrum Disorders, 2*(2), 223–236.

Olkin, R. (2004). Making research accessible to participants with disabilities. *Journal of Multicultural Counselling and Development, 32*(extra), 332–343.

Parsons, S., Guldberg, K., MacLeod, A., Jones, G., Prunty, A., & Balfe, T. (2009). *International review of the literature of evidence of best practice provision in the education of persons with autistic spectrum disorders*. Retrieved from http://www.ncse.ie/uploads/1/Autism_Report.pdf

Parsons, S., Guldberg, K., MacLeod, A., Jones, G., Prunty, A., & Balfe, T. (2011). International review of the evidence on best practice in educational provision for children on the autism spectrum. *European Journal of Special Needs Education, 26*(1), 47–63.

Passerino, L. M., & Santarosa, L. M. (2008). Autism and digital learning environments: Processes of interaction and mediation. *Computers and Education, 51*(1), 385–402.

Pink, S. (2001). *Doing visual ethnography*. London, England: SAGE.

Read, J. C., & MacFarlane, S. J. (2006). Using the fun toolkit and other survey methods to gather opinions in child computer interaction. *Proceedings of the Conference on Interaction Design and Children (IDC)* (pp. 81–88). New York, NY: ACM.

Read, J. C., MacFarlane, S. J., & Casey, C. (2002). Endurability, engagement and Expectations: Measuring children's fun. *Proceedings of the Conference on Interaction Design and Children (IDC)* (pp. 189–198). New York, NY: ACM.

Robins, B., Dautenhahn, K., te Boekhorst, R., & Billard, A. (2005). Robotic assistants in therapy and education of children with autism: Can a small humanoid robot help encourage social interaction skills? *International Journal Universal Access in the Information Society, 4*(2), 105–120.

Savolainen, H., Engelbrecht, P., Nel, M., & Malinen, O.-P. (2012). Understanding teachers' attitudes and self-efficacy in inclusive education: Implications for pre-service and in-service teacher education. *European Journal of Special Needs Education, 27*(1), 51–68.

Sze, S. (2009). Learning style and the special needs child. *Journal of Instructional Psychology, 36*(4), 360–362.

UNESCO. (1994). *The Salamanca Statement and framework for action on special needs education*. Paris, France: Author.

Vellonen V., Kärnä, E., & Virnes, M. (2012). Communication of children with autism in a technology-enhanced learning environment. *Procedia—Social and Behavioral Sciences*, *69*, 1208–1217.

Vellonen, V., Kärnä, E., & Virnes, M. (2013). Supporting the strengths and activity of children with autism in a technology-enhanced learning environment. *Proceeding of the IADIS International Conference on Cognition and Exploratory Learning in Digital Age (CELDA 2013)* (pp. 170–177). Lissabon, Portugal: IADIS Press.

Verdonschot, M. M. L., de Witte, L. P., Reichrath, E., Buntinx, W. H. E., & Curfs, L. M. G. (2009). Impact of environmental factors on community participation of persons with an intellectual disability: A systematic review. *Journal of Intellectual Disability Research*, *53*(1), 54–64.

Virnes, M., Sutinen, E., & Kärnä-Lin, E. (2008). How children's individual needs challenge the design of educational robotics. *Proceeding of the 7th Interaction Design for Children (IDC)* (pp. 274–281). New York, NY: ACM.

Voutilainen, M., Vellonen, V., & Kärnä, E. (2011). Establishing a strength-based technology-enhanced learning environment with and for children with autism. *Proceedings of World Conference on Educational Multimedia, Hypermedia and Telecommunications 2011* (pp. 601–606). Chesapeake, VA: AACE.

Walmsley, J. (2001). Normalisation, emancipatory research and inclusive research in learning disability. *Disability & Society*, *16*(2), 187–205.

Watkins, D. E. (2005). Maximizing learning for students with special needs. *Kappa Delta Pi Record*, *41*(4), 154–158.

Williams, C., Wright, B., Callaghan, G., & Coughlan, B. (2002). Do children with autism learn to read more readily by computer assisted instruction or traditional book methods? A pilot study. *Autism*, *6*(1), 71–91.

Williams, C. R. (2008). Creative engagement in interactive immersive environments. *Digital Creativity*, *19*(3), 203–211.

Williams, C. R., Petersson, E., & Brooks A. L. (2006). The picturing sound multisensory environment: An overview as entity of phenomenon. *Digital Creativity*, *18*(2), 106–114.

Williams, P. (2006). Developing methods to evaluate web usability with people with learning difficulties. *British Journal of Special Education*, *33*(4), 173–179.

Yechiam, E., Arshavsky, O., Shamay-Tsoory, S. G., Yaniv, S., & Aharon, J. (2010). Adapted to explore: Reinforcement learning in Autistic spectrum conditions. *Brain and Cognition*, *72*(2), 317–324.

CHAPTER 7

EXPERIENCES OF LEARNING

Students With Intellectual Disabilities in Higher Education in Ireland

John Kubiak and Michael Shevlin

In recent decades the international community has been promoting the benefits of tertiary education for people with disabilities as a pathway to full participation in society. Legislation has been enacted in many countries to guarantee the rights of disabled people to higher (postsecondary) education. However, despite this progress, people with intellectual disabilities (ID) continue to remain underrepresented in higher education internationally though there is evidence that these students are very gradually becoming more recognized as part of a subgroup of diverse learners in this environment. In this chapter we report on the findings of a research project that examined how learning is experienced in college by students with ID. We present a model that captures this learning in 4 categories: the cognitive stages of learning; self-regulation of learning; learning as collective meaning making, and the supportive environment and learning. We highlight that learning for this group of individuals is far more sophisticated and multifaceted than previously thought. Ultimately, the findings of this paper have broader implications for teaching and learning at all levels—primary, secondary and tertiary. If started early, the learning model outlined has the potential to enable all students to process information in a more active and reflective manner and to solve problems collectively.

Inclusive Education for Students with Intellectual Disabilities,
pp. 139–162
Copyright © 2015 by Information Age Publishing
All rights of reproduction in any form reserved.

INTRODUCTION

This paper reports on the findings of a research project conducted in one higher education institution in Ireland that focuses on facilitating the inclusion of students with intellectual disabilities (ID). The 2-year program on offer to this group of learners is entitled The Certificate in Contemporary Living (CCL) (see O'Brien et al., 2009; O'Brien, O'Keeffe, Kenny, Fitzgerald, & Curtis, 2008) which aims to promote full citizenship for its students through the development of learning networks (Kubiak & Espiner, 2009) and career opportunities (O'Brien et al., 2008). CCL students are taught in their group and also audit undergraduate courses of their choice (O'Connor, Kubiak, Espiner & O'Brien, 2012). Undergraduate students are paired with CCL students as peer mentors to encourage CCL students to engage with social activities and to support social networking on campus. Since 2008, approximately 90 students have graduated from the program, providing a rich tapestry of social capital within Irish communities and organizations. The findings of this paper—undertaken with intellectually disabled coresearchers—focus on CCL students' experiences of learning while attending college and presents a new model of how students with ID learn while in tertiary education.

In recent decades the international community has been promoting the social and economic benefits that lifelong learning offers to people with disabilities as a pathway to employment and full participation in society (United Nations Convention on the Rights of Persons with Disabilities [UNCRPD], 2006). Higher (postsecondary) education has long been considered a pathway to inclusion, independent living and competitive employment for people with disabilities, just as it has been for the general population.

It has been argued that becoming an active member of society for people with disabilities, requires the concept of embedding them within normative pathways of inclusion, that is, life avenues ordinarily pursued by individuals without disabilities (Uditsky, 1993; Uditsky & Hughson, 2012). For example in the context of education, nondisabled people's identity begins in primary school and is developed further in secondary school; this journey invariably leads onto tertiary education and/or vocational training, adult education and lifelong learning. Such normative practices are echoed in Article 24 of the UNCRPD which states that "persons with disabilities are able to access general tertiary education, vocational training, adult education and lifelong learning without discrimination and on an equal basis with others" (UNCRPD, 2006, Article 24).

Many countries have acted on the recommendations of this Convention and have endeavored to make access to education and tertiary education a reality for people with disabilities. A brief selection of examples include: the United States (Americans with Disabilities Act of 1990; Higher Education Opportunity Act, 2008); Australia (Disability Discrimination Act 1992 and Disability Standards for Education 2005), the United Kingdom (Disability Discrimination Act 2005; Equality Act 2010), and the Republic of Ireland (Report of the Commission on the Status of People with Disabilities 1996; Educational Act 1998; Education for Persons with Special Educational Needs Act 2004; Equal Status Act 2000).

Indeed it has been argued (Uditsky & Hughson, 2012) that access to education and training throughout the life span for people with disabilities is gradually becoming more widely accepted, and national codes of practice for students with disabilities in higher education have typically adopted more inclusive policies and practices to support the enrolment, progression, and subsequent employment of people with disabilities.

Since the pilot of the CCL program was set up in 2005, the National Institute for Intellectual Disability has maintained a dedicated focus on developing the capacity of people with intellectual disabilities to engage in education at third level. Indeed the CCL program has provided and continues to provide a varied program consisting of 11 modules covering transferrable skills, the expressive arts, sports and nutrition, and the humanities. This institute has also played a key role nationally in developing third level opportunities for intellectually disabled people. Under a project grant from the Irish Higher Education Authority through Strategic Innovation Funding, CCL course materials and the expertise of its teaching staff have been shared with five other third level institutes throughout Ireland.

In this chapter we first explore the landscape of international and Irish tertiary education models that are currently on offer for people with ID. Given that there is a paucity of research undertaken on how these students experience learning in a higher (postsecondary) education, we examine other studies that have explored learning in these educational contexts by using a phenomenographic approach (Marton, 1978, 1986; Marton & Booth, 1997). As these studies demonstrate that learning varies across different cultures and systems of higher education, we argue that there is a real need to closely examine the experiences of learning for people with ID and to seek a new outlook on understanding the nature of their learning from their own viewpoint. After discussing the findings of the research, we offer a model that captures how intellectually disabled students' experience learning, and conclude that the process of learning for this group of individuals is far more sophisticated and multifaceted than previously thought. Finally, in our discussion we consider the broader implications of this study for teaching and learning at all levels—primary, secondary, and tertiary.

THIRD LEVEL STUDY FOR PEOPLE WITH ID—
INTERNATIONAL MODELS

Outside of Ireland a number of tertiary educational models exist that include students with intellectual disabilities. For example, the University of Iceland offers the University program for People with Intellectual Disabilities (Stefánsdóttir, 2010). The "Up the Hill" Project at Flinders University in South Australia (Flinders University, 2011) has operated for over 10 years. In Canada, the On-Campus Program has been in operation for nearly 3 decades at the University of Alberta, Canada (Uditsky & Hughson, 2012; University of Alberta, 2006; Uditsky, Frank, Hart, & Jeffreys, 1987). Over the last decade in the United States there has been a significant growth in the number of postsecondary educational opportunities for students with ID (Hart, Grigal, & Weir, 2010), and at this time of writing over 250 programs are being offered (for a comprehensive critical review of existing U.S. programs see McEathron & Beuhring, 2011). Access to these postsecondary opportunities was given a boost from U.S. Department of Education funding that targeted 27 postsecondary education institutions to create comprehensive transition programs for students with intellectual disabilities (Nevill & White, 2011). In the following section, one of these programs is briefly described.

The "Cutting-Edge" Program

The "Cutting-Edge" program (Hafner, Moffatt, & Kisa, 2011) is offered to students with intellectual and developmental disabilities in Edgewood College, a liberal arts college in Madison, Wisconsin. Piloting inclusion for people with ID in 2007, this college was the first in Wisconsin to offer inclusion for this group of adults and became an official program of the college soon after. Cutting-Edge students attend college by "taking undergraduate courses, reside in student housing and engage in student-life events as well as pursue community service, internships and employment" (p. 18). Since 2007, Cutting Edge has served 24 people with ID who spent an average of 40 hours on campus each week, with more hours for students who live on campus. The program offers an alternative admissions process for people with ID to enter college and provides supports—such as peer mentors and faculty involvement—that make it possible for students to reach their goals. For Hafner et al. (2011, pp. 18–19), attending college is a "natural stepping stone toward independence... 79% of Cutting-Edge students lived away from parents, 29% ... lived on campus, 37% lived independently off campus ... and ... only 21% of students lived at home with their parents." Other positive effects of the program for Cutting-Edge students include: developing friendships and dating; acquiring techniques in conflict resolution; developing interpersonal communication skills, and accessing information about domestic violence and laws relating to sexual abuse. It was also found by Haffer et al. that placing Cutting-Edge students in campus also had a positive effect on other undergraduate students, peer mentors, and faculty staff.

Third Level Study for People With ID in the Republic of Ireland

Over the last number of years in the Republic of Ireland, the numbers of third level courses for people with ID have grown. The first two courses were established in 2005: the now discontinued course at University College Dublin, and the CCL at the National Institute for Intellectual Disability, Trinity College Dublin which is now the longest running course of its kind in Ireland. A part-time course in advocacy and leadership is available at Dublin City University (2009) and more recently in 2011, the National University of Ireland Galway (2011) announced the commencement of "Going to College," a 2-year university course that aims to support the civic engagement of people with intellectual disabilities through access to inclusive higher education.

Besides the university sector, other Further Education and Training Accredited Council (2006) courses exist for adults with ID. Some of these courses are provided through a number of service providing agencies, whereas other programs are provided in mainstream settings alongside the general population of adult learners, for example literacy courses at the National Adult Literacy Association (2012). Most of these educational opportunities for people with ID in the third level sector in Ireland are closely aligned with service providing agencies. Some courses were moved from inside the service agency onto a university campus in order to create a more inclusive experience for learners. However, when courses are aligned to a service provider, ultimately the choices of courses are narrowed for the individual student, as to avail of these courses requires membership of a particular service agency on the part of the adult with ID.

EXPERIENCES OF LEARNING FOR COLLEGE STUDENTS WITH ID: ADDRESING THE KNOWLEDGE GAP

Although the Irish and international examples of inclusive educational opportunities listed above are encouraging, there has been little or no research undertaken however on how students with ID experience learning in a tertiary educational environment. European studies that have explored learning in higher education for mainstream students from a phenomenographic perspective (Marton, 1978, 1986; Marton & Booth, 1997) have produced descriptive conceptions of learning that initially seem universal and hierarchically organized. For example, learning has been identified in six ways: (1) increasing one's knowledge; (2) memorizing and reproducing, (3) application, (4) understanding, (5) seeing something in a different way, and (6) changing as a person (Marton, Beaty, & Dall'Alba, 1993; Säljö 1979). These six categories can be divided into two groups: quantitative and qualitative conceptions (Boulton-Lewis, Marton, Lewis, & Wilss, 2000). The first three conception are all essentially reproductive, and reflect a lower level, quantitative view of learning (Boulton-Lewis, 1994). The latter three conceptions reflect a higher level, qualitative view of learning as an active process of seeking meaning, leading to some kind of transformation in one's view of things, or bringing about a more fundamental change: in other words changing as a person (Marton et al., 1993).

However, other phenomenographic studies undertaken outside Europe have found somewhat different results. For example, in Nepalese students, Watkins and Regmi (1992) found that a conception of learning as changing as a person had been induced by local cultural and religious traditions and this did not represent the most sophisticated development level. In China, Marton, Dall'Alba and Tse (1996) interviewed teacher educators and found that most distinguished between mechanical memorization and memorization with understanding. Some regarded memorization with understanding as a way of retaining what had already been understood, while others regarded memorization with understanding a way of attaining a deeper understanding. Marton et al. (1996) concluded that the conceptions of learning that he identified in the West were not adequate to describe learning in Chinese culture.

Consequently, there are clear messages that learning varies across different cultures and systems of higher education. It can be reasonably argued therefore, that professionals teaching people with ID in higher education do not possess adequate knowledge of how this group of adult learners experience learning while in college. For this reason, the views of students with ID in tertiary education deserve to be closely examined and a fresh perspective sought on understanding the dynamics of their experiences of learning. A specific intention in undertaking this project was to find a perspective or a model of learning that would be informative and empowering for both adult learners with ID and their teachers.

THE PRESENT INVESTIGATION: HOW STUDENTS WITH ID EXPERIENCE LEARNING IN TERTIARY EDUCATION

This study explored how CCL students experience learning while undertaking the CCL at Trinity College Dublin. This research formed part of a larger doctorate study (Kubiak, 2013) which had two main purposes: (1) to explore what can be learned about including CCL students in research with their peers; and (2) to explore the variations in CCL students' experiences of their learning. This project built on current descriptions of inclusive research (Walmsley & Johnson, 2003) and participatory research (Turnbull, Friesen, & Ramirez, 1998), as well as phenomenographic approaches to educational research which places its focus on investigating learning from the perspectives of the learners themselves (Marton & Booth, 1997; Marton & Tsui, 2004). This chapter focuses on the second purpose above and outlines how students experience learning while on the CCL program.

Three main groups of individuals participated in this study: (1) co-researchers (3 males and 3 females, $n = 6$), (2) CCL students (8 females and 10 males, $n = 18$), and (3), this paper's first author. Individual semi-structured interviews with CCL students were conducted by trained co-researchers. The interviews were transcribed verbatim by the first author and respondents' names replaced by unique identifiers (P1–P17). Data were analyzed using a phenomenographic approach (Marton & Booth, 1997); the outcomes consisted of "categories of description" (Marton & Booth, 1997, p. 126) and the "outcome space"—a "logical inclusive structure relating to the different meanings of the phenomenon (Åkerlind, 2005, p. 323). Ethical approval was gained from the School of Education ethics committee, Trinity College Dublin. Confidentiality and anonymity in reporting results were guaranteed to all participants.

RESULTS

Overview

Four categories to describe CCL students' experiences of learning were found: (1) the cognitive stages of learning, (2) self-regulation of learning, (3) learning as collective meaning making, and (4) the supportive environment and learning. These are presented and defined in Table 7.1 and discussed in the following four sections. Finally, a model entitled "the outcome space" is presented that illustrates the hierarchically structured relations between the categories.

Table 7.1.   Four Categories to Describe CCL Students' Experiences of Learning

Categories of Description	Definition
1. The cognitive stages of learning	Learning is seen as (a) increasing knowledge, (b) memorizing and reproducing knowledge, and (c) applying one's knowledge.
2. Self-regulation of learning	Learning focuses on three phases: (1) the forethought phase, (2) the performance phase and (3) the self-reflection phase. This phase also outlines students' engagement with their emotions during the performance of learning, and how feelings of self-satisfaction and positive affect enhanced their motivation, self-beliefs, self-management and goals.
3. Learning as collective meaning making	Learning moves from individual meaning to collective or shared meaning. Students participate in a dialogue with others (for example, tutors, peers, mentors, parents, work colleagues) in order to create new understandings.
4. The supportive environment and learning	Environment as a "safe-space" informed by students establishing a "group culture," i.e., "how we wish to behave together." Facilitator of learning sensitive to promoting positive student-teacher relationships that empowers students to have increasing control over their learning.

Category 1—The Cognitive Stages of Learning

This category pays attention to what is happening in the minds of the learners; their acts of learning are seen as a cognitive process. This stage is divided in to three subcategories: (a) learning as increasing one's knowledge, (b) learning as memorizing and reproducing and (c) learning and applying knowledge.

Learning as Increasing One's Knowledge

In this first subcategory, learning is viewed as adding to one's current knowledge base, whether this is through books, computers (on the internet) or auditing lectures. In this context, learning can be viewed as a passive undertaking, a process where the learner does not necessarily see him/herself as an agent of learning—rather learning takes place as a result of the delivery of knowledge by a person who remains outside the learner. For example, the following CCL student spoke about class lectures as a resource for acquiring information. She explained: *"When I was doing… Yeats in … class… I found out about his children, his son and his daugh-*

ter, and I found out what year they were born and what year they got married in" (P9).

Learning as Memorization and Reproducing

In this subcategory the knowledge that is handled by CCL students during classes is "nonproblematic," a term used by Paakkari, Tynjälä, and Kannas (2011, p. 708) that involves merely storing and remembering facts. For example, as one student explained: *"I store information into my head, long-term and short-term memory … that's how I learn* (P8).

For other CCL students the ability to remember information is enhanced by their engagement with visual images from the tutor's use of PowerPoint during delivery of the curriculum. For the following student the importance of the tutor's use of a PowerPoint in an expressive arts module was that it enabled him to memorize information on Michelangelo. He said: *"We talked about him (on) a Power Point … you can write it down and you can remember them (and) look back on it … if there was no Power Point that would make it difficult…because then I wouldn't be able to remember it and I wouldn't be able to learn it* (P4). This student's concern centered on retaining information from classes; he commented positively on the benefits of "chunking" (Gobet et al., 2001; Miller, 1956) information into manageable "bits" that builds upon what he had learned previously. He said: *"When I'm learning, I learn one thing at a time, because if I'm learning too much together I won't retain what's going on. So if I find if I learn bit by bit … I retain what I'm learning"* (P14).

Learning as Application of Knowledge

In this subcategory, students emphasized the importance of being able to apply aspects of the acquired CCL curriculum in practice. This was related to various practicalities in both classroom and home-assignment activities. However, in order to apply knowledge, an understanding of that knowledge is fundamental. For Nickerson (1985, p. 234), understanding is an active process; it requires "the connection of facts, the relating of newly acquired information to what is already known … in short, it requires not only having knowledge but also doing something with it."

For the following learner, understanding how to use computers successfully was necessary for researching home-assignments. She said: *"We're doing (computers) in class … you follow the instructions then you just click the mouse and … you can read all … sort(s) of poetry … you can look up William Shakespeare"* (P4). Furthermore the process of understanding how to apply the skills learned in the computer class in order to keep in touch with one's peers became evident in the following student's comments about using social network sites: *"We are doing Microsoft, typing in and PowerPoints, doing presentations; we are doing bloggers at the moment. There's many things I find interesting ... getting pictures on the internet ... I'm on Facebook"* (P15).

Category 2—Self-Regulation of Learning

Unlike Category 1 (learning as cognitive), which manifested the outcomes of learning, this second main category entitled "self-regulation" deals with the learning process. The social learning psychologist Zimmerman (2002) views the structure of the self-regulatory processes in terms of three cyclical phases:

1. The forethought phase (processes and beliefs that occur *before* efforts to learn)
2. The performance phase (to processes that occur *during* behavioral implementation), and
3. The self-reflection phase (processes that occur *after* each learning effort).

Figure 7.1 illustrates the phases and subphases of self-reflection for CCL students.

These phases are now discussed in turn with particular reference to CCL students' experiences of learning.

The Forethought Phase

The "forethought phase" includes the two main classes of "task analysis and self-motivation" (Zimmerman, 2002, p. 67); task analysis involves planning for goals, and self-motivation stems from students' self-efficacy beliefs.

For the following student, having clear goals was an essential part of controlling behavior, in this case it was avoiding becoming bored and lethargic: *"I hate not doing anything, I get bored easily ... (I like) a busy life ... I [like] keeping occupied"* (P1). For another student, the goal of undertaking the CCL was getting the certificate and the prospects of a dream job. He said: *"I'd do anything to pass the course.... So I can put it on my C.V. and get a good job. If you don't (pass the course) ... it's just a waste of your own time"* (P15).

For Schunk (2005), goals enhance self-regulation through their effects on motivation, and self-evaluation of progress. For the learner below determination and self-belief is the key to success: *"I just said to myself if I don't do it no one else will so I just plucked up the courage and said I'm going to do it and I'm going to pass it"* (P13).

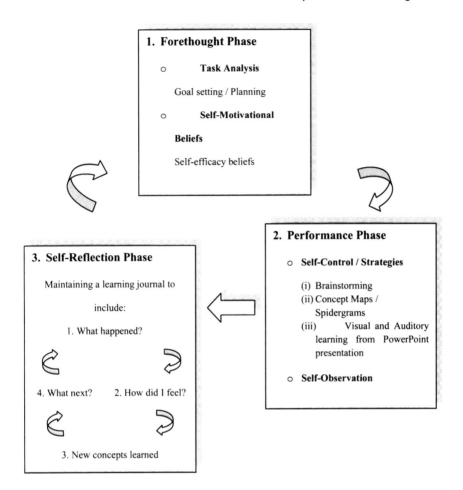

Adapted from Zimmerman (2002).

Figure 7.1.   Phases and subphases of self-regulation for CCL students.

The Performance Phase

The performance phase of self-regulation falls into two main classes: self-control and self-observation. Self-control refers to the deployment of specific methods or strategies that CCL students selected during the forethought phase. For example, brainstorming (Osborn, 1953) involves:

shouting all (of our) ideas ... about a certain topic, so say if your topic is "college," then someone would (shout) travelling, students, freebies, whatever, all that kind of thing ... and you can discuss them ... if they're on the board you don't have to try and think in your head. (P5)

Students also explained that concept maps (Novak, 1991)—also referred to as "spidergrams"—are a progression from a brainstorm: *"If I was learning about it for the first time, (I'd use) the brainstorm ... but then when you've learnt about it I'd do the spidergram"* (P5). Visual, auditory and kinaesthetic learning (Dunn & Dunn 1993) is mainly undertaken through the medium of PowerPoint presentations and follow-on exercises: *"You can see the words visually and can see pictures... on the screen—it makes it easier for you to take down notes and rewrite it in your (journal) afterwards as well"* (P13).

Self-observation refers to "self-recording personal events ... (and) cognitive tracking of personal functioning" (Zimmerman, 2002, p. 68). In this study this includes students' awareness of the importance of time management and being organized: *"I like to have things organized, have the books ready in the bag for the next day"* (P13), and taking the responsibilities of being a third-level student seriously as well as possessing an awareness of cognitive tracking, i.e. maintaining concentration in class: *"there's no point tuning out and not listening.... Listening to the tutor is good 'cause the tutors are there to help you and if you tune out you're not getting the benefits whereas if you tune in you're getting all the benefits"* (P14).

The Self-Reflection Phase

There are two main classes of the self-reflection phase processes: self-judgement and self-reaction (Zimmerman, 2002, p. 68). One form of self-judgement—self-evaluation—refers to "comparisons of self-observed performances against some standard, such as one's prior performance, another person's performance, or an absolute standard of performance" (p. 68). For the following CCL learner, what was good about self-evaluation was the enjoyment aspect of it as well as its potential for self-improvement. This student explained that he *"likes doing the reflection journals ... if we do things a certain way and then you think back, you can think back and (see) if we could have done that better, or have done it differently.... It's a way of trying to do things better"* (P9).

Self-reaction involves engaging with one's emotions during the performance of learning. This can involve being aware of and engaging with feelings of "self-satisfaction and positive affect" which according to Zimmerman can enhance motivation (p. 68). According to this student, being in touch with his emotions was very much related to understanding his own academic achievement and motivation for helping other students. He explains:

> I am a reflective person ... I think about myself and I think about others. It's important to let other people know how you're feeling so they can sympathize with you and talk you through it or be there for you if you need somebody, instead of them not knowing what is wrong (P17).

Category 3—Learning as Collective Meaning Making

This category moves from meaning making on an individual level to collective or shared meaning. The difference between this category and Categories 1 and 2 is that students do not only learn on their own, but also participate in a dialogue with others—peers, family, residential staff, and college mentors—in order to create new understandings. In this way, it is argued that there are many "teachers" who collectively create meaning both in and outside the college environment.

First, collective learning occurred for students from discussions and debates in the classroom. One student explained:

> If a few of us were in class and say if another student has an idea that I thought it was a good idea, but I didn't agree with it.... I'd put my point across and then there's a whole big debate thing about it and everyone starts joining in. (P9)

In this way there are many "teachers" in the class, all of whom form a community of learning and support.

Second, some students also tapped into the collective knowledge bank that her peers could offer, especially for home assignments. For example a student elaborated: *"we all help each other—if somebody gets stuck. (I'd say) would you help me with this essay, you can't copy off me, but I'll give you a hand"* (P1). Learning also took place outside the college in collaboration with the student's family, and/or with support from dedicated agency key-staff. One student stated that if she *"got stuck with words"* (P8) she would *"ask my parents what it means... But I try and remember the word for the next time"* (P8). Residential staff as well as volunteer college mentors also formed a very important part of the collective learning process for CCL students. For example a learner reported that: *"You can learn different stuff from your mentor.... They can let you know that you can do things in different ways.... You ask them for advice if you are having any problems with your learning. I find that very helpful"* (P13). Finally, theorists of situational and contextual learning (Brown, Collins, & Duguid, 1989; Kirshener & Whitson, 1997; Lave & Wenger, 1991) emphasize that tasks should simulate real-life situations where the knowledge is to be applied in the future. For CCL students the workplace is one real-life context where they undertake their job placement or work experience for the course. The following student explained that when *"you're in the work environment ... you know what work is actually like"* (P7). Another student's work experience led to an increase in self-confidence and self-awareness that may have not been possible anywhere else. In employment he developed a *"different attitude"* (P11) toward himself: *"This has brought me out of my shell and I find that ... people got a sense of who I am"* (P11).

Category 4—The Supportive Environment and Learning

The concept of environment, as applied to educational settings, refers to "the atmosphere, ambience, tone, or climate that pervades the particular setting" (Dorman, 2002, p. 112). Dart et al. (2000) showed the benefits of learning environments that are "safe, supportive, and that offer helpful relationships" (p. 269). It has been demonstrated that educational environments that are sensitive to promoting reciprocal student-teacher relationships ultimately result in classrooms that are learner-centered and give students greater control over their own learning (Nichols & Zhang, 2011). Such environments are also seen by Paakkari et al. (2011) as spaces that support conditions for the development of students' own views, that is "personal meanings" (p. 709) that can influence both individual students and their peers. For example, for the following student a "safe classroom space" was somewhere where she could feel comfortable to ask questions with her tutor and share ideas that were about *"important things"* (P13) with her classmates. She said: *"there's 26 of us in the group—we are a strong group and we're able to share with everyone else, and get feedback how we cope with (the demands of) college"* (P13). For this learner, feeling comfortable in a learning environment meant knowing that other students were not laughing behind her back and behaving in a judgmental or an antagonistic way. This individual also felt that the teacher was instrumental in setting up the conditions for a positive student/teacher and student/student relationship, by encouraging students to reflect on the agreed group culture, and promoting a place *"where people ... who have problems with learning ... are able to take everything at (their) own pace"* (P11).

The Outcome Space—A Model of CCL Students' Experiences of Learning

The final aim of this study was to constitute an "Outcome Space" (Åkerlind, 2005a, p. 323) that represents the core aspects of the collective ways of experiencing learning among CCL students. With reference to Järvinen and Järvinen (2000), the Outcome Space described in this current study is an inclusive, hierarchical space in which the categories further up the hierarchy include the previous or lower ones. Whilst phenomenography does not seek to generalize, it is expected however, that the "range of meanings within the sample will be representative of the range of meanings within the population" (Åkerlind, 2005b, 2005c, p. 104).

This current study's four categories of learning form a nested hierarchy (see Figure 7.2); this implies that a student who adopts Category 4 will

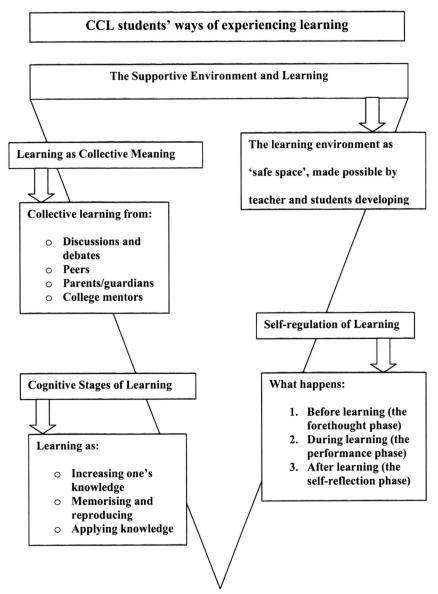

Figure 7.2.   The outcome space of CCL students' ways of experiencing learning.

also be aware of the three other categories. However, if a student adopts category 1 only, it cannot be inferred that they are aware of Categories 2, 3, and 4.

The four categories of CCL students' experiences of learning also confirm the claim of Marton et al. (1993) that there is a watershed between the categories. Biggs (1994) identified this dividing line as "quantitative" and "qualitative" perspectives. The quantitative view proposes that learning is concerned with acquisition and accumulation of content, whereas the qualitative view suggests that learning is about understanding and meaning making. In this current study the dividing line falls between category 1—the cognitive stages of learning, and Category 2—self-regulation of learning. It is also at this point in Category 2, that the nature of knowledge is seen as "problematic" (Paakkari et al., 2011, p. 708) and the role of reflection is first mentioned. The categories that follow—Categories 3 and 4—see the role of the social environment as a place for students to expand their perspectives on learning. In addition, as this dividing line is crossed, the question within the categories arises: what does a student learns *through* the CCL curriculum and its context—not what a student learns *about* the CCL curriculum.

DISCUSSION

The findings of this study have presented a number of opportunities for reflection concerning college students with ID and how they experience learning. Although the literature has shown that a number of tertiary educational opportunities exist for intellectually disabled adults, there are however a considerable number of barriers for these learners in accessing higher educations. These include systemic low expectations, a lack of awareness among transition personnel of available higher (postsecondary) educational options, and exclusionary social perceptions and conventions impeding people with ID from participating and accessing tertiary educational environments (Grigal, Hart, & Migliore, 2011). Furthermore it is argued (Folk, Yamamoto, & Stodden, 2012) that less than ideal learning environments and attitudes during early and middle school years can lead to a situation where students with ID are underprepared for college and the demands of a tertiary environment that values active participation and taking responsibility for your own learning. It is also worthwhile to note that in a study undertaken by Simpson and Spenser (2009), individuals with ID stated that their teachers, school counsellors, and parents disregarded the possibility of postgraduate education as being a viable option for them.

The findings of this research have implications for policies in relation to including people with ID in higher education and for practice within higher education. Achieving positive experiences of inclusion in tertiary environments for learners with ID means laying the groundwork early in their education. A variety of experts agree on the benefits of teachers shifting toward process-orientated instruction and involving students in learning activities that foster developmental inquiry process in order to elicit beliefs and conceptions of learning and to encourage reflection on them (Biggs, 2001; Boulhuis, 2003; Brownlee, Purdie, & Boulton-Lewis, 2001). To fulfil these objectives it is necessary for educators to structure a learning environment where students are actively encouraged to identify their learning styles and examine their approach to learning; they should also be shown how to reflect on and monitor their learning. This process needs to be underpinned by the educator's use of a variety of teaching and learning methods, such as the ones identified in this study. These include: strategies for memorization and recall that recognizes and builds on a student's learning style; the employment of multimedia and/or PowerPoint presentations; peer learning; learning through discussion; experiential learning; group work; problem-based learning; and the use of assessment procedures that both are quantitative and qualitative.

Possessing an awareness of how and why learning occurs is vital for students at all levels. Indeed it has been confirmed that an awareness of learning conceptions and epistemogical beliefs predict academic performance (Marton, Watkins, & Tang, 1997; Schommer, 1993; Van Rossum & Schenk, 1984). Therefore, the more capable students are of taking responsibility for their own learning, the more successful they can be in their academic performance. It has also been shown that as students progress through their studies, their view of learning can progress as well, becoming deeper and more sophisticated (Cano & Cardelle-Elswsr, 2004). In this current study it is worthwhile to note that second (final year) CCL students valued qualitative learning conceptions (Categories 2–4) over quantitative or a more reproductive learning conception (Category 1). A possible reason for this may be due to the nature of the assessment tasks of the program itself which values qualitative and metacognitive outcomes over more reproductive learning.

Education ought to be seen as a way of enriching the lives of students by empowering them to think about how and why they learn. The facilitator of learning should be a person who structures this environment and who instills in students the belief that they are valuable and functioning members of society. Indeed the current study has shown the benefits of a student/teacher relationship that is reciprocal and where the student/teacher hierarchy is minimized; in this way the educator learns as much from his/her students as they do from him/her.

If we hold that the prime goals of tertiary education are to help learners develop self-regulation and independence and to encourage them to be active in building their own knowledge and adopt more complex and deep learning approaches (Klatter, Lodewijks, & Cor, 2001), then teacher themselves may also require the development of more sophisticated epistemological beliefs (Brownlee et al., 2001). Studies have shown that poor academic achievement is a result of students holding immature beliefs and reproductive conceptions about their learning (Cano & Cardelle-Elawar, 2004). Consequently, educators should bear in mind that students' engagement in learning is sensitive to what they understand and what beliefs they hold about learning.

To answer "How can this be achieved?" is complex. Two suggestions are offered. Firstly it is advanced that there is a need on the part of the institution to be reflective and proactive in advancing the quality of teaching and learning—as Biggs stated "the institutional infrastructure (must be) prioritized toward best practice in teaching" (Biggs, 2001, p. 237). In a recent study of the attitudes to inclusive practices (O'Connor et al., 2012), Trinity College Dublin lecturers were partly driven by a desire to improve their instructional strategies to accommodate the diversity of students in their classes, an approach which aligned with the Trinity Inclusive Curriculum initiative. The Trinity Inclusive Curriculum aims to "break down barriers to learning by providing a range of teaching and assessment methods, allowing all students to work to their strengths" (Trinity College Dublin, 2011, para. 2). Using the universal design for instruction principles (after Shaw, Scott, & McGuire, 2001), lecturers are encouraged to create flexibility and variety in their teaching materials. Although the lecturers did not speak directly of these links, they were aware of the benefits of an inclusive approach and many had undertaken professional development workshops provided by college in this area.

Secondly, it is highlighted that teachers should shift toward process oriented instruction and involve students in learning activities that foster an inquiry process in order to elicit beliefs and conceptions of learning and to encourage reflection upon them (Biggs, 2001; Boulhuis, 2003). Explicating the process of learning instead of conceiving it simply as the memorization and reproduction of facts (which accounted for the lowest level conception in this study), requires a type of instruction which must stimulate the learning process as a thinking activity. The study outlined in this paper has reinforced the view that teaching can no longer be seen as imparting and doing things to the student, but is redefined as facilitation of self-directed learning. The students who participated in this research valued opportunities for self-directed learning and peer collaboration while also recognizing the value and importance of the self-reflective process. For Heron (1989), how people learn and how to bring about this progression should be the focus of concern, rather than the old-style preoccupation with how to teach things to people. This current chapter has also illustrated that through the use of active teaching methods (for example, Espiner, Hartnett, & Lyons, 1991; Murray, 1993) as well as instruction in self-regulation strategies (Zimmerman, 2002), students with ID have the potential to be empowered to process information in a more meaningful manner and to solve problems collectively. In this manner deep learning can result which will enable students with ID to learn social skills and clarify their opinions and perceptions on what are, often, controversial issues.

As tertiary education environments both nationally and internationally work toward increasing nontraditional student participation, a more diverse university campus which reflects a variety of perspectives and experiences is created. By including students with ID in their classes (see O'Connor et al., 2012), Trinity College Dublin lecturing staff were challenged to make their teaching and learning environments accessible to a wider range of learners by using more flexible approaches that had the ultimate benefit of engaging and motivating all students in the classroom. The above study demonstrated how the power of a tertiary education environment can contribute to drawing out the best in students with ID, as well as their peers and faculty. It is worth noting that similar gains have also been found in Canada (Uditsky & Hughson, 2012) where faculty and students without disabilities consistently remark on the benefits they derive from inclusion, such as "meaningful employment; gaining knowledge and skills; developing friendships; and increasing their sense of achievement, self-esteem, and self-confidence" (p. 229). Similarly in other studies parents report that their sons and daughters with ID have gained in maturity, independence, and capabilities (Hughson, Moodie, & Uditsky, 2006; McDonald, Mac Phearson-Court, Franks, Uditsky, & Symons, 1997). All students, not just those with an intellectual disability, deserve the chance to learn in the best environment possible and be taught by methods informed by rigorous empirical research. Within the National Institute for Intellectual Disability, students are encouraged to collaborate in research. It is through such inclusive practices that the voices of the marginalized can finally be heard by those with the power to make meaningful changes.

CONCLUSION

The intent of this chapter was to describe the experiences of learning for college students with ID. Our aim was to examine these experiences using a phenomenographic approach that foregrounded the voices and insights of these learners. It has been shown that the learning experiences of college students with ID learning are as complex as the learning experiences of any other college student. These voices have value and it is imperative from an early age that students with ID, their parents, and counsellors be involved on how to best prepare to survive in postsecondary education, and learn the skills to be successful in that setting. Furthermore, this study has demonstrated that when staff and students come together to share their expertise, ideas, and voices in the service of a shared cause, everyone gains. As one CCL student stated: *"Students are just like friends and they are there to support me and I'd do the same for them... it's important to know that you're able to ask your tutor questions without getting grief"* (P13).

ACKNOWLEDGMENTS

The two authors wish to acknowledge the CCL students and coresearchers whose participation made the study possible.

REFERENCES

Åkerlind, G. S. (2005). Variation and commonality in phenomenographic research methods. *Higher Education Research & Development, 24*(4), 321–334.

Åkerlind, G. S. (2005b). Chapter 6 learning about phenomenography: Interviewing, data analysis and the qualitative research paradigm. In J. A. Bowden & P. Green (Eds.). *Doing developmental phenomenography* (pp.63–73). Melbourne, Australia: RMIT University Press.

Åkerlind, G. S. (2005c). Academic growth and development—How do university academics experience it? *Higher Education 50,* 1–32

Americans With Disabilities Act of 1990. 42 U.S.C.A. § 12101 et seq. (West 1993).

Biggs, J. (1994). Student learning research and theory: Where do we currently stand? In G. Gibbs (Ed.), *Improving student learning: Using research to improve student learning* (pp. 1–19). Oxford, England: Oxford Centre for Staff Development.

Biggs, J. (2001). The reflective institution: Assuring and enhancing the quality of teaching and learning. *Higher Education, 41,* 221–238.

Bolhuis, S. (2003). Towards process-oriented teaching for self-directed lifelong learning: A multidimensional perspective. *Learning and Instruction, 130,* in-Ml.

Boulton-Lewis, G.M. (1994). Tertiary students' knowledge of their own learning and a SOLO Taxonomy. *Higher Education, 28,* 387–402.

Boulton-Lewis, G. M., Marton, F., Lewis, D. C., & Wilss, L. A. (2000). Learning in formal and informal contexts: Conceptions and strategies of Aboriginal and Torres Strait Islander university students. *Learning and Instruction, 10,* 393–414.

Brown, J. S., Collins, A., & Duguid, P. (1989). Situated cognition and the culture of learning. *Educational Researcher, 21*(5), 31–35.

Brownlee, J., Purdie, N., & Boulton-Lewis, G. (2001). Changing epistemological beliefs in pre-service teacher education students. *Teaching in Higher Education, 6*(2), 247–268.

Cano, F., & Cardelle-Elawar, M. (2004). An integrated analysis of secondary school students' conceptions and beliefs about learning. *European Journal of Psychology of Education, 19*(2), 167–187

Commission on the Status of People with Disabilities 1996. (Government of Ireland). Retrieved from http://lenus.ie/hse/browse?type=author&value=Commission+on+the+Status+of+People+with+Disabilities&value_lang=en_GB

Dart, B., Burnett, P.C., Purdie, N., Boulton-Lewis, G., Campbell, J., & Smith, D. (2000). Influences of students' conceptions of learning and the classroom environment on approaches to learning. *Journal of Educational Research, 93,* 262–272.

Disability Discrimination Act 1992. (Commonwealth of Australia). Retrieved from http://www.comlaw.gov.au/Details/C2010C00023

Disability Standards for Education 2005. (Commonwealth of Australia). Retrieved from http://www.comlaw.gov.au/Details/F2005L00767

Disability Act 2005. (Government of Ireland). Retrieved from http://www.oireachtas.ie/documents/bills28/acts/2005/a1405.pdf

Dorman, J. (2002). Classroom environment research: Progress and possibilities. *Queensland Journal of Educational Research, 18*(2), 112–140.

Dublin City University. (2009). *Advocacy and leadership course.* Retrieved from http://www.smh.ie/index.php?q=node/208

Dunn, R., & Dunn, K. (1993). *Teaching secondary students through their individual learning styles.* Boston, MA: Allyn & Bacon.

Education Act 1998 (Government of Ireland). Retrieved from http://www.irishstatutebook.ie/1998/en/act/pub/0051

Education for Persons with Special Needs Act 2004 (Government of Ireland). Retrieved from http://www.oireachtas.ie/documents/bills28/acts/2004/A3004.pdf

Espiner, D., Hartnett, F., & Lyons, D. (1991). *Action methods in teaching.* Auckland, New Zealand: Auckland College of Education.

Equal Status Act 2000 (Government of Ireland). Retrieved from http://www.irishstatutebook.ie/2000/en/act/pub/0008/index.html

Equality Act 2010. (United Kingdom). Retrieved from http://www.legislation.gov.uk/ukpga/2010/15/pdfs/ukpga_20100015_en.pdf

The Further Education and Training Awards Council. (2006). FETAC awards. Retrieved from http://www.fetac.ie/fetac/documents/FETAC_Awards_prepared_2006.pdf

Flinders University. (2011). Up the hill project. Retrieved from http://blogs.flinders.edu.au/flinders-news/2009/09/28/flinders-offers-unique-disabilities-program/

Folk, E. D. R., Yamamoto, K. K., & Stodden, R. A. (2012). Implementing inclusion and collaborative teaming in a model program of postsecondary education for young adults with intellectual disabilities. *Journal of Policy and Practice in Intellectual Disabilities, 9*(4), 257–269.

Gobet, F., Lane, P. C. R., Croker, S., Cheng, P. C. H., Jones, G., Oliver, I., & Pine, J. M. (2001). Chunking mechanisms in human learning. *Trends in Cognitive Sciences, 5,* 236–243.

Grigal, M., Hart, D., & Migliore, A. (2011). Comparing the transition planning, postsecondary education, and employment outcomes of students with intellectual and other disabilities. *Career Development for Exceptional Individuals, 34*, 4–17.

Hafner, D., Moffatt, C., & Kisa, N. (2011). Cutting-edge: Integrating students with intellectual and developmental disabilities into a 4-year liberal arts college. *Career Development for Exceptional Individuals, 34*, 18–30.

Hart, D., Grigal, M., & Weir, C. (2010). *Think college: A snapshot of postsecondary education for students with intellectual disabilities across the United States. Think College Fast Facts, Issue No. 2.* Boston, MA: Institute for Community Inclusion, University of Massachusetts Boston.

Heron, J. (1989). *The facilitators' handbook.* London, England: Kogan Page.

Higher Education Opportunity Act of 2008. PL 110–315, 122 Stat. 3078.

Hughson, E. A., Moodie, S., & Uditsky, B. (2006). *The story of inclusive postsecondary education in Alberta: A research report.* Edmonton, Canada: Alberta Association for Community Living.

Kirshner, D., & Whitson, J.A. (1997). *Situated cognition: Social, semiotic, and psychological perspectives.* Mahwah, NJ: Erlbaum.

Klatter, E. B., Lodewijks, H. G. L. C., & Cor, C. A. J. (2001). Learning conceptions of young students in the final year of primary education. *Learning and Instruction, 11*, 485–516.

Kubiak, J. (2013). *Intellectually disabled students' experiences of learning in tertiary education: An inclusive phenomenography* (Unpublished DEd thesis). Trinity College Dublin, Dublin, Ireland.

Kubiak, J., & Espiner, D. (2009). Pushing the boundaries of inclusion within third level education. *The Frontline of Learning Disability, 74*, 8–9.

Lave, J., & Wenger, E. (1991). *Situated learning: Legitimate peripheral participation.* Cambridge, England: Cambridge University Press.

Marton, F. (1978). *Describing conceptions of the world around us* (Report No. 66). Mölndal, Sweden: University of Göteberg, Institute of Education. (ERIC Document Reproduction Service No. ED 169 074)

Marton, F. (1986). Phenomenography—A research approach to investigating different understandings of reality. *Journal of Thought, 21*(3), 28–49.

Marton, F., & Booth, S. (1997). *Learning and awareness.* Mahwah, NJ: Erlbaum.

Marton, F., Beaty, E. & Dall'Alba, G. (1993). Conceptions of learning. *International Journal of Educational Research, 19*, 277–300.

Marton, F., Dall'Alba, G., & Tse, L. K. (1996). Memorizing and understanding: The keys to the paradox? In D. A. Watkins & J. B. Biggs (Eds.), *The Chinese learner: Cultural, psychological and contextual influences* (pp. 69–83). Hong Kong/Melbourne: University of Hong Kong, Comparative Education Research Centre/Australian Council for Educational Research.

Marton, F., & Tsui, A. B. M. (2004). *Classroom discourse and the space of learning.* Mahwah, NJ: Erlbaum.

Marton, F., Watkins, D., & Tang, C. (1997). Discontinuities and continuities in the experience of learning: An interview study of high school students in Hong Kong. *Learning and Instruction, 7*(1), 21–48.

McDonald, L., MacPherson-Court, L., Franks, S., Uditsky, B., & Symons, F. (1997). An inclusive university program for students with moderate to severe developmental disabilities: Student, parent and faculty perspectives. *Developmental Disabilities Bulletin*, *25*, 43–67.

McEathron, M., & Beuhring, T. (2011). *Postsecondary education for students with intellectual and developmental disabilities: A critical review of the state of knowledge and taxonomy to guide future research*. Retrieved from http://ici.umn.edu/products../prb/211/default.html

Miller, G. A. (1956). The magical number seven, plus or minus two: Some limits on our capacity for processing information. *Psychological Review*, *63*, 81-97.

Murray, R. (1993). *Group skills and interpersonal relationships*. Auckland, New Zealand: Auckland College of Education.

National Adult Literacy Agency. (2012). *The survey of adult skills*. Retrieved from http://www.nala.ie/resources/oecd-adult-skills-survey-piaac-factsheet-ireland

National University of Ireland Galway. (2011). *Going to College Project*. Retrieved from http://www.nuigalway.ie/about-us/news-and-events/news-archive/2011/january2011/nui-galway-launches-the-going-to-college-project-1.html

Nevill, R. E., *&* White, S. B. (2011). College students' openness toward autism spectrum disorders: Improving peer acceptance. *Journal of Autism and Developmental Disorders*, *41*, 1619–1628. doi:10.1007/s10803-011-1189-x

Nickerson, R. S. (1985). Understanding understanding. *American Journal of Education*, *93*(1), 201–239.

Nichols, J. D., & Zhang, G. (2011). Classroom environments and student empowerment: An analysis of elementary and secondary teacher beliefs. *Learning Environment Research*, *14*(3), 229–239.

Novak, J. D. (1991). Clarify with concept maps. *The Science Teacher*, *58*(7), 45–49.

Osborn, A. (1953). *Applied imagination: Principles and procedures of creative problem solving*. New York, NY: Charles Scribner's Sons.

O'Brien, P., O'Keeffe, M., Kenny, M., Fitzgerald, S., & Curtis, S. (2008). *Inclusive education: A tertiary experience and transferable model?* Lessons learned from the Certificate in Contemporary Living Programme: Dublin: National Institute for Intellectual Disability, TCD, No 3, Monograph series.

O'Brien, P., O'Keeffe, M., Healy, U., Kubiak, J., Lally, N., & Hughes, Z. (2009). Inclusion of students with intellectual disability within a university setting. *The Frontline of Learning Disability*, *74*, 6–7.

O'Connor, B., Kubiak, J., Espiner, D., & O'Brien, P. (2012). Lecturer responses to the inclusion of students with intellectually disabilities auditing undergraduate classes, *Journal of Policy and Practice in Intellectual Disability*, *9*(4), 247–256.

Paakkari, L., Tynjälä, P., & Kannas, L. (2011). Critical aspects of student teachers' conceptions of learning. *Learning and Instruction*, *21*, 705–714.

Schommer, M. (1993). Epistemological development and academic performance among secondary students. *Journal of Educational Psychology*, *S5*(3), 406–411.

Schunk, D. H. (2005). Self-regulated learning: The educational legacy of Paul R. Pintrich. *Educational Psychologist*, *40*, 85–94.

Shaw, S. F., Scott, S. S., & McGuire, J. M. (2001). Teaching college students with learning disabilities. (ED459548). Retrieved from http:// www.ericdigests.org/2002-3/college.htm

162   J. KUBIAK and M. SHEVLIN

Simpson, C. G., & Spenser, V. G. (2009). *College success for students with learning Disabilities: strategies and tips to make the most of your college. experience.* Austin, TX: Prufrock Press.

Stefánsdóttir, G. V. (2010). University program for people with intellectual disabilities at the University of Iceland. Retrieved November 29, 2013 from http://ec.europa.eu/education/grundtvig/doc/conf10/w7/empowerment.pdf

Säljö, R. (1979). *Learning in the learner's perspective: I. Some common-sense conceptions.* Reports from the Institute of Education. University of Gothenberg, 76, as summarized in Psychology: Theory and Application.

Trinity College Dublin. (2011). *Trinity inclusive curriculum.* Retrieved from http://www.tcd.ie/CAPSL/TIC/about/what/

Turnbull, P., Friesen, B. J., & Ramirez, C. (1998). Participatory action research as a model for conducting family research. RPSI. *Research and Practice from Persons with Disabilities, 23*(3), 178–188.

Uditsky, B. (1993). Natural pathways to friendships. In A. N. Amado (Ed.), *Friendships and community connections between people with and without developmental disabilities* (pp. 85–96). Baltimore, MD: Paul H. Brookes.

Uditsky, B., Frank, S., Hart, L., & Jeffreys, S. (1987). *On campus: Integrating the university environment.* In D. Baine (Ed.), *Alternative futures for the education of students with severe disabilities. Proceedings of the conference on severe and multiple handicaps: Alternative futures* (pp. 96–103). Edmonton, Alberta, Canada: Publication Services, Faculty of Education, University of Alberta.

Uditsky, B., & Hughson, E. (2012). Inclusive postsecondary education—An evidence-based moral imperative. *Journal of Policy and Practice in Intellectual Disabilities, 9*(4), 298–302.

United Nations. (2006). *Convention on the rights of persons with disabilities.* New York, NY: Author. Retrieved from http://www.un.org/disabilities/convention/conventionfull.shtml

University of Alberta. (2006). *On campus program.* Retrieved from http://www.uofaweb.ualberta.ca/oncampus/nav01.cfm?nav01=33356

Van Rossum, E. J., & Schenk, S. M. (1984). The relationship between learning conception, study strategy and learning outcome. *British Journal of Educational Psychology, 54,* 73–83.

Walmsley, J., & Johnson, K. (2003). *Inclusive research with people with intellectual disabilities: past, present and futures.* London, England: Jessica Kingsley.

Watkins, D., & Regmi, M. (1992). How universal are student conceptions of learning? A Nepalese investigation. *Psychologia, 35,* 101–110.

Zimmerman, B. J. (2002). Becoming a self-regulated learner: An overview. *Theory into practice 21*(2), 64–70.

PART III

ENABLING SELF-DETERMINATION AND AUTHENTIC PARTICIPATION IN DECISION MAKING

CHAPTER 8

INCLUDING STUDENTS WITH INTELLECTUAL DISABILITY IN DECISION MAKING AND FUTURE PLANNING DURING AND AFTER UPPER-SECONDARY EDUCATION

A Finnish Case Study

Aino Äikäs

It is an internationally accepted fact that more research is needed into how young adults diagnosed with intellectual disability experience life after education and how they are involved in the decision-making process regarding their future planning. The goals of inclusion which are connected to social justice, equality, human rights and integration to society have been slow to develop and reach full realization. In Finland, the education system can still be considered one that segregates people with disabilities. The transition from upper secondary education into a more independent adult life and subsequent entry into society is a particular challenge for young adults with intellectual disability. The main focus of the chapter is the inclusion (and

Inclusive Education for Students with Intellectual Disabilities,
pp. 165–188
Copyright © 2015 by Information Age Publishing

exclusion) of young adults in the decision-making process and the planning of their futures. The topic employs the use of a strong case study of a young adult called Oliver. The empirical part of the study consists of interviews with Oliver, his mother, and professionals who work closely with him ($N = 12$). The approach of the study is narrative and the methods of grounded theory are used in the analysis. In the chapter, I present how future planning was conducted and discuss Oliver's personal experience in the process. The influence of the disability diagnosis in relation to educational decision making is addressed, as well as the significance of using the appropriate communication method in advocating educational excellence. In addition, Oliver's experience of disability itself and how the concept is experienced and interpreted are examined. A proposal is presented concerning how people with intellectual disability could be part of an inclusive decision-making process concerning their future planning in order to realize their full, unique potential.

INTRODUCTION

A young man called Oliver (pseudonym) describes his impression of the possibilities of employment or further education after completion of upper secondary school in Finland as follows:

Aino: Did you want to attend another school or place to work?
Oliver: No (also points at the Picture Communication Symbol (PCS) "NO").[1] There seems to be no other place for me.

After finishing his upper secondary education, Oliver has become a regular at a municipal day-care unit for young adults designed to target people that fall within the spectrum of autism and challenging behavior. What happened and why? Are the possibilities really so very few in a country known for its welfare systems such as Finland as Oliver has stated? Young adults who have attended upper secondary education should have a bright future with a variety of opportunities available to them. However, the experience Oliver expressed when discussing future planning indicates a different situation for young adults with intellectual disabilities.

In this chapter I question how people with intellectual disabilities are included (or how society in fact, excludes them) in decision-making and future planning of their lives during and after upper secondary education. I argue that professionals working with students who are diagnosed with intellectual disabilities need to be provided with more methods and materials that can be utilized to help young adults achieve their goals concerning future employment or further education. In addition, I argue that young adults themselves need more opportunities to participate in the decision-making process in order to realize their full potential. In addition, I ask: is our affluent society still not capable of supporting all its members?

This topic interests me as a researcher because I had the opportunity to work on a regional project in 2009/2010 which developed models and materials for vocational education programs for individuals with intellectual and developmental disabilities that aimed to assist these young adults in the transition from upper secondary education to an independent adult lifestyle.

This chapter begins with a short review of the terminology involved in the concept of intellectual and developmental disability, the key concept of the topic. Next, there is a brief review of recent participatory research in the field of special education and disability studies. Following that is an overview of the Finnish education system and a review of several theoretical models of transition. The methods section explains how the empirical elements of the case study were conducted. The results are presented as narratives based on the methodological approach of the study. This section includes dialogue from the interviews of Oliver, his mother, and professionals that have worked with Oliver. The final section of this chapter, entitled Implications and Future Directions, outlines a number of proposals made concerning materials and methodology and also suggests an alternative approach to intellectual disability and the support provided to individuals diagnosed with intellectual disability.

THEORY AND RESEARCH

A Brief Note on Terminology

The concept of intellectual disability is a complex issue from the viewpoint of applying the term to an individual. The concept can be defined by classifications such as ICD-10 (The International Classification of Diseases, World Health Organization, 2010), DSM-V (Diagnostic and Statistical Manual of Mental Disorders V, American Psychiatric Association, 2013), classifications made by AAIDD (the American Association on Intellectual and Developmental Disabilities, Schalock, Borthwick-Duffy, & Bradley, 2010) and by ICF (International Classification of Functioning, Disability and Health, Word Health Organization, 2001) (Harris, 2006). The concept could be replaced with an alternative concept such as: individuals with cognitive differences (Biklen, 2012), people with cognitive disabilities (Kittay, 2013), or concepts such as individuals who need intensive support in everyday life. The term "intellectual disability" is used in this chapter because the individual at the core of the study was diagnosed with this particular disability at age 11, and later completed a training program in vocational education aimed at supporting students with severe disabilities (e.g. intellectual disabilities) to prepare them for work and independent life.

Students With Intellectual Disability as Participants in Research and Future Planning

What do we know about the experience of young adults diagnosed with intellectual disability in the educational system, and how they are involved in their own future planning? Previous studies that focused on the topic of educational solutions, school outcomes, or employment of individuals diagnosed with intellectual disability tend to have been conducted *about* or *on* the individuals rather than conducted *with* the individuals (Connor, Gabel, Gallagher, & Morton, 2008). Current studies in the field of disability have emphasized the belief that the people who are diagnosed with the disability are the best interpreters of the phenomenon, so research should be conducted as a cooperative effort (Johnson, Douglas, Bigby, & Iacono, 2012; Koenig 2011; Murphy, Clegg, & Almack, 2011; Wilson, Bialk, Freeze, Freeze, & Lutfiyya, 2012). In this respect, the research has also an emancipatory effect on the individuals involved, creating a positive personal result from the research (Gabel, 2005). Including these individuals in the research process has produced new insights that not only broaden the theoretical sensitivity and analytical focus of the topic, but also influence the direction of further analysis through participation in the interpretative aspect of the research (Koenig, 2011). In the chapter the desire is to include Oliver as a participant in the research so that the results are as deep and authentic as it is possible when trying to understand someone's thoughts about a certain topic.

Inclusive Education and the Finnish Education System

The aim of inclusive education is that all people are able to participate in different parts of society after education (Ainscow & César, 2006). There are clear goals of inclusion that relate to people with intellectual disability in the education system that involve equality, human rights, and societal integration (e.g., IDEA Individuals with Disabilities Education Act, 1997; UNESCO Salamanca Statement, 1994). However, these goals have materialized slowly because the education system can still be accused of segregating people in Finland. Thus, persons who have been labeled with intellectual disability find entry into society difficult. Fortunately, the education system for people with an intellectual disability has been developing at an adequate rate in Finland since 1998, when the policy of comprehensive schools (1998/628) and the policy of vocational schools (1998/630) were launched. These policies shift the responsibility of organizing education for people identified as having severe intellectual disability, from the special-care facilities to the municipalities. Individuals with severe intellectual disability are included in the so-called "mainstream" education system. This means that all students, including those with disabilities, are able to attend comprehensive schools with the support of Individualized Education Plans (IEPs) and special education classes. In addition, it was necessary to organize educational groups for these students after they completed their 12 year comprehensive education. Inclusion is clearly an aim in the background of these legislations. Physical integration increased after the legislation but according to studies by Jahnukainen and Korhonen (2003) and Hyytiäinen (2012), complete inclusion into society remains difficult to achieve. Inclusive solutions might be effective in day care or preschool settings, but the difficulties that persist in primary schools and secondary schools are the true indication that inclusive solutions for educating people with intellectual disabilities are rare.

The concept of inclusive education is an undercurrent in the legislation of Finnish education and it has been strengthened since the Basic Education Act (628/1998) Amendment 642/2010 in 2010. The Amendment featured an emphasis on inclusiveness and the response to intervention. The Tier 1-2-3 organization method of education was adopted for the curricula and put into practice. According to Grosche and Volpe (2013), the RTI-model (Response to Intervention) has the potential to influence inclusion by providing a strong implementation plan for inclusion practices; by defining the roles, responsibilities, cooperation, and collaboration of all teachers; by enabling the sharing of resources for the instruction and guidance of students with special needs, and finally, by avoiding early and unnecessary labeling of students with special needs.

Transition

Transition from upper secondary education onwards, and especially to employment, is challenging for people with disabilities in Finland. First, the model of supported employment is still seldom used as an employment method for people with intellectual disabilities. Only approximately 300 people diagnosed with intellectual disability in total have been employed by this method since the mid 1990s when the model was put in use in Finland (Pajunen et al., 2008; Ylipaavalniemi, 2001). Second, the educational institutions which organize employment tend to operate separately, and cooperation between these institutions is insufficient (Äikäs, 2012). Third, the opportunities for individuals with intellectual disability to participate in the decision-making process in relation to upper secondary education and employment are narrow and limited according to Hakala (2010). Wilson et al. (2012) illustrate that the transition from high school to adult life is a period of new opportunities, independence, and a time of disappointment and challenges for individuals with intellectual disabilities (the term "learning disability" is used in this Canadian study but the sources of disability are autism and microcephaly so it is comparable to the current topic). Access to postsecondary educational opportunities is often restricted by entrance requirements, tuition and other expenses, and a lack of support for learning and social participation. However, the young adults with intellectual disabilities pursue the same goals as other teenagers in a transition phase, such as meaningful paid employment and access to higher education. However, this is not what young adults with disabilities are able to obtain in a transition phase (Wilson et al., 2012). In addition, according to Parent and Kregel (1996) and Moore, Harley, and Gamble (2004), the service system needs improvement concerning supported employment services for individuals diagnosed with intellectual disabilities, especially severe disabilities.

An article by Certo et al. (2008) suggests two central changes that should be implemented in the transition process. First, the school to adulthood transition components of transition planning acts (e.g., the IDEIA Individuals with Disabilities Education Improvement Act, 2004) are to be strengthened. The school districts should be authorized to work with appropriate private agencies at the point of transition to produce individualized employment plans with sufficient support systems for an adult living situation. Second, the federal government as a legislator should provide access to long-term support, creating a service system which coordinates the functions of transition planning acts (e.g., IDEIA) after the completion of education. In addition, the thoughts and opinions of young adults themselves should be included in the transition planning and should be encouraged by providing materials that support the planning. For example, transition plans with appropriate alternative communication systems.

METHOD

The aim of the study is to answer the following questions: (1) How do young adults with intellectual disabilities experience education, transition periods, and the significance of education from the viewpoint of employment? (2) How are these young adults included in the decision-making process concerning their future planning? Next, the data and methods of analysis are introduced and discussed.

The Data

The empirical aspect of this study was conducted from 2005 to 2010 and the PhD dissertation took place in August 2012. The study was conducted using qualitative inquiry in order to obtain a thorough and comprehensive understanding of the phenomenon. The overarching approach of the study is narrative. The method was found appropriate for the study because narrative methodologies can provide researchers with privileged insights into how people view and make sense of the world (Lawson, Parker, & Sikes, 2006; Webster & Mertova, 2007). Furthermore, the research method can be described as a case study (Brantlinger, Jimenez, Klinger, Pughan, & Richardson, 2005).

The subject of the case study is Oliver, a 23-year-old man who was diagnosed with intellectual disability at the age of 11. Consent was given in oral form by Oliver and in written form by his mother. The informed consent principle was accomplished using PCSs (Picture Communication Symbols) with Oliver because he was familiar with the symbols. Consent was renewed at the beginning of each interview session. It is essential to take into account who gives the consent, in order to avoid questionable ethical practices (Kvale, 1996; Snelgrove, 2005). According to Oliver's mother, especially due to Oliver's severe communication problems, Oliver attended a training program in upper secondary education from 2005 to 2007 that prepares individuals with severe disabilities for work and independent life. Besides severe communication problems Oliver's adaptive functioning can be described with the expression *slow*. For example his walking and eating is independent but takes a lot of time.

Oliver's mother, the teacher and assistants of the education group, as well as the activity center personnel most likely to work with Oliver in the future were interviewed in spring 2005. These professionals were chosen to be interviewed because they were the ones working in an activity center which organizes all areas of employment services for people with intellectual disabilities. These thematic and episodic interviews lasted from 45 minutes to 1 hour 30 minutes and were all one on one. Oliver was interviewed 15 times between 2009 and 2010. The data-collection of the study applied elements of grounded theory (Strauss & Corbin, 1990). This meant that the interviews with Oliver were conducted both based on the experiences of the training program and according to themes included in the main categories which were formulated from the analysis of interviews with his mother and the professionals. The themes were the following: individual aspects, aspects in relation to the society, education and employment, and aspects related to the disability itself. The outline of the structured interview was formulated using a questionnaire. The questionnaire was designed and used in the quality of life research project conducted by the Finnish Association on Intellectual and Developmental Disabilities (FAIDD) in 1990-1992 (Matikka, 2006a, 2006b). Each interview session with Oliver lasted approximately 1 hour and 20 minutes.

In Oliver's interviews, PCSs were used as a method of augmentative and alternative communication. The significance of augmentative and alternative communication are widely recognized in studies focused on including people with disabilities in the research process (Brooks & Davies, 2007; Bunning, Heath, & Minnion, 2009; Cambridge & Forrester-Jones, 2003; Koenig, 2011; Porter et al., 2005). The augmentative and alternative communication method may include signs, graphic symbols, or technology. The essential issue to consider is the role of the researcher, particularly how they formulate questions and whether the researcher influences the answers (Brewster, 2004). In addition, it is crucial to consider beforehand what kind of symbols, concepts, or supportive equipment is necessary during interview. Lewis and Porter (2004), for instance, emphasize precise choices of vocabulary and concepts. In the interviews with Oliver, a total of 155 different PCSs were used as support. The PCSs were displayed but Oliver thought it was also important to use spoken language during the interviews. He pointed to the yes/no symbol when he was asked to answer in this manner, but he mainly used spoken language with stuttering. The total combined time of all Oliver's interviews amounted to 23 hours.

Analysis

The results of the study consist of narratives of Oliver's life written by me as a researcher based on the interviews of the above mentioned participants ($N = 12$). The analysis involved several phases. The data were first analyzed using elements of grounded theory and then were analyzed with narrative analysis. The coding and organizing of the data was done by using the Atlas.ti software. Forty-nine different types of codes, or classes of codes were found. The total number of codes in the parent's and professionals' interview data was 1120. This phase can be labeled open coding since the data were broken down, examined, compared, conceptualized, and categorized for the first time (see Strauss & Corbin, 1990). The codes were then further investigated, the data had been organized according to the quantity of codes and some codes were merged (e.g. different areas of curriculum were combined under a code "curriculum," expressions such as "talk to each other" or "speak," "sign" were combined under a code "communication").

In the second phase of analysis, the codes were organized according to coding categories. The categories were formed based on the remarks of Bogdan and Biklen (2003) on developing coding categories. The codes were added into the following categories: process, activity, event, strategy, context, relationship and social structure, definition of the situation, perspectives held by the subjects, and subjects' ways of thinking about people and objects. Strauss and Corbin (1990) suggest axial coding, which is a set of processes where the data are merged together after open coding. It is making connections between categories by utilizing a coding paradigm involving conditions, context, action, and consequences.

Concurrently conducting the coding with the elements of Grounded theory, a narrative story of Oliver's life was written. According to Polkinghorne (1988), humans are narrative beings who use many different narrative structures to provide coherence and meaning to what they experience and recognize. In this study, the story formed the basis of the results and became also a tool for accessing the credibility of the research. This can be called also the principle of evocativeness which means that by constructing the results into a form of a story it also questions how well the research narrative evokes mental images, memories or emotions related to the theme (Heikkinen, Huttunen, Syrjälä, & Pesonen, 2012).

Once the codes were organized into categories and composed into a story, the third phase of analysis began; the coding categories were organized into a model of circles which were layered on each other. The model was similar to the conditional matrix of Strauss and Corbin (1990). According to Strauss and Corbin (1990), the conditional matrix is an analytical aid, a diagram useful for understanding and considering the wide range of conditions related to the phenomenon under investigation. The matrix was also useful in attempting to comprehend the consequences of the phenomenon and it enabled the distinction and links between different levels of conditions and corresponding consequences (Strauss & Corbin, 1990).

Oliver's experiences in education, transition, employment, and disability were combined with the parent's and professionals' interpretation of his experiences and new narrative stories of Oliver's life were written. The data were then analyzed using the methods of narrative analysis according to the approaches of holistic-content and holistic-form (Lieblich, Tuval-Mashiach, & Zilber, 1998). Holistic-content analysis in this study meant that the data was observed as a whole, creating the question; what were the main themes that could be discerned in the stories regarding education, transition, employment, and disability? Holistic-form analysis was conducted with the help of Bruner's (1996) nine universals of narrative realities. This means that the stories were analyzed as a whole and the analysis concentrated on what type of interpretations could be made from the stories through the discovery of different structures, plot structures, or genres.

To enhance reliability of the analysis and the interpretations I made, the stories of Oliver's life were sent to the participants to review. Oliver's mother made some corrections to the story. Also in the beginning of each interview session with Oliver the prior interview was shortly evaluated and reviewed. Heikkinen et al. (2012) suggest that this principle of dialectics is one of the principles of validation in research conducted with a narrative approach.

RESULTS

The results of the study are presented as short narratives. The topics of the narratives are: education and transition, work and employment, the future, and the disability. According to the narrative approach, it is essential that the voices of different informants in the research can be heard and sensed in the report (Heikkinen et al., 2012). This polyphony is illustrated by the storyline composed by me, quotations from Oliver, his mother, and from the professionals working with him. The translations of the quotations from Finnish to English were done by me. The results are discussed in the Implementations and Future Directions section at the end of the chapter.

Education and Transition

When Oliver received the diagnosis of intellectual disability, it directly impacted his educational experience in that he was forced to first change education groups, and then was eventually moved to a different school. He had attended school since the age of six and learned how to read and write. He also communicated with speech at that time. According to his mother, Oliver's development gradually regressed until, by the age of 11, his communication abilities had clearly diminished. Guided by the help of professional opinions, his parents decided to go through several examinations and assessments before Oliver was finally diagnosed with intellectual disability. The mother describes the decision-making process as follows:

It was the constant movement in Oliver's schooling. If we wanted a proper curriculum he had to be separated from his friends when he had to change groups. And finally the change of the school—that he had even changed schools from the nearest school to another location. That there were no peaceful school years in Oliver's life at all.

The school Oliver finally ended up attending was a special school for students with the most severe intellectual and developmental disabilities. The school was socially and physically segregated from society, situated in the middle of nowhere. Oliver's parents thought that it was the right decision for Oliver's development. In this school he received "experiences of being better than others", as described by the mother. Oliver talks about some of his memories of early school years before he attended the special school as it follows:

> Aino: How was it in primary school, was there a lot of bullying?
> Oliver: Yes, there was quite a lot bullying. Especially during the recesses, there was bullying, calling names, calling names, and pushing.

After his final years of primary school and secondary school in the special school, Oliver attended the rehabilitation and preparation training program for youths with severe disabilities. This educational program was organized within the vocational education unit. The transition process from secondary school to vocational education was planned with the cooperation of the teacher, parents, and professionals. The duration of the program was 2 years. Some of the professionals working in the program expressed doubt about the purpose and benefit of the educational outcomes. One of the assistants describes her thoughts as follows:

> I don't know what the benefit of this type of education is for the young adults or what the benefits are for working life. I question the point ... my own opinions vary from one end to the other. Of course it is better for the young adults to come here rather than spend the whole day in their living arrangements, but ...

The special education teacher continues along the same line of thought:

> This education has become a so-called "storage place" for these young adults. Or some kind of alternative place to spend few years after secondary education. The benefit and the meaning of the training remains to be reached.

However, Oliver had positive memories of the training program and said that he studied, for example, "real estate management duties" during the course of the program. The transition planning and the transition process itself, from the program to the municipals day-care unit, was put together by the teacher, parents, and Oliver himself. Oliver told me that he visited the unit once before they decided that he would attend the unit after the program. He did not know that written transition plans were made within the transition planning, or that there would have been some form of additional materials used to help in the transition process.

Work and Employment

The municipals day-care unit that Oliver attended after his upper secondary education was catered to people within the spectrum of autism and behavior which is considered challenging as previously mentioned. The choices and possibilities available to Oliver were few, as he stated at the beginning of this chapter. In the unit, Oliver had opportunities to attend work practice once a week. The remaining four days of the week he participated in duties and chores at the unit. Oliver attended the same type of practical training during the vocational education before moving to the day-care unit. The training took place in a nearby department store and his duties were shelving and stocking goods. Oliver's experience of the work practice was positive and he was able to work independently. His experiences were also positive because the work was varied and he was given a proper amount of guidance while he was at the workplace. The guidance was organized by the day-care unit. None of the department store employees had contact with Oliver during the hours he was at work. Oliver explained the most important aspect in working life:

> Aino: What is the most important thing about work? The main priority. I have some options here which are: work-buddies (meaning colleagues), that I am able to make the decisions considering work (meaning self-determination), that chores vary (meaning variety of duties), salary, or that others value my work? (Also with PCS's)
>
> Oliver: Good buddies, that is the most important. Yes. (Points also to the PCS of friends.)

The statement that good colleagues are the most important aspect in working life and employment to Oliver is significant. The hope for social interaction and friendship is something that very often remains unobtainable for people with intellectual disabilities. The practical training or work practice provided during the vocational education and in the day-care unit were worthwhile only as daily activities but did not lead to actual, full employment. One could argue that young adults with disabilities often stay forever in a trainee role and are never able to fully experience employment unless the method of supported employment were to be completely reorganized. The young adult gets "Caught in the Continuum" as Taylor (2004) has accurately expressed.

According to the professionals interviewed in this study, one of the main reasons that full-time, long-term employment is difficult to achieve is because the transition planning does not start early enough and the cooperation between units is dysfunctional. The vocational education training program teacher describes the situation as follows: *"They don't wake up early enough to realize what kind of individuals are to be employed and what type of services these individuals need."* The other professional working in the activity center also commented:

> So we are in a school and then we are in an activity center and then we are in a third place and all these units work separately from each other. They are good places but they all are segregated and hardly ever work together. Sometimes they hardly ever meet the client. But all of the units have their own plans and curricula and the natural aspect of cooperation is missing.

What is illustrated by the above quotation is something that Oliver's mother finds very unsatisfactory. And she describes that this is the way the "client," the individual, is "being messed about in the service system."

The Future

It is clear that the employment of individuals diagnosed with intellectual disability is a difficult prospect. While these individuals do have access to upper secondary education or training programs in vocational education, after completing these programs they typically end up in segregated, disjointed environments such as activity centers for people with certain types of disabilities, or in day-care centers, as is seen in Oliver's case. These facilities are also open to people without an education. Oliver, however, had clear opinions about his future plans and hopes:

> Aino: Tell me, what is the most important thing in life? (I show PCS's of hobbies, work, home, and friends).
> Oliver: Work, garden work is. (Points also the PCS-symbol of work).

Oliver's mother expressed that the ideal situation for Oliver would be if he were employed somewhere in an integrated environment rather than in activity centers with only other individuals with disabilities. The mother described the duties in the activity center as "bagging some odds and ends" and "doing some simple duties for a few hours routinelike and then moving on to the next routine." The quality of life in this area could be

improved by appropriate working conditions and desirable work. Besides
garden work, Oliver had additional dreams which did not involve working
in an activity center or in a day-care unit. They were:

> Aino: Did you want to do something else?
> Oliver: Fireman's work. Fireman's work after a few years, some put-
> ting fires out and so on.
> Aino: Is it your dream job?
> Oliver: Yes.
> Aino: What type of education would you need for that?
> Oliver: Well, for example some courses on life saving, courses to
> extinguish fires, courses on preventing fires.

It is clear that Oliver is not capable of working as a firefighter or even
studying anything involving this type of work, but during the transition
planning period it was never proposed that some type of work could be
found or developed in assisting at a fire station, for example, in maintenance work, which Oliver had studied in vocational education. Perhaps by
planning individual duties and also including garden work in fire station.

The Disability

To Oliver the meaning of "disability" was different from the professionals' point of view. The conversation we had concerning the concept was
eye-opening and strengthened the theoretical approach to the phenomenon from a social-constructionist viewpoint.

> Aino: Do you feel that you are a disabled person?
> Oliver: No, I don't feel that way. I have never felt [that way].
> Aino: Do you feel that you are a person with intellectual disability?
> Oliver: No, I am just an ordinary young man.
> Aino: Would you like to change something about yourself?
> Oliver: Well, I'd like to be a handsome and muscular fellow.
> Aino: What would you like to say about the concept of disability to
> others?
> Oliver: Well, it wouldn't be nice to be disabled I'm sure.

The concept of disability is culturally structured and it is interpreted as
something negative, something that no one would want to deal with personally. Based on the discourse that is connected with disability terminology, expressions such as "suffers," "risk" or "captive of the wheelchair" are
terms which structure the negative stigma (Vehmas, 2005).

In addition, especially severe disability evoked insecurity among the professionals in their interviews. One of the activity centers personnel expressed that "we have large group of people and if there would be people with severe disabilities and especially people with autism it would be suffering for all. The individual with autism and all the others in the center would suffer."

Professionals in different fields have significant roles in constructing the current and often misplaced conceptions of disability. The language used by professionals reflects and constructs certain ways of perceiving those with a disability and creates actions which reflect on the individuals' lives very powerfully (Vehkakoski, 2006). For example, school, built environments, and working life have all plenty of functions which are unreachable for people with intellectual disabilities. In addition, the concept is also an individually interpreted phenomenon which can be considered an individual feature (Ferguson, Ferguson, & Taylor, 1992).

A summary of the results of the study can be seen in Figure 8.1, which illustrates that the reality and the objective are far removed from each other when considering the inclusive education and full citizenship of individuals with intellectual disabilities.

From a theoretical point of view, the possibility for a person with intellectual disability to be included and achieve full participation as a citizen (see also Duffy, 2010) and good educational opportunities in a society are numerous. Especially considering the theories of critical special education (see also Ware, 2005) and disability studies that suggest that there should be no barriers for these individuals to be active members of society. However, when observing the Finnish service system from the viewpoint of intellectual disability the truth of the matter is different. The opportunities for this group of people is narrow in relation to services provided, education groups organized, and employment possibilities, as illustrated by Oliver's story.

Based on the results of this study, the reality experienced by the young adult, his mother, and professionals is different from the objectives concerning the education, employment, and future of a young adult with intellectual disabilities. The themes in the reality section (narrow gray field) are represented mainly in the speech of the professionals. They experienced that the education is segregated and the transition from vocational education onwards is dependent on the professional's method of organizing his or her own work. The work practice sessions were also carried out in segregated environments and the future employment possibilities were in segregated activity centers rather than in an inclusive environment with a framework of employee support. The professionals also experienced especially the phenomenon of the severe disability itself as

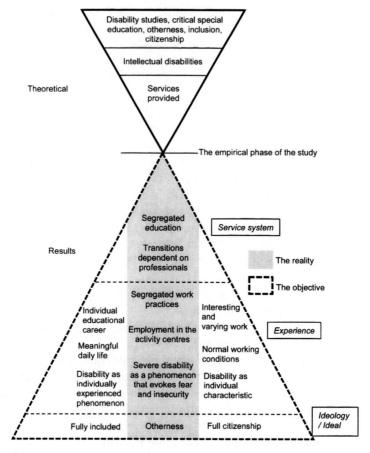

Figure 8.1.   Results and background of the study.

fearful and evoking insecurity. Based on the results of this study, this approach is interpreted as causing feelings of "otherness" in society.

Although the parent and the young adult himself spoke about the same themes, their speech included more themes in the objective section (in Figure 8.1, the area surrounding the gray section, marked with a dashed line). They experienced the service system that included the possibilities of an individual educational career and normal working conditions. They had more positive insights to the future outcomes. To them, the service system should offer the possibilities of a meaningful daily life and future which included interesting and varying work. The meanings were much more objective according to their speech. The phenomenon of the disability was experienced individually and through individual characteristics by Oliver and also by his mother. The results of this study indicate that the young adult and the parent experienced good possibilities and positive insights of full inclusion and full citizenship (Duffy, 2010) in the life of a young adult even though the reality is rather different.

IMPLICATIONS AND FUTURE DIRECTIONS

Next I observe how future planning was conducted, what elements should be taken into closer consideration and what Oliver experienced. In addition, some suggestions are presented and implications proposed.

The Influence of the Diagnosis Must Be Recognized. The meaning and impact of the diagnosis in relation to educational decision making is discussed in the following section. Medicalization has influenced the decision-making process from the point of view of educational solutions which have primarily been made in the past (Thomas & Loxley, 2007). It is clear that someone with a particular diagnosis would be assigned to an education group designed for individuals with a similar diagnosis. Oliver was forced to change education groups and finally transferred to a different school after he received the diagnosis. This is how society operated in Oliver's primary school years (the 1990s) and this remains how the system functions today, in 2013. What if the inclusive education system was the reality, and individuals with intellectual disability were able to attend their nearest school and participate in the so-called "normal" classroom experience with the kids in their neighborhood?

Experience of Disability Must Be Taken Account. Disability itself is a complex phenomenon. Oliver experiences disability as an individual feature and it is not the primary feature he has in mind when he talks about himself. In fact, he referred to himself as "just an ordinary young man". The theoretical structures behind the phenomenon are also very complex. According to Vehmas (2005), it is possible to find at least two approaches in the background that follow the social-constructionist approach and the materialistic approach to the disability. First, the materialistic approach (also called the social model of disability) suggests that the core of the phenomenon of disability lies in society and not in the individuals. In other words, the society creates disabilities. Disability results in acts of segregation and exclusion of these individuals from participation in society's functions. Different actors in society have created a majority of functions that are not accessible to all members. The restrictive environments created by society can be seen in all of its spheres. They can vary from individual prejudice and institutionalized prejudice, to buildings and public transportation which are not accessible with wheelchair, to segregated educational programs and employment possibilities that do not exist (Määttä, 1981; Oliver, 1996; Vehmas, 2005).

Second, from a theoretical standpoint, the other approach to the phenomenon is that disability is structured by the language, ideals, and values. The language not only illustrates the world of disability but also creates structures for that world. In the process, the reality and the knowledge are structured in social interactions and created by individuals. From this point of view, disability is not a universal phenomenon but gets its forms and features from certain social contexts (Barnes, Mercer, & Shakespeare, 2005). This social-constructionist approach views the disability as always combined with certain cultural environments and the beliefs and values of the society (Barnes et al., 2005). The disability is thus a culturally constructed phenomenon. The meaning of "disability" varies depending on which different cultural lenses are used in approaching this topic.

These two views outline the fact that the disability is a phenomenon that can be interpreted in many ways. Also, the theoretical opinions of the phenomenon vary. Could disability and especially the phenomenon of intellectual disability be interpreted as a minority group in our society? Individuals with disabilities report that the negative attitudes towards people with disabilities and discriminative actions of others are more restrictive than the disability itself (Hahn, 1986). Is it possible that if individuals with intellectual disability were seen as a minority group, the possibility to be included would be greater?

Appropriate Communication Methods Are Crucial. In light of advocating educational excellence and learning environments, it is very important that the appropriate communication method for the individual is determined at an early age. Oliver was diagnosed at age 11 with intellectual disability due to his extensive communication problems that had gradually intensified. At the beginning of primary school, Oliver used spoken language as a means of communication but by the time he was diagnosed professionals considered that he might have autism rather than intellectual disability. However, the diagnosis of intellectual disability was eventually provided. The methods used to help Oliver's social interaction seldom involved the use of PCSs or a communicator using the PCSs as communication support. At the time, he was told to use methods that he found too restrictive in comparison with his competence and understanding. According to Stock, Davies, Wehmeyer, and Lachapelle (2011), a substantial amount of attention is paid to provide access to the basic features of independent communities for individuals with hearing, vision, or physical disabilities but less attention is paid to access for people with intellectual disabilities. The research summarizes that the most important outcome of the study was the realization that technology was able to help in, for example, using public transportation to make the community more accessible. New technology and new applications of existing technology can be used more widely as alternative or augmentative communication methods.

How to Participate in Decision making and Future Planning? How can people with intellectual disability be active participants in the decision-making process concerning their future planning in order to reach their full potential? Murphy et al. (2011) explain that there are two main discourses that address adulthood from a viewpoint of intellectual disability. One positions the young people as adults entitled unequivocally to self-determination, and invokes policy injunctions to do so. The second viewpoint qualifies the young adult status and claims to self-determination, emphasizing the obdurate reality of intellectual disability. These findings raise a difficult question about the young adult's position in the transition phase and decision-making process. Could inclusive research be the solution to the issue? The creative strategies that include people with intellectual disabilities in research projects from the beginning should be implemented in the Finnish context more widely. Inclusive research would be an appropriate approach to research that aims to influence the students with intellectual disabilities by empowering them. Emancipatory research and participatory research are the overlapping themes and all methods have the mutual aim to involve people in the research projects at every phase, represent their views, and improve the lives of those who participate in the process (Nind, 2013).

In addition, the critical elements in the planning phase that would be most effective in advocating educational opportunities according to Hartman (2009) should include: student-centered planning, functional community-referenced skill development, connections with adult service providers, participation in employment before graduation, school-business partnerships, trainings in self-determination and advocacy, and training or college opportunities.

Developing evidence-based and research-derived transition planning materials in cooperation with young adults is one solution. Also, portfolios of the young adults' history including all work practice materials, evaluations, and assessments of the young adult in cooperation with a professional, should be made accessible and easy to interpret in order to serve the needs of the young adults. After all, serving the needs of young adults is the most important goal of the future planning.

NOTE

1. PCS – Picture Communication Symbols. DynaVox Mayer-Johnson, 2100 Wharton Street, Suite 400, Pittsburgh, PA 15203, USA, Phone: 1 (800) 588-

4548, Fax: 1 (866) 585-6260, E-mail: mayer-johnson.usa@dynavox-tech.com, Web site: www.mayer-johnson.com

REFERENCES

Äikäs, A. (2012) *Toiselta asteelta eteenpäin. Narratiivinen tutkimus vaikeavammaisen nuoren aikuisen koulutuksesta ja työllistymisestä* [Life after upper secondary education. A narrative study of the education and employment of a severely disabled young adult] (Doctoral dissertation). University of Eastern Finland, Joensuu, Finland). Retrieved from http://epublications.uef.fi/pub/urn_isbn_978-952-61-0776-9/urn_isbn_978-952-61-0776-9.pdf

Ainscow, M., & César, M. (2006). Inclusive education ten years after Salamanca: Setting the agenda. *European Journal of Psychology of Education 21*(3), 231–238.

American Psychiatric Association. (2013). *DSM-5. Diagnostic and statistical manual of mental disorders* (5th ed.). Arlington, VA: Author.

Barnes, C., Mercer, G., & Shakespeare, T. (2005). *Exploring disability. A sociological introduction*. Cambridge, England: Polity Press.

Biklen, D. (2012). *After intellectual disability: The case for presuming competence and the possibility of social inclusion* [Lecture in IISS-seminar]. Institute of Inclusive Science and Solutions, Joensuu, Finland.

Bogdan, R. C., & Biklen, S. K. (2003). *Qualitative research in education: An introduction to theory and methods*. Needham Heights, MA: Allyn & Bacon.

Brantlingen, E., Jimenez, R., Klingner, J., Pugach, M., & Richardson, V. (2005). Qualitative studies in special education. *Exceptional Children, 71*(2), 195–207.

Brewster, S. J. (2004). Putting words into their mouths? Interviewing people with learning disabilities and little/no speech. *British Journal of Learning Disabilities 32*, 166–169.

Brooks, M., & Davies, S. (2007). Pathways to participatory research in developing a tool to measure feelings. *British Journal of Learning Disabilities, 36*, 128-133.

Bruner, J. (1996). *The culture of education*. Cambridge, MA: Harvard University Press.

Bunning, K., Heath, B., & Minnion, A. (2009). Communication and empowerment: A place for rich and multiple media? *Journal of Applied Research in Intellectual Disabilities 22*, 370–379.

Cambridge, P., & Forrester-Jones, R. (2003). Using individualised communication for interviewing people with intellectual disability: A case study of user-centred research. *Journal of Intellectual and Developmental Disability, 28*(1), 5–23.

Certo, N. J., Luecking, R. G., Murphy, S., Brown, L., Courey, S., & Belanger, D. (2008). Seamless transition and long-term support for individuals with severe intellectual disabilities. *Research & Practice for Persons with Severe Disabilities, 33*(3), 85–95.

Connor, D. J., Gabel, S. L. Gallagher, D. J., & Morton, M. (2008). Disability studies and inclusive education—Implications for theory, research and practice. *International Journal of Inclusive Education, 12*(5–6), 441–457.

Duffy, S. (2010). The citizenship theory of social justice: Exploring the meaning of personalization for social workers. *Journal of Social Work Practice, 24*(3), 253–267.

Ferguson, P. M., Ferguson, D. L., & Taylor, S. J. (1992). The future of interpretivism in disability studies. In P. M. Ferguson, D. L. Ferguson & S. J. Taylor (Eds.) *Interpreting disability: A qualitative reader* (pp. 259–302). New York, NY: Teachers College Press.

Gabel, S. (Ed.). (2005). Introduction: Disability studies in education. In *Disability studies in education. Readings in theory and method* (pp. 1–20). New York, NY: Peter Lang.

Grosche, M., & Volpe, R. J. (2013). Response-to-intervention (RTI) as a model to facilitate inclusion for students with learning and behavior problems. *European Journal of Special Needs Education, 28*(3), 254–269.

Hahn, H. (1986). Public support for rehabilitation programs: The analysis of U.S. disability policy. *Disability, Handicap & Society, 1*(2), 121–137.

Hakala, K. (2010). Discourses on inclusion, citizenship and categorizations of 'special' in education policy: The case of negotiating change in the governing of vocational special needs education in Finland. *European Educational Research Journal, 9*(2), 269–283.

Harris, J. C. (2006). *Intellectual disability. Understanding its development, causes, classification, evaluation, and treatment.* New York, NY: Oxford University Press.

Hartman, M. A. (2009). Step by step: Creating a community-based transition program for students with intellectual disabilities. *Teaching Exceptional Children, 41*(6), 6–11.

Heikkinen, H. L. T., Huttunen. R., Syrjälä, L., & Pesonen, J. (2012). Action research as narrative: five principles for validation. *Educational Action Research, 20*(1), 5–21.

Hyytiäinen, M. (2012). *Integroiden, segregoiden ja osallistaen. Kolmen vaikeasti kehitysvammaisen oppilaan opiskelu yleisopetuksessa ja koulupolku esiopetuksesta toiselle asteelle* [Integrated, segregated and included. Studying in basic education and a school-path from pre-school to upper secondary of three students with severe intellectual and developmental disabilities] (Doctoral dissertation). University of Eastern Finland, Joensuu, Finland. Retrieved from http://epublications.uef.fi/pub/urn_isbn_978-952-61-0686-1/urn_isbn_978-952-61-0686-1.pdf

Individuals with Disability Education Act Amendments of 1997 (IDEA 1997). (1997).105th Congress. Public Law No: 105-17.

Individuals with Disabilities Education Improvement Act 2004 (IDEIA 2004). 108th Congress. Public Law No: 108-108th-446. (2004).

Jahnukainen, M., & Korhonen, A. (2003). Integration of students with severe and profound intellectual disabilities into the comprehensive school system: Teachers' perceptions of the education reform in Finland. *International Journal of Disability, Development and Education, 50*(2), 169–180.

Johnson, H., Douglas, J., Bigby, C., & Iacono, T. (2012). Social interaction with adults with severe intellectual disability: Having fun and hanging out. *Journal of Applied Research in Intellectual Disabilities, 25*, 329–341.

Kittay, E. F. (2013, May). *Quality of life and the desire for the normal*. Keynote lecture presented at the Nordic Network on Disability Research conference (NNDR). Naantali, Finland.

Koenig, O. (2011). Any added value? Co-constructing life stories of and with people with intellectual disabilities. *British Journal of Learning Disabilities, 40*, 213-221.

Kvale, S. (1996). *InterView: An introduction to qualitative research interviewing*. Thousand Oaks, CA: SAGE.

Lawson, H., Parker, M., & Sikes, P. (2006). Seeking stories: Reflections on a narrative approach to researching understandings of inclusion. *European Journal of Special Needs Education, 21*(1), 55–68.

Lewis, A., & Porter, J. (2004). Interviewing children and young people with learning disabilities: Guidelines for researches and multi-professional practice. *British Journal of Learning Disabilities, 32*, 191–197.

Lieblich, A., Tuval-Mashiach, R., & Zilber, T. (1998). *Narrative research. Reading, analysis and interpretation*. Thousand Oaks, CA: SAGE.

Määttä, P. (1981). *Vammaiset – suuri vähemmistö. Mitä on hyvä tietää vammaisuudesta?* [The disabled—A Great minority. What is good to know about disability?]. Jyväskylä, Finland: Gummerus.

Matikka, L. (2006a). *Quality of life of the mentally disabled: Mildly disabled* [computer file]. FSD2207, version 1.0 (2006-11-17). Helsinki: Finnish Association on Intellectual and Developmental Disabilities [producer], 1991. Tampere: Finnish Social Science Data Archive [distributor], 2006.

Matikka, L. (2006b). *Quality of life of the mentally disabled: severely disabled* [computer file]. FSD2208, version 1.0 (2006-11-17). Helsinki: Finnish Association on Intellectual and Developmental Disabilities [producer], 1991. Tampere: Finnish Social Science Data Archive [distributor], 2006.

Moore, C. L., Harley, D. A., & Gamble, D. (2004). Ex-post-facto analysis of competitive employment outcomes for individuals with mental retardation: national perspective. *Mental Retardation, 42*(4), 253–262.

Murphy, E., Clegg, J., & Almack, K. (2011). Constructing adulthood in discussions about the futures of young people with moderate-profound intellectual disabilities. *Journal of Applied Research in Intellectual Disabilities, 24*, 61–73.

Nind, M. (2013, May). *Understanding quality in inclusive research: A process of dialogue*. Paper presentation at the Nordic Network on Disability Research conference, Naantali, Finland.

Oliver, M. (1996). *Understanding disability: From theory to practice*. Basingstoke, England: Macmillan.

Pajunen, T., Vuorenpää, K., Nikula, L., Österlund, K., Mäenpää, M., Ahlstén, M., & Seppälä, H. (2008). *Työllä osallisuutta? Yhteisvastuukeräysten 2008 -hankkeiden loppuraportti* [Inclusion through employment? Report of an employment project organized by the Finnish Association on Intellectual and Developmental Disabilities and Church]. Retrieved from http://www.kvtl.fi/media/Tyo/tyolla_osallisuutta_loppuraportti_netti.pdf

Parent, W., & Kregel, J. (1996). Consumer satisfaction: a survey of individuals with severe disabilities who receive supported employment services. *Focus on Autism and Other Developmental Disabilities, 11*(4), 207–222.

Polkinghorne, D. E. (1988). *Narrative knowing and the human sciences.* Albany, NY: State University of New York.

Porter, J., Aspinall, A., Parsons, S., Simmonds, L., Wood, M., Culley, G., & Holroyd, A. (2005). Time to listen. *Disability and Society, 20*(5), 575–585.

Schalock, R. L., Borthwick-Duffy, S. A., Buntinx, W. H. E., Coulter, D. L., & Craig, E. M. (2010). *Intellectual disability: Definition, classification, and systems of supports* (11th ed.). Washington, DC: American Association on Intellectual and Developmental Disabilities.

Snelgrove, S. (2005). Bad, mad and sad: developing a methodology of inclusion and a pedagogy for researching students with intellectual disabilities. *International Journal of Inclusive Education, 9*(3), 313–329.

Stock, S. E., Davies, D., K., Wehmeyer, M., L., & Lachapelle, Y. (2011). Emerging new practices in technology to support independent community access for people with intellectual and cognitive disabilities. *NeuroRehabilitiation, 28*, 261-269.

Strauss, A., & Corbin, J. (1990). *Basics of qualitative research: Grounded Theory procedures and techniques.* Thousand Oaks, CA: SAGE.

Taylor, S. (2004). Caught in the continuum: A Critical analysis of the principle of the least restrictive environment. *Research & Practice for Persons with Severe Disabilities 2004, 29*(4), 218–230. (Reprinted from *The Journal of The Association for the Severely Handicapped, 13*(1), Spring, 1988).

Thomas, G., & Loxley, A. (2007). *Deconstructing special education and constructing inclusion* (2nd ed.). Berkshire, England: Open University Press, McGraw-Hill.

UNESCO Salamanca Statement. (1994). *The Salamanca Statement and framework for action on special needs education.* Retrieved from http://www.unesco.org/education/pdf/SALAMA_E.PDF

Vehkakoski, T. (2006). *Leimattu lapsuus? Vammaisuuden rakentuminen ammatti-ihmisten puheissa ja teksteissä* [Stigmatized childhood? Constructing disability in professional talk and texts]. Jyväskylä Studies in Education, Psychology and Social Research 297. Jyväskylä, Finland: University of Jyväskylä.

Vehmas, S. (2005). *Vammaisuus. Johdatus historiaan, teoriaan ja etiikkaan* [Disability. Introduction to history, theory and ethics]. Helsinki, Finland: Gaudeamus.

Ware, L. (2005). Many possible futures, many different directions: Merging critical special education and disability studies. In S. Gabel (Ed.), *Disability studies in education. Readings in theory and method* (pp. 103–124). New York, NY: Peter Lang.

Webster, L., & Mertova, P. (2007). *Using narrative inquiry as a research method. An Introduction to using critical event narrative analysis in research on learning and teaching.* New York, NY: Routledge.

Wilson, H., Bialk, P., Freeze, T. B., Freeze, R., & Lutfiya, Z. M. (2012). Heidi's and Philip's stories: Transitions to post-secondary education. *British Journal of Learning Disabilities, 40*, 87–93.

World Health Organization. (2001). *ICF. International classification of functioning, disability and health* [Online version]. Retrieved from http://apps.who.int/classifications/icfbrowser/

World Health Organization. (2010). *ICD-10. International statistical classification of diseases and related health problems* (10th Revision). Retrieved from http://apps.who.int/classifications/icd10/browse/2010/en

Ylipaavalniemi, P. (2001). *Vammaisten ja vajaakuntoisten työllistämisen kokonaiskartoitus* [Surveying of the employment of the disabled]. Ministry of Social Affairs and Health. Survey No. 6. Helsinki, Finland: Vates-foundation.

CHAPTER 9

SELF-DETERMINATION AND INCLUSIVE EDUCATION FOR STUDENTS WITH INTELLECTUAL DISABILITY

Karrie A. Shogren and Michael L. Wehmeyer

This chapter focuses the emergence of strengths-based approaches to intellectual disability, and the role of positive psychology and self-determination in the implementation of such approaches. Specifically, the social-ecological model and its implications for identifying needed supports that address the mismatch between personal capacities and environmental demands is described as are ways to identify needed supports for participation and learning in inclusive contexts. The third generation of inclusive practice, focused on the total education program—where, how, and what students are taught—is introduced. Research on the role of self-determination in promoting valued postschool outcomes is described and the self-determined learning model of instruction is highlighted as a means to promote self-determination and student involvement in inclusive settings, building on student strengths to create strengths-based systems of supports

Inclusive Education for Students with Intellectual Disabilities,
pp. 189–210
Copyright © 2015 by Information Age Publishing
All rights of reproduction in any form reserved.

INTRODUCTION

Advances in the disability field are necessitating the development of new models for supporting students with intellectual disability to be included in the general education classroom and curriculum. Pressures for change have emerged on multiple fronts, including worldwide efforts focused on creating inclusive educational opportunities for students with intellectual disability. For example, Article 24 of the United Nations Convention on the Rights of Persons with Disabilities (CRPD) affirms the right of persons with disabilities to education and emphasizes that "States Parties shall ensure an inclusive education system at all levels." The CRPD further states State Parties shall ensure that:

(a) Persons with disabilities are not excluded from the general education system on the basis of disability, and that children with disabilities are not excluded from free and compulsory primary education, or from secondary education, on the basis of disability;
(b) Persons with disabilities can access an inclusive, quality and free primary education and secondary education on an equal basis with others in the communities in which they live;
(c) Reasonable accommodation of the individual's requirements is provided;
(d) Persons with disabilities receive the support required, within the general education system, to facilitate their effective education;
(e) Effective individualized support measures are provided in environments that maximize academic and social development, consistent with the goal of full inclusion (United Nations, 2006).

Traditional models of creating segregated educational programs based on disability label are no longer an acceptable solution. Instead, new educational models are needed that are inclusive, individualized and strengths-based, and focused on self-determination and empowerment.

This chapter will review the emergence of strengths-based approaches for understanding intellectual disability and describe the role of positive psychology in the adoption of a strengths-focus in the disability field. Next, the current status of inclusive education and the role of positive psychology in developing new strategies for providing individualized strengths-based supports will be highlighted. Finally, the role of self-determination and student-directed learning in promoting valued inclusive outcomes will be described and strategies to make self-determination a reality for students with intellectual disability introduced.

STRENGTHS-BASED APPROACH TO INTELLECTUAL DISABILITY

Historically, disability, and particularly intellectual disability, has been conceptualized as an extension of the medical model and understood in terms of disease and disorders. Such models focused on "imperfections within the individual … [that result] in actions or behaviors that fall significantly short of what one would want or expect" (Danforth, 2001, p. 349). Under such models, the primary goal of identifying disability is to quantify the deficits and implement strategies for remediation. The focus of intervention, therefore, is on the deficit. For example, for people with intellectual disability, the predominant focus throughout much of the 20th century was on quantifying intellectual functioning through IQ scores to identify the extent of the intellectual deficit. In recent history, under this model, students with intellectual disability would then be assigned to segregated programs based on their level of intellectual functioning (Snell & Luckasson, 2009; Wehmeyer et al., 2008). And, if the deficit could not be remediated (or was perceived to be irremediable), students with intellectual disability would typically remain in these programs, with limited access to their peers or inclusive environments, throughout their education. Segregated programs are characterized by assumptions about limitations in outcomes linked to deficits in functioning.

Deficit-based approaches, however, have been challenged. During the latter part of the 20th century, social and political movements (Wehmeyer, Bersani, & Gagne, 2000) emerged within the disability field that prompted increased focus on the role of the environment in shaping the experiences of people with disabilities. Conceptualizations of disability began to shift and researchers and advocates began to assert that barriers experienced by people with disabilities were not inherent to them as persons, but instead resulted from oppression, discrimination, and segregation that limited opportunities for personal growth and development.

This recognition, that disability was not inherent to the person, but instead was a state of functioning (Luckasson et al., 1992; Luckasson et al., 2002) shaped by environmental circumstances, led to the development of new models of conceptualizing disability. While previous conceptualizations of intellectual disability placed exclusive focus on differences in intellectual and adaptive functioning, these new conceptualizations of disability emphasized the person-environment interaction and incorporated a social-ecological model of human functioning (Bronfenbrenner, 1979; Schalock et al., 2010; World Health Organization, 2007).

Social-Ecological Model

The social-ecological model defines disability is a state of functioning resulting from the interaction of personal capacities and environmental or contextual demands. The social-ecological model of disability has been integrated into World Health Organization's *International Classification of Impairment, Disability and Health* (World Health Organization, 1980, 2001, 2007) and the American Association on Intellectual and Developmental Disabilities' definition and classification framework for intellectual disability (Luckasson et al., 1992; Luckasson et al., 2002; Schalock et al., 2010).

The social-ecological model emphasizes the importance of identifying mismatches between personal capacities and environmental demands and identifying the supports needed to address these mismatches. It:

> (a) exemplifies the interaction between the person and their environment; (b) focuses on the role that individualized supports can play in enhancing individual functioning; and (c) allows for the pursuit and understanding of "disability identity" whose principles include self-worth, subjective well-being, pride, common cause, policy alternatives, and engagement in political action. (Schalock et al., 2007, p. 117)

From a social-ecological perspective, the ultimate goal of identifying disability is to build systems of supports that promote optimal human functioning. The purpose of diagnosis and classification is to identify needed supports to enhance human functioning (Thompson et al., 2009). In the education context, these supports may be instruction to promote new skill development, environmental modifications through universal design, natural supports, technology supports, or any other resources and strategies to "promote the development, education, interests, and personal well-being of an individual and that enhance human functioning" (Schalock et al., 2010, p. 175).

The American Association on Intellectual and Developmental Disabilities (Schalock et al., 2010; Thompson et al., 2009) has developed a process for assessing, planning, monitoring, and evaluating individualized supports that begins with identifying desired life experiences and goals, moves on to assessing supports needed to achieve these desired life experiences and goals, and developing, implementing, and evaluating a plan to make those outcomes occur. This process clarifies that the only purpose of identifying deficits or limitations experienced by a person in a given environments is to develop a profile of needed supports to promote optimal human functioning, it also emphasizes the importance of building on strengths and capacities that an individual has to promote personally valued outcomes. This process has been applied to the planning of individualized educational supports. Schalock and colleagues (2012) emphasize the importance of identifying supports for participation and for learning in inclusive contexts, and the role of structuring the environment through collaborative teaming and planning to promote access to inclusive environments for students with intellectual disability.

Positive Psychology

The growing emphasis within the intellectual disability field on building on strengths and capacities mirrors in many ways, the emergence of the field of positive psychology. The term "positive psychology" was coined to describe the movement away from a focus on deficits and damage toward a psychology focused on human strengths and virtues. In 1998, while President of the American Psychological Association, Martin Seligman stated that "psychology has moved too far away from its original roots, which were to make the lives of all people more fulfilling and productive, and too much toward the important, but not all important, area of curing mental illness" (Seligman, 1999, p. 559). Seligman called for a "reoriented science that emphasizes the understanding and building of the most positive qualities of an individual" (Seligman, 1999, p. 559), which he called "positive psychology." Seligman (1998) defined the mission of positive psychology as "to measure, understand and then build the human strengths and the civic virtues" (p. 2). It is important to note that, researchers make clear that "positive psychologists do not ignore the negative in life" (Diener, 2009, p. 10), instead positive psychology focuses on the positive in life—the things that make life good—but also explores ways to approach problems that emerge in life from a positive, strengths-based perspective.

These emerging conceptualizations of positive psychology have had a substantial impact on research and practice. While research on constructs associated with positive attributes and values had existed throughout the history of psychology, never before had a positive, strengths based model of understanding human functioning, rather than a disease model, been described and systematically integrated into research and practice in the field. And, since Seligman's presidential address, there has been significant grown in research on strengths (Yen, 2010). Hart and Sasso (2011), in a review of the positive psychology literature, found over 20,000 articles published since Seligman's 1998 presidential address, with a steady increase in articles over time. This has also been reflected in research in the intellectual disability field. Shogren et al. (2006) reviewed 30 years of research on intellectual disability published in the top journals in the field and found that when articles focused on a human capacity in people with intellectual disability, 35% of articles adopted a strengths perspective, however, this focus changed significantly over time, from a low of 22% of articles in 1975–1984 to a high of 50% of articles in 1995–2004. This suggested that more and more research is adopting a strengths-based approach to understand the experiences of people with intellectual disability. Further, in more recent publications, more emphasis was being placed on issues related to participation in inclusive environments, versus historical research that tended to focus more on deficits in intellectual or adaptive functioning (Shogren et al., 2006). Research focused on self-determination, which has been identified as a highly relevant construct in the field of positive psychology, also increased over time (Shogren, 2013a; Shogren et al., 2006). This suggested that the social-ecological model and positive psychological research are promoting more emphasis on inclusive, individualized and strengths-based approaches and focused on self-determination and empowerment.

STRENGTHS-BASED APPROACH TO INCLUSIVE EDUCATION

Changing understandings of disability, the shift toward a supports model, and the growing field of positive psychology with its focus on strengths-based approaches, creates opportunities for a shift in focus toward building systems of supports for students with intellectual disability in inclusive settings that facilitate positive outcomes. In terms of building strengths-based approaches to providing supports in inclusive environments, we first discuss how inclusive education has evolved over time, and how positive psychology and the social-ecological model are influencing the current generation of inclusive practices.

Turnbull, Turnbull, Wehmeyer, and Shank (2004) argued that we are currently in the "third generation of inclusive practice." The first generation focused primarily on getting students into inclusive environments. This generation of practice focused on addressing the question of "where" to provide educational services and supports. The second generation of inclusive practice focused both on "where" but also on "how" by emphasizing the importance of identifying and implementing supports for participation and learning that facilitate student success in general education classrooms. Various supports for learning and participation were identified through research and practice, including coteaching, differentiation, universal design, collaborative planning and teaming, and family professional partnerships. In both first and second generation inclusive practices, the primary focus was on where students were receiving their education and how to support success in that environment. As emphasized in the CRPD, a key element of inclusive education is ensuring equal access to the same environments as age peers and having necessary supports to be successful in those settings. The third generation of inclusive practices, however, while retaining a focus on "where" and "how" also began to emphasize the "what" of education, specifically examining how to provide access to grade-level curriculum for students with intellectual disability with appropriate supports and modifications.

Application of the Social-Ecological Model and Positive Psychology to Third Generation Inclusive Practices

The current generation of inclusive practices focuses on the total education program—where, how and what students are being taught. All three elements are critical. Research has established that for students to have access to challenging, grade-level curriculum they must be in the general education classroom (Lee, Wehmeyer, Soukup, & Palmer, 2010; Wehmeyer, Lattin, Lapp Rincker, & Agran, 2003). The focus must be both on supports for participation in the general education classroom *and* supports for learning in the general education curriculum. Identifying supports for participation and learning requires the adoption of a social-ecological model to promote success through the identification of needed supports. By identifying support needs based on the demands of the environment and the curriculum and the personal capacities of the student, an individualized supports plan can be developed that is relevant to the classroom and curriculum.

An individualized supports plan is inherently strengths based. A key assumption of the social-ecological model is that "within an individual, limitations often coexist with strengths" (Schalock et al., 2010, p. 1). This drives the creation of total education programs that are individualized and strengths based. A key element of an individualized and strengths-based total education program is self-determination, a key construct associated with positive psychology. Self-determination not only promotes valued transition and postschool outcomes, but also has been linked with greater access to the general education curriculum in inclusive classrooms (Shogren, Palmer, Wehmeyer, Williams-Diehm, & Little, 2012). With the focus on strengths and supports in the social-ecological model, it is important to consider how students can become their own supports, how they can take an active role in planning for their education and their future, and learn skills and develop attitudes that enable them to be a causal agent, or a person that makes things happen in his or her life.

SELF-DETERMINATION AND STUDENT-DIRECTED LEARNING

Promoting the self-determination of students with disabilities is recognized as best practice in special education services (Wehman, 2012) and is a key element of an individualized, strengths-based total educational program. Self-determination is a valued outcome of secondary education (Alwell & Cobb, 2006; Wehmeyer et al., 2012) as well as a predictor of positive postschool outcomes, including employment and community participation (Shogren, Wehmeyer, Palmer, Rifenbark, & Little, in press; Wehmeyer & Palmer, 2003; Wehmeyer & Schwartz, 1997). Researchers have also found that when students are taught self-determination skills they make more progress on goals linked to the general education curriculum (Shogren et al., 2012).

Self-determination has been situated as a key construct within positive psychology and the social-ecological model of human functioning. Several theoretical frameworks for self-determination had been forwarded in psychology and in the disability field. Within psychology, *self-determination theory* (SDT; Deci & Ryan, 1985, 2002; Ryan & Deci, 2000) proposed three basic psychological needs—competence, autonomy, and relatedness—that are either supported or challenged by social contexts and that congruence between one's basic needs and social contexts spur personal agency that, ultimately, results in improved overall well-being. Essentially, SDT holds that people's basic needs for competence, autonomy, and relatedness drive them toward action, and when environments are supportive of such action, overall well-being is improved.

Within the disability field, the functional theory of self-determination (Wehmeyer, 2003) has become one of the most widely cited by emphasizing the importance of defining the construct and its essential characteristics to facilitate the identification of skills and attitudes that enables the development of self-determined behavior and can be supported in education and other contexts to enable children, youth, and adults with disabilities to act as causal agents over their lives. The functional theory of self-determination builds on foundational understandings of self-determination as motivated by the basic psychological needs of competence, autonomy, and relatedness from SDT, but focuses on *how* people become self-determined, that is how people define the actions and beliefs necessary to engage in self-caused, autonomous action that addresses basic psychological needs.

Functional Theory of Self-Determination

Self-determination is a general psychological construct within the organizing structure of theories of human agency which refers to self- (vs.

other-) caused action—to people acting volitionally, based on their own will. Human agency refers to the sense of personal empowerment involving both knowing and having what it takes to achieve goals. Human agentic theories share the meta-theoretical view that organismic aspirations drive human behaviors. The concept of causal agency is central to the functional theory. *Causal agency* implies that it is the individual who makes or causes things to happen in his or her life.

The functional theory of self-determination defines self-determined behavior as "volitional actions that enable one to act as the primary causal agent in one's life and to maintain or improve one's quality of life" (Wehmeyer, 2005, p. 117). Within this theoretical perspective, self-determined behavior refers to actions that are identified by four *essential characteristics*: (1) the person acted *autonomously*; (2) the behavior(s) are *self-regulated*; (3) the person initiated and responded to the event(s) in a *psychologically empowered* manner; and (4) the person acted in a *self-realizing* manner. These four essential characteristics describe the *function* of the behavior that makes it self-determined or not. That is, it is the function that the behavior serves for the individual that defines it as self-determined, not any specific class of behaviors themselves.

Self-determination emerges across the lifespan as children and adolescents learn skills and develop attitudes and beliefs that enable them to be causal agents in their lives. These are the *component elements* of self-determined behavior, and include choice making, problem solving, decision making, goal setting and attainment, self-advocacy, and self-management skills. Although not an exhaustive list, Table 9.1 highlights the component elements particularly important to the emergence of self-determined behavior. A number of instructional strategies and curricula have been developed to teach these skills, although a complete review is beyond the scope of this chapter. The centrality of these elements in promoting positive outcomes for individuals with disabilities is further reinforced by other bodies of research, such as work in organizational psychology on psychological empowerment (Seibert, Wang, & Courtright, 2011; Spreitzer, 1995, 2008). Readers are also referred to other sources for more information on evidence-based strategies to teach specific self-determination skills to students with intellectual disability (Algozzine, Browder, Karvonen, Test, & Wood, 2001; Shogren, 2013b; Wehmeyer & Field, 2007). We will, however, describe in the following section a model of instruction that has been developed and focuses on enabling teachers to move away from traditional (i.e., teacher directed) instruction to student-directed instruction by creating supports and opportunities for students with intellectual disability to learn and apply self-determination skills to learning.

Table 9.1.   Component Elements of Self-Determined Behavior

- Choice-making skills
- Decision-making skills
- Problem-solving skills
- Goal-setting and attainment skills
- Independence, risk-taking and safety skills
- Self-observation, evaluation and reinforcement skills
- Self-instruction skills
- Self-advocacy and leadership skills
- Internal locus of control
- Positive attributions of efficacy and outcome expectancy
- Self-awareness
- Self-knowledge

Self-Determined Learning Model of Instruction

The Self-Determined Learning Model of Instruction is a model of instruction that focuses on enabling teachers to support student-directed learning in the context of the general education classroom and curriculum. A model of instruction can be defined as "a plan or pattern that can be used to shape curriculums (long term courses of study), to design instructional materials, and to guide instruction in the classroom and other settings" (Joyce & Weil, 1980, p. 1). Such models are derived from theories about human behavior, learning, and cognition. Effective teachers typically use multiple models of teaching in the classroom to support unique and diverse characteristics of learners within the classroom. However, many of the most common models of teaching, particularly in special education (e.g., role playing, assertiveness training, operant conditioning) tend to be teacher directed. And, even within these models, self-determination skills (e.g., self-advocacy, goal setting, etc.) can be taught. However, unless students are directing their own learning, the opportunities to develop causal agency are limited.

The Self-Determined Learning Model of Instruction (Mithaug, Wehmeyer, Agran, Martin, & Palmer, 1998) was developed to address this need, and is based on the component elements of self-determination, the process of self-regulated problem solving, and research on student-directed learning. It is appropriate for use with students with and without disabilities across a wide range of content areas, and enables teachers to engage students in the totality of their educational program by increasing opportunities to self-direct learning and, in the process, to enhance student self-determination. The model can be individualized to the unique needs of students with intellectual disability, by adding additional supports, including supports for learning and participation in the process (Mithaug et al., 1998)

Implementation of the model consists of a three-phase instructional process. This process is depicted in Figure 9.1 (Wehmeyer, Agran, Palmer, & Mithaug, 1999). Each instructional phase presents a problem to be solved by the student. The student solves each problem by posing and answering a series of four *student questions* per phase that students learn, modify to make their own, and apply to reach self-selected goals. Each question is linked to a set of *teacher objectives*. Each instructional phase includes a list of *educational supports* that teachers can use to enable students to self-direct learning. In each instructional phase, the student is the primary agent for choices, decisions, and actions, even when eventual actions are teacher directed.

The student questions in the model are constructed to direct the student through a problem-solving sequence in each instructional phase. The solutions to the problems in each phase lead to the problem-solving sequence in the next phase. Teachers implementing the model teach students to solve a sequence of problems to construct a means-ends chain—a causal sequence—that moves them from where they are (an actual state of not having their needs and interests satisfied) to where they want to be (a goal state of having those needs and interests satisfied). Its function is to reduce or eliminate the discrepancy between what students want or need and what students currently have or know. We construct this means-ends sequence by having students answer the questions that connect their needs and interests to their actions and results via goals and plans.

To answer the questions in this sequence, students must regulate their own problem solving by setting goals to meet needs, constructing plans to meet goals, and adjusting actions to complete plans. Thus, each instructional phase poses a problem the student must solve (What is my goal? What is my plan? What have I learned?) by, in turn, solving a series of problems posed by the questions in each phase. The four questions differ from phase to phase, but represent identical steps in the problem-solving sequence. That is, students answering the questions must: (1) identify the problem, (2) identify potential solutions to the problem, (3) identify barriers to solving the problem, and (4) identify consequences of each solution. These steps are the fundamental steps in any problem-solving process and they form the means-end problem-solving sequence represented by the student questions in each phase and enable the student to solve the problem posed in each instructional phase.

Because the model itself is designed for teachers to implement, the language of the student questions are, intentionally, not written to be understandable by every student nor does the model assume that students

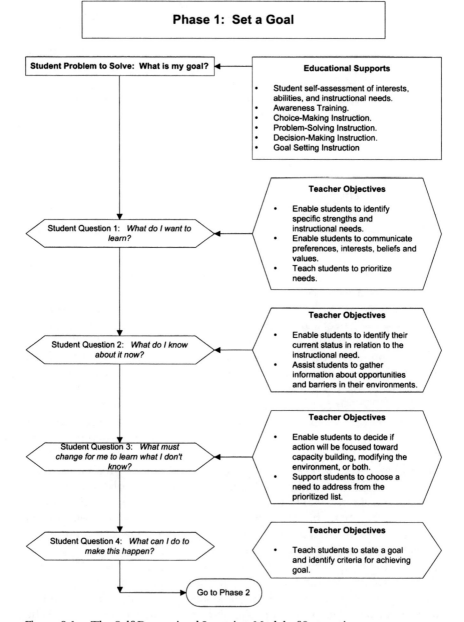

Figure 9.1.   The Self-Determined Learning Model of Instruction.

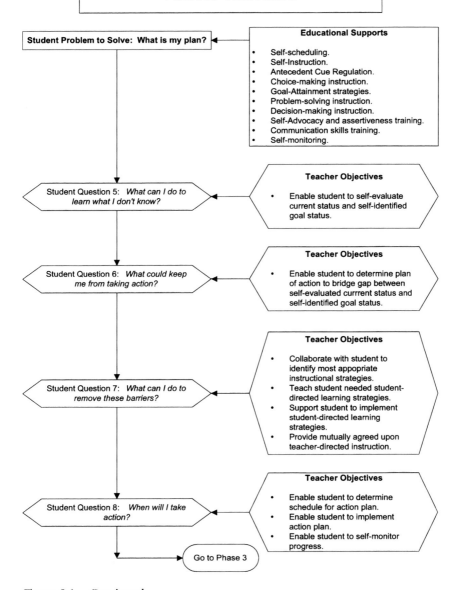

Figure 9.1.   Continued.

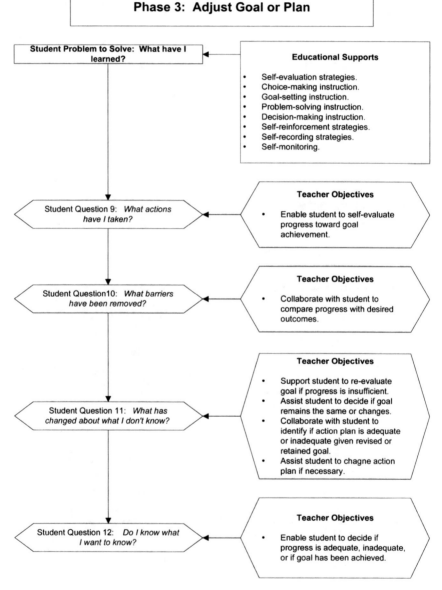

Figure 9.1.   Continued.

have life experiences that enable them to fully answer each question. The student questions are written in first-person voice in a relatively simple format with the intention that they are the starting point for discussion between the teacher and the student. Some students will learn and use all 12 questions as they are written. Other students will need to have the questions rephrased to be more understandable. Still other students, due to the intensity of their instructional needs, may have the teacher paraphrase the questions for them.

The first time a teacher uses the model with a student, the initial step in the implementation process is to read the question with or to the student, discuss what the question means and then, if necessary, change the wording to enable that student to better understand the intent of the question. Such wording changes must, however, be made such that the problem-solving intent of the question remains intact. For example, changing Student Question 1 from "What do I want to learn?" to "What is my goal?" changes the nature of the question. The teacher objectives associated with each student question provide direction for possible wording changes. It is perhaps less important that actual changes in the words occur than that students take ownership over the process and adopt the question as their own, instead of having questions imposed on them. Going through this process once, as the student progresses through the model, should result in a set of questions that a student accepts as his or her own.

The teacher objectives within the model are just that—the objectives a teacher will be trying to accomplish by implementing the model. In each instructional phase, the objectives are linked directly to the student questions. These objectives can be met by utilizing strategies provided in the educational supports section of the model. The teacher objectives provide, in essence, a road map to assist the teacher to enable the student to solve the problem stated in the student question. For example, regarding the first student question: What do I want to learn? Teacher objectives linked to this question comprise the activities in which students should be engaged in order to answer this question. In this case, it involves enabling students to identify their specific strengths and instructional needs, to identify and communicate preferences, interests, beliefs and values, and to prioritize their instructional needs. As teachers use the model it is likely that they can generate more objectives that are relevant to the question, and they are encouraged to do so.

The emphasis in the model on the use of instructional strategies and educational supports that are student directed provides another means of teaching students to teach themselves. As important as this is, however, not every instructional strategy implemented will be student directed. The purpose of any model of teaching is to promote student learning and growth. There are circumstances in which the most effective instructional method or strategy to achieve a particular educational outcome will be a teacher-directed strategy. Students who are considering what plan of action to implement to achieve a self-selected goal can recognize that teachers have expertise in instructional strategies and take full advantage of that expertise.

Research on the Impact of Self-Determination on Academic and Transition Outcomes

Teaching the skills associated with self-determination has been identified as a key element of a total education program that can augment efforts to promote access to general education classrooms and curriculum for students with disabilities. Researchers have found that teaching self-determination skills can promoting increased academic skills (Konrad, Fowler, Walker, Test, & Wood, 2007), attainment of academic and transition goals (Agran, Blanchard, & Wehmeyer, 2000; McGlashing-Johnson, Agran, Sitlington, Cavin, & Wehmeyer, 2003; Shogren et al., 2012; Wehmeyer, Palmer, Agran, Mithaug, & Martin, 2000), and access to the general education curriculum (Lee, Wehmeyer, Palmer, Soukup, & Little, 2008; Shogren et al., 2012) for students with intellectual disability. A curriculum augmentation is type of curriculum modification that expands the curriculum, teaching students additional skills that enable them to more effectively engage and progress in the general education curriculum (Wehmeyer, Lattin, & Agran, 2001). Teaching self-determination skills such as problem-solving, goal-setting, and self-management skills augments the curriculum by providing students with strategies to set goals related to academic and transition content, to solve problems encountered in the process of working toward those goals, and to monitor and evaluate progress toward goals, critical skills for academic and life success (Wehmeyer, Lance, & Bashinski, 2002). And, research has established that the Self-Determined Learning Model of Instruction can act as an effective curriculum augmentation. Shogren and colleagues (2012) conducted a group randomized control study of the impact of the Self-Determined Learning model of Instruction (SDLMI) on access to the general education curriculum and goal attainment with 312 students with intellectual and learning disability. Students who were randomly assigned, by their high school campus, to intervention with the SDLMI made significantly more progress on education goals and had significantly greater increases in their access to the general education curriculum than students assigned to the control group. Students with intellectual disability, however, tended to make more progress on transition (e.g., employment, residential, advocacy) goals than students with learning disabilities and students with learning disabilities tended to make significantly more progress on traditional academic goals. Students with both disability labels, however, demonstrated significantly greater access to the general education curriculum over time although overall access remained low. Overall, these findings suggest that for students with intellectual, as well as other, disability labels, the SDLMI is a powerful model for teaching promoting self-determination and academic and transition outcomes.

Researchers have also shown when self-determination interventions are systematically implemented in schools, changes in student self-determination result (Wehmeyer, Palmer, Shogren, Williams-Diehm, & Soukup, 2013; Wehmeyer et al., 2012). For example, Wehmeyer et al. (2012) reported the results of a group randomized control study of the efficacy of the SDLMI (Wehmeyer, Palmer, et al., 2000) for improving student self-determination outcomes with 312 high school students with intellectual and learning disabilities. Students were randomly assigned, by their high school campus, to either receive instruction with the SDLMI or to the control group, who continued with typical models of instruction already used in the classroom. The study continued for two years, and students with intellectual and learning disability in the treatment group reported significantly greater increases in self-determination, with the greatest growth in the second year of instruction. Students with intellectual disability started with lower initial levels of self-determination, but showed significant gains over time, although those gains did not elevate them to the same level as students with learning disabilities in the treatment group. However, this research establishes that the SDLMI is relevant and instructionally relevant for students with intellectual disability, and leads to significant gains in self-determination.

Despite this research, as well as research that has suggested that teaching self-determination skills can impact teacher attitudes and perceptions of student potential (Shogren, Plotner, Palmer, Wehmeyer, & Paek, in press) as well as valued postschool outcomes, such as employment and community participation (Shogren, Wehmeyer, et al., in press), research has suggested limited use of curriculum augmentations for students with disabilities, and particularly students with intellectual disability at the elementary, middle, and high school level (Lee et al., 2010; Soukup, Wehmeyer, Bashinski, & Bovaird, 2007; Wehmeyer et al., 2003). This is troubling given the emerging evidence that by building on student strengths using a social-ecological perspective of identifying needed supports for learning and participation to augment the curriculum by teaching students to direct their own learning can lead to enhanced student self-determination (Wehmeyer et al., 2013) and attainment of educationally relevant goals (Agran et al., 2000; Agran, Cavin, Wehmeyer, & Palmer, 2006; Wehmeyer, Palmer, et al., 2000).

CONCLUSION

There is a growing push for inclusive educational opportunities for all students across the world. The emergence of the social-ecological model and positive psychology have created opportunities to build systems of support that focus on strengths and student self-determination and empowerment in the context of general education classrooms and curriculum. Models of instruction, such as the Self-Determined Learning Model of Instruction, provide an opportunity to support students to learn to be causal agents over their lives in learning in the general education classroom and curriculum.

REFERENCES

Agran, M., Blanchard, C., & Wehmeyer, M. L. (2000). Promoting transition goals and self-determination through student self-directed learning: The self-determined learning model of instruction. *Education and Training in Mental Retardation and Developmental Disabilities, 35*(4), 351–364.

Agran, M., Cavin, M., Wehmeyer, M. L., & Palmer, S. B. (2006). Participation of students with severe disabilities in the general curriculum: The effects of the self-determined learning model of instruction. *Research and Practice for Persons with Severe Disabilities, 31*, 230–241.

Algozzine, B., Browder, D., Karvonen, M., Test, D. W., & Wood, W. M. (2001). Effects of interventions to promote self-determination for individuals with disabilities. *Review of Educational Research, 71*, 219–277. doi:10.3102/00346543071002219

Alwell, M., & Cobb, B. (2006). A map of the intervention literature in secondary special education transition. *Career Development for Exceptional Individuals, 29*, 3–27.

Bronfenbrenner, U. (1979). *The ecology of human development: Experiments by nature and design*. Cambridge, MA: Harvard University Press.

Danforth, S. (2001). A pragmatic evaluation of three models of disability in special education. *Journal of Development and Physical Disabilities, 13*(4), 343–359.

Deci, E. L., & Ryan, R. M. (1985). *Intrinsic motivation and self-determination in human behavior*. New York, NY: Plenum.

Deci, E. L., & Ryan, R. M. (Eds.). (2002). *Handbook of self-determination research*. Rochester, NY: University of Rochester Press.

Diener, E. (2009). Positive psychology: Past, present, and future. In S. J. Lopez & C. R. Snyder (Eds.), *The Oxford handbook of positive psychology* (2nd ed., pp. 7–11). Oxford, England: Oxford University Press.

Hart, K. E., & Sasso, T. (2011). Mapping the contours of contemporary positive psychology. *Canadian Psychology, 52*, 82–92. doi:http://dx.doi.org/10.1037/a0023118

Joyce, B., & Weil, M. (1980). *Models of teaching* (2nd ed.). Englewood Cliffs, NJ: Prentice Hall.

Konrad, M., Fowler, C. H., Walker, A. R., Test, D. W., & Wood, W. M. (2007). Effects of self-determination interventions on the academic skills of students with learning disabilities. *Learning Disability Quarterly, 30*, 89–113. doi:10.2307/30035545

Lee, S. H., Wehmeyer, M. L., Palmer, S. B., Soukup, J. H., & Little, T. D. (2008). Self-determination and access to the general education curriculum. *The Journal of Special Education, 42*(2), 91–107.

Lee, S. H., Wehmeyer, M. L., Soukup, J., & Palmer, S. B. (2010). Impact of curriculum modifications on access to the general education curriculum for students with disabilities. *Exceptional Children, 76*(2), 213–233.

Luckasson, R., Borthwick-Duffy, S., Buntinx, W. H. E., Coulter, D. L., Craig, E. P. M., Reeve, A., ... Tasse, M. J. (2002). *Mental retardation: Definition, classification, and systems of support* (10th ed.). Washington, DC: American Association on Mental Retardation.

Luckasson, R., Coulter, D. L., Polloway, E. A., Reiss, S., Schalock, R. L., Snell, M. E., ... Stark, J. A. (1992). *Mental retardation: Definition, classification, and systems of supports* (9th ed.). Washington, DC: American Association on Mental Retardation.

McGlashing-Johnson, J., Agran, M., Sitlington, P., Cavin, M., & Wehmeyer, M. L. (2003). Enhancing the job performance of youth with moderate to severe cognitive disabilities using the self-determined learning model of instruction. *Research and Practice for Persons with Severe Disabilities, 28*(4), 194–204.

Mithaug, D., Wehmeyer, M. L., Agran, M., Martin, J. E., & Palmer, S. B. (1998). The self-determined learning model of instruction: Engaging students to solve their learning problems. In M. L. Wehmeyer & D. J. Sands (Eds.), *Making it happen: Student involvement in educational planning, decision-making and instruction* (pp. 299–328). Baltimore, MD: Brookes.

Ryan, R. M., & Deci, E. L. (2000). Self-determination theory and the facilitation of intrinsic motivation, social development, and well-being. *American Psychologist, 55*, 68–78.

Schalock, R. L., Borthwick-Duffy, S., Bradley, V., Buntix, W. H. E., Coulter, D. L., Craig, E. P. M., ... Yeager, M. H. (2010). *Intellectual disability: Definition, classification, and systems of support* (11th ed.). Washington, DC: American Association on Intellectual and Developmental Disabilities.

Schalock, R. L., Luckasson, R., Bradley, V., Buntinx, W., Lachapelle, Y., Shogren, K. A., ... Wehmeyer, M. L. (2012). *User's guide for the 11th edition of intellectual disability: Diagnosis, classification and systems of support*. Washington, DC: American Association on Intellectual and Developmental Disabilities.

Schalock, R. L., Luckasson, R. A., Shogren, K. A., with, Borthwick-Duffy, S., Bradley, V., ... Yeager, M. H. (2007). The renaming of mental retardation: Understanding the change to the term intellectual disability. *Intellectual and Developmental Disabilities, 45*, 116–124.

Seibert, S. E., Wang, G., & Courtright, S. H. (2011). Antecedent and consequences of psychological and team empowerment in organizations: a meta-analytic review. *Journal of Applied Psychology, 96*, 981–1003.

Seligman, M. E. P. (1998). What is the 'good life'? *APA Monitor, 29*(10), 2.

Seligman, M. E. P. (1999). The president's address. *American Psychologist, 54*(8), 559–562.

Shogren, K. A. (2013a). Positive psychology and disability: A historical analysis. In M. L. Wehmeyer (Ed.), *The Oxford handbook of positive psychology and disability* (pp. 19–33). New York, NY: Oxford University Press.

Shogren, K. A. (2013b). *Self-determination and transition planning*. Baltimore, MD: Brookes.

Shogren, K. A., Palmer, S. B., Wehmeyer, M. L., Williams-Diehm, K., & Little, T. D. (2012). Effect of intervention with the self-determined learning model of instruction on access and goal attainment. *Remedial and Special Education, 33*, 320–330. doi:10.1177/0741932511410072

Shogren, K. A., Plotner, A. J., Palmer, S. B., Wehmeyer, M. L., & Paek, Y. (in press). Impact of the self-determined learning model of instruction on teacher perceptions of student capacity and opportunity for self-determination. *Education and Training in Autism and Developmental Disabilities*.

Shogren, K. A., Wehmeyer, M. L., Palmer, S. B., Rifenbark, G. G., & Little, T. D. (in press). Relationships between self-determination and postschool outcomes for youth with disabilities. *Journal of Special Education*.

Shogren, K. A., Wehmeyer, M. L., Pressgrove, C. L., & Lopez, S. J. (2006). The application of positive psychology and self-determination to research in intellectual disability: A content analysis of 30 years of literature *Research and Practice for Persons with Severe Disabilities, 31*, 338–345.

Snell, M. E., Luckasson, R. A., with, Borthwick-Duffy, S., Bradley, V., Buntix, W. H. E., ... Yeager, M. H. (2009). The characteristics and needs of people with intellectual disability who have higher IQs. *Intellectual and Developmental Disabilities, 47*(3), 220–233.

Soukup, J. H., Wehmeyer, M. L., Bashinski, S. M., & Bovaird, J. (2007). Classroom variables and access to the general curriculum of students with intellectual and developmental disabilities. *Exceptional Children, 74*, 101–120.

Spreitzer, G. M. (1995). Psychological empowerment in the workplace: Dimensions, measurement and validation. *Academy of Management Journal, 38*, 1442–1465.

Spreitzer, G. M. (2008). Tacking stock: A review of more than twenty years of research on empowerment at work. In J. Barling & C. L. Cooper (Eds.), *Handbook of organizational behavior* (pp. 54–72). Thousand Oaks, CA: SAGE.

Thompson, J. R., Bradley, V., Buntinx, W. H. E., Schalock, R. L., Shogren, K. A., Snell, M. E., ... Yeager, M. H. (2009). Conceptualizing supports and the support needs of people with intellectual disability. *Intellectual and Developmental Disabilities, 47*(2), 135–146.

Turnbull, A. P., Turnbull, H. R., Wehmeyer, M. L., & Shank, M. (2004). *Exceptional Lives* (5th ed.). Columbus, OH: Merrill/Prentice Hall.

United Nations. (2006). Convention on the Rights of Persons with Disability. Retrieved March 28, 2008, from http://www.un.org/disabilities/convention

Wehman, P. (2012). *Life beyond the classroom: Transition strategies for young people with disabilities* (5th ed.). Baltimore, MD: Paul H. Brookes.

Wehmeyer, M. L. (2003). A functional theory of self-determination: Model overview. In M. L. Wehmeyer, B. Abery, D. E. Mithaug, & R. Stancliffe (Eds.), *Theory in self-determination: Foundations for educational practice* (pp. 182–201). Springfield, IL: Charles C. Thomas.

Wehmeyer, M. L. (2005). Self-determination and individuals with severe disabilities: Re-examining meanings and misinterpretations. *Research and Practice for Persons with Severe Disabilities, 30*, 113–120.

Wehmeyer, M. L., Agran, M., Palmer, S. B., & Mithaug, D. (1999). *A teacher's guide to implementing the self-determined learning model of instruction: Adolescent version*. Lawrence, KS: Beach Center on Disability, University of Kansas.

Wehmeyer, M. L., Bersani, H., Jr., & Gagne, R. (2000). Riding the third wave: Self-determination and self-advocacy in the 21st century. *Focus on Autism and Other Developmental Disabilities, 15*(2), 106–115.

Wehmeyer, M. L., Buntix, W. H. E., Lachapelle, Y., Luckasson, R. A., Schalock, R. L., Verdugo, M. A., … Yeager, M. H. (2008). The intellectual disability construct and its relation to human functioning. *Intellectual and Developmental Disabilities, 46*, 311–318.

Wehmeyer, M. L., & Field, S. (2007). *Self-determination: Instructional and assessment strategies*. Thousand Oaks, CA: Corwin Press.

Wehmeyer, M. L., Lance, G. D., & Bashinski, S. (2002). Promoting access to the general curriculum for students with mental retardation: A multi-level model. *Education and Training in Mental Retardation and Developmental Disabilities, 37*(3), 223–234.

Wehmeyer, M. L., Lattin, D., & Agran, M. (2001). Achieving access to the general curriculum for students with mental retardation: A curriculum decision-making model. *Education and Training in Mental Retardation and Developmental Disabilities, 36*(4), 327–342.

Wehmeyer, M. L., Lattin, D. L., Lapp Rincker, G., & Agran, M. (2003). Access to the general curriculum of middle school students with mental retardation: An observational study. *Remedial and Special Education, 24*(5), 262–272.

Wehmeyer, M. L., & Palmer, S. B. (2003). Adult outcomes for students with cognitive disabilities three-years after high school: The impact of self-determination. *Education and Training in Developmental Disabilities, 38*, 131–144.

Wehmeyer, M. L., Palmer, S. B., Agran, M., Mithaug, D. E., & Martin, J. E. (2000). Promoting causal agency: The self-determined learning model of instruction. *Exceptional Children, 66*, 439-453.

Wehmeyer, M. L., Palmer, S. B., Shogren, K. A., Williams-Diehm, K., & Soukup, J. (2013). Establishing a causal relationship between interventions to promote self-determination and enhanced student self-determination. *Journal of Special Education, 46*, 195–210. doi:10.1177/0022466910392377

Wehmeyer, M. L., & Schwartz, M. (1997). Self-determination and positive adult outcomes: A follow-up study of youth with mental retardation or learning disabilities. *Exceptional Children, 63*, 245–255.

Wehmeyer, M. L., Shogren, K. A., Palmer, S. B., Williams-Diehm, K., Little, T. D., & Boulton, A. (2012). Impact of the self-determined learning model of instruction on student self-determination: A randomized-trial placebo control group study. *Exceptional Children, 78*, 135–153.

World Health Organization. (1980). *The international classification of impairment, disability and handicap*. Geneva, Switzerland: Author.

World Health Organization. (2001). *International classification of functioning, disability, and health*. Geneva, Switzerland: Author.

World Health Organization. (2007). *International classification of functioning, disability and health: Children and youth version*. Geneva, Switzerland: Author.

Yen, J. (2010). Authorizing happiness: Rhetorical demarcation of science and society is historical narratives of positive psychology. *Journal of Theoretical and Philosophical Psychology, 30*, 67–78.

CHAPTER 10

THE NEXT FRONTIER

Advancing Quality of Life and Self-Determination by Explicating the Self-Concepts of Children With Mild Intellectual Disabilities

Danielle Tracey, Rhonda G. Craven, and Herb Marsh

Enhancing children's self-concepts has been cast as a critical goal of education. Over the last 3 decades significant advances in self-concept theory, measurement and research have bolstered our understanding and educational practice to support the well-being of children. Progress with children with mild intellectual disabilities, however, has been slow due in part to weaknesses in measurement and theory. It is vital that decision making, and service and policy developments are informed by direct input from children with mild intellectual disabilities. This necessity is endorsed by both the United Nations Convention on the Rights of the Child (United Nations, 1989) and the Organisation for Economic Co-operation and Development's (2013) call to ensure the robust measurement of subjective well-being. This chapter provides a critique of the importance of positive self-concepts, the advances achieved within the field, and the progress that has been made with research methodology for children with mild intellectual disabilities. A body of research attests that children with mild intellectual disabilities can indeed reliably report their multidimensional self-concepts, and that

Inclusive Education for Students with Intellectual Disabilities,
pp. 211–227

psychometrically valid measures are available for use with these children. Researchers and practitioners are encouraged to apply robust self-concepts measurement tools to explicate the life experiences of children with mild intellectual disabilities and champion their self-determination and quality of life.

INTRODUCTION

Cultivating children's positive self-concepts is a critical goal of education throughout the developed world (Marsh & Craven, 2006). Despite significant advances in self-concept theory, measurement, research, and practice, progress with children with mild intellectual disabilities has been slow (Tracey, Marsh, & Craven, 2003). This is regrettable as the development of positive self-concepts is related to the attainment of an enhanced quality of life and thus a construct of salience for children with mild intellectual disabilities. Of particular importance for this vulnerable population, it is imperative that service and policy developments, and decision making, are shaped directly by children's input (Oliver, 1997). Providing children with mild intellectual disabilities with a reliable avenue to communicate their self-concepts will champion their participation in decision making processes and provide robust data to inform and evaluate services and policy that strive to enhance their quality of life.

This chapter provides a critique of the importance of positive self-concepts, the advances achieved within the field, and the progress that has been made with research methodology for children with mild intellectual disabilities. Our thesis is that research has now determined that children with mild intellectual disabilities can indeed reliably report their multidimensional self-concepts, and valid measures are available for this purpose. The onus is now on researchers to capitalize on recent advancements and boost the rigor they apply to their investigation of the self-concepts of children with mild intellectual disabilities. Such research will ensure that the voices and perceptions of children with mild intellectual disabilities are promoted, and that life outcomes are improved by providing direct insight into the reported self-concepts of these children.

A SIGNIFICANT ISSUE OF OUR TIME

Few would challenge the assertion that children with intellectual disabilities are one of the most vulnerable groups within our society. With this in mind, fundamental principles emanating from the United Nations (UN) Convention on the rights of the child (UN, 1989) and the UN Convention on the rights of persons with disabilities (UN, 2006) serve as beacons for practitioners, policy makers, and researchers alike who seek to work with and enhance the lives of children with intellectual disabilities. Most pertinent to the current discussion are the UN's fundamental principles that champion the rights of children with disabilities to freely express their views on issues and decisions that affect them, and to have their opinion taken into account. To accomplish this goal, the UN asserts that children with disabilities must be provided with the necessary assistance so that they are able to convey their views in a manner that is appropriate for their age and maturity—regardless of their disability.

Regrettably, it appears that policy, practice, and research is struggling to meet the expectations of the fundamental rights advocated by the UN. Inclusion International (2006) initiated a global study to capture the experience of people with intellectual disabilities across five global regions: the Americas, Africa and the Indian Ocean, Europe, Middle East and North Africa, and Asia Pacific. The study concluded that across all five global regions, people with intellectual disabilities are denied rights of participation and self-determination. More specifically, their ideas and needs are not heard; they do not have autonomy to make decisions for themselves; and they are not actively engaged as partners in policy development.

Significant government reforms, however, are beginning to emerge that promote self-determination and societal participation for people with intellectual disabilities. In Australia, both the National Disability Strategy 2010-2020 (Council of Australian Governments, 2011) and the National Disability Insurance Scheme Act 2013 signal a climate of change whereby the experience of people with disabilities is on the national agenda. The National Disability Strategy presents a national commitment to a unified approach to improving the lives of people with disabilities, while the National Disability Insurance Scheme provides national disability support that promotes the individual needs and choices of people with disabilities. Such initiatives are encouraging.

It is crucial that the emerging climate of change extends to the conceptualization, conduct, and dissemination of research. Research has the potential to both reflect and influence community perspectives, policy, and practice. As such, research promises to be a powerful tool to advance the inclusion, self-determination, and quality of life of children with mild intellectual disabilities. In recognition of the valuable role of research, and the current dearth of quality international and national studies in the disability field, The National Disability Research and Development Agenda (Council of Australian Governments, 2011) was endorsed by the Australian Disability Ministers in 2011. This agenda advocates that research should center on substantive issues that confront people with disabilities and utilize methodologies that encourage the establishment of research and development partnerships with people with disabilities as a matter of urgency.

SELF-CONCEPT RESEARCH AGENDA

Self-concept development has been consistently recognized as having a significant influence on one's quality of life, and as such, has become a flourishing area of research and a key construct of interest in the burgeoning positive psychology movement (Marsh, Xu, & Martin, 2012). Over the past 30 years advances in self-concept theory and measurement have served as a catalyst for the increasing commitment to boosting the self-concepts of children and youth within educational practice and policy. Unfortunately, these advances have not been mirrored in research and practice with children with mild intellectual disabilities, and methodological rigor has been slow (Huck, Kemp, & Carter, 2010). The central purpose of this chapter is to elucidate the current state of self-concept research with children with mild intellectual disabilities and encourage further rigorous research that has substantive applications. To inform this discussion, it is important to firstly consider the significant progress that has been made within the broader self-concept research field in the hope that children with mild intellectual disabilities may benefit from these innovations.

The Centrality of Self-Concepts

In their seminal review, Shavelson, Hubner, and Stanton (1976) defined self-concept as how a person feels about themselves in specific life areas. This self-perception is established via experience with and interpretations of one's environment. They advocated that evaluations by significant others, reinforcements, and attributions for one's behavior influence self-concept and that one's self-concept influences how a person behaves. Hence the construct of self-concept has been conceptualized as a powerful entity within each of us (Marsh, 2007).

The psychological research literature boasts an abundance of both theoretical and empirical inquiries into the self-concepts of children. The vastness of this line of inquiry can be attributed to the recognition by researchers and practitioners alike that self-concept shares positive relations with many desirable life outcomes. There is also a new positive revolution sweeping psychology that emphasizes how individuals get the most out of life and manage to stay healthy and happy in the face of adversity.

Individual resources, psychological strengths, and positive psychological factors like self-concept act as critical "buffers" and lead to more positive outcomes. Positive self-beliefs are at the heart of the positive psychology movement (Marsh & Craven, 2006) and have been demonstrated "to impact on a wide range of critical well-being outcomes and serve as an influential platform for enabling full human potential" (Craven & Marsh, 2008, p. 104). Numerous studies have identified strong relations between self-concept and outcomes such as well-being (Marsh, Trautwein, Lüdtke, Köller, & Baumert, 2006), coursework selection, completion of high school, adaptive academic behaviors, coping mechanisms, enhanced academic achievement, and reduced mental health problems (e.g., Marsh & Craven, 2006). Self-concept and performance are also known to be reciprocally related (Marsh & O'Mara, 2008; Möller, Retelsdorf, Köller, & Marsh, 2011) whereby they share a dynamic causal relation (Marsh & Craven, 2006).

Positive self-concepts are also cast as a means through which a young person develops into adulthood with the capacity to establish healthy relationships, acquire more responsibilities and increase their active participation in society (Harter, 1998). Hence, self-concepts are a worthy area of investigation to promote the quality of life for all children, especially those who are vulnerable and experience disadvantage.

Advances in Self-Concept Research

Self-concept is one of the oldest and most extensively examined constructs in educational psychology, and over the past 30 years in particular, important advances in theory, research and methodology have been made (Marsh et al., 2012). Both theoretical and empirical work has endorsed a multidimensional, hierarchical model of self-concepts whereby individuals conceptualize their self-perception in distinct ways across academic, social, and physical domains (Marsh & Hattie, 1996; Shavelson et al., 1976). This advancement in theory served as a catalyst for the rise of multidimensional instruments to accurately capture the differentiation that is evident in one's self-concept. Researchers now attest that measures of self-concept are more meaningful and useful when they are domain specific relative to specific contexts or particular skills rather than a measure that represents one's global self-concept (Bong & Skaalvik, 2003).

Advances in methodology have stimulated important substantive developments that encourage self-determination and quality of life for children without disabilities. Indeed, "such methodological evolvement provides unprecedented opportunities for substantive researchers to pursue quantitatively sophisticated research" (Marsh et al., 2012, pp.

451–452). Researchers in educational psychology have applied these theoretical and methodological advances to both construct specific interventions, and evaluate interventions and policy (O'Mara, Marsh, Craven, & Debus, 2006). Self-concept research now sees methodological rigor applied to critical educational issues with the goal of enhancing self-determination and quality of life for children without disabilities. Unfortunately, this research rigor has not been realized with children with mild intellectual disabilities. A critique of what has been achieved in the following section will provide researchers with an understanding of the gains that have been made and illuminate the next steps for researchers to effect change for children with mild intellectual disabilities.

SELF-CONCEPT RESEARCH WITH CHILDREN WITH MILD INTELLECTUAL DISABILITIES

Despite considerable efforts across the arenas of education, health, and government policy to assist children with intellectual disabilities, these children continue to be susceptible to a life of adversity. Across the globe, young people with intellectual disabilities are vulnerable to poverty and exclusion (Inclusion International, 2006) and lowered standards of community participation and quality of life (Australian Government, 2009; Kiddle & Dagnan, 2011; Oseburg, Dijkstra, Groothoff, Reijneveld, & Jansen, 2011; Pricewaterhouse Cooper, 2011). This dire situation not only places a horrendous burden on children and their families, but on society as a whole.

Given this pressing disadvantage faced by children with mild intellectual disabilities, there has been a focus on their personal adjustment. Arguments both for and against inclusive education for children with intellectual disabilities have been based on the anticipated effects on the children's self-concepts (e.g., the big-fish-little-pond effect, Marsh, 1984; and labeling theory, Goffman, 1963). Although it is pleasing that self-concepts have received such attention in the literature, much of this discussion has been based on a human rights argument rather than on empirical evidence (Huck, Kemp, & Carter, 2010). In addition, historically, empirical investigations of self-concepts have been plagued with methodological problems. Self-concept research, therefore, needs further and more rigorous investigation to be positioned as an outcome measure for quality of life and to bolster successful inclusion (Huck et al., 2010). In the next section, we offer a critique of past and current self-concept research with children with mild intellectual disabilities to consider the history of where we have been, how we have evolved, and most importantly, where we can head in the future in order to advance self-determination and quality of life for this vulnerable population.

Early Research: The Rejection of Self-Reports of Children with Mild Intellectual Disabilities

In early research (and indeed in some current research), proxies were used to report on children's self-concepts (e.g., Katz & Yekutiel, 1974; Larson & Lapointe, 1986; Turk, Khattran, Kerry, Corney, & Painter, 2012). Such methodology was driven by a deficit model whereby children with mild intellectual disabilities were perceived as incapable of either constructing or expressing their self-concepts. Despite the acknowledgement that findings are strengthened by converging multiple perspectives from multiple stakeholders (Creswell, 2009), in capturing what is essentially an internal subjective state, it is critical that the individual's perception is acquired through appropriate methodology when attempting to evaluate the self-concepts of children with mild intellectual disabilities. As highlighted by Hensel (2001), when seeking to gather an understanding of an individual's subjective experience, the inquiry is incomplete without considering how the very people themselves perceive and evaluate their experiences.

Engagement in self-reports requires a level of both cognitive and verbal literacy skills that children with intellectual disabilities may not possess (Albuquerque, 2012; Axford, 2008). As a result, they are likely to be excluded from having a direct voice in research. Ironically, it is disadvantaged and minority groups such as children with mild intellectual disabilities who need to have a strong voice to guide policy and practice concerning them. For example, Oliver (1997) argued that disability research that does not actively involve individuals with disabilities is nothing more than a "rip off." Oliver (1997) contends that without such direct involvement, research has little chance of accurately portraying the issues that are deemed important to individuals with disabilities and thus their quality of life or policy impacting upon their lives is unlikely to change in any real way. Researchers now stress the importance of gathering information directly from individuals with disabilities. This has also occurred as a result of the shift in service development and policy that values a greater focus on individuals with disabilities making decisions about their own lives (Finlay & Lyons, 2001). Researchers are charged with the task of constructing methodology that is able to reliably and validly evaluate the self-concepts of children with mild intellectual disabilities if research is to adequately capture their voices and serve their needs as an instrument to improve life outcomes.

Reliance on Preexisting Self-Concept Measures

As efforts to accurately obtain these self-reported self-concepts emerged, measurement and methodology became the weakest link hindering this line of research (Bear, Minke, & Manning, 2002). This early research was limited by weaknesses in self-concept theory and research prevalent at the time and characterized by research based on small sample sizes, dubious administration procedures, and weak statistical analysis tools. Many researchers (e.g., Fink, 2000; Paterson, McKenzie, & Lindsay, 2012) continued to measure self-concept as a unidimensional construct, despite consistent and strong theoretical propositions and empirical findings confirming that perceptions of the self are multidimensional (Humphrey, Charlton, & Newtown, 2004).

In an effort to obtain such self-perceptions, some researchers administered standardized self-concept measures to individuals with intellectual disabilities without testing or justifying the suitability of their use with this population (e.g., Begley, 1999; Chiu, 1990; Jiranek & Kirby, 1990; Stringer & Heath, 2008; Thompson, Lampron, Johnson, & Eckstein, 1990; Tymchuk, 1991). As highlighted by Byrne (1996) tests that have been designed and validated on the general population may not be appropriate for specific populations. Byrne (1996) also lamented that there appeared to be a critical void in self-concept measures for young people with intellectual disabilities. More recently, Finlay and Lyons (2001) asserted that despite the widespread use of self-report questionnaires with individuals with intellectual disabilities, few researchers question or demonstrate that they are valid for use. Indeed Finlay and Lyons (2001) go on to caution that questionnaires developed for individuals without disabilities are unlikely to be appropriate for individuals with intellectual disabilities.

The Emergence of Validated Self-Concept Measures for use With Children With Mild Intellectual Disabilities

Recently researchers (Albuquerque, 2012) have emphasized the need to prioritize the design and validation of assessment tools that provide insight into subjective components for individuals with intellectual disabilities. This urgency is grounded on the belief that direct service delivery, the evaluation of services, practices, and social policies can be based on the findings of such self-reported data. For example, there has been an emerging interest in the attainment of quality of life for individuals with intellectual disabilities (WHOQOL Group, 1995). Albuquerque (2012) argues that for this goal to be pursued in both research and practice, the first priority must be to design and validate assessment tools to provide insight into subjective components for individuals with intellectual disabilities. Only then, can such subjective, self-reported experiences be used to direct organizational delivery, evaluate services, and practices, and inform social policies (Albuquerque, 2012).

As researchers strived to address the dearth of self-concept measurement tools for children with mild intellectual disabilities, researchers turned their attention to statistically test whether preexisting scales were valid for use with children with mild intellectual disabilities, that is, to confirm that there was equivalence or invariance across the construct structure for the two groups (e.g., Little et al., 1990; Silon & Harter, 1985). Silon and Harter (1985) examined whether the Perceived Competence Scale for Children, designed to assess the self-perceptions of children without disabilities, could be successfully used with 126 children with mild intellectual disabilities aged 9 to 12 years. Their analysis found that the measure was inappropriate for children with mild intellectual disabilities as fewer scale factors were revealed in comparison to the number of factors confirmed for children without intellectual disabilities. The limited number of confirmed factors mirrored the multidimensionality of self-concept reported by younger typically developing preschool and kindergarten children (as measured by Harter & Pike's [1984] Pictorial Scale of Perceived Competence and Social Acceptance for Young Children). Silon and Harter (1985) concluded that "it appears that retarded children do not make distinctions about specific competence domains but rather simply make judgements about one's competence at activities in general, regardless of their nature. Thus they think one is either competent or not" (p. 223). Such a conclusion has significant ramifications for how researchers, practitioners, and policy makers consider the capacity of children with mild intellectual disabilities to contribute personal insight to inform key decisions about their life and future well-being.

Tracey et al. (2003) were able to counter the widely cited claims that children with mild intellectual disabilities cannot accurately report a differentiated multiple self-concept. The Self Description Questionnaire I–Individual Administration (SDQI-IA) (Marsh, Craven, & Debus, 1991) was individually administered to 211 children with mild intellectual disabilities from across 25 schools in New South Wales, Australia. The age of the participants ranged from 7 years 5 months to 13 years (with a mean age of 10 years and 3 months, SD of 1.48). Results provided clear support for the a priori eight-factor solution, modest correlations between the factors (*Mdn r* = .42), substantial reliabilities (0.88 for the subscales and 0.95 for the total scales), and invariance of the factor solution over gender, age, and educational placement (regular vs. special, segregated classes). The SDQI-IA demonstrated strong psychometric properties (reliability, multidimensional factor structure, convergent and discriminant validity), thus verifying it as a reliable and valid measure of the multidimensional self-concepts of children with mild intellectual disabilities. Interestingly, Tracey et al. (2003) found that children could discriminate between their self-concepts in the areas of: physical appearance, physical ability, peer relationships, parent relationships, reading, math, general school, and general self. These are the same eight factors as reported for children without disabilities. The average correlation between factors demonstrated that children were able to differentiate between the multiple facets of self-concept. Similarly, the correlations between the nonacademic and academic factors confirmed a hierarchical framework of self-concepts. This suggests that children with mild intellectual disabilities develop and report their self-concept in a similar way to children without intellectual disabilities.

Tracey et al.'s (2003) findings may be attributed to the modifications made to the SDQI-IA's administration and question format in order to successfully elucidate self-reports from children with mild intellectual disabilities. Following piloting, an individual interview, two-step response format was adopted. In contrast, Silon and Harter (1985) did not alter the content or administration format prior to administering their measure for children with mild intellectual disabilities. Silon and Harter (1985) concluded that children with mild intellectual disabilities could not report a multifaceted self-concept, whereas an alternative conclusion could be that their measure and procedures were unable to gather the children's self-perception accurately.

It is now established that the multidimensional self-concept that is well-documented for children without disabilities, is also evident for children with mild intellectual disabilities, and that these self-concepts can be reliably measured. Furthering our capacity to accurately measure the subjective perceptions of children with intellectual disabilities, many empirical studies now ensure that the measures they utilize for individuals with intellectual disabilities embody sound psychometric properties as a key feature of their work (e.g., Donohue, Wise, Romski, Henrich, & Sevcik, 2010; Maiano, Morin, Begarie, & Ninot, 2011; von der Luft, BeBoer, Harman, Koenig, & Nixon-Cave, 2008).

Donohue et al. (2010) examined the nature of self-concept development and its measurement for 38 children aged 7 to 13 years with mild intellectual disabilities. They utilized both the Pictorial Scale of Perceived Competence and Social Acceptance for Children (Harter & Pike, 1984) and the SDQI-IA (Marsh et al., 1991) which provide a four-factor and eight-factor structure, respectively. They concluded that both scales evidenced sound reliability and validity for use with children with mild intellectual disabilities, but identified preferences for the shorter and picture-based administration format of Harter and Pike's (1984) measure. We note, however, that Donohue et al. (2010) did not actually perform a factor analysis on responses to either instrument. Hence, there is no basis to replicate studies showing support for the a priori factor structure of the SDQI-IA (Marsh et al., 1991) or the failure to support the a priori factor structure based on the Harter and Pike (1984) instrument. Indeed, a critical limitation of this study—like much of the research in this area—is that the sample size is too small even to apply appropriate factor analysis (e.g., Marsh, 2007; Marsh, Hau, Balla, & Grayson, 1998).

In contrast, self-concept researchers have emphasized the need to measure self-concept domains with as much specificity as possible in order to target intervention and inform intervention effects (Marsh, 2007). It seems logical, therefore, to select a measure that provides the greatest differentiation within self-concept to advance research and practice. The SDQI-IA (Marsh et al., 1991) measures eight dimensions of self-concept (peer and parent relationships, physical ability and appearance, reading, math, general school and general self-concept) whereas the Pictorial Scale of Perceived Competence and Social Acceptance for Children (Harter & Pike, 1984) measures four domains only (cognitive and physical competence, and maternal and peer acceptance). The Harter and Pike (1984) scale underestimates the capacity of children with mild intellectual disabilities to delineate between lower order hierarchy of self-concept and may mask important issues or impacts from intervention.

Future Directions for Self-Concept Research With Children With Mild Intellectual Disabilities

Considerable advances in self-concept research, theory, and practice with children with mild intellectual disabilities have been made. Exemplary studies have utilized large sample sizes, adapted their administration procedure, and applied sophisticated confirmatory analysis. Research can now capitalize on these methodological advances to progress substantive issues that will promote the participation and quality of life for children with mild intellectual disabilities.

In 2013 an audit of disability research in Australia was commissioned by the Disability Policy and Research Working Group, Department of Ageing, Disability and Home Care. The audit identified gaps in disability research and posed research challenges for the future (Llewellyn, 2014). First, although the disability reform agenda is founded on key principles such as empowerment, self-determination and participation, the audit found that the investigation of such constructs are relatively scant in the research evidence base. With the development of psychometrically sound measures of self-concepts, such research agendas may be bolstered.

Second, the audit declared that the majority of study designs and aims describe the problem, rather than seeking to produce evidence based solutions (Llewellyn, 2014). This aligns with the current state of self-concept research for children with mild intellectual disabilities. Recent research investigating the self-concepts of children with mild intellectual disabilities appears to have largely capitalized on advances in measurement to ascertain their levels of self-concepts and how these levels compare to that of their peers, most notably those without disabilities (e.g., Donohue et al., 2010; Fiasse & Nader-Grosbois, 2012; Huck et al., 2010; Mueller & Thompson, 2009; Varsamis & Agaliotis, 2011). This body of research has generated relatively consistent support for two main findings. First, children with mild intellectual disabilities appear to report lowered academic self-concepts when compared to their peers without intellectual disabilities. Second, consistent with the big-fish-little-pond effect (Marsh et al., 2008) and social comparison theory (Festinger, 1954) students with mild intellectual disabilities report higher academic self-concepts when placed in support units with other students with mild intellectual disabilities (Tracey et al., 2003). This line of inquiry is helpful in placing the spotlight on the issues that confront children with mild intellectual disabilities, and has fuelled some debate around inclusive education. But more can be done.

The self-concept research agenda for children without intellectual disabilities is now positioned to capitalize on 3 decades of theory and measurement innovations to action and evaluate interventions, services, and policy in order to boost the self-determination and quality of life for these children. With the confronting disadvantage faced by children with mild intellectual disabilities, and the climate of encouraging self-determination and quality of life, researchers can now enhance the evidence base to inform the development and evaluation of service delivery and social policy.

CONCLUSION

The inquiry into the personal adjustment of children with mild intellectual disabilities is a worthwhile endeavor that has aspired to understand and enhance the lives of these vulnerable children. The theoretical and empirical exploration of self-concepts has featured as a prolific area of research over an extended period of time. This is not surprising given the recognition of the disadvantage encountered by these children and the multiple life outcomes informed by one's self-concept (Branden, 1994).

This work should be celebrated and encouraged. Unfortunately, substantial progress in these endeavors has been hampered by methodological flaws inherent within this body of research. Research has now provided sound multidimensional self-concept measurement tools for children with mild intellectual disabilities, and the time is right for researchers to capitalize on such advances.

In the current climate of empowerment and self-determination for individuals with disabilities, the opportunity is here to reform and strengthen the self-concept research agenda by fostering rigor in our work and applying this rigor to address substantive issues faced by children with mild intellectual disabilities. The Organisation for Economic Co-operation and Development (2013) has recently championed the need to measure subjective well-being in a way that provides robust data and allows researchers to better measure how individuals evaluate and experience their lives. This commitment encourages researchers and policy makers to move beyond traditional ways of measuring economic performance and encompass measures of subjective well-being. It is now recognized that gathering reliable data about subjective well-being, such as self-concepts, can serve as both an important indicator of performance and outcomes, as well as a guide for influencing social policy, service delivery, and people's choices. When it comes to vulnerable members of our society, such as children with mild intellectual disabilities, this need becomes even more pressing. Although this journey is unchartered and possibly turbulent, it is a journey worth pursuing.

REFERENCES

Albuquerque, C. P. (2012). Psychometric properties of the Portuguese version of the quality of life questionnaire (QOL-Q). *Journal of Applied Research in Intellectual Disabilities, 25*, 445–454.

Australian Government. (2009). *Shut out: The experience of people with disability and their families in Australia* (National Disability Strategy Consultation Report). Prepared by the National People with Disabilities and Carer Council.

Axford, N. (2008). *Exploring concepts of child well-being: Implications for children's services.* Bristol, England: The Policy Press.

Bear, G., Minke, K., & Manning, M. (2002). Self-concept of students with learning disabilities: A meta-analysis. *School Psychology Review, 31*(3), 405–427.

Begley, A. (1999). The self-perceptions of pupils with down syndrome in relation to their academic competence, physical competence and social acceptance. *International Journal of Disability, Development and Education, 46*, 515–529.

Bong, M., & Skaalvik, E. (2003). Academic self-concept and self-efficacy: How different are they really? *Educational Psychology Review, 15*, 1–40.

Branden, N. (1994). *Six pillars of self-esteem.* New York, NY: Bantam.

Byrne, B. (1996). *Measuring self-concept across the life span: Issues and instrumentation.* Washington, DC: American Psychological Association.

Chiu, L. (1990). Self-esteem of gifted, normal, and mildly mentally handicapped children. *Psychology in the Schools, 27,* 263–268.

Council of Australian Governments. (2011). *National Disability Strategy 2010— 2020.* Commonwealth of Australia.

Craven, R. G., & Marsh, H. W. (2008). The centrality of the self-concept construct for psychological wellbeing and unlocking human potential: Implications for child and educational psychologists. *Educational and Child Psychology 25*(2), 104–118.

Creswell, J. W. (2009). *Research design: Qualitative, quantitative, and mixed methods approaches* (3rd ed.). Thousand Oaks, CA: SAGE.

Donohue, D., Wise, J. C., Romski, M., Henrich, C. C., Sevcik, R. (2010). Self-concept development and measurement in children with mild intellectual disabilities. *Developmental Neurorehabilitation, 13*(5), 322–334.

Festinger, L. (1954). A theory of social comparison processes. *Human Relations, 7,* 117–140.

Fiasse, C., & Nader-Grosbois, N. (2012). Perceived social acceptance, theory of mind and social adjustment in children with intellectual disabilities. *Research in Developmental Disabilities: A Multidisciplinary Journal, 33*(6), 1871–1880.

Fink, R. (2000). Gender, self-concept and reading disabilities. *Journal of the International Academy for Research in Learning Disabilities, 18,* 15–33.

Finlay, W., & Lyons, E. (2001). Methodological issues in interviewing and using self-report questionnaires with people with mental retardation. *Psychological Assessment, 13*(3), 319–335.

Goffman, E. (1963). *Stigma: Notes on the management of a spoiled identity.* Englewood Cliffs, NJ: Prentice-Hall.

Harter, S. (1998). The development of self-representations. In N. Eisenberg (Ed.), *Handbook of child psychology* (Vol. 3., pp. 553–617). New York, NY: Wiley.

Harter, S., & Pike, R. (1984). The pictorial scale of perceived competence and social acceptance for young children. *Child Development, 55,* 1969–1982.

Hensel, E. (2001). Is satisfaction a valid concept in the assessment of quality of life of people with intellectual disabilities? A review of the literature. *Journal of Applied Research in Intellectual Disabilities, 14,* 311–326.

Huck, S., Kemp, C., & Carter, M. (2010). Self-concept of children with intellectual disability in mainstream settings. *Journal of Intellectual and Developmental Disability, 35*(3), 141–154.

Humphrey, N., Charlton, J., & Newton, I. (2004). The developmental root of disaffection? *Educational Psychology: An International Journal of Experimental Educational Psychology, 24*(5), 579–594.

Inclusion International. (2006). *Hear our voices: A global report: People with an intellectual disability and their families speak out on poverty and exclusion.* London, England: Author.

Jiranek, D., & Kirby, N. (1990). The job satisfaction and/or psychological well being of young adults with mental retardation and nondisabled young adults in either sheltered employment, competitive employment or unemployment. *Australia and New Zealand Journal of Developmental Disabilities, 16,* 133–148.

Katz, S., & Yekutiel, E. (1974). Leisure time problems of mentally retarded graduates of training programs. *Mental Retardation*, *12*(3), 54–57.

Kiddle, H., & Dagnan, D. (2011). Vulnerability to depression in adolescents with intellectual disabilities. *Advances in Mental Health & Intellectual Disabilities*, *5*, 3–8.

Larson, C. P., & Lapointe, Y. (1986). The health status of mild to moderate intellectually handicapped adolescents. *Journal of Mental Deficiency Research*, *30*(2), 121–128.

Little, T., Widaman, K., Farren, A., MacMillan, A., Hemsley, R., & MacMillan, D. (1990). *The factor structure and reliability of the Self Description Questionnaire (SDQII) in an early adolescent population, stratified by academic level, ethnicity and gender.* Riverside, CA: University of California.

Llewellyn, G. (2014). *Report of audit of disability research in Australia.* Sydney, Australia: Centre for Disability Research and Policy, University of Sydney.

Maiano, C., Morin, A., Begarie, J., & Ninot, G. (2011). The intellectual disability version of the very short form of the physical self-inventory (PSI-VS-ID): Cross-validation and measurement invariance across gender, weight, age and intellectual disability level. *Research in Developmental Disabilities: A Multidisciplinary Journal*, *32*(5), 1652–1662.

Marsh, H. W. (1984). Self-concept, social comparison and ability grouping: A reply to Kulik and Kulik. *American Educational Research Journal*, *21*, 799–806.

Marsh, H. W. (2007). *Self-concept theory, measurement and research into practice: The role of self-concept in educational psychology.* Leicester, United Kingdom: British Psychological Society.

Marsh, H. W., & Craven, R. G. (2006). Reciprocal effects of self-concept and performance from a multidimensional perspective: Beyond seductive pleasure and unidimensional perspectives. *Perspectives on Psychological Science*, *1*(2), 133-163.

Marsh, H. W., Craven, R. G., & Debus, R. L. (1991). Self-concepts of young children 5 to 8 years of age: Measurement and multidimensional structure. *Journal of Educational Psychology*, *83*(3), 377–392.

Marsh, H. W., & Hattie, J. (1996). Theoretical perspectives on the structure of self-concept. In B. A. Bracken, (Ed.) *Handbook of self-concept.* New York, NY: Wiley.

Marsh, H. W., Hau, K-T., Balla, J. R., & Grayson, D. (1998). Is more ever too much? The number of indicators per factor in confirmatory factor analysis. *Multivariate Behavioral Research*, *33*, 181–220.

Marsh, H. W., & O'Mara, A. (2008). Reciprocal effects between academic self-concept, self-esteem, achievement, and attainment over seven adolescent years: Unidimensional and multidimensional perspectives of self-concept. *Personality and Social Psychology Bulletin*, *34*, 542–552.

Marsh, H. W., Seaton, M., Trautwein, U., Lüdtke, O., Hau, K. T., O'Mara, A. J., & Craven, R. G. (2008). The big-fish-little-pond-effect stands up to critical scrutiny: Implications for theory, methodology, and future research. *Educational Psychology Review*, *20*(3), 319–350.

Marsh, H. W., Trautwein, U., Lüdtke, O., Köller, O., & Baumert, J. (2006). Integration of multidimensional self-concept and core personality constructs:

construct validation and relations to well?being and achievement. *Journal of Personality, 74*(2), 403–456.

Marsh, H. W., Xu, M., & Martin, A. J. (2012). Self-concept: A synergy of theory, method, and application. In K. R. Harris, S. Graham, T. Urdan, C. B. McCormick, G. M. Sinatra, & J. Sweller (Eds.). *APA educational psychology handbook, Vol. 1. Theories, constructs, and critical issues* (pp. 427–458). Washington, DC: American Psychological Association.

Möller, J., Retelsdorf, J., Köller, O., & Marsh, H.W. (2011). The reciprocal internal/external frame of reference model. *American Educational Research Journal, 48*(6), 1315–1346.

Mueller, C. E., & Thompson, P. H. (2009). Psychosocial adjustment of adolescents and young adults with intellectual disabilities. *Journal of Mental Health Research in Intellectual Disabilities, 2*(4), 294–311.

National Disability Insurance Scheme Act 2013 (Cth) (Austl.).

Oliver, M. (1997). Emancipatory research: Realistic goal or impossible dream? In C. Barnes & G. Mercer (Eds.), *Doing disability research* (pp. 15–31). Leeds, England: The Disability Press.

O'Mara, A. J., Marsh, H. W., Craven, R. G., & Debus, R. L. (2006). Do self-concept interventions make a difference? A synergistic blend of construct validation and meta-analysis. *Educational Psychologist, 41*(3), 181–206.

Organisation for Economic Co-operation and Development. (2013). *OECD Guidelines on Measuring Subjective Well-being.* http://dx.doi.org/10.1787/9789264191655-en

Oseburg, B., Dijkstra, G. J., Groothoff, J. W., Reijneveld, S. A., & Jansen, D. E. M. C. (2011). Prevalence of chronic health conditions in children with intellectual disability: A systematic literature review. *Intellectual and Developmental Disabilities, 49*, 59–85.

Paterson, L., McKenzie, K., & Lindsay, B. (2012). Stigma, social comparison and self-esteem in adults with an intellectual disability. *Journal of Applied Research in Intellectual Disabilities, 25*, 166–176.

Pricewaterhouse Cooper (2011). *Disability expectations: Investigating in a better life, and a stronger Australia.* Australia: Pricewaterhouse Cooper.

Shavelson, R. J., Hubner, J. J., & Stanton, G. C. (1976). Validation of construct interpretations. *Review of Educational Research, 46*, 407–441.

Silon, E., & Harter, S. (1985). Assessment of perceived competence, motivational orientations, and anxiety in segregated and mainstreamed educable mentally retarded children. *Journal of Educational Psychology, 77*, 217–230.

Stringer, R., & Heath, N. (2008). Academic self-perceptions and its relationship to academic performance. *Canadian Journal of Education, 31*(2), 327–345.

Thompson, R. J., Lampron, L. B., Johnson, D. F., & Eckstein, T. L. (1990). Behavior problems in children with the presenting problem of poor school performance. *Journal of Pediatric Psychology, 15*, 3–20.

Tracey, D., Marsh, H., & Craven, R. G. (2003). Self-concepts of preadolescents with mild intellectual disabilities: Issues of measurement and educational placements. In H. Marsh, R. G. Craven, & D. McInerney (Eds.), *International advances in self research* (pp. 203–229). Greenwich, CT: Information Age.

Turk, V., Khattran, S., Kerry, S., Corney, R., & Painter, K. (2012). Reporting of health problems and pain by adults with an intellectual disability and by their carers. *Journal of Applied Research in Intellectual Disabilities, 25*(2), 155–165.

Tymchuk, A. J. (1991). Self-concepts of mothers who show mental retardation. *Psychological Reports, 68*, 503–510.

United Nations (1989). *The United Nations convention on the rights of the child.* New York: UNICEF.

United Nations. (2006). *The United Nations Convention on the Rights of Persons With Disabilities.* New York, NY: UNICEF.

Varsamis, P., & Agaliotis, I. (2011). Profiles of self-concept, goal orientation, and self-regulation in students with physical, intellectual, and multiple disabilities: Implications for instructional support. *Research in Developmental Disabilities, 32*, 1548–1555.

Von der Luft, G., DeBoer, B. V., Harman, L. B., Koenig, K. P., & Nixon-Cave, K. (2008). Improving the quality of studies on self-concept in children with cerebral palsy. *Journal of Developmental Physical Disabilities, 29*, 581–594.

WHOQOL Group. (1995). The World Health Organization Quality of Life Assessment (WHOQOL): Position paper from the World Health Organization. *Social Science & Medicine, 41*, 1403–1409.

PART IV

THE AGENCY OF PARENTS AND EDUCATORS AS ADVOCATES FOR THE INCLUSIVE EDUCATION OF STUDENTS WITH INTELLECTUAL DISABILITIES

CHAPTER 11

PARENT ADVOCACY FOR INCLUSIVE EDUCATION IN THE UNITED STATES

Meghan M. Burke

Parent advocacy has paved the way for individuals with intellectual disabilities to be educated alongside their peers without disabilities. Indeed, inclusion is a hallmark of special education policy in the United States. However, parents encounter various barriers when advocating on behalf of their children with disabilities. Such barriers are exacerbated among minority, low-income, and non-English speaking families. In this chapter, I discuss the historical importance of parent advocacy with respect to inclusion. Based upon the lawsuits of parents against school districts, special education law and, correspondingly, the expectation of inclusive practices were instituted for students with disabilities. Unfortunately, parents face many barriers in effective advocacy. I identify barriers with respect to attitude, knowledge, and logistics. Still further, I demonstrate how these barriers are further exacerbated among disenfranchised families. I highlight additional challenges in advocacy that low-income, minority, and non-English speaking families face. I then identify gaps in the existing research with respect to: absence of a clear definition of advocacy, lack of research delineating the relation between advocacy and inclusive practices, and need for targeted support for vulnerable families. Based upon my observations of the literature, I discuss directions for the future including: developing an operational definition of advocacy, documenting the relation between parent advocacy

Inclusive Education for Students with Intellectual Disabilities,
pp. 231–248
Copyright © 2015 by Information Age Publishing

and inclusion, and providing targeted support for marginalized populations.

INTRODUCTION

In the United States, many parents of students with intellectual disabilities (ID) advocate for their children to receive services and be included with their peers without disabilities. My interest in advocacy stems from first-hand experience. My brother, Ryan, has Down syndrome, a genetic syndrome often resulting in an intellectual disability. When Ryan was three years old, my parents felt he should be educated in a preschool with his peers without disabilities. The school district disagreed, arguing that Ryan should be in a special education, self-contained classroom. Unable to come to an agreement, we filed a due process hearing against our school district. After prevailing several times and the school district, in return, appealing, we prevailed at the 7th Circuit Court Appeals resulting in a landmark case for inclusion on behalf of students with ID (*Board of Education of LaGrange School District V. Ryan B*, 1999).

Since prevailing in our court case, we moved to another school district, which promoted inclusive practices for students with all types of disabilities. Ryan did well in an inclusive setting until eighth grade. At junior high graduation, we came to another crossroads. In our district, the public high school tended to segregate students with ID. Again, we faced the option of advocating for Ryan to be placed in an inclusive setting. Instead of pursuing another battle with the school district, we developed a program for students with ID at a nearby, private high school. There, Ryan was the first student with ID to attend the school with his peers without disabilities. Since then, the program has welcomed more than 10 other students with ID.

Ryan's story of inclusion is one of many. In fact, parent advocacy instigated the beginning of inclusive practices. In 1971, a group of parents of students with ID filed suit against the school system arguing that their children should be educated in the public schools (*Parc v. Commonwealth of Pennsylvania*; hereafter Parc). Those parents prevailed, establishing a landmark case for inclusive education for students with ID. A few years later, in 1975, Congress passed the first federal special education law—now known as The Individuals with Disabilities Education Act (IDEA). Indeed, many of the premises of the Parc case were embedded in the special education legislation. One of those principles is the concept of the least restrictive environment. Under IDEA, each child with a disability is entitled to be educated, to the maximum extent appropriate, with peers without disabilities.

While IDEA has several regulations geared to ensure that children with ID receive appropriate services, students with ID are disproportionately more likely to be educated in self-contained, special education classrooms (U.S. Department of Education, 2011). IDEA expects parents to advocate on behalf of their children (Turnbull, Huerta, & Stowe, 2005). However, many parents struggle to advocate for their children with ID to be educated in inclusive settings. Parents face attitudinal, logistical, and knowledge barriers in advocating on behalf of their children. Still further, marginalized parents (e.g., parents who are from low-income backgrounds or have less education) face even greater obstacles in advocacy.

This chapter focuses on the advocacy of parents of students with ID for their children to be included with their peers without disabilities. While parents have spearheaded inclusive education for students with ID, students with ID continue to be segregated from their peers and many parents struggle with learning how to advocate for their children. This chapter begins by discussing the history of parent advocacy including the Parc decision as well as the benefits of advocacy for parents and their children. Then, I discuss the barriers to advocacy for parents especially those who are from marginalized populations. I review the literature about parent advocacy identifying gaps in the current research and discussing new directions in research and practice stemming from that research. Finally, I conclude with future directions for the field. For the ease of the reader, we list the acronyms used in this paper are listed in Table 11.1.

Table 11.1.   List of Acronyms

Term (Acronym)	Definition
Least restrictive environment (LRE)	To the maximum extent appropriate, every child should be educated with his/her non-disabled peers
Intellectual disability (ID)	A cognitive disability related to impairments in adaptive behavior and intellectual functioning that occurred before the age of 18
Individualized Education Program (IEP)	A plan for a child with a disability outlining the present levels of performance, goals and objectives, services and placement
Free Appropriate Public Education (FAPE)	Every child with a disability in the United States is entitled to an education at no cost by the public school
Individuals with Disabilities Education Act (IDEA)	The federal special education act in the United States
Parent Training and Information Center (PTI)	A federally funded agency designed to educate parents about their special education rights

REVIEW OF THE LITERATURE

History of Parent Advocacy

The Parc decision was followed by a national parent movement to advocate for children with ID to be included in the public school system. By 1972, parent organizations had filed 27 similar educational suits arguing for their children to be educated by the public schools (Melnick, 1995). One of those cases was *Mills v. D.C. Board of Education* (1972). From this decision, parents were accorded procedural safeguards (i.e., due process). By having dispute resolution options, parents have recourse when they disagree with the school system. Several principles of the Parc and Mills decision (e.g., inclusion and procedural safeguards, respectively) were then incorporated into the Education for All Handicapped Children Act (now known as IDEA) when it was passed in 1975.

In both its initial passage and continuing today, IDEA has several protections for parents. In fact, one of the six components of IDEA is parent participation (Turnbull, Turnbull, Erwin, Soodak, & Shogren, 2011). In conjunction with the school, IDEA requires parents to make decisions about their child's education. To this end, parents have the right to participate in hearings, be members of the IEP team, have access to school records, and participate on state and district advisory committees. Still further, before conducting any evaluations or implementing the initial placement of the child, the school must have parental consent.

To aid in teaching parents how to advocate for their children, Part D of IDEA requires each state to have at least one Parent Training and Information Center (PTI). Parents of students with disabilities usually staff these agencies. The purpose of a PTI is to educate parents about their special education rights by enabling parents to understand: their child's disability, necessary follow-up support, ways to communicate with the school, strategies to participate in the decision-making process, information about available services and resources, and provisions of IDEA (Turnbull et al., 2011). To date, there are more than 70 PTIs across the country, which continue to educate parents of students with ID about how to advocate for their children.

The need for parent advocacy continues today especially with respect to Individualized Education Programs (IEPs) for students with ID. IEPs are the individualized plans for students with disabilities. The plan includes: present levels of performance, goals and objectives, related services, and placement. Unfortunately, many IEPs are not written or implemented in compliance with IDEA. IEPs are often missing essential components (Simon, 2006). The social, emotional, and behavioral needs of the student are insufficiently addressed by many IEPs (Butera, Klein, McMullen, & Wilson, 1998). The goals and objectives are likely to be written just to comply with IDEA mandates, not to fulfill the spirit of the law (Grigal, Test, Beattie, & Wood, 1997). Related to placement, some special education, self-contained classrooms have been found to offer no more than babysitting services to the students with disabilities (Williams, 2007). Given the challenges in having an appropriate IEP, parent advocacy may be necessary.

Benefits of Parent Advocacy

As demonstrated by the Parc and Mills cases, when parents advocate on behalf of their children with ID, systemic change can occur. With the Parc and Mills cases, parents forged the way for not only their own children but also for other children to be educated by the public school system. Furthermore, the cases served as the impetus and model for the eventual passage of IDEA in 1975. Such legal advocacy demonstrates the sweeping changes parents can make for students with disabilities.

On an individual level, many benefits can also result from effective parent advocacy. Without parent advocacy, IDEA may not be implemented as comprehensively in the school system (Rice, 2006). When parents are involved, students are more prepared for program placements (Wolery, 1989) and, relatedly, students are less likely to receive inappropriate IEPs (Fish, 2008). Parent advocacy may enable children with disabilities to receive adequate services (Duquette, Stodel, Fullarton, & Haggland, 2011). Additionally, when parents effectively advocate, they demonstrate greater satisfaction with the services their children receive (Rehm, Fisher, Fuentes-Afflick, & Chesla, 2013).

In addition to the benefits of parent advocacy for children with disabilities, parent advocacy may also have positive outcomes for parents themselves. When parents advocate, they may be more likely to receive respect from they school system (Duquette et al., 2011). Furthermore, parents who advocate may develop a large parent support network allowing them to network with professionals, other parents, and agencies (Wang, Mannan, Poston, Turnbull, & Summers, 2004). Such extended networks may enable parents to have greater support in rearing their children with ID.

Barriers to Parent Advocacy

Parents encounter several barriers to meaningful advocacy related to attitude, logistics and knowledge. With respect to attitude, many parents feel inadequate in the school setting. Institutional structures seem to contribute to this power differential. For example, historically, parents have been viewed as ancillary to the school and, in some cases, as hindrances to the school's daily operations (Leiter & Krauss, 2004). Typically, parents are viewed as receivers of information (Smith, 1990). As such, schools may not expect or encourage parents to be active providers of information at IEP meetings. Still further, parents may not advocate because they feel they lack the legitimacy that the school professionals possess (Kalynpur, Harry, & Skrtic, 2000).

Attitudinal barriers also encompass feelings of disrespect at special education meetings. Many parents report feeling disrespected by professionals (Rock, 2000; Simon, 2006; Soodak & Erwin, 2000). For example, when professionals do not attend IEP meetings or choose to leave the meeting before it is over, parents may feel disrespected. Alternatively, when professionals arrive late to special education meetings, parents may feel their time is not valued (Blue-Banning, Summers, Frankland, Nelson, & Beagle, 2004). Such actions may reflect attitudinal barriers which inhibit parent advocacy.

Regarding logistics, many parents face tangible barriers in even attending IEP meetings, which is the primary forum for parent advocacy. For example, many parents lack childcare, and transportation to be able to attend IEP meetings (Friesen & Huff, 1990). Furthermore, IEP meetings tend to be scheduled during the school day, which, for many adults, conflict with their normal working hours. Some parents lack work flexibility to attend IEP meetings (Lynch & Stein, 1987). Without being able to attend IEP meetings, parents have fewer opportunities to advocate for services and inclusive placements.

Still further, parents struggle becoming educated about their special education rights in order to advocate. Indeed, many parents do not know how to advocate for their children (Turnbull & Turnbull, 2003). For example, the procedural safeguards given to parents are written, on average, at a 16th grade level (Mandic, Rudd, Hehir, & Acevedo-Garcia, 2010). For many parents, such safeguards are inaccessible. Another reason parents struggle to learn their special education rights is their lack of familiarity with professional jargon. Many evaluation and eligibility reports include technical terms which parents are unfamiliar with (Lytle & Bordin, 2001). Parents may feel uncomfortable or embarrassed to ask questions about such jargon in special education meetings. The knowledge barrier proves to be a significant obstacle in parents effectively advocating for their children.

Marginalized Populations

Such barriers become compounded among marginalized populations such as families in poverty. Indeed, many parents of individuals with ID are likely to be from households below the poverty line (Emerson, 2007). Such families are even more likely to face logistical struggles due to lacking the resources to afford childcare and transportation to attend IEP meetings (Friesen & Huff, 1990). Additionally, they are less likely to have flexible work hours enabling them to attend IEP meetings (Harry, 2002). Given that less formal education is comorbid with poverty, these individuals may also be less likely to understand their procedural safeguards and, more broadly, their special education rights.

Furthermore, individuals with ID are disproportionately more likely to be from minority backgrounds (Losen & Orfield, 2002). Even though minority families are over represented in the special education system, they are least likely to advocate and have their voices heard (Harry, 2002). In a review of the literature, Harry (2002) identified six barriers minority families face with respect to parent involvement: (1) cultural differences in definitions and interpretations of disabilities, (2) cultural differences in family-coping styles and disability-related stress, (3) cultural differences in parental interaction styles as well as expectations of participation and advocacy, (4) different access to information and services, (5) negative professional attitudes to and perceptions of families' roles in special education, and (6) dissonance of the cultural fit of programs. Other studies have identified further challenges which fit into these six larger issues: caution about sharing information (Cartledge, Kea, & Simmons-Reed, 2002); feelings of intimidation (Cartledge et al., 2002); unfamiliarity with acronyms (Park & Turnbull, 2001) and; documents are not available in other languages (Shapiro, Monzon, Rueda, & Blacher, 2004).

The school system faces many challenges in working with minority families. For example, the school system perspective of minority families may be that they are less committed and less skilled at parenting (Cartledge et al., 2002). Furthermore, research has found that some schools perceive minority families as passive and uninvolved (Harry, Allen, & McLaughlin, 1995; Harry, Kalyanpur, & Day, 1999). Additionally, the school system as a whole may engage in culturally insensitive or ethnocentric practices (Rock, 2000). Furthermore, the teaching pool is not racially or culturally diverse and, within the existing teaching pool, few teachers are prepared to teach minority students and work with their families (Thorp, 1997).

Another marginalized group of parents includes parents who do not speak English. These parents face tremendous obstacles in effectively advocating for their children. For example, IEP documents do not have to be translated in parents' native languages (Harry et al., 1995). While interpreters are required to attend IEP meetings, they are frequently unavailable for informal communication between the parent and the school thereby reducing parent-school communication (Hughes, Valle-

Riestra, & Arguelles, 2002). Still further, many interpreters struggle to adequately translate IEP meetings as special education has many technical terms (Hughes et al., 2002). As such, families may not receive all of the necessary information about their child in these meetings, thereby reducing their ability to effectively advocate.

GAPS IN THE LITERATURE

While history and research has shown the importance of parent advocacy with respect to inclusion as well as the barriers to advocacy especially among vulnerable populations, there are several gaps in the literature. Below, I discuss the: absence of a definition of advocacy, need for a research to document the relation between advocacy and supports for inclusion, and demand for targeted advocacy interventions for disenfranchised families.

Absence of an Operational Definition of Advocacy

While IDEA expects parents to advocate on behalf of their children with ID and many parents feel the need to advocate, the literature has yet to agree upon an operational definition of advocacy. Few studies have tried to systematically define advocacy. In one of the few studies to date, Nachshen, Anderson, and Jamieson (2001) developed a Parent Advocacy Scale (PAS) focusing on five dimensions of advocacy. Developed using 26 participants who completed semi structured interviews, the PAS represents a measure of global advocacy, quantifying membership in organizations, roles in organizations, number of advocacy actions, focus of advocacy, and feelings toward advocacy. The PAS, however, is not specific to special education, nor does it include questions about participation at IEP meetings, special education knowledge, or use of an advocate. As such, the PAS may not be specific enough to measure special education advocacy.

Additionally, a taxonomy of advocacy was created based upon the evaluation of a Partners in Policymaking Program in Illinois (Balcazar, Keys, Bertram, & Rizzo, 1996). The purpose of the Partners program was to involve and empower parents and other family members of individuals with disabilities in public policy. From this training, Balcazar and colleagues identified three developmental stages of the participants: beginner, involved, and activist. Beginner participants were involved in one disability organization, received few services, and were more passive. Comparatively, involved participants belonged to more than one organization, were active members, and obtained services as needed. The most advanced developmental stage was activist; individuals who belonged to several organizations, held leadership roles, and obtained services for others. The developmental stage reflects the pathway to advocacy development. However, this pathway is not specific to special education advocacy.

Two other scales have been developed which examine parent knowledge and participation in the IEP process. Lo (2005) had parents complete 12 true/false questions about special education law, and Plunge and Kratochwill (1995) asked parents to answer 13 true/false statements about special education knowledge and 17 questions about their levels of participation in special education meetings. Both Lo (2005) and Plunge and Kratochwill (1995) focused on parents' knowledge of special education as a proxy for parent advocacy. While Plunge and Kratochwill also asked questions about parent involvement, none of their questions asked directly about advocacy. While these measures provide some insight into parent participation and knowledge, they were not intended to capture parent advocacy in its entirety.

More recently, Trainor (2008) reveals four approaches to parent advocacy. Based upon focus groups and interviews with parents of individuals with disabilities, the four types of advocacy were: intuitive advocates, disability experts, strategists, and agents for systemic change. Intuitive advocates, for example relied on their own insights about their children and developing relationships with professionals whereas disability experts relied on information about their child's disability. Conversely, strategists relied on understanding their rights accorded to them by IDEA to advocate for their children. Finally, agents of change encompassed individuals who advocated not only for changes for their own children but in the larger system itself. While Trainor's sample was diverse reflecting both culturally and socioeconomically different families, her sample did not include Asian American families. From other studies, we know that Asian American families experience unique obstacles in advocacy (e.g., Lo, 2005). As such, the lack of Asian American representation affects the generalizability of this study. Also, while more general advocacy strategies were listed (e.g., understanding your child's disability), few observable advocacy methods were offered. However, this study does provide a jumping off point to examine specific advocacy strategies with respect to each type of advocacy.

Different than the above mentioned qualitative study, Burke and Hodapp (in press) developed a quantitative advocacy scale. Their eight-item scale focuses on activities related to acquiring special education legal knowledge. Such items include: searched the internet for special education rights; called an agency to ask about special education; talked with another parent about special education rights; read a copy of your special education rights; attended a workshop about special education rights; used an advocate or attorney to attend an IEP meeting; had someone else (not an advocate) attend an IEP meeting with you and; had difficulty reading and understanding special education rights. This is the one of the few scales that has been used with a national sample of parents of students with disabilities. However, this scale focuses on methods about acquiring special education knowledge; the scale does not address empowerment and assertiveness, which are necessary components of advocacy.

Effect of Advocacy Upon Inclusion

In tandem with the lack of a clear definition of advocacy, we also do not have a clear link between advocacy and more inclusive placements. Aside from case-law decisions, few studies have demonstrated that parent advocacy relates to students with ID being included in the regular education classroom. In one study by Ryndak, Downing, Morrison, and Williams (1996), 13 parents shared their perceptions of special education and regular education placements for their children with significant disabilities. In the special education classroom, many parents reported that their children received repetitive, meaningless, and non functional work. As such, at the surface level, it seems that many parents may recognize the need for their children to be educated in inclusive settings and, subsequently, to advocate for their children with ID to be placed in regular education classrooms.

However, placement and inclusion are two separate concepts. To date, parents have advocated for placement of their children with ID in regular education classrooms. However, parents must also advocate for their children with ID to be included with the necessary supports in the regular education classroom. Such advocacy may require asking for: certain kinds of instruction, paraprofessional support, and training. To date, few studies have examined how or if parents advocate for true, meaningful inclusion of their students with ID in the regular education classroom.

Advocating for Instructional Methods

Research has shown that students with ID can learn academic content in areas such as reading, math, science, and social studies (Browder, Spooner, Wakeman, Trela, & Baker, 2006). Interventions such as prompting have been found to be effective in teaching students with ID sight words. By enabling students to read and be educated in inclusive classrooms, they are more prepared to enter the community as adults

(Bochner, Outhred, & Pieterse, 2001). Unfortunately, some students with ID are still believed to be incapable of becoming literate. As such, parent advocacy may prove to be necessary to ensure these students are held to high expectations by being expected to read (with the appropriate supports) and access the general classroom. Still further, parents may also have to advocate for specific evidence-based teaching methods (e.g., prompting) to be used in the regular education classroom.

Advocating for Paraprofessional Support and Training

A paraprofessional is a person who "works in a school in an instructional capacity alongside school professionals and is supervised by the certified or licensed professionals who hold ultimate responsibility for the student and programmatic outcomes" (French, 1999, p. 65). Because of the cost of paraprofessionals to the school district, schools may be reluctant to offer paraprofessional support to students with ID. As such, parent advocacy may be necessary.

The duties of paraprofessionals span a broad range including: modifying curriculum, addressing student behavior, leading small-group work, meeting students' physical and health needs, and facilitating communication (Downing, Ryndak, & Clark, 2000; French, 1999; Marks, Schrader, & Levine, 1999). Even with so many responsibilities, paraprofessionals receive little training and little is known about the qualities and skills paraprofessionals need to support students with severe disabilities (Downing et al., 2000; Giangreco, Broer, & Edelman, 2002). Consequently, if the school agrees to provide a paraprofessional, parents may need to advocate for training, restricted responsibilities, and necessary skills of the paraprofessional to ensure that the appropriate amount and type of support is provided to the student with ID.

Ways to Reach out to Marginalized Populations

To date, much of the research about marginalized families has been descriptive. We understand that marginalized families are disproportionately more likely to have children with ID and they face greater barriers to advocacy. The literature, however, lacks clear ways to support marginalized families in advocacy. One potential intervention is a special education advocate. Because families struggle to advocate for their own children, a special education advocate may be able to step into that role and assist families in securing appropriate services in the most inclusive setting. By having an advocate, parents may feel less stress, as they are no longer alone in negotiating with the school system (Wang, Mannan, Poston, Turnbull, & Summers, 2004). To date, the special education advocacy field is largely unsupervised and unregulated (Wheeler & Marshall, 2008). However, a few special education and advocacy trainings exist (Burke, 2013).

Two of the prominent special education advocacy trainings include the Special Education Advocacy Training (SEAT) and the Volunteer Advocacy Project (VAP). The SEAT is a national, web-based training. It includes 115 hours of instruction and 115 hours of a practicum with a special education attorney. The VAP is a statewide training in Tennessee; it is comprised of 40 hours of instruction in addition to the shadowing of a special education advocate. The VAP has been demonstrated to improve the special education knowledge and advocacy skills of its participants (Burke, Goldman, Hart, & Hodapp, 2015).

While these trainings are potential interventions for marginalized families, there are some concerns. First, the VAP is currently restricted to Tennessee, thereby reducing its availability to support families across the country. While the SEAT training is countrywide, it has yet to document its effectiveness in training individuals to become advocates. But most importantly, neither training has a high percentage of minority families as its participants. In the VAP, over 85% of the participants are from White backgrounds (Burke et al., 2015). Similarly, over half of the SEAT participants in its first cohorts were Caucasian (Burke & Wheeler, 2008). Clearly, there is a need for minority and other marginalized families to have special education advocacy training; programs like the SEAT and the VAP offer a jumping off point to configuring support for these families but more targeted intervention is needed to ensure that their needs are met.

FUTURE DIRECTIONS FOR FIELD

This chapter has described the importance of parent advocacy in establishing inclusive education for students with ID. From the landmark case-law decisions to the initial passage of IDEA, parents were the trailblazers of inclusion for students with ID. While advocacy proved crucial to starting the movement to educate students with ID, parents also encounter many barriers to effective advocacy. Parents struggle with attitudinal, logistical, and knowledge obstacles making it difficult to advocate for their children. Furthermore, such obstacles are further exacerbated among marginalized populations such as parents from low-income, minority, and/or non-English speaking backgrounds. What is additionally striking, is that individuals with ID are significantly more likely to be from marginalized populations making it especially crucial to identify and eliminate these barriers to advocacy.

While the literature has demonstrated the importance and challenges to parent advocacy, more research is needed. For example, there is limited research related to an operational definition of advocacy. Still further, research has yet to explore the link between parent advocacy and inclusive placements. Finally, while it is known that marginalized populations are more likely to have children with ID and these families face additional barriers, little research has proposed interventions to help these families advocate.

Here, I detail directions for future research and implications for the field. More specifically, I discuss the need for additional research about observable advocacy strategies. Then, I discuss the need for research clearly linking parent advocacy to greater inclusion for students with ID. Finally, I discuss ways for practitioners to support marginalized parents of students with ID in advocacy.

Observable Advocacy Strategies

Neither policy nor research provides a clear definition of advocacy. While it is clear that IDEA expects parents to advocate for their children, IDEA does not provide explicit guidance for how that advocacy can occur (Kalyanpur et al., 2000). Furthermore, research has yet to offer an operationalized definition of advocacy. Various types of advocacy have been characterized (Trainor, 2008) and advocacy scales have been developed (e.g., Burke & Hodapp, in press; Lo, 2005). However, there remains no agreed upon definition for advocacy. Future research should delineate an operational definition of advocacy.

Furthermore, research provides few examples of observable advocacy strategies. IDEA affords parents certain legal advocacy strategies including procedural safeguards, informed consent, and access to school records. However, informal advocacy strategies are insufficiently documented in the literature. How can parents assertively but not aggressively advocate for inclusion in IEP meetings? Additional descriptive research is needed to see what advocacy strategies parents use to secure services.

To identify the advocacy strategies used by parents, research should begin with the PTIs. Each year, every PTI has to submit an annual report to the Office of Special Education Programs detailing the number of parents trained (Turnbull et al., 2011). In addition to this report, PTIs may offer the strategies used by parents they work with. Given that there is a PTI in every state, this would result in a national sample of advocacy strategies. Using the PTIs as resource will provide a preliminary description of advocacy strategies.

Clear Link between Advocacy and Inclusive Outcomes

In addition to the lack of research operationalizing advocacy, little research connects advocacy to inclusive outcomes for youth with ID. Within the context of special education, there is a link between advocacy and services. Parent advocacy seems to improve placements (Wolery, 1989) and the quality of the IEP (Fish, 2008). At a systems change level, advocacy seems to lead to more inclusive placements. For example, some of the lawsuits filed by families have resulted in more inclusive placements for students with ID (e.g., Parc and Mills decisions).

However, at the individual level, the connection between parent advocacy and inclusion is less clear. Little research has quantitatively examined the relation between advocacy and the placement of the child. While it seems that parents do advocate for more inclusive placements, it is less clear whether greater parent advocacy does indeed relate to more inclusive settings. Additionally, research needs to examine how parent advocacy can ensure that the student with ID is not simply "placed" in a regular education classroom but rather is fully included. To do this, research needs to discern whether parent advocacy for inclusion encompasses relevant supports (e.g., a paraprofessional).

Furthermore, it is unknown whether there are any mediating factors in this relationship. For example, when a child is younger and the parent advocates, is the child more likely to be in an inclusive placement? Does the age of the child with ID mediate the effectiveness of parent advocacy? Future research is needed to delineate the relation between parent advocacy and the degree of inclusion of the child with ID as well as any potential mediators.

Targeted Support for Marginalized Families

The SEAT and the VAP offer jumping off points to targeting support for marginalized families. Similar to the teaching pool, many parents may want advocates who reflect their own cultural background and experiences (Thorp, 1997). To meet the needs of minority families, more minority parents need to attend trainings like the SEAT or the VAP. These minority parents can then serve their peers in the role of an advocate. Such trainings should make efforts to encourage the attendance of minority and other disenfranchised parents at these trainings. For example, targeting minority organizations for recruitment may help increase the diversity at advocacy trainings. Additionally, having speakers at the trainings who reflect various cultural backgrounds may help attract more diverse participants. Concerted attempts to attract a more diverse pool of participants may help provide additional support for typically marginalized families.

Additionally, a targeted effort should be made to train bilingual individuals to become advocates. As stated earlier, the translation of IEP meetings can be difficult due to the jargon involved. Regular translators may struggle to interpret such technical terms. However, a bilingual advocate who is well-versed in special education law can more accurately interpret the conversation at the IEP meetings. Furthermore, because the written documents are not translated, by having a bilingual advocate available, the parent can ask questions about the evaluation and IEP documents to the advocate in forums other than the IEP meeting.

In the United States, since the 1970s, parents have spearheaded the movement to include students with ID in regular education classrooms. Primarily through legal and individual advocacy efforts, students with ID are being educated with their non disabled peers. However, parents, especially disenfranchised parents, face barriers to effective parent advocacy. Furthermore, there are several gaps in the parent advocacy literature such as the absence of: an operationalized definition of advocacy, a clear link between advocacy and the degree of inclusion for students with ID, and resources and supports for marginalized populations. Future research should focus on identifying observable advocacy strategies as well as delineating the link between parent advocacy and inclusion for students with ID. Additionally, practitioners should make concerted efforts to provide support to vulnerable families in learning how to effectively advocate on behalf of their children with ID.

ACKNOWLEDGMENTS

Preparation for this article was supported in part by Grant No. H133P110004 from the National Institute on Disability and Rehabilitation Research. The findings and conclusions in this paper are those of the author and do not represent the official position of any other entity.

REFERENCES

Balcazar, F. E., Keys, C. B., Bertram, J. F., & Rizzo, T. (1996). Advocate development in the field of developmental disabilities: A data based conceptual model. *Mental Retardation, 34*, 341–351.

Blue-Banning, M., Summers, J. A., Frankland, H. C., Nelson, L. L., & Beagle, G. P. (2004). Dimensions of family and professional partnerships: Constructive guidelines for collaboration. *Exceptional Children, 70*, 167–184.

Board of Education of LaGrange School District No. 105 v. Illinois State Board of Education and Ryan B. (1999). 184 F. 3d 912.

Bochner, S., Outhred, L., & Pieterse, M. (2001). A study of functional literacy skills in young adults with Down syndrome. *International Journal of Disability, Development, and Education, 48,* 67–90.

Browder, D. M., Spooner, F., Wakeman, S., Trela, K., & Baker, J. N. (2006). Aligning instruction with academic content standards: Finding the link. *Research and Practice for Persons with Severe Disabilities, 31,* 309–321.

Burke, M. M. (2013). Improving parental involvement: Training special education advocates. *Journal of Disability Policy Studies, 23,* 225–234.

Burke, M. M., Goldman, S. E., Hart, M., & Hodapp, R. M. (2015). Evaluating the efficacy of a special education advocacy training program. Manuscript submitted for review.

Burke, M.M. & Hodapp, R.M. (in press). The nature, correlates, and conditions of parent advocacy in special education. *Exceptionality.*

Burke, M. M., & Wheeler, B. (2008, November). *Two training models for special education advocates: Working with families of children with disabilities.* Paper presented at Association of University Centers on Disabilities, Washington, D.C.

Butera, G., Klein, H., McMullen, L., & Wilson, B. (1998). A statewide study of FAPE and school discipline policies. *The Journal of Special Education, 32,* 108–114.

Cartledge, G., Kea, C., & Simmons-Reed, E. (2002). Serving culturally diverse children with serious emotional disturbance and their families. *Journal of Child and Family Studies, 11,* 113–126.

Downing, J.E., Ryndak, D.L., & Clark, D. (2000). Paraeducators in inclusive classrooms. *Remedial and Special Education, 21,* 171–181.

Duquette, C.A., Stodel, E. J., Fullarton, S., & Haggland, K. (2011). Educational advocacy among adoptive parents of adolescents with fetal alcohol spectrum disorder. *International Journal of Inclusive Education, 16,* 1203–1221.

Emerson, E. (2007). Poverty and people with intellectual disabilities. *Mental Retardation and Developmental Disabilities Research Reviews, 13,* 107–113.

Fish, W. W. (2008). The IEP meeting: Perceptions of parents of students who receive special education services. *Preventing School Failure, 53,* 8–14.

French, N. K. (1999). Paraeducators: Who are they and what do they do? *Teaching Exceptional Children, 32,* 65–69.

Friesen, B. J., & Huff, B. (1990). Parents and professionals as advocacy partners. *Preventing School Failure, 34,* 31–39.

Giangreco, M. F., Broer, S. M., & Edelman, S. (2002). That was then, this is now! Paraprofessional supports for students with disabilities in general education classrooms. *Exceptionality, 10,* 47–54.

Grigal, M., Test, D. W., Beattie, J., & Wood, W. M. (1997). An evaluation of transition components of individualized education programs. *Exceptional Children, 63,* 357–372.

Harry, B. (2002). Trends and issues in serving culturally diverse families of children with disabilities. *Journal of Special Education, 36,* 131–147.

Harry, B., Allen, N., & McLaughlin, M. (1995). Communication versus compliance: African-American parents' involvement in special education. *Exceptional Children, 61*, 364–378.

Harry, B., Kalyanpur, M., & Day, M. (1999). *Building cultural reciprocity with families: Case studies in special education.* Baltimore, MD: Paul H. Brookes.

Hughes, M. T., Valle-Riestra, D. M., & Arguelles, M. E. (2002). Experiences of latino families with their child's special education program. *Multicultural Perspectives, 4,* 11–17.

Kalyanpur, M., Harry, B., & Skrtic, T. (2000). Equity and advocacy expectations of culturally diverse families' participation in special education. *International Journal of Disability, Development, and Education, 47,* 119–136.

Leiter, V., & Krauss, M. W. (2004). Claims, barriers, and satisfaction: Parents' requests for additional special education services. *Journal of Disability Policy Studies. 15,* 135–146.

Lo, L. (2005). Barriers to successful partnerships with Chinese-speaking parents of children with disabilities in urban schools. *Multiple Voices, 8,* 84–95.

Losen, D. J., & Orfield, G. (2002). *Racial inequity in special education.* Boston, MA: Harvard Educational Publishing Group.

Lynch, L. W., & Stein, R. C. (1987). Parent participation by ethnicity: A comparison of Hispanic, Black, and Anglo families. *Exceptional Children, 54,* 105–111.

Lytle, R. K., & Bordin, L. (2001). Enhancing the IEP team: Strategies for parents and professionals. *Teaching Exceptional Children, 33,* 40–44.

Mandic, C. G., Rudd, R., Hehir, T., & Acevedo-Garcia, D. (2010). Readability of special education procedural safeguards. *Journal of Special Education, 30,* 1–9.

Marks, S. U., Schrader, C., & Levine, M. (1999). Paraeducator experiences in inclusive settings: Helping, hovering, or holding their own? *Exceptional Children, 65,* 315–330.

Melnick, R. S. (1995). Separation of powers and the strategy of rights: The expansion of special education. In M. K. Landy & M. A. Levin (Eds.), *The new politics of public policy* (pp. 23–46). Baltimore, MD: The John Hopkins University Press.

Mills v. District of Columbia Bd. Of Education., 348 F. Supp. 866 (D.D.C., 1972).

Nachshen, J., Anderson, J., & Jamieson, J. (2001). The parent advocacy scale: Measuring advocacy in parents of children with special needs. *Journal on Developmental Disabilities, 81,* 93–105.

Plunge, M. M., & Kratochwill, T. R. (1995). Parental knowledge, involvement, and satisfaction with their child's special education services. *Special Services in the Schools, 10,* 113–138.

Parc v. Commonwealth of Pennsylvania. (1971). 343 F. Supp. 279. (U.S. Dist. LEXIS 13874).

Park, J., & Turnbull, A.P. (2001). Cross-cultural competency and special education: Perceptions of experiences of Korean parents of children with special needs. *Education and Training in Mental Retardation and Developmental Disabilities, 36,* 133–147.

Rehm, R. S., Fisher, L. T., Fuentes-Afflick, E., & Chesla, C. A. (2013). Parental advocacy styles for special education students during the transition to adulthood. *Qualitative Health Research, 23,* 1377–1387.

Rice, M. (2006). The parent teacher team: Establishing communication between home and school. *Exceptional Parent, 36,* 49.

Rock, M. L. (2000). Parents as equal partners. *Teaching Exceptional Children, 32,* 30.

Ryndak, D. L., Downing, J. E., Morrison, A. P., & Williams, L. J. (1996). Parents' perceptions of educational settings and services for children with moderate or severe disabilities. *Remedial and Special Education, 17,* 106–118.

Shapiro, J., Monzon, L. D., Rueda, R., Gomez, J. A., & Blacher, J. (2004). Alienated advocacy: Perspectives of latina mothers of young adults with developmental disabilities on service systems. *Mental Retardation, 42,* 37–54.

Simon, J. B. (2006). Perceptions of the IEP requirement. *Teacher Education and Special Education, 29,* 225–235.

Smith, S. W. (1990). Individualized education programs (IEPs) in special education—from intent to acquiescence. *Exceptional Children, 76,* 75–100.

Soodak, L. C., & Erwin, E. J. (2000). Valued member or tolerated participant: Parents' experiences in inclusive early childhood settings. *The Journal of the Association for Persons with Severe Handicaps, 25,* 29–41.

Thorp, E. K. (1997). Increasing opportunities for partnership with culturally and linguistically diverse families. *Intervention in School and Clinic, 32,* 261–269.

Trainor, A. A. (2008). Diverse approaches to parent advocacy during special education home-school interactions: Identification and use of cultural and social capital. *Remedial and Special Education, 31,* 34–47.

Turnbull, R. H., & Turnbull, A. P. (2003). Reaching the ideal. *Education Next, 3,* 32–37.

Turnbull, R. H., Turnbull, A. P., Erwin, E. J., Soodak, L. C., & Shogren, K. A. (2011). *Families, professionals, and exceptionality: Positive outcomes through partnerships and trust* (6th ed.). Upper Saddle River, NJ: Pearson.

Turnbull, R. H., Huerta, H., & Stowe, M. (2005). *The Individuals with Disabilities Education Act as amended in 2004.* Lawrence, KS: Beach Center on Disability.

U. S. Department of Education. (2011). *Historical State-Level IDEA data files.* Retrieved on October 2, 2013, from http://tadnet.public.tadnet.org/pages/712.

Wang, M., Mannan, H., Poston, D., Turnbull, A., & Summers, J. (2004). Parents' perceptions of advocacy activities and their impact on family quality of life. *Research and Practice for Persons with Severe Disabilities, 29,* 144–155.

Wheeler, B., & Marshall, D. (2008, March). *Special education advocacy training (SEAT).* Presentation at the Council of Parent Attorneys and Advocates Conference, Anaheim, CA.

Williams, E. R. (2007). Unnecessary and unjustified: African-American parental perceptions of special education. *The Educational Forum, 71,* 250–261.

Wolery, M. (1989). Transitions in early childhood special education: Issues and procedures. *Focus on Exceptional Children, 22,* 1–16.

CHAPTER 12

SPECIAL EDUCATION TEACHERS OF CHILDREN WITH INTELLECTUAL AND DEVELOPMENTAL DISABILITIES, AND TEACHERS IN INCLUSIVE AND REGULAR CLASSROOMS

Differential Views Toward Inclusive Education

Frances Lai Mui Lee, Alexander Seeshing Yeung, Danielle Tracey, Katrina Barker, Jesmond C. M. Fan

Despite a general advocacy of inclusive education worldwide, teachers may hold different views toward inclusive education. Investigations of teachers' views are important for the provision of support to children with intellectual and developmental disabilities. Compared to studies in Western contexts, little is known about Asian teachers in special education, and even less about early childhood teachers. In Hong Kong, preprimary education settings

Inclusive Education for Students with Intellectual Disabilities,
pp. 249–272

have a choice to opt in to an "integrated program" whereby special education teachers and regular classroom teachers work together in an inclusive classroom or opt out to have regular teachers teach in regular classrooms. A sample of preprimary teachers in Hong Kong were surveyed ($N = 436$) with regard to their perceptions of inclusive education. Analysis confirmed 5 factors of interest: government support, knowledge, self-efficacy, individualized curriculum, and resistance to inclusive education. The main results indicated that special education teachers and their collaborating regular teachers in inclusive classrooms were higher in knowledge, efficacy, individualized curriculum, and lower in resistance than teachers in regular classrooms. All 3 teacher types showed similarly low scores for government support. More experienced teachers tended to have better knowledge about special education, but this difference was small. The results imply that resources need to be allocated to develop regular teachers who teach in regular classrooms. Strategies may include the collaboration of special education and regular teachers to promote inclusive education and improve their self-development, curriculum implementation, and views toward inclusive education. Teachers in general seemed to desire more government support. A range of hypotheses and strategies are explored to address this interesting finding. In sum, the study is well positioned to provide practical recommendations about how best to support and develop teachers' perception and knowledge in the area of inclusive education. With the recognition that teachers are an essential ingredient to the success of inclusive education and maximizing outcomes for children with intellectual and developmental disabilities, this endeavor is critical to advancing preprimary education in Hong Kong.

INTRODUCTION

There is a general advocacy of inclusive education worldwide promoting the inclusion of children with intellectual and developmental disabilities in regular classrooms with children without special educational needs. The movement to include children with special educational needs in general education classrooms is evident in schools across the United States, United Kingdom, and other countries (Bruneau-Balderrama, 1997; Department for Education and Skills, 1997). For Hong Kong, the "Code of Practice on Education" enacted in 2001 provided practical guidance for education sectors to develop policies and enable people with disabilities and their parents and related parties to understand their rights and responsibilities (Forlin, 2010). The vision for inclusive education was further demonstrated by the Inclusive Education Implementation Guide (Education Department, 2000) which heightened the enforcement of the government's policy for inclusion (Forlin, 2010).

In recent years, there has been a remarkable movement of children with special educational needs away from segregated settings and into regular classrooms (Ainscow, 1997; Avramidis, Bayliss, & Burden, 2000). It is a strong belief that every child should be an equally valued member of the school community (Bryant, Smith, & Bryant, 2008). Educators generally recognize that including children with special educational needs in regular classrooms can provide them with the opportunity to learn in natural and stimulating settings (Black-Hawkins, Florian, & Rouse, 2007). The advantages of inclusive education are evident in the literature. Research indicates that children with disabilities make developmental gains in inclusive settings and the effectiveness of teaching is rated higher when children with and without disabilities form the classroom community (Baker-Ericzen, Mueggenborg, & Shea., 2009; DeVore & Russell, 2007; Purcell, Horn, & Palmer, 2007).

The development of inclusive education at the school level is impacted by several factors such as government policies, resources, support offered by school administrators and the degree of collaboration among teachers and school personnel (Gavish & Shimoni, 2011; Kavale & Forness, 2000). However, as teachers are the major agents of change in student development, teachers' attitudes (Campbell & Gilmore, 2003) and knowledge regarding the inclusion of children with diverse needs (Sukbunpant, Arthur-Kelly, & Dempsey, 2013) and teachers' sense of efficacy (Sharma, Loreman, & Forlin, 2012) are critical factors determining the success of inclusion.

The purpose of the research reported here is to examine the views of different types of teachers toward inclusion, and whether their teaching experience matters in formulating such views. The importance of the study is bolstered as it centers on the underresearched context of preprimary settings in Hong Kong.

TEACHERS' VIEWS TOWARD INCLUSIVE EDUCATION

Research shows that the success of inclusion is significantly influenced by the attitudes of the teachers who are directly involved (Avramidis & Kalyva, 2007; Jordan, Schwartz, & McGhie-Richmond, 2009; Rakap & Kaczmarek, 2010). Buell, Hallam, Gamel-McCormick, and Scheer (1999) reported that teachers with positive views of inclusion are more likely to support children in inclusive settings, and to adapt learning materials to accommodate their needs. Ross-Hill (2009) thus cautioned that inclusive education cannot be implemented without the support of teachers.

However, a review of the literature showed that the teachers' attitudes toward inclusive education vary. Whereas several studies indicated that teachers generally have a positive attitude toward including children with special educational needs (Black-Hawkins et al., 2007), other studies reported teachers' unwillingness to include children with special educational needs in their classrooms (Forlin, 2001). Even if some teachers generally endorse the idea of inclusive education, their positive attitudes toward inclusion in their classroom are affected by many factors including the type and severity of the child's disability and the amount of additional time they need to spend with the child (Scruggs & Mastropieri, 1996). For example, Avramidis and Norwich (2002) argued that the more severe the disability, the greater the obligation associated with the child and the more negative are the teachers' attitudes toward inclusion. Moreover, teachers considered children with emotional and behavioral difficulties to be the most challenging (Avramidis et al., 2000; Forlin, 2001; Kniveton, 2004).

Influential Factors

Factors affecting teachers' views toward inclusion are various. Some factors are associated with the elements necessary for individualized curricula. For example, a number of studies have reported that teachers do not find sufficient time to work within an inclusive model (Paliokosta & Blandford, 2010; Scruggs & Mastropieri, 1996; Smith & Smith, 2000; Valeo, 2008); or lack adequate collaboration between teachers (Bouillet, 2013; Hamaidi, Homidi, & Reyes, 2012) and believe that the class size and student-teacher ratio in a class with children with special educational needs are too big (Smith & Smith, 2000).

Other than curriculum- and resource-related factors, some factors are associated with teachers' value of inclusion. For example, some regular teachers in Valeo's (2008) study expressed their belief that children with special educational needs learn better in special classes than regular classes even though they may not have adequate experience with children with disabilities. Minke, Bear, and Deemer (1996) also claimed that regular teachers' resistance to inclusion may be due to their belief that instruction and curriculum for children with special educational needs is not likely to work in the regular classroom.

Some other factors are related to teachers' knowledge and self-efficacy. For example, many teachers often do not feel that they have the expertise necessary for teaching children with special educational needs (Westwood, 2013). For some teachers, the intensity of children's educational needs could increase pressure in their teaching (Buysse, Wesley, Keyes, & Bailey, 1996). Apart from these, there are also external factors affecting the implementation of inclusive education including fragmented laws and regulations as perceived by teachers (Slavica, 2010).

Government Support

Following the advocacy of inclusive education in most countries, relevant policies have been mandated to ensure that children with special educational needs are provided with adequate educational opportunities. Vaillant (2011) argues that the success of inclusion is not simply a matter of teachers' competence and capacities, but it requires changes in educational policies that can improve teachers' social status and their professional preparation for inclusive education. He believes that it is not an easy task to make education inclusive, and it could fail easily if not all parties acknowledge the important role of the classroom teacher. Hence, government needs to support and empower inclusive teachers through appropriate provision of supportive legislation and policy frameworks (Brady & Opertti, 2011). Indeed, government policy relating to inclusion has been a primary issue in recent years. However, as cautioned by Lindsay (2003), "Inclusion is the policy framework. What is at issue is the interpretation and implementation of inclusion in practice" (p. 10). In order to ensure the success of inclusion, the teachers must not only support the policy themselves, but should also believe that they are capable of putting the policy into practice (UNESCO, 2005).

Knowledge and Self-Efficacy in Inclusion

An individual's perceptions of the self are known to be influential to their behaviors and attitudes (Craven & Yeung, 2008). What teachers believe about their instructional capacity has a significant impact on their willingness to put into practice instructional reform to achieve student academic success (Ross & Bruce, 2009). In a study by Avramidis, Bayliss, and Burden (2000), respondents who perceived themselves to have "generic" teaching skills appeared more positive to the idea of inclusion (p. 204). In a study by Mitchell and Hedge (2007), preschool teachers with a graduate degree expressed that they did not feel comfortable with the idea of inclusion because they felt unprepared to work in an inclusive setting. Teachers in most countries are frequently found to express that they do not have the expertise needed to teach children with special educational needs (Westwood, 2013). Hutzler, Zach, and Gafni (2005) investigated the influence of self-efficacy toward the participation of children with special educational needs in regular classes, and found that teachers with low self-efficacy tend to see a child with special educational needs as someone who will cause trouble, rather than someone who will launch a challenge for their professional performance. Teachers need to feel that they are empowered, so as to apply their new skills and competence in any setting successfully (Hegarty, 1994).

The Inclusive Curriculum

As Blanco (2009) noted, inclusion is not about individualized educational provision, but rather diversified and personalized programs within a common curriculum framework. Moving away from a standardized curriculum structured around the logic of a homogeneous group of average learners, the inclusive curriculum aims for a curriculum design based on the diverse needs of all children. Inclusive curriculum recognizes that all learners are diverse and educators need to design and implement lessons appropriate for all children (Brady & Opertti, 2011). In an inclusive classroom, teachers should actively analyze their modes of instruction and provide personal and meaningful learning for their students.

However, implementing an inclusive curriculum is challenging to both special and regular teachers. Special education teachers are expected to focus on the individual child who has special educational needs whereas the regular teachers might treat each child in the class as equivalent. In an inclusive classroom, collaboration and team work provide an opportunity for teachers to expand their knowledge and share ideas and strategies. As mentioned by Robinson and Buly (2007), coteaching is an opportunity for regular education and special education teachers to work together, to share ideas, and to design meaningful lessons for children with special educational needs. It can increase teacher effectiveness (Goodwin, 1999), and build stronger connections among the teaching staff, which leads to a more positive and cohesive learning environment for children with or without special educational needs.

THE ROLE OF DIFFERENT TEACHERS IN INCLUSIVE CLASSROOMS

During the past decades, research indicated the critical roles of special education teachers in inclusive education. The practice of inclusive education has increased expectations of special education teachers in teaching children with special educational needs. However, regular teachers also have a significant role to play. An issue is how different types of teachers may work collegially together to benefit all children. Webb, Neumann, and Jones (2004) measured the attitudes of special and regular education teachers in the inclusive classroom and found conflicting views regarding the practices of special and regular education teachers. In terms of attitudes, while special education teachers generally had a positive attitude toward inclusion, regular education teachers did not.

Historically, regular and special education teachers have distinct roles and work separately. Regular education teachers provide instruction in the regular classroom while special education teachers deliver programs in a self-contained classroom. Current practices of including children with special educational needs require teachers to support all children regardless of their developmental abilities. The roles and responsibilities for both the special education and regular education teacher have therefore undergone a drastic transformation. For regular education teachers, they have to play a dual role of advancing the knowledge and skills of the entire class and also differentiating their instruction to meet the needs of children with special educational needs. Special education teachers need to provide individual programs for individual children while also supporting the regular education teachers in managing all of the tasks for children with special educational needs (Boe, Shin, & Cook, 2007; Jorgensen, Schuh, & Nisbet, 2006; Klor, 2007).

INCLUSIVE EDUCATION IN EARLY CHILDHOOD SETTINGS IN HONG KONG

Before providing the details of the current investigation, it is important that readers are familiar with the complexity of inclusive education in early childhood settings in Hong Kong. First, kindergartens have a choice to opt in to implement an "integrated program" whereby special education teachers and regular teachers work together in an inclusive classroom, or opt out to allow teachers in regular classrooms to teach children with or without special educational needs. Second, early childhood education in Hong Kong is not mandatory, although over 95% of children attend kindergarten at the age of 3. Third, there is no definite requirement regarding the degree of inclusion and how it operates.

Since the 1970s, the Social Welfare Department provided early interventions and training for young children with special educational needs. In 1978, the integrated programs were introduced (Social Welfare Department, 2004). Children with mild disabilities were included in regular schools together with their peers without disabilities, but they also received a session of individual training in a school day. Preschools that joined the scheme received extra funding to hire a special education teacher to provide individual training for children with special educational needs. For other nonintegrated preschools, they had no special education teachers even though there were young children with special educational needs in their classrooms.

In 2009, the Education Bureau implemented the "Comprehensive Child Development Services" to help early childhood educators understand the characteristics of children with special educational needs and proposed a referral to parents for further assessment of their children. Under the scheme, early childhood teachers are expected to identify children with early signs of developmental disabilities. Besides, "teachers also need to manage the children's learning, emotional and behavioral problems in the classroom in order to help them adapt to school life and learn more easily" (Education Bureau, 2009, p. 50). According to government policy, regular education teachers are required to participate in many facets of inclusive education. Apart from being the main teachers for children with or without special educational needs, they need to identify children's diverse needs and help them learn in a regular classroom setting. Special education teachers take on the role of supporting the regular education teachers and modeling how to meet the needs of children with special educational needs in their classrooms.

In a nutshell, teachers working in Hong Kong preschool settings can be differentiated in three types based on their working experiences with children with special educational needs: regular teachers and special education teachers working in inclusive classrooms, and regular teachers working in regular classrooms. Our review of the literature has revealed that teachers' attitudes (e.g., Avramidis & Kalyva, 2007) and sense of efficacy (e.g., Hutzler et al., 2005) are significant factors in determining the success of inclusion. Nevertheless, how these three different types of teachers in an early childhood setting may differ in their attitudes is unclear. The authors endeavored to reveal potentially different views of teachers in inclusive and regular classrooms. It was hypothesized that teachers who have had different experiences with inclusive education would demonstrate different attitudes to inclusion. That is, teachers with more opportunities working with children with special educational needs would reflect a greater understanding of this work, report a greater sense of efficacy, and be more supportive of inclusion.

THE PRESENT INVESTIGATION

The objectives of the present study are to develop a measure to assess the five key factors of interest, and then examine teachers' views toward inclusion of children with intellectual and developmental disabilities: government support (an external-referenced factor), knowledge, and self-efficacy (self-referenced factors), individualized curriculum (an action-referenced factor), and resistance to inclusive education (a value factor). Specifically, we hypothesized that: (1) the measure used to examine the five factors of interest would have good reliability and the factors would be confirmed as five distinct factors, thus providing a valid measure for group comparisons, (2) special education teachers and their collaborating regular teachers in inclusive classrooms would have higher perceptions of knowledge and efficacy, advocate more individualized curriculum, and would be lower in resistance to inclusion than teachers in regular classrooms. As there is no clear evidence from the literature showing teachers' perceptions of government support, we left this as a research question: Do the three teacher types differ in their perceptions of government support for inclusion? The findings could provide a possible direction for teacher education to enhance positive attitudes toward inclusion to benefit young children with intellectual and developmental disabilities.

METHOD

Instrument

Data were collected using a questionnaire that was developed by the researchers. The survey questions were created from a review of current literature that identified teachers' attitudes. The survey asked the teachers about their perceptions of inclusive education whereby children with intellectual and developmental needs were placed within regular classrooms together with other children. Five factors were of particular interest in the present study: (a) government support, (b) knowledge, (c) efficacy, (d) adapted curriculum, and (e) noninclusive attitude. The scales and items used in the study are presented in Table 12.1. The participants responded to each of 20 items on a 5-point scale of 1-5: (1) *strongly disagree*, (2) *disagree*, (3) *neutral*, (4) *agree*, or (5) strongly *agree*. Other collected information included age, teaching experience, and training in special education. The scales (Table 12.1) were:

- *Government support*. Four items related to the support obtained from the government: guidelines for action, continual assessment support, and schooling arrangements.
- *Knowledge*. Four items aimed to examine teachers' understanding and knowledge of government policy, referral procedures and resources.
- *Efficacy*. Five items asked teachers to evaluate their abilities and competency of teaching, helping and providing suitable learning materials.

- *Adapted curriculum*. Three items were about curriculum adaptation and classroom activities for students.
- *Noninclusive attitude*. Four items asked teachers the extent to which they did not endorse inclusive education. That is, teachers were asked to show how strong they felt against placing children with special educational needs in a regular classroom.

Procedure

To meet the aims of the research, 520 printed surveys were sent to the principals and teachers of mainstream preprimary education organizations in Hong Kong. A high return rate of over 95% left us with a total of 436 surveys to assess. Over 90% of the respondents were females, which is typical of the teaching population in preprimary education in Hong Kong —age ranging from 20 to 50 years, mostly between 20 and 40 years (68%). About half of the participants had less than 10 years' teaching experience whereas the other half had over 10 years' experience. We examined the responses of special education teachers ($n = 73$), regular classroom teachers working in an inclusive classroom ($n = 79$), and regular teachers teaching in regular classrooms ($n = 284$).

Statistical Analysis

The responses were coded so that higher scores depicted a stronger reflection of the attitude measured. We first examined the descriptive statistics, then tested the ability of the items to form the five factors and subsequently examined the alpha reliability of each a priori factor formed from the respective items (Table 12.1). Finally, based on the established factors, we conducted group comparisons to test our hypothesis and answer our research question.

Factor Analysis. Underpinned by previous research a clear a priori hypothesis was established for the newly developed scales and consequently analyses proceeded with confirmatory factor analysis (CFA). We examined the structure of a confirmatory factor analysis model with the 20 items forming five factors, allowing each item to load on to one factor only. Then we compared it against a single-factor model. The procedures for conducting CFA have been described elsewhere (e.g., Byrne, 1998; Jöreskog & Sörbom, 2006) and are therefore not detailed here. The CFA was conducted with the LISREL software (Jöreskog & Sörbom, 2006). Following widely accepted criteria for assessing model fit, CFI and TLI values of .90 or above and RMSEA values of below .08 were used as

Table 12.1.   Scales

Scale		Items	Alpha
Government support	1.	Government provides adequate service for identification and referral.	.87
	2.	Government provides clear guidelines for assessing children with special needs.	
	3.	Government provides adequate resources to help children with learning diversity.	
	4.	Government policy regarding children with SEN is well defined.	
Knowledge	1.	I understand government policies regarding support of diversity of children's learning needs.	.81
	2.	I know the procedures for assessing children's diverse needs in learning.	
	3.	I am competent with referral procedures for children with diverse needs.	
	4.	I have a good understanding of government resources for children with diverse needs.	
Efficacy	1.	In an inclusive education environment, I can help children more readily accept other children.	.68
	2.	I can help children with or without special needs learn together.	
	3.	I can help all children of varying abilities improve in learning.	
	4.	In teaching, I use various methods to help different children with various learning needs.	
	5.	I will find out how to design curriculum to suit various learning needs of children	
Adapted curriculum	1.	My school adapts the curriculum and teaching to suit children's needs.	.79
	2.	Children have suitable group learning activities.	
	3.	Children are engaged in individualized learning programs.	
Noninclusive	1.	Placing children with learning needs in special schools will prevent them from being discriminated.	.64
	2.	Children with special needs will upset normal classroom routines and progress.	
	3.	Children with special needs are a burden to the teacher in the mainstream classroom.	
	4.	Children with special needs should be taught separately because it is not easy to change the mainstream environment just for them.	

Note: Items were randomized.

indication of acceptable model fit (see Bentler, 1990; Browne & Cudeck, 1993; Byrne, 1998).

Group Comparisons. When the five factors were established, the item scores for each factor were averaged to form a factor score for group comparisons. To answer the research question, a MANOVA was conducted.

The factor scores for the five factors (government, knowledge, efficacy, curriculum, and noninclusive) were the dependent variables. Teacher type (special education teacher of children with intellectual and developmental disabilities, regular teachers in inclusive classrooms, and teachers in regular classrooms), experience (<10 years, >10 years teaching), and the teacher × experience interaction term were the independent variables.

RESULTS

Preliminary Analysis

Table 12.1 presents the scales and their reliabilities estimates. All the five a priori factors had acceptable alpha reliabilities ($\alpha > .60$; Clark & Watson, 1995). The mean factor scores are reported in Table 12.2. It can be seen that the teachers were generally high in knowledge ($M = 3.23$), efficacy ($M = 3.68$), and individualized curriculum ($M = 4.33$), all above the midpoint of 3 on a 5-point scale. However perceived government support was generally low ($M = 2.62$), well below the midpoint; whereas noninclusive attitude was also high ($M = 3.44$), also above the midpoint.

Factor Analysis. Confirmatory factor analysis was conducted forcing each item to load onto its respective factor only (Model 1). This model converged to a proper solution with five distinct factors providing an acceptable fit ($\chi^2 = 373.76$, $df = 160$, $TLI = .908$, $CFI = .922$, $RMSEA = .055$). The parameter estimates are presented in Table 12.2. Model 2 testing a single-factor model did not provide a good fit ($\chi^2 = 1703.92$, $df = 170$, $TLI = .377$, $CFI = .443$, $RMSEA = .144$). Hence Model 1 was supported (Table 12.2). In Model 1, the factor loadings were all acceptable (all > .40). The factor correlations were reasonable, ranging from $-.40$ to $.47$, indicating that all factors were clearly distinguishable from each other.

Several important findings were observed from the latent factor correlations (Table 12.2), one of which was the significantly positive correlation between efficacy and knowledge ($r = .47$). This positive correlation implies that teachers' sense of efficacy is likely to be associated with their knowledge about special educational needs. Another important finding was the negative correlation between teachers' efficacy and noninclusive attitude ($r = -.40$). This implies that the more positive the teachers are about their efficacy in teaching children with special educational needs, the less resistant to inclusion they tend to be. The positive correlation between efficacy and curriculum ($r = .31$) also implies that teachers who are positive about their efficacy are more likely to advocate individualized

Table 12.2. CFA Model

	Government	Knowledge	Efficacy	Curriculum	Noninclusive	Uniqueness
M	2.62	3.23	3.68	4.32	3.46	
SD	(0.65)	(0.60)	(0.43)	(0.53)	(0.57)	
Variable Factor Loadings						
Government1	.71*					.66*
Government2	.76*					.39*
Government3	.84*					.63*
Government4	.86*					.29*
Knowledge1		.76*				.26*
Knowledge2		.79*				.19*
Knowledge3		.59*				.22*
Knowledge4		.72*				.53*
Efficacy1			.51*			.47*
Efficacy2			.70*			.63*
Efficacy3			.66*			.61*
Efficacy4			.44*			.63*
Efficacy5			.41*			.32*
Curriculum1				.66*		.41*
Curriculum2				.80*		.41*
Curriculum3				.78*		.41*
Noninclusive1					.51*	.41*
Noninclusive2					.56*	.41*
Noninclusive3					.43*	.41*
Noninclusive4					.72*	.41*
Factor Correlations						
Knowledge	.46*					
Efficacy	.35*	.47*				
Curriculum	-.21*	.03	.31*			
Noninclusive	.16*	-.03	-.40*	-.16*		

Note: N = 436. Parameters estimates are completely standardized. *p < .05.

261

curriculum. Finally, the positive correlations of government support with knowledge and efficacy (rs = .46 and .35, respectively) seem to suggest that for teachers to feel stronger support from the government, they need to be positive about their knowledge and efficacy.

Group Comparisons

The means and standard deviations of the five factors in different groups are given in Table 12.3. A 3 (type) × 2 (experience) MANOVA was conducted. Apart from the main effect of type on government support which was not statistically significant, $F(2, 430)$ = 2.48, MSE = 0.42, p > .05, all the main effects of type were statistically significant, $Fs(2, 430)$ = 11.63, 15.57, 6.29, and 16.53, respectively for knowledge, efficacy, curriculum, and noninclusive, ps < .05 (Table 12.3). Post-hoc simple contrasts found a consistent pattern showing that special education teachers and teachers in inclusive classrooms were both higher in Knowledge, Efficacy, and Curriculum than teachers in regular classrooms (Table 12.3). In contrast, special education teachers (Ms = 3.38 and 3.29) and teachers in inclusive classrooms (Ms = 3.27 and 3.09) were both lower in noninclusive than teachers in regular classrooms (Ms = 3.52 and 3.60), suggesting that teachers in regular classroom have higher tendencies of resistance to inclusive education.

The main effect of experience was statistically significant for Knowledge, $F(1, 430)$ = 5.04, MSE = 0.34, p < .05, although the effect size was small, η^2 = .01. There was a general pattern showing that more experienced teachers tended to have better knowledge, which was consistent across three teacher types (Table 12.3). The main effects of experience were not significant for any of the other four factors, p > .05. For the type × experience interaction effects, none was statistically significant, indicating that teacher type differences were quite consistent across experience groups whereas differences due to experience were also consistent across teacher types.

DISCUSSION AND IMPLICATIONS

Evidence shows that teachers' attitudes toward inclusion are significantly associated with their self-efficacy and perception of government support regarding special education (Avramidis et al., 2000; Clough & Lindsay, 1991; Ross & Bruce, 2009). In particular, while knowledge and self-efficacy are positively correlated (r = .47) supporting previous research demonstrating positive relations between an individual's ability and sense of com-

Table 12.3. Means and Standard Deviations for 5 Factors by Teacher Type and Teaching Experience

		Total	SEN Teacher		Teacher Inclusive		Teacher Regular		MANOVA Results *p < .05; **p < .001						
			<10yrs	>10yrs	<10yrs	>10yrs	<10yrs	>10yrs	Type (T)		Experience (E)		T x E		MSE
									F	η^2	F	η^2	F	η^2	
	N	436	44	29	39	40	122	162							
Government support	M	2.62	2.70	2.68	2.58	2.63	2.60	2.54	2.48	.01	1.75	.00	0.63	.00	0.42
	SD	(0.65)	(0.60)	(0.57)	(0.66)	(0.65)	(0.90)	(0.64)							
Knowledge	M	3.23	3.29	3.37	3.33	3.62	3.09	3.18	11.63**	.05	5.04*	.01	0.90	.00	0.34
	SD	(0.60)	(0.56)	(0.49)	(0.43)	(0.51)	(0.61)	(0.63)							
Efficacy	M	3.68	3.80	3.77	3.87	3.86	3.61	3.58	15.57**	.07	0.26	.00	0.02	.00	0.17
	SD	(0.43)	(0.37)	(0.36)	(0.37)	(0.40)	(0.41)	(0.47)							
Curriculum	M	4.32	4.49	4.46	4.40	4.44	4.30	4.22	6.29*	.03	0.14	.00	0.46	.00	0.28
	SD	(0.53)	(0.48)	(0.50)	(0.38)	(0.43)	(0.54)	(0.58)							
Noninclusive	M	3.46	3.38	3.29	3.27	3.09	3.52	3.60	16.53**	.07	0.95	.00	2.00	.00	0.30
	SD	(0.57)	(0.50)	(0.60)	(0.50)	(0.63)	(0.52)	(0.57)							

Note: SEN Teacher = Teachers of students with special educational needs. Teacher inclusive = Teachers teaching in inclusive classrooms. Teacher regular = Teachers teaching in regular classrooms.

petence (Craven & Yeung, 2008), self-efficacy was found to be the strongest correlate of attitude toward inclusion ($r = -.40$ with noninclusive; Table 12.2). The positive relation between self-efficacy and advocacy of inclusion is also consistent with previous research (e.g., Hutzler et al., 2005; Westwood, 2013).

In general, Hypothesis 1 was supported. That is, the measure of the five factors of interest (government support, knowledge, efficacy, adapted curriculum, and noninclusive attitude) demonstrated good psychometric properties. The fit of the model was good, the items for each factor loaded appropriately on the designated factor, and the five latent factors were clearly distinguishable from each other. The strength of the CFA model provided us with a strong basis for subsequent group comparisons. Hypothesis 2 was supported. Special education teachers and their collaborating regular teachers in inclusive classrooms were found to display higher perceptions of knowledge ($Ms > 3.18$) and efficacy ($Ms > 3.61$), advocate more individualized curriculum ($Ms > 4.30$), and were less resistant to inclusion ($Ms < 3.52$) than teachers in regular classrooms (Table 12.3). For the research question, as shown in Table 12.3, teachers—irrespective of type—did not seem to have favorable perceptions of government support for inclusion ($Ms < 3$ on a scale of 1 to 5). This implies that either the government need to provide more support or that this kind of support should be clearly made known to teachers in more tangible ways.

Some interesting findings emerged from the CFA model (Table 12.2). First, teachers' knowledge of government policy was found to be positively correlated with their perception of government support ($r = .46$), which is quite logical. It is unclear whether a better knowledge of policy leads to a more favorable perception of government support or better support from the government leads to better knowledge of policy, which would require longitudinal data to resolve. Nevertheless, it seems quite clear that both improved support and enhanced knowledge may work together to bring better benefits.

Second, the correlations of noninclusive attitudes with the other four factors displayed an interesting pattern. Efficacy is clearly the strongest correlate ($r = -.40$). That is, teachers' higher efficacy beliefs about their ability to work with children with varying needs are negatively related to negative attitudes toward inclusion. This implies that by improving teachers' perceived capability of working with children with special educational needs, they would more likely advocate inclusion; and by promoting their acceptance of inclusion, teachers may increase their sense of competence working with children with special educational needs. Although not as strong as efficacy, curriculum is also a significant correlate of noninclusive attitude ($r = -.16$). This suggests that teachers in schools that adapt curriculum and teaching to suit children with special educational needs are more likely to accept inclusion. Nevertheless, the positive correlation between noninclusive attitude and government support is surprising ($r = .16$). The positive correlation suggests that the more supportive the government, as perceived by the teachers, the less likely it is for teachers to adopt a positive attitude toward inclusion. This interesting finding may best be explained in terms of Forlin's (2010) research on some of the implications associated with developing and implementing quality inclusive education. Forlin (2010) has raised concerns about whether increasing bureaucracy, which is often associated with developing and implementing inclusive practices, serves to support or hinder inclusion. Specifically Forlin (2010) states "A top-down bureaucratic approach to education in Hong Kong makes it challenging for schools" (p. 181). When governments are perceived to mandate laws and monitor the details and implementation of these, teachers perceive that they have limited control and less flexibility in their classrooms. In this study, perhaps the teachers viewed government support in terms of external monitoring and implementing mandated policies which may lead them to adopt less positive attitudes toward inclusion. In recent years, some international education systems have been responsive to this concern from the profession and to address it, they have been proactive in minimizing their external monitoring. An alternative explanation to teachers forming less positive attitudes toward inclusion with government support is possible. Perhaps government support through the increase in resources promotes wider inclusion of children and consequently teachers struggle with the challenge of supporting children with more complex special educational needs who previously did not attend their education setting. Perhaps those teachers who strongly advocate inclusion take more of a critical stance on government support and identify shortcomings more readily. The finding is interesting and warrants attention in further research studies.

Third, teachers' sense of efficacy was found to be related to their schools' adaptation of curriculum to suit individual needs ($r = .31$). This implies that curriculum adaptation may benefit from the expertise of teachers who have a high level of efficacy, and through the practice of adapting curriculum to suit diverse needs, teachers may build their capacity and a sense of efficacy at the same time.

Fourth, the significantly negative correlations of noninclusive attitude to efficacy and curriculum ($rs = -.40$ and $-.16$) together with the significantly positive ($r = .16$) and near-zero ($r = -.03$) correlations to government support and knowledge of policy imply that to promote advocacy for inclusion, the most salient are teacher- and teaching-related factors. Whereas initiatives to increase knowledge of policy may have no direct bearing on attitudes toward inclusion, further investment in terms of services and resources may even downplay the concept and practice of inclusion.

The group comparisons also found some interesting patterns. Consistent across all five factors, teachers' years of teaching experience did not seem to be a significant factor that makes any difference. The only significant main effect of experience was found for knowledge of policy (Table 12.3) but the effect was small ($\eta^2 = .01$), and none of the interaction effects were statistically significant. Hence the group differences attributed to teacher type are quite consistent for all five factors irrespective of teaching experience.

Consistent across four factors (knowledge, efficacy, curriculum, and noninclusive), teachers who worked in inclusive classrooms (special education and regular teachers) had more favorable perceptions (i.e., more positive knowledge, efficacy, and curriculum; more negative noninclusive). However, for perceptions of government support, they were equally unfavorable (Table 12.3). As previous researchers have suggested, regular teachers who work in schools adopting inclusive education have many opportunities to talk with special education teachers, work together, and evaluate each other's teaching practices (McLaughlin & Talbert, 2001) and thereby benefit from an increase in their level of efficacy, knowledge and positive attitudes toward children with special educational needs. This finding has an important practical implication. Collaborating with special education teachers appears critically important for preschool regular teachers, given the specific challenges linked to the preschool teaching environment in Hong Kong, such as a lack of government support and lack of preparation (Cheuk & Hatch, 2007), at least from the teachers' perspective. Collaboration provides regular and special education teachers with reinforcement and expands their knowledge of pedagogy, all of which increase teachers' efficacy in teaching young children.

Mittler (2000) argued that even for teachers who have the knowledge and skills necessary for the inclusive classroom, they may not be confident with their competence. A similar notion was also suggested by Slavica (2010) who found that more than half of the teachers who had attended seminars and workshops still claimed to be unprepared for inclusive education. One may argue that apart from knowledge and skills, regular education teachers need authentic experiences with children to build up their sense of competence working in inclusive settings. Indeed, a study by Leroy and Simpson (1996) showed that when teachers' experience with children with special educational needs is increased, their confidence of teaching these children was also raised. Nevertheless, our data did not support this claim. For teachers in inclusive classrooms, whether special education or regular teachers, years of teaching did not make any difference for all factors examined here. Instead, as Avramidis et al. (2000) have suggested, it is probably through the implementation of inclusion and the collaborative experience in such settings that teachers' expertise is developed, resulting in a more positive attitude toward inclusion.

Hence, direct experience is probably more important for increasing teachers' efficacy and confidence, but when teachers teach in an inclusive classroom, it is necessary to provide adequate supports from special education professionals. In the present study, the comparison of the views held by different types of teachers revealed that special education teachers and regular education teachers in inclusive classroom were more positive in knowledge, efficacy and curriculum than teachers in traditional regular classroom. Also, they showed lower tendencies of resistance to inclusive education when compared with their counterparts. The findings imply that special education teachers are crucial in the implementation of inclusive education. The development of more inclusive classrooms requires teachers to cater for diverse student needs through the adaptation or differentiation of the curriculum (Forlin, 2004). However, there is a big gap between what regular teachers know and do in regular classrooms and what needs to be done in an inclusive classroom. In an attempt to bridge this gap, the collaboration between special education and regular teachers has become an essential element of successful inclusion. As such, coteaching opportunities and programs of mentorship and communities of learning amongst colleagues may be a helpful strategy.

Generally speaking, special education teachers are more familiar with special educational needs than regular education teachers. Their knowledge and skills about how to teach children with a specific disability (e.g., intellectual disability) can help teachers in regular classes develop their capability to be inclusive. As traditionally special education teachers are expected to be responsible to cater for children with special educational needs while regular education teachers will take the responsibility of catering for all students in the class, both special education and regular education teachers may have a generally clear role to play. However, these roles are not always clear cut. Therefore, it is necessary for both types of teachers to collegially revisit and clarify their own role and responsibility when working together in an inclusive classroom. Communication between educators is crucial for ensuring good quality teaching and learning for children with special educational needs (Barrell, 2010). Despite competing pressures of the teaching profession, it is important to find the time to engage in collaborative discussions because of the benefits associated with the conversations. "Collaborative discussion of pedagogy supports a move from a focus on individual teacher practices to broader teaching and learning issues and collective purposes" (Deppeler, 2012, p. 132). Interestingly, the effects of teaching experience did not seem to be a significant factor in the present study. Hence, while more experienced teachers tend to have better knowledge regardless of their inclusive experience, it is unclear whether more experienced teachers could contribute positively to building the capacity of less experienced teachers to benefit inclusive education.

CONCLUSION

The study has identified the relations of some important factors of concern to teachers regarding inclusive classrooms. Among those influential factors, teachers' self-efficacy and exposure to curriculum adaptation seem to be most salient in relation to their views toward inclusion. Findings regarding teachers in varying settings suggest that collaboration of special education and regular education teachers may enhance the knowledge and efficacy of teachers, adaptation of curriculum, and a more positive attitude to inclusion, all of which will benefit the promotion of inclusive education. The main target of such strategies is the regular teacher who does not work in a designated inclusive setting, although still works with children with special educational needs—as they appear to rate their knowledge, advocacy for individualized curriculum and inclusion lowest when compared to their colleagues.

Changing attitudes is difficult, particularly for those teachers whose efficacy and knowledge are low. The typical way of attempting to bring developments in inclusive education is to focus on improving teachers' knowledge and skills. Providing new knowledge for teachers has been seen as necessary, but not sufficient for improvement. When teachers acquire new knowledge and they are supported in implementing new practice, then attitudes and efficacy will change over time. In the same token, if teachers already have positive attitudes and they are supported in implementing new practices, then they are motivated to acquire new knowledge and skills.

The present study has significant implications for early childhood policymakers, school leaders, educators, and researchers alike. Since current reforms in inclusive education in Hong Kong have focused mainly on improving the training of teachers, the findings of the present study recommend that promoting collaboration between special education and regular education teachers may be a potential avenue to support and improve teachers' efficacy and attitudes.

Teachers' views on inclusion continue to be a potent construct in empirical studies of teachers' inclusive practices. The current study provides a sound measure for future research to implement to examine these perspectives. The research efforts in the field of preschool inclusive education should continue investigating specific features of the collaboration that may enhance teachers' self-efficacy and advocacy of inclusion, as well as the perception toward, and role of government support in Hong Kong.

ACKNOWLEDGMENT

This research was supported by the Democratic Alliance for the Betterment and Progress of Hong Kong. The authors would like to thank the school principals and staff involved, especially Ms Florence Ng who has contributed to various components of the research, and also Zhu Chen who has assisted with the manuscript.

REFERENCES

Ainscow, M. (1997) Towards inclusive schooling. *British Journal of Special Education, 24*(1), 3–6.

Avramidis, E., Bayliss, P., & Burden, R. (2000). A Survey into mainstream teachers' attitudes towards the inclusion of children with special education needs in the ordinary school in one local education authority. *Educational Psychology, 20*(2), 191–211.

Avramidis, E., & Kalyva, E. (2007). The influence of teaching experience and professional development on Greek teachers' attitudes towards inclusion. *European Journal of Special Needs Education, 22*(4), 367–389.

Avramidis, E., & Norwich, B. (2002) Teachers' attitudes towards integration/inclusion: A review of the literature. *European Journal of Special Needs Education, 17*(2), 129–147.

Baker-Ericzen, M. S., Mueggenborg, M. G., & Shea, M. M. (2009). Impact of trainings on child care providers' attitudes and perceived competence toward inclusion. What factors are associated with change? *Topics in Early Childhood Special Education, 28*(4), 196–208.

Barrell, R. (2010). The importance of interpersonal skills. In F. Hallett & G. Hallett (Eds.), *Transforming the role of the SENCO: Achieving the National Award for SEN Coordination* (pp. 168–173). Berkshire, England: Open University Press.

Bentler, P. M. (1990). Comparative fit indexes in structural models. *Psychological Bulletin, 107*(2), 238–246.

Black-Hawkins, K., Florian, L., & Rouse, M. (2007). *Achievement and inclusion in schools.* London, England: Routledge.

Blanco Guijarro, R. (2009). Conceptual framework of inclusive education. In C. Acedo, M. Amadio, & R. Opertti (Eds.), *Defining an inclusive education agenda: Reflections around the 48th session of the International Conference on Education* (pp. 11–20). Geneva, Switzerland: UNESCO IBE.

Boe, E. E., Shin, S., & Cook, L. H. (2007). Does teacher preparation matter for beginning teachers in either special or general education? *The Journal of Special Education, 41*, 158–170.

Bouillet, D. (2013). Some aspects of collaboration in inclusive education—Teachers' experiences. *C.E.P.S. Journal, 30*(2), 93–117.

Brady, J., & Opertti, R. (2011). Developing inclusive teachers from an inclusive curricular perspective. *Prospects, 41*(3), 459–472.

Browne, M. W., & Cudeck, R. (1993). Alternative ways of assessing model fit. In K. A. Bollen & J. S. Long (Eds.), *Testing structural equation models* (pp. 136–162). Beverly Hills, CA: SAGE.

Bruneau-Balderrama, O. (1997). Inclusion: Making it work for teachers, too. *Clearing House, 70*(6), 328–331.

Bryant, D. P., Smith, D. D., & Bryant, B. R. (2008). *Teaching students with special needs in inclusive classrooms.* Boston, MA: Pearson Education.

Buell, M. J., Hallam, R., Gamel-McCormick, M., & Scheer, S. (1999). A survey of general and special education teachers' perceptions and inservice needs concerning inclusion. *International Journal of Disability, Development and Education, 46*(2), 143–156.

Buysse, V., Wesley, P., Keyes, L., & Bailey, D. (1996). Assessing the comfort zone of child care teachers in serving young children with disabilities. *Journal of Early Intervention, 20*(3), 189–203.

Byrne, B. M. (1998). *Structural equation modeling with LISREL, PRELIS, and SIMPLIS: Basic concepts, applications, and programming.* Mahwah, NJ: Erlbaum.

Campbell, J., & Gilmore, L. (2003). Changing student teachers' attitudes toward disability and inclusion. *Journal of Intellectual and Developmental Disability, 28*(4), 369–379.

Cheuk, J., & Hatch, J. A. (2007). Teachers' perceptions of integrated kindergarten programs in Hong Kong. *Early Child Development and Care, 177*(4), 417–432.

Clark, L. A., & Watson, D. (1995). Constructing validity: Basic issues in objective scale development. *Psychological Assessment, 7*(3), 309–319.

Clough, P., & Lindsay, G. (1991). *Integration and the support service: Changing roles in special education.* London, England: Routledge.

Craven, R. G., & Yeung, A. S. (2008). International best practice in effective educational interventions: Why self-concept matters and examples from bullying, peer support, and reading research. In D. M. McInerney, V. E. Shawn, & M. Dowson (Eds.), *Research on sociocultural influences on motivation and learning. Vol. 8: Teaching and learning: International best practice* (pp. 267–294). Greenwich, CT: Information Age.

Deppeler, J. (2012). Developing inclusive practices: Innovation through collaboration. In C. Boyle & K. Topping (Eds.). *What works in inclusion?* (pp.125–138). Berkshire, England: Open University Press.

DeVore, S., & Russell, K. (2007). Early childhood education and care for children with disabilities: Facilitating inclusive practice. *Early Childhood Education Journal, 35*(2), 189–198.

Department for Education and Skills. (1997). *SEN Green Paper: Excellence for all.* London, England: Author.

Education Bureau. (2009). *Comprehensive child development service.* Hong Kong, China: Author.

Education Department. (2000). Towards Integration [Compact disk]. Hong Kong, China: CDC.

Forlin, C. (2001). Inclusion: Identifying potential stressors for regular class teachers. *Educational Research, 43*(3), 235–245.

Forlin, C. (2004). Promoting inclusivity in Western Australian schools. *International Journal of Inclusive Education, 8*(2), 185–202.

Forlin, C. (2010). Developing and implementing quality inclusive education in Hong Kong: Implications for teacher education. *Journal of Research in Special Education Needs*, *10*(s1), 177–184.

Gavish, B., & Shimoni, S. (2011). Elementary school teachers' beliefs and perceptions about the inclusion of children with special needs in their classrooms. *Journal of International Special Needs Education*, *14*, 49–59.

Goodwin, R. (1999). *Personal relationships across cultures*. London, England: Routledge.

Hamaidi, D., Homidi, M., & Reyes, L. V. (2012). International view of inclusive education: A comparative study of early childhood educators' perceptions in Jordan, United Arab Emirates, and The United States of America. *International Journal of Special Education*, *27*(2), 94–101.

Hegarty, S. (1994). Keys to integration. In C. Meijer, S. J. Pijl, & S. Hegarty (Eds.), *New perspectives in special education: A six-country study* (pp. 79–94). New York, NY: Routledge.

Hutzler, Y., Zach, S., & Gafni, O. (2005). Physical education students' attitudes and self-efficacy towards the participation of children with special needs in regular classes. *European Journal of Special Needs Education*, *20*(3), 309–327.

Jordan, A., Schwartz, E., & McGhie-Richmond, D. (2009). Preparing teachers for inclusive classrooms. *Teaching and Teacher Education*, *25*(4), 535–542.

Jöreskog, K. G., & Sörbom, D. (2006). *LISREL 8.80 for Windows*. Lincolnwood, IL: Scientific Software International.

Jorgensen, C. M., Schuh, M. C., & Nisbet, J. (2006). *The inclusion facilitator's guide*. Baltimore, MD: Paul H. Brookes.

Kavale, K. A., & Forness, S. R. (2000). The great divide in special education: Inclusion, ideology, and research. In T. E. Scruggs & M. A. Mastropieri (Eds.), *Advances in learning and behavioral disabilities* (Vol. 14, pp. 179–215). Stamford, CT: JAI Press.

Klor, G. (2007). *Getting to know special ed: The general educator's essential guide*. Horsham, PA: LRP.

Kniveton, B. H. (2004). Adolescent perceptions of the importance of teachers as a therapeutic support in coping with their problems. *Emotional and Behavioural Differences*, *9*(4), 239–248.

Leroy, B., & Simpson, C. (1996). Improving student outcomes through inclusive education. *Support for Learning*, *11*, 32–36

Lindsay, G. (2003). Inclusive education: A critical perspective. *British Journal of Special Education*, *30*(1), 3–12.

McLaughlin, M., & Talbert, J. (2001). *Professional communities and the work of high school teaching*. Chicago, IL: University of Chicago Press.

Mittler, P. (2000). *Working towards inclusion: Social contexts*. London, England: David Foulton.

Minke, K. M., Bear, G. G., & Deemer, S. M. (1996). Teachers' experiences with inclusive classrooms: Implications for special education reform. *The Journal of Special Education*, *30*(2), 152–186.

Mitchell, L. C., & Hegde, A. V. (2007). Beliefs and practices of in-service preschool teachers in inclusive settings: Implications for personnel preparation. *Journal of Early Childhood Teacher Education*, *28*(4), 353–366.

Paliokosta, P., & Blandford, S. (2010). Inclusion in school: A policy, ideology or lived experience? Similar findings in diverse school cultures. *British Journal of Learning Support, 25*(4), 179–186.

Purcell, M., Horn, E., & Palmer, S. (2007). A qualitative study of the initiation and continuation of preschool inclusion programs. *Exceptional Children, 74*, 85–99.

Rakap, S., & Kaczmarek, L. (2010). Teachers' attitudes towards inclusion in Turkey. *European Journal of Special Needs Education, 25*(1), 59–75.

Robinson, L., & Buly, R. (2007). Breaking the language barrier: Promoting collaboration between general and special educators. *Teacher Education Quarterly, 34*(3), 83–94.

Ross, J. A., & Bruce, C. D. (2009). Student achievement effects of technology-supported remediation of understanding of fractions. *International Journal of Mathematical Education in Science and Technology, 40*(6), 713–727.

Ross-Hill, R. (2009). Teacher attitude towards inclusion practices and special needs students. *Journal of Research in Special Educational Needs, 9*(3), 188–198.

Scruggs, T., & Mastropieri, M. A. (1996). Teacher perceptions of mainstreaming/inclusion, 1958-1995: A research synthesis. *Exceptional Children, 63*(1), 59–74.

Sharma, U., Loreman, T., & Forlin, C. (2012). Measuring teacher efficacy to implement inclusive practices. *Journal of Research in Special Educational Needs, 12*(1), 12–21

Slavica, P. (2010). Inclusive education: Proclamations or reality (primary school teachers' view). *US-China Education Review, 7*(10), 62–69.

Smith, M. K., & Smith K. E. (2000). "I believe in inclusion, but ...": Regular education early childhood teachers' perceptions of successful inclusion. *Journal of Research in Childhood Education, 14*(2), 161–180.

Social Welfare Department. (2004). *Handbook on rehabilitation services.* Retrieved from   http://www.swd.gov.hk/tc/index/site_pubsvc/page_rehab/sub_listofserv/id_serpresch/

Sukbunpant, S., Arthur-Kelly, M., & Dempsey, I. (2013). Thai preschool teachers' views about inclusive education for young children with disabilities. *International Journal of Inclusive Education, 17*(10), 1–13.

UNESCO. (2005). *Guidelines for inclusion: Ensuring access to education for all.* Paris, France: Author.

Vaillant, D. (2011). Preparing teachers for inclusive education in Latin America. *Prospects, 41*(3), 385–398.

Valeo, A. (2008). Inclusive education support systems: Teacher and administrator views. *International Journal of Special Education, 23*(2), 8–16.

Webb, P., Neumann, T, M., & Jones. L. C. (2004). Politics, school improvement, and social justice: A triadic model of teacher leadership. *The Educational Forum, 68*(3), 254–262.

Westwood, P. (2013). *Inclusive and adaptive teaching: Meeting the challenge of diversity in classroom.* New York, NY: Routledge.

CHAPTER 13

PARENT'S CAPABILITIES AND INSTITUTIONAL CONDITIONS FOR CHILDREN WITH INTELLECTUAL DISABILITIES IN AUSTRIAN SCHOOLS

Michaela Kramann and Gottfried Biewer

This chapter highlights parental views on the process of school placement. In the 1990s Austria established a system of integrative classes which get supported by additional teaching resources. The parents got the legal right to select whether their children with disabilities should attend integrative or special school settings. From a capabilities approach perspective, this system could deliver a chance for free choice of educational and life options. But the analyses of interviews with parents reveals hidden institutional factors which undermine parents' school choice. Whereas special schools deliver a wide range of therapies and support, mainstream schools confront parents with additional problems as transport, missing day care in the afternoon, insufficient material equipment and often they also have to be persuaded to receive children with disabilities. It depends on the engagement of the school staff and parents if emerging problems can be solved. Only those parents who have the resources to engage in their children's school career in

Inclusive Education for Students with Intellectual Disabilities,
pp. 273–293
Copyright © 2015 by Information Age Publishing
All rights of reproduction in any form reserved.

a certain way, are able to act as advocates for their children within a selective school system. Hence, the legal right of choice between alternative ways of education does not provide equivalent alternatives. From an institutional perspective, the unequal conditions between inclusive and special classes are a barrier for societal development toward equity in education.

INTRODUCTION

It is incredible how much time we spent on things like making an appeal against some decisions. You have to start immediately to look for another school because you cannot send your child to a school where there is a principal against whom you started legal actions because your child will suffer. (Parent comment)

The demand for inclusive education is a global one (Artiles & Dyson, 2006), but the narratives of people involved in this process of institutional change, reveal hidden effects. This chapter describes the experiences of parents with the developing integrative education system in Austria's capital city, Vienna, and focuses on school placement issues. Though this contribution refers only to data collected in Vienna, they are embedded in an international and comparative study and the results generated may be of interest beyond this national context and lead to a better understanding of the local mechanisms that undermine the implementation of inclusive education.

HISTORY OF CHANGE FOR STUDENTS WITH INTELLECTUAL DISABILITIES IN RELATION TO EQUITY ISSUES IN EDUCATION

Austria, with only 8.5 million inhabitants, is a small country in the center of Europe; it has a strong tradition of special needs education and the current education system includes integration and special school settings. The social and cultural model by Artiles, Kozleski, and Waitoller (2011) helps to connect historical developments in education systems with equity issues. Some main structures of the current Austrian school system have strong historical roots that can even be traced back to the era of the Danube monarchy, and legislation from the late 18th and the 19th centuries (Luciak & Biewer, 2011), of which the decision to have free and compulsory education was one.

When referring to schooling of children with disabilities, Austria was one of the first European countries where ambitious educational models emerged. Some schools were able to receive state support, like the first school for the deaf that was founded by the Austrian emperor Joseph II in

1779 (Ellger-Rüttgardt, 2008), whereas others only survived through private and church funding.

One of the most remarkable educational experiments for children with intellectual disabilities was undertaken in the 19th century by Jan Daniel Georgens and Heinrich Marianus Deinhardt. It was the common education of both children with and without intellectual disabilities and was commenced in 1856 and existed in several areas in and near Vienna for 9 years until 1865 when it had to be discontinued due to economic reasons. This approach also led to a series of lectures in the Austrian Academy of Science in the late 1850s (Biewer, 2010), which were written down and printed in two books of more than 900 pages (Georgens & Deinhardt, 1861, 1863). This publication was regarded as the first elaborated conceptual design on scientific special education in German-speaking countries.

It is remarkable that the first draft of a publication on scientific remedial education was connected with a practical experiment on the common education of children with and without intellectual disabilities. Although it led to a sophisticated theory, this ambitious model was unable to survive in the social and educational environment of Austria in the 19th century. In the following decades children with intellectual disabilities were cared for in clerical or state institutions, led by clergymen or physicians. Often the education offered was of poor quality. Nevertheless, the strong foundations of Austrian remedial education since the late 18th century gave rise to some ambitious educational models at the beginning of the 20th century and in the 1920s and 1930s (Möckel, 2007).

A shift came in the year 1938 when Austria became part of the German Reich. In the early 1940s all inhabitants of institutions for people with intellectual disabilities were murdered under the national-socialist euthanasia program. Only a small number of persons who remained in their families survived the Third Reich (Ellger-Rüttgardt, 2008; Möckel, 2007). Hence, after the World War II in 1945, there were very few persons with intellectual disabilities still alive in Germany and Austria (Klee, 2001).

It took more than one decade for societal awareness of the necessity of education for children with intellectual disabilities emerged. It was the work of parents' associations that in the 1960s and 1970s led to schools for children with intellectual disabilities to be opened all over the country. Most were government funded and some were run by the church. Over the years they became well equipped and parents were content with the overall service provision (Biewer, 2010).

In the 1980s Austria and the other two German-speaking neighboring countries, Germany and Switzerland, had a well-developed, countrywide special school system that was regarded as a success by state institutions as well as by teachers and parents. But the 1980s also was a time of doubt as to whether special education really was the best way to educate children with disabilities. Starting in the late 1970s, parent initiatives proclaimed new manners of education and united with progressive teachers. In 1984, the first integration class for children with and without disabilities was established; without a legal basis it was the result of concerted action by parents, reform-orientated teachers and the media (Anlanger, 1993). In the following years an increasing number of integration classes were established as pilot projects, and in 1993 school legislation was changed. As a result of the parents' movement for integration, parents had the right to select whether their child should attend a special school or receive education in an integrative setting. This important change in school legislation shifted educational pathways for children with disabilities and brought sustainable effects over the next two decades. In the following years integration classes of four to six children with special educational needs were established all over the country. They were equipped with two teachers, a regular teacher and a full-time special education teacher. This type of integration class still exists today. Compared with integration in other countries, the provision of professional personal resources is relatively high (Biewer, 2006).

After the year 2000, discussion on inclusive education also reached Austria. Before, there had been no awareness of the difference between integrative and inclusive education structures. Austria was among the 88 States Parties, which signed the UN Convention on the Rights of Persons with Disabilities (UNCRPD) and its Optional Protocol on March 30, 2007, the day of submission. In September 2008, Austria ratified both documents, and with this legal act Austria committed to inclusive education, as mentioned in Article 24 of the UNCRPD (Biewer, 2011). Discussion on the consequences of inclusion for the reform of the hitherto integrative system of education for children with disabilities that had started a few years earlier is still going on. As a consequence of the discussion on the implementation of the UNCRPD there is a debate on the demand for the abolition of special schools. Representatives of the special school system, as well as some parents, argue for free choice between different school types, also because of the lack of resources in current integration classes, and the fear that the implementation of inclusive school structures will worsen the support situation.

The legal right of parents to select between integration and special schooling may be regarded as a real choice between different options and an expression of freedom which could have the potential to overcome a conflict between two totally different educational pathways—the segregative and the inclusive one.

Nevertheless, state laws and school administrative regulations require individual statements on students as having special educational needs in order for there to be additional educational provision in integrative classrooms. So the philosophy of integrative education is to work with two different groups. The inclusive approach, that all schools shall change their structure in order to meet all learners' needs is, in fact, more a claim with little impact on current school structures.

Furthermore, the integrative school system produces certain effects that have an impact on student's educational trajectories. The "hidden" preconditions for enabling parents to send their child to an integration class are overlooked and not made transparent so that the impression of freedom of choice remains. Therefore, it is argued that the freedom of "choice" between the different school types cannot be realized by all parents because of underlying structures within the school system, which undermine the parents' decision on the school placement of their children. Hence, it will be shown that equity in education is not provided for all in this system of "choice" in Austria.

THEORETICAL FRAMEWORK

Equity issues are strongly connected with political philosophy. In this area the capabilities approach (Nussbaum, 2011), developed by Sen (1992/ 2009) and Nussbaum (2007), can provide a new view on disability. Though Sen's capability approach was developed to analyze different concepts in a welfare economy, it has the potential to be combined with disability issues (Mitra, 2006). Terzi (2010) used the capabilities approach to develop a new perspective on disability and education.

The situation where children attend separate or inclusive settings may appear as a simple fact, but from a capabilities perspective, this may have different meanings. Sen stated that starvation could be the effect of the absence of food as a result of poverty. In this case there is no choice. The same physiological functions could also result from a decision to fast on religious or other grounds. In this case the person had a choice.

If you transfer this view to the field of education, it may be the question of whether parents really had a choice between two options or if the parental decision resulted from constraints, produced by the education system. Consistently, the choice of possibilities offered in a given society realizing what one values to do and to be, is at the center of interest. So it is worth considering the narratives of parents on the school placement of their children.

METHODOLOGICAL ISSUES IN A COMPARATIVE STUDY

The CLASDISA project[1] looks at the life world of children with disabilities and their micro systems. Based on the International Classification of

Functioning, Disability and Health, Children & Youth Version (WHO, 2007) where participation is defined as "involvement in a life situation," the research project CLASDISA investigates children with disabilities (hearing, visual, physical, intellectual impairment) in education in countries with different societal and cultural backgrounds (Ethiopia, Thailand, and Austria). Therefore, barriers to and facilitators of the participation of students with disabilities in school life are identified and described from several perspectives (based on case studies of children, their parents and teachers). Although we describe here the full CLASDISA project, this chapter represents an initial dissemination effort and will more specifically focus on the perspective of the parents forming the Austrian sample.

In collecting and analyzing qualitative data as well as in developing theory, the project refers to a grounded theory methodology (Bryant & Charmaz, 2007). Due to grounded theory methodology, theories shall emerge from the data by means of a system of coding, memo writing and continuous comparison of data and results of analyses. For this research the constructivist version of the grounded theory of Charmaz (2006) led the investigation. Quotations from interview texts were the subject of initial, focused and axial coding, until saturation of the theoretical categories were able to be achieved. The project used the qualitative data analysis software Atlas.ti, and the following contribution will present some findings, using a few cases for demonstrating the data-based results. More than other grounded theory methodology versions the constructivist approach of Charmaz (2006) regards researchers and participants as co-constructors of theory.

The volume of qualitative data that emerged in the project was large and it was collected at different stages during the research process. At the end, the data set included more than 100 narratives and guided interviews from each country with children with disabilities, their parents and teachers. In order to gather the children's perspective, adapted techniques (e.g., the use of Playmobil School, cue cards) were developed (see, e.g., Darbyshire, MacDougall, & Schiller, 2005). Additionally, interviews with experts, as well as with stakeholders in the field of disability and education, document analysis and observations were added in order to obtain further information about the cases involved. Using a mixed-methods approach, quantitative data (questionnaires for parents and teachers) was also collected for affirmative purposes.

Although this contribution refers only to a small number of cases, the content is the result of the comparison of the data in three different countries. It is embedded in the analyses of the large data sets. The findings from Austria seem to be country specific, but they also resulted from a comparison between the findings in the two other countries. Due to the grounded theory methodology the respective cases were selected through theoretical sampling and represent a specific issue of the findings from the project. In this contribution the conflict between parents and the Austrian school system will be demonstrated. Hence, the focus is on the Austrian data. The grounded theory approach enables the construction of meaning and the development of a theory together with the participants in the course of simultaneous data collection and analysis that is still ongoing in Vienna. The field researcher went to the field and started to search for comprehensive cases (including children with disabilities, at least one of their parents and a teacher) in order to gain insights from several perspectives into the participation of children with disabilities in school. Children with physical, visual, hearing and intellectual disabilities were included, some also being described as having social-emotional problems, cultural and language differences or multiple disabilities. In order to be able to contrast the different views on participation of children with disabilities in school a relatively diverse sample was collected. In the end, 22 children in compulsory education between the ages of 7 and 13 were interviewed, 16 comprehensive cases (children, parent, teacher) took part in the study and additional interviews were collected (e.g. principals). Figure 13.1 demonstrates the diversity of the Austrian children that were interviewed in regard to diversity categories like gender, first language spoken and the school type they attended.

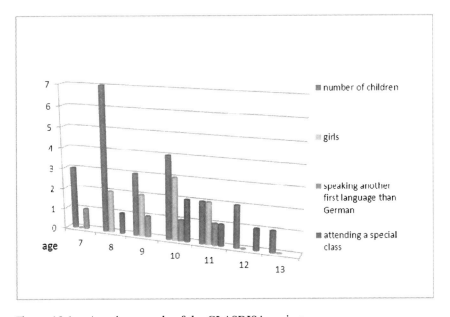

Figure 13.1.   Austrian sample of the CLASDISA project.

Nevertheless, several groups of people were difficult to reach and therefore (almost) missing in the sample, namely, parents with rare or no contact with the school and people who had problems with the German language and verbal communication. Especially those children with intellectual disabilities who were regarded by the school as being unable to make their "voice" heard were not submitted to the sample in the first place. It was necessary to clarify that the ability of communication was not a precondition for choosing children as participants.

Already after the first narrative and guided interviews about the participation of children in school (using overall questions in the guided interviews about school, material and assistive devices, teachers, peers and wishes for the future) social participation and the role of parents as a facilitating factor for children's school achievement and placement was highlighted. Hence, theory development focused on these topics in the subsequent interviews and theoretical sampling was also done with regard to the handling of school-parents-cooperation and placement, as well as to social participation of the children in school, which was the most important topic for the children.

Although the analysis is still ongoing, some categories and memo writing already reveal interesting insights into parents' influence on their children's educational opportunities. Especially the categories "fighting for the child," "highlighting engagement," "searching for information," or "receiving information" and "realizing/investing in educational opportunities for the child" will be demonstrated in the next sections with regard to school placement.

Therefore, the following presentation of intermediary results is based on the narratives of parents about school-parents cooperation and school choice in Austria. In order to demonstrate the view of parents of children with intellectual disabilities, examples from two cases are provided as illustration. Nevertheless, the problems with the school system seemed to be rather similar in all groups and the categories were developed on the basis of all interviews. Theory building has not yet been completed, but the insights based on the reported narratives of parents and teachers already provided some important insights into a school system which privileges certain parents and their children more than others when it comes to the freedom of school choice. These insights are interesting in their own right as a valuable topic for discussion and reflection with regard to the equity of education, and not just as the final results of the study. The last section will reflect on equal access to education of children with intellectual disabilities and possible solutions to overcome inequality.

PARENTAL PERSPECTIVES

In the following sections it will be demonstrated how parents handle challenges when it comes to choosing a school for their child.

Parents Being Engaged in the Choice of School

The category "highlighting engagement" is based on teachers and parents' narratives about the importance of personal engagement on the part of teachers as well as on that of parents for children's achievement. The relevance of parental engagement was emphasized, and parents were mentioned as one, if not the most important facilitating, factor for children's participation in school, as well as for children's school success by both parents and teachers. It will be demonstrated that this engagement already starts with parental influence in their children's school placement.

The following interview sequence places us in the live experience of a mother when talking about different types of access to education for her children, one with intellectual disabilities, the other one "healthy," as she terms it.

> My second child is 'healthy' and attends an academic secondary school in Vienna ... you know, everything works automatically. That hurts. Because I have two different children and when talking about the one ["healthy"] child a phone call is enough [for being registered in school]. It just works. When talking about the other child [the one with an intellectual disability] each step has to be fought for, whether it's the administration, school barriers etc.

This quotation demonstrates parents have to engage differently to ensure the school placement of their children when one child does not fit into the regular school system as easily as others do.

According to parents and teachers' narratives, the influence of parents starts with the will and the interest to engage in their children's school lives. When people are perceived as not having this "interest" in the child they are judged very negatively by those who practice this sort of engagement, as has already been illustrated by others (see, for example, Ong-Dean, 2009). Nevertheless, we need to ask whether it is just the lack of "interest" or if it is more than that, which prevents parents from engaging in the school lives of their children. The project sample consists mainly of parents with a great deal of contact with the school. Looking at parents who described their engagement in school, the following characteristics were found: such parents believed in the important role of education for their children's future and invested in finding an appropriate school. School placement is an important factor that may facilitate or hinder the participation of children with disabilities in further education and employment (Powell, 2003), and these parents were quite aware of this. Additionally, the parents who fought for their children's school careers believed in their own power to realize change for the benefit of their children and sometimes even for other children who faced similar challenges. Handling the disability of their children was something they accepted to a certain extent but they also knew that the situation of their children could be greatly influenced, and took this as their responsibility. The parents considered themselves to be advocates for their children, and thus were able to and had to have an impact on the children's future lives in the best possible way, including the important issue of their school careers.

As has already been stated in relation to parental involvement in school (Hornby & Lafaele, 2011), parents' belief in their role in their children's education, parents' belief in their own ability to work together effectively with school, as well as parents' belief in the possibility of influencing the development of their children in school, have a big impact on parental involvement in school. This was also obvious from the CLAS-DISA project when looking at parents who engaged in their children's school achievements and also in school placement. Hence, parents who were aware of their power, believed in the importance of education, the changeability of disability and school achievement, and in their own ability and duty to decide what was best for their children's education (even when considering information from "experts"), showed the sort of engagement which was said to be necessary for supporting the school success of children with disabilities. In the following sections we consider the activities with which parents engaged, starting with the acquisition of knowledge.

Gaining Knowledge about Education Possibilities

Before deciding if a certain school was a good place for one's child, parents had to know their selection criteria, such as the distance of the school from home, good team teaching in integration classes, and they had to search for a school which fulfilled these wishes. The category "searching for and receiving information" applies to interview sequences in which parents were talking about their struggle in gaining relevant information for their decision on school placement and support. Parents stated that information was not easily accessible, and without the appropriate knowledge, they said it was difficult to orient themselves in the education system.

> Because we heard someone say: "Oh yes, they have a list [of schools that offer integration]." But it's very difficult to get this information and we're really, we constantly have to talk to people.

Therefore, the above mentioned "engaged" parents were talking about their active search for information, using the Internet as well as social (e.g. friends, other parents), institutional (e.g. therapists, kindergarten teachers) or even their professional networks. Furthermore, they were describing their contact with the Ministry of Education, their engagement in meeting principals and their personal visits to schools in order to explore the school situation. Especially experiences by trusted others (also therapists) or their own were seen as more reliable than official information like the school homepages when searching for a school. In other words, information was sought from all sorts of more or less valued sources.

Moreover, knowledge as a basis for argument in favor of the schools, classes and curricula of one's choice was sought when it was unable to be found right from the outset. Some parents even went through legal texts to obtain information and prepare themselves for discussions with education experts. Indeed, the language used by parents in the interviews was full of legal expressions and arguments, as well as expert knowledge, for example, regarding the disability of the child or the school system and rights in Austria. Parents acquired a great deal of knowledge, which they regarded as important for performing their role as advocates for their children.

Other parents, on the other hand, reported on several barriers to obtaining relevant information, such as being isolated and not having well-informed networks. Another barrier mentioned was not speaking and understanding the language in which the information was provided and communication was taking place. This might not just be true when speaking another first language, but also when, for example, trying to read and understand the legal texts.

Parents needed to know how to access information in a given environment, whether the information they needed to seek was reliable, and which information they needed next for being able to influence the school placement of their children. On obtaining all the relevant information they had sought, parents discovered many barriers in the Austrian education system and that there were unequal conditions between integration and special schooling, and so they highlighted these in the interviews.

Being Able to Realize Educational Options

The category "realizing/investing in educational opportunities for the child" will be addressed with respect to the process parents undergo when confronted with the education system. The Austrian school system can constitute a barrier to inclusion (Altrichter & Feyerer, 2011) because of its highly competitive and selective orientation. Not only are there secondary schools for varying achievement levels but there are also different special schools and different curricula geared toward the different "special educational needs" of students.

First, the process of labelling for obtaining resources was a topic of which parents were critical. They also questioned decisions based on the labelling and testing process. Parents stated that the classification of the child as having special educational needs was the beginning of the problems with the school system, that is, having to fight for being able to attend preparatory class or repeating a class when the label of SEN had already been given (due to the unavailability of integration classes). The classification process for having access to relevant resources in school was criticized as a stigmatizing act in which testing rather than getting to know the student over a longer period of time was used as a basis for argumentation for school placement and curricula. Moreover, the stressful act of being tested had to be undergone several times, for school as well as for after-school care.

> I don't know how many exams with psychologists, with principals, with professors with—you know—all types of academics ... and it's a bit humiliating because you're the one with the problem.... You. And she's now at an age where she knows [M: she knows exactly] and it's a big topic for her. Why am I different? Why do I have this problem? ... And then you have the same thing ... you have to do the same thing all over again for after-school care. It's just, it's just a joke.

The labeling of children as having special educational needs confronted parents and children with the disability and was described as a painful, deficit-oriented confrontation with difference. Parents also tried to find a basis for their arguments when the testing was used to encourage parents to put their children in special classes or to apply a curriculum with which the parents did not agree.

Second, parents reported on how they handled problems when they found a school that they considered appropriate for their child. Once the special educational needs (SEN) label had been received, the opportunities included attendance at integration classes, special support (for several hours) in mainstream schools, the admission to schools for children with disabilities or to specialized schools for certain disabilities, and home-schooling, as one mother summarizes it. But if one wanted to place one's child in a regular school next door, the principal's position toward opening an integration class played a major role, as will be illustrated by the next interview sequence.

> In theory, every school can open an integration class. So we went to the first primary school that we could see and asked the principal. And then she clearly said something she wasn't supposed to say.... "No. In our school, there will be no integration class, definitely not."

Attitudes of professionals are important facilitating or hindering factors when it come to the admission of children to an integration class, as is also shown in the literature (e.g. Meijer, 2003). A quite dramatic metaphor expressed by one of the mothers illustrates how she perceived the participation of children with disabilities in Austrian society and in the school system.

> In the meantime I have the feeling that a Trojan [laughing] has been put into society and that people are more conscious and open when meeting people with disabilities—children ... that there's not always so much fear and distance any more.... I hope that it won't change and that it will even progress.

The metaphor of a "Trojan" says a great deal about the struggle people with disabilities face when it comes to their right to participation in Austrian society, and in the regular education system. The Trojan, the computer virus or the Trojan horse, is used as a symbol for people with disabilities in society, entering an area where they are not welcome and destroying the old order completely. Nevertheless, the mother used the "Trojan" to depict how people realized that the perceived enemy was nothing to fear. In this sense, contact with people with disabilities in society, being within the system, and not being segregated, should have the power to change their participation in important societal areas like school. Therefore, after having done the labelling of the child, parents are confronted with attitudes toward inclusion in the Austrian school system when contacting mainstream schools next door to them.

Not surprisingly, parents in the sample searched for schools that already had experience and had made adaptations for children with disabilities. But they also argued that there were not many schools which already possessed these qualities in Vienna in the regular school system. In the rest of Austria the situation was described as being even worse. Furthermore, parents talked about the challenge of the school having to be within the scope of responsibility of the district in which the child lived, although some managed to be able to attend schools in Vienna or in a certain district in which they did not live. Parents also reported on their efforts in organizing transportation, assistive devices and therapies for their children and in providing schools with teaching materials or information they found important for the school achievement of their children. Furthermore, parents also went to the Ministry of Education to argue against the possibilities offered and for the necessity of facilitating alternatives.

Another important issue reported was the barrier that there had to be a certain number of children with SEN in order to establish an integration class and to obtain the necessary resources such as a second teacher, namely, a special education teacher, in class. Parents experienced a great deal of uncertainty as to whether such a class could even be opened in the schools they wanted their children to attend. Parents even described the existence of an informal list in some (private) schools where parents registered their children, sometimes years before entering school, in order to secure a place for their children should an integration class be opened.

> And the big problem in the Austrian school system is also that there's a formal bureaucratic way—what's in the law. And then there's an informal way. So you need to know how the informal way works because otherwise even if you follow the formal way you'll just end up with having no place, so you need to secure your place in an informal way at the right time, that's the big, big problem ... and the thing is with the private schools: you can be registered on the informal list, but with the public schools you can't do that. They don't accept it.

The possibility of a special teacher who comes to school at certain times per week instead of an integration class seemed to be of less interest for schools and parents because they desired full-time support from a second professional. Nevertheless, if this possibility was chosen and there was no special teacher in class for several hours or in after-school care, parents also reported that the child could no longer participate or that school refused to guarantee achievement. One mother decided not to work but to take her child home during the time in which no special teacher was available in order to support the child herself. Parents also reported that their children would have been able to attend an integration class but that there were no integration opportunities for after-school care and the children would not have been able to be with their class mates in the afternoon anymore. All these were barriers to parents choosing to place their children in an integration class of a regular school.

Furthermore, parents described the conflicts inherent in having to accommodate having children in several schools, working and having to organize their daily lives, as well as the demands of having to search for an appropriate school.

> But this doesn't help you very much if you don't know to organize your whole life around these questions.

In sum, the search for an integrative setting in mainstream schools required certain characteristics like being able to cope with negative attitudes, to organize adaptations, to make time, and to organize daily life with respect to school demands or being able to argue for the relevance of facilitating alternative education possibilities.

Parents also choose special school settings. Special schools are at times more appealing to parents because of the lack of resources and inferior quality standards in integration (Altrichter & Feyerer, 2011). Parents and teachers reported the benefits of special schools, such as affordable therapies, information, networks and support for the disability with which they were most specialized. The smaller number of students in special classes was also associated with a more individualized education. Interviewees (children although not the ones in the study with intellectual disability) talked about the feeling of security as well as having more quiet working conditions and personal contact with the teacher as being important advantages in a small (special) class. It is easy to see what a special school can offer parents and children who feel unsure and cannot obtain the relevant information, support and therapies themselves.

Also reported were the positive effects of large classes, such as learning social competence from others and that integration schools provided information and support through the high spirit of engagement of the school staff. The preconditions for facilitating support for children with disabilities within these two school types are not provided at the same level. This should not just depend on additional personal effort from teachers, parents and schools but should be provided without hindering policies. On the other hand, not offering as much adaptation as is done in a "special environment" of a special school was described in the interviews as one reason why integration classes were perceived to be more similar to living in society (e.g., the code "being perceived more like reality," "preparing children for leaving the protected area of this school"). The higher the education, the more pressure was reported in mainstream schools to fit to the norm (and the employment market). Parents talked about the education legislation and indicated that after the fifth grade a clearance for the label of special educational needs for children with disabilities (physical, visual, hearing) could be achieved, but that this was not the case for children with intellectual disabilities. Despite the possibility of having individual adaptations of the school program when keeping the label of special educational needs, a lack of concrete specifications was reported by parents as well. So everything was possible and nothing could be taken for granted, everything was up to the decision making of each individual. The higher the education, the more children had to fit into the mainstream classes and the lower the availability of integration possibilities, according to the narratives. Additionally, the difficult and time consuming search for a new school offering integration started again after primary school, whereas children could stay longer in special schools. Especially if interests and future employment wishes were to guide the decision for the next school type, as is common for children without disabilities, the availability of a school offering integration and/or adaptations might "turn to zero" as one mother put it. So it did not become easier for the parents when planning their children's school careers. Moreover, parents criticized that there was no law for the integration of children with disabilities after the 10th grade and that there was no possibility of obtaining the general qualification for university entrance in special schools. In a nutshell, the issue demonstrated by parents in Austria was not so much whether children with intellectual disabilities had access to education in general but rather, whether all children had equal access to inclusive and higher education.

The decision between integration and special education is not just between two different types of schooling but between two different "worlds" with different availability of resources and adaptations and different possibilities for higher education. In sum, parents who believe in their influence on their children's education, who can afford financial resources, time and energy, and are able to organize their lives in relation to the education issues for adapting to regular schools have a big advantage. But even more is needed if parents decide to fight for their children's school careers, against the limitations of Austria's school policies.

Coping with Challenges to Realize One's Decision

Some parents addressed the importance of fighting for their children's education. The category "fighting for the child" was linked to passages in which parents were talking about the school system, the search for a school and support for their child in general. Additionally, combat vocabulary was used by parents, such as "being a death sentence" or "having ammunition" in order to argue and push teachers, principals and politicians to ensure what they believed to be the best possible conditions for their children's school careers.

But fighting requires certain characteristics and power in order to be successful. Parents and teachers argued that having a high status in society or contact to the media facilitated realizing one's goal by using pressure as a method. Even if not possessing these advantages, it was evident that it was necessary to be aware of the fight against people who had a higher hierarchical status. Parents who fought for their children's school placement and curricula against educational policies assumed that their resoluteness to take action against the authorities, their confident appearance, as well as their knowledge (e.g. about the legislation) and argumentation helped them change the educational possibilities for their children and perhaps also for other children in a similar position.

Nevertheless, fighting was not perceived as the best strategy in all situations. The question was posed whether a combat for the child's placement against the will of schools was really a good strategy if afterwards the child had to be in an environment where it was not accepted and welcomed. The attitudes of the child's teachers were perceived as being important for working together and supporting the child in school.

Fighting against segregative education in Austria needs a great deal of engagement and resources on the part of the parents. Furthermore, on having reached the goal of having one's child in an integration (maybe even preparatory) class, and also finding a secondary school and after-school care with integration and adaptations, et cetera, the daily engagement and cooperation with the school is another issue of importance when regarding parents' influence on their children's school careers (see, e.g., Hornby & Lafaele, 2011).

IMPLICATIONS AND CONSEQUENCES

When comparing the development in Austria with that in other neighboring countries like Germany or Switzerland, a much stronger development toward inclusion over more than 2 decades becomes evident. The establishment of new forms of education was the result of a parental movement, fighting against school administration and for the right of their children to attend the same schools as all others. Service provision for students with disabilities in Austria seems to be attractive because of the two-teacher-system in integrative classrooms, especially for teachers and parents from other countries where children with disabilities enjoy less support from educators in their classroom. But the system emerged in the 1990s when there was no doubt about classifying children. The difference between inclusion as the right to be involved in every life area and integration as the provision of special support to special children in mainstream settings becomes clear in the current discussion on the UN Convention on the Rights of Persons with Disabilities (UNCPRD). The narratives of the parents reveal the contradictions in the old integration system.

Experiences from parents show that there are not the same educational opportunities for children with and without disabilities in Austria. Parents complain that policies are not implemented with the corresponding commitment and that appropriate resources are lacking in mainstream education settings. School legislation requires the necessity of conferring a "special educational needs" status for obtaining appropriate support, and there is also disregard for higher education opportunities for children with disabilities, all which can be seen as structural barriers (Grubich, 2011). Parents and some teachers fight for equal educational possibilities, which at times requires social and economic capital (Ong-Dean, 2009).

The preliminary results of the CLASDISA study in Austria show that there is an ongoing conflict between parents and the education system related to classifications, adaptations and the placement of children with disabilities. Although parents have the legal right to select between integrative and special school settings, it is a challenging task to find an appropriate place in an integration class of a mainstream school. In the system of integration classes parents contribute a great deal toward ensuring the necessary resources and support for their children.

The system of choice between integrative and special school classrooms presupposes parents' abilities to deal with institutional barriers and thus is highly socially selective. Children of parents with lower socioeconomic status attend less often regular or integration schools, and more often attend special schools, even if parents decline the latter option. This reveals nothing less than social inequality in education (Szumsky & Karwowski, 2012). It is therefore important to uncover at least some mechanisms behind this failure of providing equity for all. According to the narratives of parents in the CLASDISA project, the hidden effects behind the promulgated freedom of choice are based on the different ways of accessing information, the different amounts of engagement necessary for finding a school place, as well as the different provision and manners of obtaining resources. Sometimes even a different perception of the responsibility in educating children with disabilities between special and integration schools in Vienna results not just in unequal school opportunities for children both with and without disabilities, but also for children with and without parents who are able to cope with these challenges within the education system. The belief in the importance of education, in one's ability and one's right to change the child's situation, the ability to have access to relevant information and resources, and also the will and ability to stand up for one's view against the will of authorities are all needed for fighting for educational opportunities. Furthermore, parents are seen as the most important factor for their children's school achievement (Jeynes, 2012) in whatever placement they may be. Therefore, cooperation between schools and parents is important. Also, when the child is already in school parents engage in supporting the school and the learning of the child. The disadvantages when parents do not have the necessary capabilities and resources cannot be underestimated.

Inclusive and special school settings still work under different institutional conditions. Special schools for children with intellectual disabilities have day-care in the afternoon and there are no restrictions to access. Special therapies are provided and parents can be sure that their children are welcomed. It is therefore not surprising that parents resist initiatives for closing down special schools for students with intellectual disabilities. The parental choice for their children's educational trajectories, provided for under Austrian school legislation is more a simulation of two different options than a real choice. So it may not come as a surprise that an unpublished statistical overview of the Vienna school administration shows that schools for children with intellectual disabilities are the only special school type with a slowly increasing number of students.

There were parents who had confidence in the integration school of their children: they felt immediately welcome, received information and support from schools offering integration classes each year and which invested in good school-parent cooperation through adapting to the parents' needs (e.g., time, presence of other parents), and adapting to the children's needs although sometimes acting against policies of school organization. Yet, there was still the fight for resources requiring the investment of time, effort, et cetera in order to adapt to the possibilities of parents, schools or both. This shows us that school has the potential to override educational trajectories, but that there also has to be more support for these schools. Recommendations would be to ensure that schools feel obliged and ready to take all children, that the path to resources and to adaptations not be paved with bureaucratic stumbling stones, but that all schools should easily be able to make the adaptations necessary for greater autonomy so that children's needs become more important than school policies (e.g., providing integration classes each year no matter how many children with SEN status start school).

ACKNOWLEDGMENT

This contribution refers to the project "Classifications of disabilities in the field of education in different societal and cultural contexts," financed by the Austrian Science Fund, project number P22178.

NOTE

1. Information is available on the project website: http://classifications-of-
disabilities.univie.ac.at/

REFERENCES

Altrichter, H., & Feyerer, E. (2011). Auf dem Weg zu einem inklusiven Schulsys-
tem? [Towards an inclusive school system?]. *Zeitschrift für Inklusion, 4.*
Retrieved from http://www.inklusion-online.net/index.php/inklusion-online/
article/view/73/73

Anlanger, O. (1993). *Behinderten Integration. Geschichte eines Erfolges* [Integration of
the disabled. History of a success.] Wien, Austria: Jugend & Volk.

Artiles, A., & Dyson, A. (2006). Inclusive education in the globalization age. The
promise of comparative cultural-historical analysis. In D. Mitchell (Ed.), *Con-
textualizing inclusive education. Evaluating old and new international perspectives*
(pp. 37–62). London, England: Routledge.

Artiles, A. J., Kozleski, E. B., & Waitoller, F. R. (Eds.). (2011). *Inclusive education.
examining equity on five continents.* Cambridge, MA: Harvard Education Press.

Biewer, G. (2006). Schulische integration in Deutschland und Österreich im Ver-
gleich [Comparison of school integration in Germany and Austria]. *Erziehung
und Unterricht, 156*(1–2), 21–28.

Biewer, G. (2010). *Grundlagen der Heilpädagogik und Inklusiven Pädagogik* [Basic
knowledge in remedial and inclusive education] (2nd ed.). Bad Heilbrunn,
Germany: Klinkhardt.

Biewer, G. (2011). Die UN-Behindertenrechtskonvention und das Recht auf Bil-
dung [The UN Convention on the Rights of Persons with Disabilities and the
Right to Education]. In O. Dangl & T. Schrei (Eds.), *Bildungsrecht für alle*
[Right to education for all?] (Vol. 51–62). Wien, Berlin: Lit.

Bryant, A., & Charmaz, K. (Eds.). (2007). The SAGE Handbook of Grounded
Theory. London: SAGE.

Charmaz, K. (2006). *Constructing grounded theory. A practical guide through qualitative
analysis.* Thousand Oaks, CA: SAGE.

Darbyshire, P., MacDougall, C., & Schiller, W. (2005). Multiple methods in qualitative research with children: More insight or just more? *Qualitative Research,
5*(4), 417–436.

Ellger-Rüttgardt, S. L. (2008). *Geschichte der Sonderpädagogik* [History of special
education]. München, Basel: Reinhardt.

Georgens, J. D., & Deinhardt, H. M. (1861). *Die Heilpädagogik - Mit besonderer
Berücksichtigung der Idiotie und der Idiotenanstalten. Erster Band.* [Remedial education - With a focus on idiocy and asylums for idiots. First volume]. Leipzig,
Germany: Fleischer. Online: https://fedora.phaidra.univie.ac.at/fedora/get/
o:89383/bdef:Asset/view

Georgens, J. D., & Deinhardt, H. M. (1863). *Die Heilpädagogik - Mit besonderer
Berücksichtigung der Idiotie und der Idiotenanstalten* [Remedial education - With

a focus on idiocy and asylums for idiots. Second volume]. Leipzig, Germany: Fleischer.   Online: https://fedora.phaidra.univie.ac.at/fedora/get/o:89776/bdef:Asset/view

Grubich, R. (2011). Zur schulischen Situation von Kindern und Jugendlichen mit sonderpädagogischem Förderbedarf (SPF) in Österreich – Analyse im Lichte der UN-Konvention über die Rechte von Menschen mit Behinderung [The school situation of children and young people with special educational needs (SEN) in Austria - Analysis referring to the UN Convention on the Rights of Persons with Disabilities]. *Zeitschrift für Inklusion, 2*. Retrieved from http://www.inklusion-online.net/index.php/inklusion-online/article/view/90/90

Hornby, G., & Lafaele, R. (2011). Barriers to parental involvement in education: an explanatory model. *Educational Review, 63*(1), 37–52.

Jeynes, W. H. (2012). A meta-analysis of the efficacy of different types of parental involvement programs for urban students. *Urban Education, 47*(4), 706–742.

Klee, E. (2001). *"Euthanasie" im NS-Staat* ["Euthanasia" in the NS-State] (10 ed.). Frankfurt, Germany: Fischer.

Luciak, M., & Biewer, G. (2011). Equity and inclusive education in Austria: A comparative analysis. In A. J. Artiles, E. B. Kozleski, & F. R. Waitoller (Eds.), *Inclusive education. examining equity on five continents* (pp. 17–44). Cambridge, MA: Harvard Education Press.

Meijer, C. J. W. (2003). *Special needs education across Europe*. Middelfart, Denmark: European Agency for Development in Special Needs Education.

Mitra, S. (2006). The capability approach and disability. *Journal of Disability Policy Studies, 16*(4), 236–247.

Möckel, A. (2007). *Geschichte der Heilpädagogik* [History of Remedial Education] (2nd ed.). Stuttgart, Germany: Klett-Cotta.

Nussbaum, M. (2007). *Frontiers of justice: Disability—nationality—species membership*. Cambridge, MA; London: The Belknap Press of Harvard University Press.

Nussbaum, M. C. (2011). *Creating capabilities. The human development approach*. Cambridge, MA; London: The Belknap Press of Harvard University Press.

Ong-Dean, C. (2009). *Distinguishing disability: Parents, privilege, and special education*. Chicago, IL: The University of Chicago Press.

Powell, J. (2003). Constructing disability and social inequality early in the life course: The case of special education in Germany and the United States. *Disability Studies Quarterly, 23*(2), 57–75.

Sen, A. (2009). *Inequality reexamined*. Oxford, England: Oxford University Press. (Original work published 1992)

Szumski, G., & Karwowski, M. (2012). School achievement of children with intellectual disability: The role of socioeconomic status, placement, and parents' engagement. *Research in Developmental Disabilities, 33*(5), 1615–1625.

Terzi, L. (2010). *Justice and equity in education. A capability perspective on disability and special educational needs*. London, England: Continuum.

WHO (Ed.). (2007). *International classification of functioning, disability and health—Children & youth version. ICF-CY*. Geneva, Switzerland: WHO Press.

CHAPTER 14

THE ROAD TO INCLUSION FOR CHILDREN WITH AUTISM SPECTRUM DISORDERS

Llyween Couper

This chapter explores the implications that inclusion has for all those involved in the lives of children with autism spectrum disorders. The journey often begins with parents who notice difference and ends with a student attending, participating and contributing in a mainstream school. While inclusion is viewed as a right for all children and fits well with the values and beliefs of many communities it is still a challenge to achieve. The movement of students from education in a special facility to inclusion in their local mainstream school is a worldwide trend. In some countries this began with legislation as a human rights issue and in others began with parents simply wanting all their children to attend the local school. New Zealand began the journey toward inclusion with the 1989 Education Act that embedded parental choice in law stating, "People who have special education needs have the same rights to enroll and receive education at state schools as people who do not." The aim was to achieve in 10 years, a world class inclusive education system that provided learning opportunities for all children. For some families, schools and communities, inclusion has been easy and the destination of inclusion has already been reached despite confusions between the Ministry of Education's aims, values and policy and current research. While much has been achieved new research and theories require

Inclusive Education for Students with Intellectual Disabilities,
pp. 295–319

continual change, reflection and evaluation. The journey toward inclusion can be illusive with a destination that may also keep changing.

FOREWORD

Inclusion has always been an uphill battle for the parents of any child with special needs despite entitlement to enrol children in the local school. The overall aim of the chapter is to describe the important roles of everyone in the search for inclusion for children with autism spectrum disorders. The chapter first explores the expectations of parents who choose to enroll their children in mainstream schools and then explores the frustrations, challenges, and problems that can arise for both the families and their school communities as they support the learning of a child with ASD. Children who are autistic and nonverbal, often need support not only in the classroom but also in the playground where interaction with peers can happen. Unfortunately as this chapter suggests, it can also be where they are isolated and vulnerable. Addressing the challenges of isolation, lack of adequate support and peer acceptance is complex and ongoing, often further complicated by the differences between government educational policies and current research findings. For many years there have been issues with funding, assessment, resources, adequate training and professional development. As described it has not been a smooth journey. I am the grandparent of a nonverbal child with ASD and I know the enormous load this has placed on his school and family. This is well researched and sympathetically covered in the following chapter.

—Janet Sutherland
Auckland, New Zealand

INTRODUCTION

For more than 30 years the movement of students with special needs from education in a special facility to inclusion in their local mainstream school has been a worldwide trend (Ofsted, 2004, p. 679; Sigafoos et al., 2010). For example, in 1997, there was a 16% increase in the number of children with autism spectrum disorders (ASD) attending mainstream schools within the United Kingdom (Department for Education and Employment, 1997; Keen & Ward, 2004). By 2010, the majority of students (70%) with ASD in England attended mainstream rather than specialist schools (Department for Education, 2010).

In New Zealand the reported prevalence of children diagnosed with ASD is rising and is now estimated to be prevalent in 1 in every 100 school aged children (Ministry of Health, 2013). Currently, approximately 95% of all children with special needs, including those with ASD, attend mainstream schools (Ministry of Education, 2012b). This historical and current trend toward including children with ASD and other special education needs in mainstream schools has implications for students, parents, schools, teachers, teacher educators, and support agencies.

This chapter will describe the implications that inclusion has for those involved in the lives of children with ASD. First, it will describe the challenges of defining inclusion and the roles of teachers in achieving an inclusive environment for children with ASD. Second, it will outline the expectations of parents, their experiences of raising a child with ASD, and their interactions with support agencies.

INCLUSION

What is Inclusion?

The terms "inclusion" and "inclusive education" have led to common misunderstandings in both public forums and research contexts (Higgins, MacArthur, & Morton, 2008). Inclusion is a deliberate approach that requires that all students are accepted and take a full and active part in school life as valued members of ordinary classrooms in regular schools (Ballard, 2004; Slee, 2001). Inclusion is described by Ainscow, Booth, and Dyson (2006) as the culture of the entire school which values equity, participation, community, compassion, respect for diversity, sustainability, and where entitlement to an education is considered a vital characteristic of the school. Higgins, MacArthur, and Kelly (2009, p. 6) state that "Inclusive education stands in contrast to "special" education, where disabled students are educated in separate schools or classes or treated very differently in the classroom to regular students."

Furthermore, inclusion is achieved by more than supporting students with ASD to attend and access the curriculum. Some recommend the use of assessment tools such as narrative assessment (Ministry of Education, 2009) that evaluates student's progress and is "relevant and responsive to the students themselves and acknowledges learning in a positive way" (Higgins, Mitchell, & Sanderson, 2005, p. 15). The importance of assessment as a tool that celebrates the progress of every student is seen as the starting point for an education system that is more inclusive and more responsive to diversity (Bartolo, Annemieke, & Hofsass, 2007).

For some families, schools, and communities, attaining an inclusive environment has been easy and the goal of inclusion reached despite a lack of clarity between the Ministry of Education's aims, values, policy, and current research. Because inclusion can mean different things in different places, and even between different schools in the same community, the goal of inclusion can often feel like an illusion. While defining and delivering inclusion is still a challenge, and despite the exclusion stories that surface, all students in New Zealand are entitled to attend their local school and be taught by a registered teacher using the New Zealand curriculum. Recently the Ministry of Education clarified expectations from schools in New Zealand by describing inclusion as a place where learners are present, and fully participating and achieving (Ministry of Education, 2012a). This includes all students despite their level of ability or disability. The complexity of catering for the educational needs of children with ASD has required educators to identify new possibilities and alternative ways of teaching especially for participation in social learning activities (Peters, Forlin, McInerney, & Maclean, 2013). In the New Zealand Ministry of Health and Education ASD Guidelines (Ministries of Health and Education, 2008), there is agreement that best practice for learners with ASD is achieved in settings that include other children. The authors describe an ever expanding number of teaching and learning strategies that includes those using typically developing peers.

The History of Inclusion

In New Zealand, the 1989 Education Act began the journey toward educational inclusion enabling students with special needs to be enrolled at their local schools just like those who did not have special needs (Education Act, 1989) However, it was not until almost a decade later that the direction of policy and practice in New Zealand schools really began to change, beginning with the release of the Ministry of Education's Special Education 2000 (SE2000) policy. This legislation reaffirmed the understanding that all students would be welcome to enrol and attend their local school and that young children and students with special needs have the same right to a high quality education as do other children of the same age without special needs (Ministry of Education, 1997). Since then, principals, teachers, and teacher aides have endeavoured to create inclusive schools with inclusive school communities while battling with issues of eligibility, funding allocations, assessment, purchase of resources, access to professional agencies and external support, as well as professional development shifting the view of disability from an exclusionary to an inclusionary paradigm (Kearney & Kane, 2006).

The Special Education 2000 policy (Ministry of Education, 1997) which is a funding policy, not a professional practice policy, required schools to become familiar with changes to funding for students with special education needs. However, it also required teacher identification, assessment, and teaching and learning plans, to be implemented for students that had previously not been their responsibility.

Historically students with ASD have been seen as "too cognitively impaired" or "not ready for instruction" (Mirenda, 2003a, p. 271). Based on many unsubstantiated claims, Edelson (2006) found that students with ASD are still claimed to be mentally retarded. They are presumed by these nonempirical sources "to be less able than their peers to learn to read, write or do mathematics, think critically, solve problems, perform functional life skills and demonstrate age appropriate receptive and expressive language skills" (McSheehan, Sonnenmeier, & Jorgensen, 2009, p. 416). However, there is significant research (Jorgensen, 2005; Kasa-Hendrickson, 2005) around presumed competence that supports the idea that students with cognitive disabilities, including ASD, can learn academic content that includes reading, mathematics, and science (Browder, Spooner, Ahlgrim-Delzell, Wakeman, & Harris, 2008; Browder, Wakeman, Spooner, Ahlgrim-Delzell, & Algozzine, 2006; Courtade, Spooner, & Browder, 2007). Therefore, we can assume that all students can learn and that despite their abilities or disabilities everyone should have that opportunity (Finke, McNaughton, & Drager, 2009).

Parental Choice of School Setting

Despite the challenges involved in supporting the learning and development of children with complex educational needs, these children and their families are entitled to attend their local school and experience learning alongside their peers (Higgins et al., 2008). This may be a challenge for even the most inclusive school community, teachers, peers, parents, boards of trustees, and supporting agencies. Parent choice is a Ministry of Education commitment enabling parents to choose between their local schools, and any other school of their choice including a special school specifically catering for the needs of their child with ASD. In many situations it is more convenient and desirable for all children in the family to attend their local school or conversely to travel by taxi to a special school. The decision may reflect the parent's values and beliefs around what constitutes an inclusive society as well as their expectations from their chosen school. Sometimes the reputation of the local school and the perceived attitudes and philosophies of teachers are considered to be the most important factors in making the placement decision

(Morton & McMenamin, 2009). In some locations the reality is that there are limited choices especially when finding a suitable secondary school that provides an inclusive environment for their child's postprimary education (Higgins et al., 2008).

CHALLENGES IN TEACHING STUDENTS WITH AUTISM SPECTRUM DISORDERS

As described above, there are an increasing number of students with ASD now attending their local school rather than special units or special schools (Dybvik, 2004; Keen & Ward, 2004; Ofsted, 2004; Sigafoos et al., 2010). As a result, the focus on inclusion in education is presenting some teachers with new demands as they manage the learning needs of a greater number of students with complex needs like those with ASD (Batten & Daly, 2006). For example, research shows that:

- Half of the students with ASD do not develop speech or have limited speech and language abilities (Mirenda, 2003b). Many of these students fall into the most challenging cohort for any classroom teacher.
- Many students with ASD have numerous learning and development needs which require a comprehensive educational programme focussed on teaching new skills (Sigafoos et al., 2010).
- Students with ASD can have both learning and behavioral characteristics that require different approaches to learning and behavior at home and school.
- Some students display excessive behaviors such as self–injury, extreme tantrums, and repetitive movements.
- Many students with ASD have difficulty attending for any length of time, lack control or the expression of emotions, and need to be taught skills in social competence and self-care.

Students who are unable to speak have limited means of communicating with others with significant deficits in speech, language, and communication development. Prelinguistic behaviors become frustrating for everyone as they are difficult to interpret (van der Meer & Rispoli, 2010). It is often unclear whether young children who lack speech will remain at a prelinguistic level (Romski et al., 2009). Although a child's communication ability may change with maturity and intervention, improvement is considered an essential step toward enabling students with autism who are nonverbal to access the curriculum, to manage their behavior, and to interact socially with their teachers, immediate and extended family, and peers.

Teachers' Attitudes

Many researchers find that the strongest predictor of successful inclusion is teachers' positive attitudes (Rodriguez, Saldana, & Moreno, 2012). However, additional research has found that even teachers who were considered to be professionally competent often believed that they were unable to manage the complex learning needs of students with ASD. They also viewed special needs and inclusion as the domain of a few members of staff and not the concern of every teacher, including themselves (Florian, 2012). It has been observed that teachers' attitudes toward inclusion are influenced by variables such as experience, training, and perceptions of available resources and support (Werts, Wolery, Snyder, & Caldwell, 1996).

Teachers of children with ASD consider the presence and collaboration of support staff to be very important (Rowley et al., 2012). However, teachers' as well as support staff's attitudes can change over time from initial resistance to more favorable perceptions as they become accustomed to having students with disabilities, including those with ASD, in their classes (Giangreco, 1993). Promoting understanding of diversity and difference within the peer group is seen as critical as this means the teacher also has support for inclusion from the class members (Finke et al., 2009). Generally it is agreed that students with ASD can be successfully included in their local mainstream school when there is a commitment to do so and inclusion is "saturated" in all areas of school life, practice, and support structures (Morewood, Humphrey, & Symes, 2011).

As teachers become more accountable for the learning experiences of all their students, they are expected to individualize learning and recognize the needs of learners within their care. Good teaching in an inclusive classroom requires continually balancing the needs of the individual with the needs of the rest of the class. Unfortunately, it also requires teachers to assess and report according to national standards which is yet another balancing act as infinitesimal but significant progress is measured.

Collaboration

Team communication and collaboration are identified as critical elements in the inclusion process (Finke et al., 2009; Rodriguez et al., 2012). While the support of experts and other practitioners is valuable, it works best for teachers when there is a shared vision for inclusion that includes those closest to the child and is based on the day to day experiences of the learners.

In New Zealand the Principles of the Treaty of Waitangi are often used as a guide to effective collaboration and partnerships (Bishop & Glynn, 1999). The framework is based on three principles: partnership, protection, and participation. Strong partnerships do not harbor unequal power relationships, protection requires decisions to enhance student mana (self-belief) and cultural identity, and successful participation is possible when input and presence is valued. These three principles can be fundamental guidelines for effective meetings such as Individual Education Plans or any form of collaborative gathering (Ministry of Education, 2011). Building a team that is collaborative requires a strong commitment to a shared belief in inclusion as well as a willingness to work together for the benefit of the school, the student, and their family and whanau (Maori extended family members).

Different or the Same?

It is suggested by some writers that the field of education is at a critical juncture as the number of students diagnosed with ASD is increasing (McSheehan, Sonnenmeier, & Jorgensen, 2009). How to best educate all students in regard to this increase poses important questions such as: do we focus on student deficits and remediation? Do we expect students to demonstrate specific skills before allowing them to be educated in an inclusive school? "Or do we develop approaches that foster skill development and engagement with typical peers in natural settings?" (McSheehan et al., 2009, p. 434). The latter includes successful and complete inclusion in the whole school environment; the classroom, the playground, school camps, assemblies, and other extracurricula activities.

The conflict is between acknowledging that learners on the autism spectrum are a distinct group of learners requiring a special pedagogical approach and an argument that most teaching strategies are relevant and effective for all pupils irrespective of social background, ethnicity, gender, or disability (Florian, 2012; Norwich & Lewis, 2005). Some researchers argue that interventions for children with ASD are so complex that they require specialized training for teachers, low teacher-student ratio, and many hours of intervention (Machalicek, O'Reilly, Beretvas, Sigafoos, & Lancioni, 2007; Machalicek et al., 2008; Scheuermann, Webber, & Goodwin, 2003). Students with ASD are also culturally and linguistically diverse (Machalicek et al., 2007) but we are reminded by Garcia et al. (2010) that teacher educators are still professionally and ethically responsible for ensuring teachers are prepared to successfully serve students with ASD.

A study that investigated general classroom teachers' perspectives of inclusion (Finke et al., 2009) found that teachers who promoted an understanding of diversity within their classrooms showed an increased awareness that they were teachers for all students and embraced the benefits of inclusion despite the challenges. They used programmes that required different levels of support and learning styles, and promoted student independence by adapting the curriculum. A teacher in the study described successful inclusion for children with ASD:

> Our students with special needs are never pulled out of the classroom. They are able to spend all day with their peers and do not miss out on any lessons. The service provider meets the student's needs within the lesson that is taking place and teaches skills in context. (Finke et al., 2009, p. 118)

Teacher Training

For many years researchers have been vigorously reminding special educators that they need to understand the complex interplay between disability, language, and culture (Cloud, 1993; Garcia & Dominguez, 1997; Garcia & Malkin, 1993). Teacher training needs to deal with the skills and knowledge gap that undermines teacher confidence and students' success (Morewood et al., 2011). Morewood et al. (2011) argue that if teachers do not understand the diagnosis of autism they will have difficulty anticipating, recognizing, and understanding the degree of difference when confronted with a child with ASD.

The typical cognitive profile and learning style of students with ASD can challenge professional assumptions about teaching and learning (Jordan, 2005). The preference for routine, predictability, and low sensory stimulation is hard to achieve in a noisy, colorful, changeable, mainstream classroom (Carrington & Graham, 2001). Finding time to gain an understanding of the task ahead when a student with ASD becomes part of the class as well as time to develop a relationship with the student, parents, and other service providers is challenging for even the most skilled teacher. Sometimes new skills to prepare appropriate learning tasks and curriculum adaptations for the student are required. However, teachers cannot make inclusion work in isolation (Ravet, 2011) and a strong relationship with an ASD network is considered the most relevant support for teachers (Rodriguez et al., 2012).

Teachers' Aides

Teachers everywhere argue that teacher aid support is critical to the successful inclusion of pupils with ASD (Rodriguez et al., 2012) but the research presents a mixed picture (Symes & Humphrey, 2011). Some argue that the practice may unfortunately reproduce the problems the educators set out to solve (Black-Hawkins & Florian, 2012). For example, although teachers' aides can provide a secure feeling for students who move from teacher to teacher (which is important for students who like routine and predictability), some studies show that the more teachers' aide support the student receives the less progress they make. This is because they receive less teacher attention (Blatchford et al., 2009). Teachers' aide support can also reduce student independence (Howes, 2003) leading to supported students becoming socially excluded as teachers' aides unwittingly reduce opportunities for peer interactions (Alston & Kilham, 2004; McVittie, 2005).

Furthermore, some schools provide a teacher's aide to support the student during time in the playground. This is an example of well-intentioned practice that can actually reinforce the isolation of the student by not only linking the student with the teacher's aide rather than his/her peers but also perpetuating the notion that students with ASD are needy and different (Alston & Kilham, 2004; Anderson, Moore, Godfrey, & Fletcher-Flinn, 2004; McVittie, 2005). More research confirms that training is necessary as increased teachers' aide contact can lead to supported students being socially excluded and rarely encouraged to participate in typical play or any interactions with peers. It has also been shown that teachers' aides sometimes actively discourage participation in certain activities as they see their role as protectors rather than supporters (Anderson et al., 2004).

Therefore, support from teachers' aides for the teachers of students with ASD needs to be grounded in a shared understanding of the aims and expectations of inclusion within the school. Successful student learning requires all educators to presume competence not incompetence (Jorgensen, McSheehan, & Sonnenmeier, 2007) without an overreliance on teacher aide support. Educators who make decisions that presume competence are more likely to promote a student's full membership of the classroom which includes access to the general school curriculum (Jorgensen et al., 2007).

Students With ASD and Their Peers

Students have to be physically included in the classroom and the playground to interact with their classmates and to gain acceptance by their peers. There are symbols of belonging, such as having a desk, doing class jobs, having your name called at roll call, and going on trips or camps. In the early days of inclusive practice it was found by Williams and Downing (1998) that once relationships were established, students became more positive, behavior problems were lowered, and students became socially included in the class (Rowley et al., 2012). The successful inclusion of students is also influenced by the teacher modelling acceptance, tolerance, and celebrating diversity. Peer acceptance and positive interactions between the child with ASD and the peer group makes a significant difference to the whole class culture as well as to the student with autism.

Unfortunately when students see others behaving differently, being treated differently, looking different, speaking differently, and supported by different staff with no explanations they behave defensively. They frequently avoid contact and resort to age old negative behaviors like teasing and bullying (Zablotsky, Bradshaw, Anderson, & Laws, 2013). Isolating behavior can be fueled by a "them" and "us" mentality generated by labelled students being frequently withdrawn from the class by specialist teachers and teacher aides for reasons unknown to the mainstream peers. When peers have an understanding of ASD, or any other disability, their negative behaviors such as rejection, teasing, and bullying which are usually fuelled by ignorance are often replaced with friendly, supportive, and accepting behaviors (Doll & Brehm, 2010; MacArthur & Gaffney, 2001).

Peers may struggle to cope with a student with autism in their mainstream class especially when this includes language and communication impairments (Laws, Bates, Feuerstein, Mason-Apps, & White, 2012). A teacher will probably change the way she/he teaches when a student with ASD joins the class and this may include spending less time with existing students and more time with the student with ASD. Peers may become aware of the extra stress that may occur for their teacher and feel uncomfortable and even distressed themselves with the behaviors of the student with ASD. In the author's experience, peers are sometimes frightened and avoid physical contact or being in close proximity with students with ASD, and like their parents, may believe that this student is stopping their class from learning or engaging in activities that they enjoy. Some students may feel that extra adults in their room such as teacher aides or specialist teachers are an intrusion or an unwanted distraction, and they may come to feel that the student with ASD does not belong in their class (Finke et al., 2009). Some teachers see the benefits for the classmates of ASD students. They see the development of a greater sense of individual difference, compassion, and understanding of individual needs (Finke et al., 2009). Classmates are able to develop academic and leadership skills through their interactions with children with ASD, with opportunities to act as role models, to learn to work alongside the student with autism, and sometimes to be the expert (Finke et al., 2009). In addition, some research suggests that teaching strategies that are effective for "special" children such those with ASD may also be effective for all learners as the needs associated with ASD are shared by other learners (Ravet, 2011). Some believe that this even contributes to the teacher's professional growth and learning (Syriopoulou-Delli, Cassimos, Tripsianis, & Polychronopoulou, 2012).

ASD and Inclusion in the Playground

Parents who enrol their students in mainstream schools are often hopeful for opportunities of social interaction and play between their child and other typically developing peers (Anderson et al., 2004). Many want friendships to develop and enjoy play time in the playground. Very little research has investigated the experiences of students with ASD in their school playgrounds in spite of the increased numbers of students attending mainstream schools (Ingram, Dickerson Mayes, Troxell, & Calhoun, 2007). The physical design of playgrounds and equipment has also been neglected by researchers as contributors to increasing playful social interactions between students with and without ASD (Yuill, Strieth, Roake, Aspden, & Todd, 2007).

Researchers identify the playground as the setting where students with ASD are frequently victims of bullying (Doll & Brehm, 2010; MacArthur & Gaffney, 2001; Rowley et al., 2012). Students with ASD may experience feelings of anxiety, isolation, and vulnerability in the playground because they often lack sufficient communication skills to engage easily with their peers. They may also have impairments in play skills such as symbolic, sociodramatic play, including imaginative or pretend play (Brewster & Coleyshaw, 2010; Lydon, Healy, & Leader, 2011). This results in feelings of anxiety and fear when even the simplest game requires interaction with a peer. Most students, including those with ASD, want to have friends and belong to a friendship group (Brewster & Coleyshaw, 2010). Limited play opportunities and time outside are a concern for some researchers (Pellegrini, 2008; Pellegrini & Blatchford, 2002) who have found trends toward shortening break times for all students including those with disabilities such as ASD (Woolley, Armitage, Bishop, Curtis, & Ginsborg, 2006). Break times are reduced based an assumption that time in the classroom is necessary for "real" teaching as the curriculum expands and also that negative behavior will decrease (Pellegrini, 2005). In the United Kingdom only one in six schools have kept the afternoon break (Woolley et al., 2006). Yet it is the school playground where friendships can develop naturally (Bauminger & Kasari, 2000) and when friends and siblings are around, bullies are deterred (MacArthur & Gaffney, 2001).

Research has shown that students with ASD can identify feelings of loneliness and exclusion (Brewster & Coleyshaw, 2010). According to Doll and Brehm (2010) moving these isolated students into the everyday play of their classmates is one of the signs of an effective inclusive school. Such a move may also provide an opportunity for students with ASD to see and learn skills together with their peers in social and emotional competence, communication, and play. For this reason, the school playground is considered just as significant as the classroom as an environment in which to develop these skills (Woolley et al., 2006).

All students, including those with ASD, have the right to engage in play and leisure activities as described in the United Nations Convention on the Rights of the Child (Commisioner for Children, 1989). Yet some students still spend their time in the playground in isolation, being shadowed by a teacher's aide or even removed from the playground to "play" on a computer or for physiotherapy or some other individual procedure. The more students with ASD are isolated from their peers, the more likely they are to develop rigid play routines that lack pretence or social interaction as they need their peers to serve as models in the playground (Hess, 2006). Engaging in play activities helps all students to get to know and accept one another, and through this, create a sense of belonging. Therefore, time in the playground with their peers is extremely important for students with ASD, and diminishing such time to engage in other solitary activities should be avoided (Terpstra, Higgins, & Pierce, 2002).

A recent investigation (Couper, Sutherland, & van Bysterveldt, 2013) explored ways to increase interactive play activities and decrease the ritualistic behaviors of three students who were nonverbal and autistic. The students used iPads with a small menu of their preferred playground options from which they selected one or two activities prior to entering their school playgrounds. Adding one or two other choices for some of their time in the playground not only increased the chances of their engagement with their peers and their teachers but also began to remove the label of difference by reducing ritualistic behaviors (Couper et al., 2013).

AUGMENTATIVE ALTERNATIVE COMMUNICATION AS AN AID TO INCLUSION

The development of functional spoken language is challenging for many children with ASD with over a quarter identified as nonverbal (Lord, Risi, & Pickles, 2004) creating a serious barrier to any form of communication with others. However, various options have been developed to establish augmentative and alternative communication (AAC). These supports which include manual signing speech generating devices and picture exchange can help students with ASD communicate competently, to access the curriculum, and to actively participate in the social and instructional life of the classroom. Teachers in a study that explored their experiences of teaching classes that included students with autism using AAC made positive comments about increased interactions with typically developing peers allowing everyone to develop socially and academically (Finke et al., 2009). These findings challenge long-held beliefs about disability and the cognitive ability of children with ASD such as that they are "too cognitively impaired" or "not ready for instruction" (Miranda, 2003a).

Providing opportunities for student voice and controllability are thought to enhance the effectiveness of AAC interventions (Cini, 2007; Sigafoos, 2006). The likelihood that the new skill will be generalized and sustained is increased enabling greater participation and improved learning outcomes (McSheehan et al., 2009). Some recent studies show that students can demonstrate a degree of preference for different AAC options (van der Meer, Sutherland, O'Reilly, Lancioni, & Sigafoos, 2012). This empowers students with ASD and provides them with a degree of self-determination (van der Meer, Sigafoos, O'Reilly, & Lancioniet al., 2011). However, some students need support in determining a preference as many students with ASD have not had direct responsibility for their own progress. They may not even be aware of the significance of their disability or the need for change (Russell, 1996). Choice making interventions provided by new technology can enable students to indicate wants and needs and in many instances also avoid difficulties associated with problematic behaviors (Sigafoos, O'Reilly, & Lancioni, 2009).

Recently, there has been rapid and widespread development in mobile technology. Increased availability of iPads and other tablet devices are making significant changes in the lives and learning for students with ASD, especially for those who are nonverbal. Researchers see an urgent need for collaboration among stakeholders to support research and determine the most effective approaches to interventions, practice, and participation of students using AAC (McNaughton & Light, 2013).

THE COST OF ASD FOR PARENTS, FAMILIES, AND SUPPORT SERVICES

Parents are often first to notice differences in their child but may not be involved in the assessment and intervention process that follows the diagnosis of ASD. However, it is generally believed that the participation model which uses information gathered from a wide range of sources and encourages family involvement in the assessment and intervention process strengthens family functioning (Dunst, Johanson, Trivette, & Hamby, 1991).

Bevan-Brown (2004) found that many parents became aware that their children had difficulties before they were 2 years old yet diagnosis of ASD did not happen until much later. Factors included long waiting lists, rural locations, the caution of medical professions to label, and "red tape." Generally, early diagnosis of ASD can result in fewer challenging behaviors and better outcomes for families and whanau (Maori extended family members) but in New Zealand it is the parent's choice if, and when, to consult a general practitioner (Ministries of Health and Education, 2008).

The need for a diagnosis can enable families and teachers to make sense of the condition, to gain financial support, and to use coping strategies (Ravet, 2011). However, a diagnosis of disability may not only be stigmatizing but also dictate school placement despite parent choice. In Iran, all students are screened for ASD at an early age where a compulsory national screening programme began in 1993 for all students aged 5-6 years (Samadi, Mahmoodizadeh, & McConkey, 2011). The survey which was completed by parents was part of the screening procedure but the results are believed to be influenced by the parents' responses as they wanted their students to attend a mainstream school rather than a special school.

A family's experience of living with a child with ASD may be an ongoing challenge which can be associated with maternal psychological distress, reduced marital happiness, and reduced family adaptability and cohesion (Bromley, Hare, Davison, & Emerson, 2004). Researchers suggest that the stress experienced by the parents of a child with ASD exhibiting difficult behaviors and deficits, as well as lack of community support, is far greater than any other disability or special needs (Schieve, Blumberg, Rice, Visser, & Boyle, 2007). The difficulty of coping with destructive, unsafe, demanding, self-injurious, and frustrating behaviors was reported in a New Zealand study that invited 17 families to describe what had been helpful and unhelpful in their experiences of raising a child with ASD (Bevan-Brown, 2004). Cultural issues also arose as parents and case workers often had conflicting priorities. Other issues included: insurance claims that were challenged, other parents' with negative attitudes, exclusion from schools and kindergartens, shopping that included tantrums, and feelings that they had to "fight" for everything, even appropriate treatment at the dentist.

In New Zealand, some financial assistance is provided to families such as the child disability allowance, travel allowances, and some funding for practical resources such as fences at home or school. However, families have identified significant other financial costs in raising a child with ASD. Parents in the Bevan-Brown (2004) study outlined above, agreed that damage to their clothes, toys, their home, and furniture were the main extra expenses but transport and health care costs also caused a significant financial drain. It was also noted that parents who have a child with ASD are rarely able to manage both parents working which creates further financial problems as ASD is well acknowledged to be a costly disorder (Ministries of Health and Education, 2008, p. 64). Similarly, studies in Canada (Siklos & Kerns, 2006) and America (Kogan et al., 2008) also have found that compared with other special healthcare needs, children with ASD were more likely to live in families that experienced financial problems.

ASD and Support Agencies

It is well documented throughout the world that there is a significant increase in the numbers of students identified as ASD (Avchen et al., 2011; Fombonne, 2005; Samadi et al., 2011). This increase may not be attributed solely to growth in the disorder as other factors such as greater diagnostic precision, more expansive diagnostic criteria, and more public attention may be contributing to the increase (Hattier & Matson, 2012). The increase means that more students are in need of services and accommodation. While it is agreed that early detection and intervention for those with ASD is a top priority (Matson, 2007; Matson, Dixon, & Matson, 2005; Volkmar & Pauls, 2003), the life-long nature of the disorder (Howlin, Goode, Hutton, & Rutter, 2004) requires an intensive allocation of resources (Jarbrink, Fombonne, & Knapp, 2003; Leslie & Martin, 2007). This has caused strain on current services in terms of cost, provision, and the organization of health, social, and educational support for students with ASD (Kogan et al., 2008).

Research in New Zealand which gathered information from the parents around their experiences of their child's diagnosis and intervention, found delays were many and varied, and not all were as a result of the limited capacity of the agencies involved (Bevan-Brown, 2004). A mother participating in the study believed that the high turnover rate of various professionals made it too difficult to build rapport. Other parents found that the appropriate services were not easy to access because of: organizational rules and regulations, gate-keeping, geographic locations, and the health of their child.

Access to care is identified as a significant concern by several researchers (Cassidy, McConkey, Truesdale-Kennedy, & Slevin, 2008; Kogan et al., 2008; Kohler, 1999). It is also suggested that "health capture" of services is responsible for restricting access to activities unless they are physio-therapy or occupational therapy. An example of health capture is when activities such as piano or classical ballet are agreed to be effective activities but are not funded because they are not provided by traditional health care professionals. While it is understood that some parents have multiple roles when their child has ASD, the degree to which they are involved will differ. For example, some parents may prefer to be "Mum" and "Dad" and not become involved with facilitating their education (Ministries of Health and Education, 2008). The roles and responsibilities of everyone may change over time reflecting the needs of the child and their families.

Students in rural locations are often disadvantaged with limited access to support groups, playgroups, and parent organizations or speech language therapists. Parents also felt that some medical personnel were overly cautious with labeling and adopted a "wait and see" approach (Bevan-Brown, 2004). A major problem reported by parents in the study was the lack of information about services and entitlements which was not confined to the early years (Bevan-Brown, 2004).

This problem necessitates an examination of the unmet needs of students with ASD (Brown, Ouellette-Kuntz, Hunter, & Kelley, 2010). Service providers need to rethink eligibility criteria and develop resources and services that are responsive to the needs of their client group (Krauss, Gulley, Sciegaj, & Wells, 2003). Key actions identified for supporting New Zealand families (Ministries of Health and Education, 2008) particularly during the diagnosis stage of students with ASD included:

- easy access for families to information and supports relating to their needs;
- immediate appointment of a key worker who has ASD expertise for coordination of interventions and supports for the child and family, with an outline of agreed times and dates;
- care plan developed with, and for, the family which includes care management for complex situations and ongoing needs; and
- consideration of the needs of siblings as part of the care plan.

All agencies need to consider the practical, emotional, and cultural needs of family members in their service and the central role that families have in the life of their child with ASD. Planning and the provision of supports and services needs to be guided by the families' knowledge, beliefs, aspirations, values, and culture (Ministries of Health and Education, 2008, p. 65).

CONCLUSION

When a student is diagnosed with ASD the parents begin a journey that includes many difficult decisions and significant lifestyle changes for the whole family. The journey is a long winding road for most families and an unexpected, anxious time. While the diagnosis is a relief for some, no one can prepare family members for the future which is as variable, and at times as hazardous, as it is for all students. Regardless of anything else, when students with ASD attend their local school with their siblings, they become part of that school community and this is the very beginning of their journey with the end goal of inclusion. There may be some pot holes and even some detours but the destination will be reached when everyone works toward the same goal. Attainment of that goal is defined by the student and the context in which he/she participates.

It has also been a long and bumpy road for educators and school communities who, over the last 20 years have had to rethink their roles and responsibilities, and question their values and beliefs about inclusion. Inclusion is complex and not just about placing a student with special needs in a mainstream school with extra support. French and Swain (2004, p. 169) state that "Inclusion demands major changes within society itself and should not be viewed in a vacuum."

Change was thrust upon New Zealand schools and their communities 20 plus years ago, and for some this has been hard but for others an easy, comfortable transition. Despite the numerous guidelines, curriculum changes, legislation and ministry policies, it is the caring relationships of classroom teachers, teachers' aides, taxi drivers who transport children between home and school, neighbors, parents, grandparents, siblings, and whanau of children with ASD who demonstrate and define inclusion. The destination of inclusion is not illusive, it is reached every day when students with ASD are able to live, learn, and play together with their family and peers.

REFERENCES

Ainscow, M., Booth, T., & Dyson, A. (2006). *Improving schools, developing inclusion.* London, England: Routledge.

Alston, J., & Kilham, C. (2004). Adaptive education for students with special needs in the inclusive classroom. *Australian Journal of Early Childhood, 29*(3), 24–33.

Anderson, A., Moore, D. W., Godfrey, R., & Fletcher-Flinn, C. M. (2004). Social skills assessment of children with autism in free-play situations. *Autism, 8*(4), 369–385.

Avchen, R. N., Wiggins, L. D., Devine, O., Braun, K. V., Rice, C., Hobson, N. C., … Yeargin-Allsopp, M. (2011). Evaluation of a records-review surveillance system used to determine the prevalence of autism spectrum disorders. *Journal of Autism and Developmental Disorders, 41,* 227–236.

Ballard, K. (2004). Children and disability: Special or included? *NZ: Waikato Journal of Education, 10,* 315–326.

Bartolo, P., Annemieke, M. L., & Hofsass, T. (Eds.). (2007). *Responding to student diversity teacher education and classroom practice.* Malta: Faculty of Education, University of Malta.

Batten, A., & Daly, J. (2006). *Make school make sense: Autism and education in Scotland: The reality for families today.* London, England: National Autistic Society.

Bauminger, N., & Kasari, C. (2000). Loneliness and friendship in high-functioning children with autism. *Child Development, 71*(2), 447–456.

Bevan-Brown, J. (2004). *Maori perspectives of autistic spectrum disorder.* Massey, New Zealand: Maori Education Research Matauranga Maori.

Bishop, R., & Glynn, T. (1999). *Culture counts: Changing power relations in education.* Palmerston North, Wellington, New Zealand: Dunmore Press.

Black-Hawkins, K., & Florian, L. (2012). Classroom teachers' craft knowledge of their inclusive practice. *Teachers and Teaching, 18*(5), 567–584.

Blatchford, P., Bassett, P., Brown, P., Martin, C., Russell, A., & Webster, R. (2009). *Deployment and impact staff project.* Nottingham, England: Institute of London, University of London.

Brewster, S., & Coleyshaw, L. (2010). Participation or exclusion? Perspectives of pupils with autistic spectrum disorders on their participation in leisure activities. *British Journal of Learning Disabilities, 39,* 284–291.

Bromley, J., Hare, D. J., Davison, K., & Emerson, E. (2004). Mothers supporting children with autism spectrum disorder. *Autism, 8,* 409–423.

Browder, D. M., Spooner, F., Ahlgrim-Delzell, L., Wakeman, S. Y., & Harris, A. (2008). A meta-analysis on teaching mathematics to students with significant cognitive disabilities. *Exceptional Children, 74*(4), 407–432.

Browder, D. M., Wakeman, S., Spooner, F., Ahlgrim-Delzell, L., & Algozzine, B. (2006). Research on reading instruction for individuals with significant cognitive disabilities. *Exceptional Children, 72,* 392–408.

Brown, H. K., Ouellette-Kuntz, H., Hunter, D., & Kelley, E. (2010). Assessing need in school-aged children with an autism spectrum disorder. *Research in Autism Spectrum Disorders, 4,* 539–547.

Carrington, S., & Graham, L. (2001). Perceptions of school by two teenage boys with Asperger syndrome and their mothers: A qualitative study. *Autism, 5*(1), 37–48.

Cassidy, A., McConkey, R., Truesdale-Kennedy, M., & Slevin, E. (2008). Preschoolers with autism spectrum disorders: The impact on families and the supports available to them. *Early Childhood Development and Care, 178,* 115–128.

Cini, J. (2007). Understanding the impact of context on children's attributional style. In P. Bartolo, A. Mol Lous, & T. Hofsäss (Eds.), *Responding to students diversity: Teacher education and classroom practice* (pp. 203–235). Malta: Faculty of Education, University of Malta.

Cloud, N. (1993). Language, culture and disability: Implications for instruction and teacher preparation. *Teacher Education and Special Education, 16*(1), 60–72.

Commisioner for Children. (1989). *United Nations Convention of the Rights of the Child*. Wellington, New Zealand: Author.

Couper, L., Sutherland, D., & van Bysterveldt, A. (2013). Children with autism spectrum disorders in the mainstream playground. *Kairaranga, 14*(1), 25–31.

Courtade, G., Spooner, F., & Browder, D. M. (2007). Review of studies with students with significant cognitive disabilities which link to science standards. *Research and Practice for Persons with Severe Disabilities, 32*, 43–49.

Department for Education. (2010). *Children with special education needs: An analysis*. Nottingham, England: DFE Publications.

Department for Education and Employment. (1997). *Excellence for all children: Meeting special educational needs*. London, England: Author.

Doll, B., & Brehm, K. (2010). *Resilient playgrounds*. New York, NY: Routledge.

Dunst, C., Johanson, C., Trivette, C., & Hamby, D. (1991). Family-oriented early intervention policies and practice: Family-centred or not? *Exceptional Children, 58*, 115–134.

Dybvik, A. C. (2004). Autism and the inclusion mandate: What happens when children with severe disabilities like autism are taught in regular classrooms? Daniel knows. *Education Next, 4*(1), 43–51.

Edelson, M. G. (2006). Are the majority of children with autism mentally retarded? A systematic evaluation of the data. *Focus on Autism and Other Developmental Disabilities, 21*, 66–83.

Education Act. (1989). Retrieved from http://www.legislation.govt.nz/act/public/1989/0080/latest/DLM175959.html

Finke, E., McNaughton, D., & Drager, K. (2009). "All children can and should have the opportunity to learn": General education teachers' perspectives on including children with autism spectrum disorder who require AAC. *Augmentative and Alternative Communication, 25*(2), 110–122.

Florian, L. (2012). Preparing teachers to work in inclusive classrooms key lessons for the professional development of teacher educators from Scotland's inclusive practice project. *Journal of Teacher Education, 63*(4), 275–285.

Fombonne, E. (2005). The changing epidemiology of autism. *Journal of Applied Research in Intellectual Disabilities, 18*, 281–294.

French, S., & Swain, J. (2004). Controlling inclusion in education: Young disabled people's perspectives. In J. Swain, S. French, C. Barnes & C. Thomas (Eds.), *Disabling barriers-enabling environments* (2nd ed., pp. 169–175.). London, England: SAGE.

Garcia, S. B., & Dominguez, L. (1997). Cultural contexts which influence learning and academic preparation. *Child and Adolescent Psychiatric Clinics of North America, 6*(3), 621–655.

Garcia, S. B., & Malkin, D. H. (1993). Toward defining programmes and services for culturally and linguistically diverse learners in special education. *Teaching Exceptional Children, 26*(1), 52–58.

Garcia, S. B., O'Raghallaigh, M., Aguilar, J., Pierce, N., Baker, S., & Sorrells, A. M. (2010). Preparing special educators to work with students with autism spectrum disorders in culturally and linguistically diverse settings: An evolving teacher education model at the University of Texas at Austin. In V. Green & S. Cherrington (Eds.), *Delving into diversity: An international exploration of issues of diversity in education* (pp. 247–254). New York, NY: Nova Science.

Giangreco, M. F. (1993). Using creative problem solving methods to include students with severe disabilities in general education classroom activities. *Journal of Educational and Psychological Consultation, 4*(2), 113–135.

Hattier, M. A., & Matson, J. L. (2012). Examination of the relationship between communication and socialization deficits in children with autism and PDD-NOS. *Research in Autism Spectrum Disorders, 6*, 871–880.

Hess, L. (2006). I would like to play but I don't know how: A case study of pretend play in autism. *Child Language Teaching and Therapy, 22*(1), 97–116.

Higgins, N., MacArthur, J., & Kelly, B. (2009). Including disabled children at school: Is it really as simple as 'a, c, d'? *International Journal of Inclusive Education, 13*(5), 471–487.

Higgins, N., MacArthur, J., & Morton, M. (2008). Winding back the clock: The retreat of New Zealand inclusive education policy. *New Zealand Annual Review of Education, 17*, 145–167.

Higgins, N., Mitchell, J., & Sanderson, D. (2005, December). *Action research in action: Reducing the isolation of teachers and disabled students in a Student Support Centre.* Paper presented at the New Zealand Association for Research in Education, Dunedin, New Zealand.

Howes, A. (2003). Teaching reforms and the impact of paid adult support on participation and learning in mainstream schools. *Support for Learning, 18*(4), 147–153.

Howlin, P., Goode, S., Hutton, J., & Rutter, M. (2004). Adult outcome for children with autism. *Journal of Child Psychology and Psychiatry, 45*(2), 212–229.

Ingram, D. H., Dickerson Mayes, S., Troxell, L. B., & Calhoun, S. L. (2007). Assessing children with autism, mental retardation and typical development using the Playground Observation Checklist. *Autism, 11*(4), 311–319.

Jarbrink, K., Fombonne, E., & Knapp, M. (2003). Measuring the parental service, cost impacts of children with autism spectrum disorder: A pilot study. *Journal of Autism and Developmental Disorders, 33*, 395–402.

Jordan, R. (2005). Autistic spectrum disorders. In A. Lewis & B. Norwich (Eds.), *Special teaching for special children? Pedagogies for inclusion.* Maidenhead, United Kingdom: Open University Press.

Jorgensen, C. M. (2005). The least dangerous assumption: A challenge to create a new paradigm. *Disability Solutions, 6*(3), 1–15.

Jorgensen, C. M., McSheehan, M., & Sonnenmeier, R. M. (2007). Presumed competence reflected in students' educational programs before and after the Beyond Access professional development intervention. *Journal of Intellectual and Developmental Disabilities, 32*, 248–262.

Kasa-Hendrickson, C. (2005). 'There's no way this kid's retarded': Teachers' optimistic constructions of students' ability. *International Journal of Inclusive Education, 9*(1), 55–69.

Kearney, A., & Kane, R. (2006). Inclusive education policy in New Zealand: Reality or ruse? *International Journal of Inclusive Education 10*(2–3), 201–219.

Keen, D., & Ward, S. (2004). Autistic spectrum disorder: A child population profile. *Autism, 8*(1), 39–48.

Kogan, M. D., Strickland, B. B., Blumberg, S. J., Sing, G. K., Perrin, J. M., & van Dyck, P. C. (2008). A national profile of health care experiences and family impact of autism spectrum disorder among children in the United States, 2005–2006. *Paediatrics, 122,* 1149–1158.

Kohler, F. W. (1999). Examining the services received by young children with autism and their families: A survey of parent responses. *Focus on Autism and other Developmental Disabilities, 14,* 150–158.

Krauss, M. W., Gulley, S., Sciegaj, M., & Wells, N. (2003). Access to special medical care for children with mental retardation, autism, and other special health care needs. *Mental Retardation, 41,* 329–339.

Laws, G., Bates, G., Feuerstein, M., Mason-Apps, E., & White, C. (2012). Peer acceptance of children with language and communication impairments in a mainstream primary school: Associations with type of language difficulty, problem behaviours and a change in placement organization. *Child Language Teaching and Therapy, 28*(1), 73–86.

Leslie, D. L., & Martin, A. (2007). Health care expenditures associated with autism spectrum disorders. *Archives of Pediatrics and Adolescent Medicine, 161,* 350–355.

Lord, C., Risi, S., & Pickles, A. (2004). Trajectory of language development in autistic spectrum disorders. In M. L. Rice & S. F. Warren (Eds.), *Developmental language disorders: From phenotypes to etiologies* (pp. 7–29). Mahwah, NJ: Erlbaum.

Lydon, H., Healy, O., & Leader, G. (2011). Comparison of video modelling and pivotal responses training to teach pretend play skills to children with autism spectrum disorder. *Research in Autism Spectrum Disorders, 5,* 872–884.

MacArthur, J., & Gaffney, M. (2001). *Bullied and teased or just another kid.* Wellington, New Zealand: New Zealand Council for Educational Research.

Machalicek, W., O'Reilly, M. F., Beretvas, N., Sigafoos, J., & Lancioni, G. E. (2007). A review of interventions to reduce challenging behaviour in school settings for students with autism spectrum disorders. *Research in Autism Spectrum Disorders, 1,* 229–246.

Machalicek, W., O'Reilly, M. F., Beretvas, N., Sigafoos, J., Lancioni, G. E., & Sorrells, A. (2008). A review of school based instructional interventions for students with autism spectrum disorders. *Research in Autism Spectrum Disorders, 2,* 395–416.

Matson, J. L. (2007). Determining treatment outcome in early intervention programs for children with autism spectrum disorders: A critical analysis of measurement issues in learning based interventions. *Research in Developmental Disabilities, 28,* 207–218.

Matson, J. L., Dixon, D. R., & Matson, M. L. (2005). Assessing and treating aggression in children and adolescents with developmental disabilities: A 20-year overview. *Educational Psychology, 25*(2–3), 151–181.

McNaughton, D., & Light, J. (2013). The iPad and mobile technology revolution: Benefits and challenges for individuals who require argumentative and alternative communication. *Augmentative and Alternative Communication, 29*(2), 107–116.

McSheehan, M., Sonnenmeier, R. M., & Jorgensen, C. M. (2009). Membership, participation, and learning in general classrooms for students with autism spectrum disorders who use AAC. In P. Mirenda & T. Iacono (Eds.), *Autism spectrum disorders and AAC* (pp. 413–439). Baltimore, MD: Paul Brookes.

McVittie, E. (2005). The role of teaching the assistant: An investigative study to discover if teaching assistants are being used effectively to support children with special needs in mainstream schools. *Education 3-13: International Journal of Primary, Elementary and Early Years Education, 33*(3), 26–31.

Ministries of Health and Education. (2008). *New Zealand Autism spectrum disorder guideline*. Wellington, New Zealand: Ministry of Health.

Ministry of Education. (1997). *Special Education 2000 Policy*. Wellington, New Zealand: Learning Media.

Ministry of Education. (2009). Narrative assessment: A guide for teachers. Retrieved May 28, 2009, from http://www.inclusive.org.nz/__data/assets/pdf_file/0010/57925/Narrative-Assessment_a-guide-for-teachers.pdf

Ministry of Education. (2011). *Collaboration for success: Individual education plans*. Wellington, New Zealand: Learning Media.

Ministry of Education. (2012a). *The New Zealand curriculum update*. Retrieved from http:/nzcurriculum.tki.org.nz/curriculum_updates

Ministry of Education. (2012b). *Taskforce mandate for action inclusive education*. Wellington, New Zealand: Author.

Ministry of Health. (2013). Autism. Retrieved from www.health.govt.nz

Mirenda, P. (2003a). He's not really a reader ...: Perspectives on supporting literacy development in individuals with autism. *Topics in Language Disorders, 23*, 271–282.

Mirenda, P. (2003b). Toward functional augmentative and alternative communication for students with autism: Manual signs, graphic symbols, and voice output communication aids. *Language, speech, & Hearing Services in Schools, 34*(3), 203–216.

Morewood, G. D., Humphrey, N., & Symes, W. (2011). Mainstreaming autism: Making it work. *GAP, 12*(2), 62–68.

Morton, M., & McMenamin, T. (2009). Families choices: Choosing school(s): Part 1: Literature review, interviews and design of questionnaire. Retrieved from http://ir.canterbury.ac.nz/handle/10092/5220

Norwich, B., & Lewis, A. (Eds.). (2005). *How specialized is teaching pupils with disabilities and difficulties?* Maidenhead, United Kingdom: Open University.

Ofsted. (2004). *Special educational needs and disability: Towards inclusive schools*. London, England: Author.

Pellegrini, A. (2008, Fall). The recess debate. A disjuncture between educational policy and scientific research. *American Journal of Play*, 181–191.

Pellegrini, A., & Blatchford, P. (2002). Time for a break. *The Psycholgist, 15*(2), 60–62.

Pellegrini, A. D. (2005). *Recess: Its role in education and development*. Mahwah, NJ: Erlbaum.

Peters, B., Forlin, C., McInerney, D., & Maclean, R. (2013). Social interaction and cooperative activities: Drawing plans as a means of increasing engagement for children with ASD. *International Journal of Whole Schooling, 9*(2), 61–86.

Ravet, J. (2011). Inclusive/exclusive? Contradictory perspectives on autism and inclusion: The case for an integrative position. *International Journal of Inclusive Education, 15*(6), 667–682.

Rodriguez, I. R., Saldana, D., & Moreno, F. M. (2012). Support, inclusion and special education teachers' attitudes toward the education of students with autism spectrum disorders. *Autism Research and Treatment, 2012*, 1–7.

Romski, M., Sevcik, R., Smith, A., Barker, R., Folan, S., & Barton-Husley, A. (2009). The system for augmenting language. Implications for young children with autism spectrum disorders. In P. Mirenda & T. Iacono (Eds.), *Autism spectrum disorders and AAC* (pp. 219–245). Baltimore, MD: Paul H. Brookes.

Rowley, E., Chandler, S., Baird, G., Simonoff, E., Pickles, A., Loucas, T., & Charman, T. (2012). The experience of friendship, victimization and bullying in children with autism spectrum disorder: Associations with child characteristics and school placement. *Research in Autism Spectrum Disorders, 6*, 1126–1134.

Russell, P. (1996). Listening to children with disabilities and special educational needs. In R. Davie, G. Upton, & V. Varma (Eds.), *The voice of the child: A handbook for professionals* (pp. 107–119). London, England: Falmer.

Samadi, S., Mahmoodizadeh, A., & McConkey, R. (2011). A national study of the prevalence of autism spectrum disorder among five-year-old children in Iran. *Autism, 16*(5), 5–14.

Scheuermann, B., Webber, J. B. E. A., & Goodwin, M. (2003). Problems with personal preparation in autism spectrum disorders. *Focus on Autism and Other Developmental Disabilities, 18*, 197–206.

Schieve, L. A., Blumberg, S. J., Rice, C., Visser, S. N., & Boyle, C. (2007). The relationship between autism and parenting stress. *Paediatrics, 119*, 114–121.

Sigafoos, J. (2006). Self-determination: Can we let the child determine the "best" treatment? *Paediatric Rehabitulation, 9*, 1–2.

Sigafoos, J., Lang, R., Davis, T., Rispoli, M., Tait, K., Cannella-Malone, H., ... Lancioni, G. (2010). Developmental and physical disabilities. In V. A. Green & S. Cherrington (Eds.), *Delving into diversity: An international exploration of issues of diversity in education* (pp. 119–128). New York, NY: Nova Science.

Sigafoos, J., O'Reilly, M. F., & Lancioni, G. E. (2009). Functional communication-training and choice-making interventions for the treatment of problem behaviour in individuals with autism spectrum disorders. In P. Mirenda & T. Iacono (Eds.), *Autism spectrum disorders and AAC* (pp. 333–353). Baltimore, MD: Paul H Brookes.

Siklos, S., & Kerns, K. A. (2006). Assessing need for social support in parents of children with autism and Down syndrome. *Journal of Autism and Developmental Disorders, 36*, 921–933.

Slee, R. (2001). Social justice and the changing directions in educational research: The case of inclusive education. *International Journal of Inclusive Education, 5*(2–3), 167–177.

Symes, W., & Humphrey, N. (2011). School factors that facilitate or hinder the ability of teaching assistants to effectively support pupils with autism spectrum disorders (ASDs) in mainstream secondary schools. *Journal of Research in Special Educational Needs, 11*(3), 153–161.

Syriopoulou-Delli, C., Cassimos, D., Tripsianis, G., & Polychronopoulou, S. (2012). Teachers' perceptions regarding the management of children with autism spectrum disorders. *Journal of Autism Developmental Disorders, 42,* 755–768.

Terpstra, J., Higgins, K., & Pierce, T. (2002). Can I play?: Classroom-based interventions for teaching play skills to children with autism. *Focus on Autism and Other Developmental Disabilities, 17,* 119–126.

van der Meer, L., & Rispoli, M. (2010). Communication interventions involving speech-generating devices for children with autism: A review of the literature. *Developmental Neurorehabilitation, 13*(4), 295–306.

van der Meer, L., Sigafoos, J., O'Reilly, M., & Lancioni, G. (2011). Assessing preferences for AAC options in communication interventions for individuals with developmental disabilities: A review of the literature. *Research in Developmental Disabilities, 32,* 1422–1431.

van der Meer, L., Sutherland, D., O'Reilly, M., Lancioni, G., & Sigafoos, J. (2012). A further comparison of manual signing, picture exchange and speech generating devices as communication modes for children with autism spectrum disorders. *Research in Autism Spectrum Disorders, 6,* 1247–1257.

Volkmar, F. R., & Pauls, D. (2003). Autism. *Lancet, 362*(9390), 1133–1141.

Werts, M. G., Wolery, M., Snyder, E. D., & Caldwell, N. K. (1996). Teachers' perceptions of the supports critical to the success of inclusion programs. *Journal of the Association for Persons with Severe Handicaps, 21*(1), 9–21.

ABOUT THE CONTRIBUTORS

Aino Äikäs works as a university lecturer and a teacher educator in the School of Educational Sciences and Psychology, in the Department of Special Education in the University of Eastern Finland in Joensuu. She earned her doctoral dissertation in August 2012 and concentrated on the future outcomes of young adults with severe intellectual disabilities. Her primary research interest in the field of special education and disability studies concentrates on the inclusive education and transition from school to working life from the viewpoint of intellectual disabilities. She has experience of working as a special education teacher in secondary school. She also has working experience of planning officer in ESF-project, which concentrated on the development of equal educational and employment opportunities, and promoting social inclusion. She is planning an inclusive research project with a colleague aiming to study how to execute participatory research with individuals with intellectual disabilities. [aino.aikas@uef.fi]

Lucie Leclair Arvisais is a planning, programing, and research officer for Pavillon du Parc Rehabilitation Centre (RC) in western Quebec, Canada. She has over 30 years of experience in the field of intellectual disabilities. She received a National Consortium for Social Integration award for her research on aging and intellectual disabilities. In the last few years, her major contribution was the development and implementation of the inclusive Intensive Early Intervention program for all children 2 to 5 years of age with a developmental or intellectual disability receiving services from the RC. She was responsible for setting program objectives based on best practices, developing the clinical process, and training early childhood educators. The program won two excellence awards in 2011, one from the Quebec Ministry of Health and Social Services and another from the Public Administration of Quebec. [lucie_leclair-arvisais@ssss.gouv.qc.ca]

Katrina Barker is a senior lecturer in educational psychology in the School of Education at the University of Western Sydney. Her expertise in teaching educational psychology to preservice teachers has been recognized with an Australian Government Office for Learning and Teaching citation Award in 2010 and she has been nominated for UniJobs Australia Top Ten Lecturer of the Year Award in 2008 through to 2013. Katrina's research focus links well to her teaching as it relates to achievement motivation, self-concept, school retention, classroom management, teacher self-efficacy, and more recently inclusive education.
[k.barker@uws.edu.au]

Sheila Bennett is a professor and former chair in the Department of Teacher Education. Professionally, Sheila has worked as a classroom and special education teacher, school board resource person, and faculty member. She has been active in the field of special education for many years and has been involved in policy and practical issues in the field. She has been cochair of the Special Education Transformation Document as well as coauthor of Special Education in Ontario Schools, Sheila has dedicated her career to working with educators and students in her chosen field.
[sbennett@brocku.ca]

Kathryn W. Best is a doctoral student in the School of Education, Special Education & Disability Policy Department at Virginia Commonwealth University. She is currently the director of the Academic Resource Center at Trinity Episcopal School. Her research interests include universal design for learning, universal design for transition, and professional development.
[kwbest@vcu.edu]

Gottfried Biewer is a professor and chair for Special Needs and Inclusive Education at the University of Vienna. With more than 90,000 students this institution is one of the largest universities in Europe and the leading research institution in Austria. During the last years Professor Biewer lead several large projects for the Austrian Science Fund, the European Science Foundation, and the Austrian Development Cooperation. In these projects his main international cooperation partners came from Ireland, Spain, the Czech Republic, Thailand, and Ethiopia. The main areas of his research are inclusive education, comparative research in special needs education, vocational participation of persons with intellectual disabilities, life course research with persons with disabilities, and education of persons with disabilities in developing countries. Professor Biewer is co-

convenor of network 4 (inclusive education) of the European Educational Research Association.
Website: http://homepage.univie.ac.at/gottfried.biewer/
[Gottfried.Biewer@univie.ac.at]

Meghan M. Burke is an assistant professor in the Department of Special Education at the University of Illinois at Urbana-Champaign. Previously, she was a postdoctoral fellow in the Department of Disability and Human Development at the University of Illinois at Chicago. Her fellowship was supported by the National Institute on Disability and Rehabilitation Research. She graduated from Vanderbilt with her PhD in special education. Her research areas include family-school partnerships, families of individuals with disabilities, and special education advocacy. Dr. Burke conducts research with community organizations to better understand parent advocacy and its impact upon individuals with disabilities and their families. Her awards include the Anne Rudigier Award from the Association for University Centers in Disabilities. She has several grants related to advocacy and families of individuals with disabilities. Dr. Burke is also a certified special education teacher and a board certified behavior analyst.
[meghanbm@illinois.edu]

Soh Mee Choo is the chief executive officer at Apex Harmony Lodge, a purpose-built facility that caters to the special needs of individuals with dementia. Prior to her current position, she was with the Ministry of Education, Singapore, and was the former principal of Delta Senior School (DSS) at the Association for Persons with Special Needs (APSN) in Singapore. Among Ms. Soh's many invaluable contributions and legacies to DSS and APSN, she led the development of a prototype field-tested transition program for her students with mild intellectual disabilities, which is featured in this chapter. Many of students at DSS and their families have benefited immensely from this program.
[meechoo.soh@apexharmony.org.sg]

Llyween Couper is a PhD candidate in the School of Health Sciences at the University of Canterbury New Zealand. The focus of her study is finding the preferred communication choices of nonverbal children with autism spectrum disorders. Part of this study is exploring the experiences of the participants in their mainstream playgrounds. In 2014 she presented a paper at the International School Psychology Conference in Lithuania titled When Research Benefits the Participants which described her study and the impact on schools in which the study was located. In 2013 the findings were presented at the Disability in Education Confer-

ence in Christchurch and at the International Association of Special Education in Vancouver and the New Zealand Academic Research in Education Conference in Dunedin. Results are published in *Kairaranga, 14*(1) 2013. Children with autism spectrum disorders in the mainstream playground. Prior to her PhD study Llyween had a career in special education supporting teachers in inclusive settings. During a teacher's sabbatical she designed and trialled, A Practical Guide to Conducting a Playground Audit. The results titled, Putting Play Back into the Playground were presented at The International School Psychology Association Conference in Dublin in 2010 and published in *Kairaranga, 12*(1) 2011.
[llyween.couper@pg.canterbury.ac.nz]

Rhonda G. Craven is a professor and the director in the Institute Director of the Institute for Positive Psychology and Education at the Australian Catholic University. She is a highly accomplished researcher, having successfully secured over 8.68 million dollars in nationally and highly competitive funding for 49 large-scale research projects including 29 Australian Research Council grants. This performance is arguably one of the strongest for an Australian educational researcher. She is the recipient of the Meritorious Service to Public Education Award, the Betty Watts Award (Australian Association for Research in Education), the Vice Chancellor's Award for Excellence in Postgraduate Research Supervision and Training, and the Vice Chancellor's Award for Excellence in Social Justice Research. Her research interests include: the structure, measurement, development, and enhancement of self-concept and key psychosocial drivers of well-being and performance; the effective teaching of Indigenous Studies and Indigenous students; maximizing life potential and enabling people to not just succeed but flourish in diverse settings; and interventions that make a tangible difference in educational and industry settings.
[rhonda.craven@acu.edu.au]

Jesmond C. M. Fan is a lecturer of the School of Continuing Education at Hong Kong Baptist University, where she teaches special education to in-service and preservice teachers. Prior to her current position, she worked as a special education teacher at the elementary and secondary levels in a special school. She has taught children with intellectual disabilities, physical disabilities, learning disabilities, and autism. She also has worked as a former teacher and special needs facilitator at a nonprofit organization where provides vocational and educational programs for adults with special needs. She received her postgraduate diploma of education from the

University of Hong Kong and master degree from the University of Leeds. Her research interests include special educational needs, inclusive education, and curriculum adaptation.
[jesmond@hkbu.edu.hk]

Tiffany L. Gallagher is an associate professor in the Teacher Education Department at Brock University. She teaches courses in educational psychology and language arts methods. Tiffany's research interests include inclusive literacy assessment, reading and writing strategy instruction, the roles of the instructional coach and the special education teacher, and education for students with learning and intellectual disabilities. Tiffany has worked closely with several school boards in the Southern Ontario as a consultant researcher for projects that these school boards were implementing in the areas of inclusion, professional development, and literacy for struggling students.
[tiffany.gallagher@brocku.ca]

Geert Van Hove is a professor, working in the field of disability and inclusive education at Ghent University and in the field of disability studies at the Free University of Amsterdam (Endowed Chair from Disability Studies in the Netherlands). He works together with families and persons with disabilities in an attempt to close the gap between academia and activism.
[Geert.VanHove@UGent.be]

Eija Kärnä is a professor of special education and works in the Faculty of Philosophy at the University of Eastern Finland. During her career Professor Kärnä has worked on several international development and research projects and conducted multidisciplinary research with researchers from several scientific fields (e.g., linguistics, psychology, nursing science, computer science). Currently she leads several multidisciplinary research projects on inclusive technology with and for children with special educational needs. The projects are funded by highly nationally competitive funding. Her research interests are particularly in inclusive learning environments, communication and interaction of individuals with severe developmental disabilities and autism spectrum disorders, and in participatory research and design of technology for and with individuals with special needs.
[eija.karna@uef.fi]

Michaela Kramann is working at the Department of Education in the research unit Special Needs and Inclusive Education at the University of Vienna. She studied psychology as well as education with a focus on special education. Her first master thesis was about the influence of the

Roma culture on school achievement and the other about different information processing of reading material of children with different teaching
methods and reading skills. Additionally she finalized her postgraduate
studies for clinical and health psychology. At the moment she is part of
three research projects in the field of participation and inclusion of people with disabilities and socioemotional problems in education and voca-
tion. She is also member of a group discussing on international special
education. Her main research areas are inclusive education, intercultural
education, research with children, as well as disability and education.
[Michaela.Kramann@univie.ac.at]

John Kubiak, DEd, lectures in the National Institute for Intellectual Disability, Trinity College Dublin. He is coordinator of the Certificate in Contemporary Living (CCL) program and supervises at masters level. John's
doctoral research was conducted with the input of CCL students and has
resulted in a model of how students with intellectual disabilities learn
while in tertiary education. In 2012 John was a recipient of Trinity's prestigious Provost Teaching Award which is designed to recognise and
reward staff who have made an outstanding contribution in the pursuit of
teaching excellence. In May 2013 John was awarded a postdoctorate
research position and bursary from Trinity's School of Education. His
research interests include: inclusion in higher education; inclusive
research; learning and people with intellectual disabilities.
[kubiakj@tcd.ie]

Levan Lim, PhD, is an associate professor and head of the Early Childhood and Special Needs Education Academic Group at the National Institute of Education, Nanyang Technological University, Singapore. He
obtained his PhD in special education from Lehigh University, Pennsylvania. His teaching areas and research interests have included disability
studies, inclusion, transition and curriculum reform, persons with severe
disabilities, teacher education for special needs, and intentional communities. He has been an editorial board member of several international
journals in special and inclusive education such the *International Journal of
Inclusive Education*.
[levan.lim@nie.edu.sg]

Frances Lai Mui Lee has been actively involved in education for many
years. She has been involved in education for many years. Her experience
involves classroom teaching, instructional design, and academic staff
development. Her academic and professional interests are in the areas of

guidance and counseling, gifted education, inclusive education and learners with special needs. She has also studied self-concept of students in Hong Kong and the Chinese mainland. She teaches in the areas of early childhood education and offers courses on special education and parent education. She is actively involved in the MEd (early childhood education), and the postgraduate diploma and undergraduate in education (early childhood education) at universities in Hong Kong, Macau, and Mainland China.
[franceslee422@gmail.com]

Christophe Maïano is an associate professor at the Département de Psychoéducation et de Psychologie at the Université du Québec en Outaouais (Québec, Canada) and holds an adjunct appointment at the Institute for Positive Psychology and Education (IPPE) at the Australian Catholic University that is related to ongoing research collaborations with IPPE's members. Christophe's expertise broadly covers psychosocial interventions, adapted physical activity interventions, and health prevention and education interventions, all aimed at improving the physical and psychological well-being of individuals with an intellectual disability (ID), physical health problems, or mental health disorders. His current research projects are centered on: (a) the assessment of multidimensional self-conceptions, mental health, and well-being in youth with or without an ID; (b) the identification of social factors (social comparison, stereotypes, significant others, friends, school, etc.) related to the development of multidimensional self-conceptions in youth with or without an ID; (c) the interrelations between these social factors and multidimensional self-conceptions and the more global biopsychosocial adaptation of these youth (physical fitness, obesity, eating disorders, depression, well-being, etc.); and (d) the effects and efficacy of physical activity and physical activity interventions for furthering positive outcomes for youth with physical, psychological, or social disabilities or disadvantages.
[christophe.maiano@uqo.ca]

Herb Marsh, professor, holds a joint appointment at the Institute for Positive Psychology and Education at the Australian Catholic University and an emeritus professor at Oxford University. He is an "ISI highly cited researcher" (http://isihighlycited.com/) with 842+ publications, 62,000+ citations and an H-index = 124 in Google Scholar (Google Citations), co-edits the *International Advances in Self Research* monograph series, and has been recognized as the most productive educational psychologist in the world and the 11th most productive researcher across all disciplines of psychology. He founded and directs the SELF Research Centre that has 500+ members and satellite centers at leading universities around the

world, and coedits the SELF monograph series. He coined the phrase substantive-methodological research synergy which underpins his research efforts. In addition to his methodological focus on structural equation models, factor analysis, and multilevel modelling, his major substantive interests include self-concept and motivational constructs; evaluations of teaching/educational effectiveness; developmental psychology; sports psychology; the peer review process; gender differences; peer support and anti-bullying interventions.
[herb.marsh@acu.edu.au]

Alexandre J. S. Morin is a research professor at the Institute for Positive Psychology and Education at the Australian Catholic University. He is a highly productive researcher having produced more than 100 articles, many of which are in top-tier journals, and book chapters with reputable publishers. His research has also attracted multiple prestigious external grants in Canada (e.g., Social Sciences and Humanities Research Council of Canada) and Australia (e.g., Australian Research Council). He defines himself as a lifespan developmental psychologist, with broad research interests anchored in the exploration of the social determinants of psychological well-being and psychopathologies at various life stages and various settings, such as schools and organizations. Most of his research endeavours are anchored in a substantive-methodological synergy framework, and thus represent joint ventures in which new methodological developments are applied to substantively important issues. A significant part of his current research program aims to understand how to foster more positive futures for children with intellectual disabilities through the identification of drivers of psychosocial and physical well-being.
[alexandre.morin@acu.edu.au]

Claude Louise Normand is an associate professor in the Department of Psychoeducation and Psychology at the Université du Québec en Outaouais in Gatineau, Canada. She was educated in developmental psychology, and her research interests include parenting children with special needs and especially the social participation of children and adolescents with an intellectual or developmental disability. She has developed a questionnaire on barriers and accommodations to the inclusion and social participation of children (0–14 years of age) with a global developmental delay, an intellectual disability, or autism spectrum disorder. She is responsible for the data analyses of the developmental measures from the intensive early intervention programs offered by the regional rehabilitation centre in western Quebec.
[claude.normand@uqo.ca]

Philip D. Parker is currently an Australian Research Council DECRA funded research fellow at the Institute for Positive Psychology and Education (IPPE). Philip's research uses large longitudinal databases from Australia, United States, United Kingdom, Switzerland, Germany, and Finland where he focuses on career pathways, personality, and well-being issues related to youths' transition from school to work or further education with a particular focus on minority and marginalized groups. Philip studied psychology at the SELF research centre at the University of Western Sydney and completed his PhD at the University of Sydney on the role of motivational constructs and processes in the development of teacher burnout and subjective well-being. Philip was previously a Jacob's foundation funded postdoctoral research fellow in the PATHWAYS to Adulthood program.
[philip.parker@acu.edu.au]

Julie Ruel, PhD, is an associate researcher at Pavillon du Parc Rehabilitation Center for people with intellectual disabilities or autistic spectrum disorders, in the province of Québec, Canada. She is cochair holder of the Interdisciplinary Chair in Literacy and Inclusion attached to Université du Québec en Outaouais, where she is also an adjunct professor. During the past 10 years she has been conducting research on the topics of early intervention and school transitions. She instigated the systematic data collection leading to the evaluation of an inclusive Intensive Early Intervention program. Her doctoral research examined the transition to kindergarten, with particular emphasis on the role of networking of stakeholders from the education, social services and health sectors, working with the parents, in easing the transition of children with special needs. She is the primary author of the *Carte routière vers le préscolaire* [Roadmap to Kindergarten].
Website: w3.uqo.ca/transition/
[julie_ruel@ssss.gouv.qc.ca]

Inge Van de Putte supports children, parents, and schools in the processes of inclusive education. The past years she did research about teacher education training. She focused on the competence of teachers in inclusive education and developed a support concept for teachers while working with diverse students. Support of teachers, and the position of special needs coordinators are the topics in her current PhD research project in the field of disability studies. In her research and publications she finds the transfer to practice very important.
[inge.vandeputte@UGent.be]

Elisabeth De Schauwer is working in the field of disability studies at Ghent University. Her research centers around "difference" and the influence on relationships. She is interested in finding and strengthening theoretical and pragmatic links between pedagogy and other disciplines like philosophy, feminism, and anthropology. She works closely together with children, parents, and schools in the praxis of inclusive education. Activism, research, and teaching go hand in hand. Following people and their stories is a never ending source of inspiration for her daily work and life. [Elisabeth. De Schauwer@UGent.be]

LaRon A. Scott is an assistant professor in the School of Education, Special Education & Disability Policy Department at Virginia Commonwealth University. He is currently the coordinator for the special education-general curriculum master's program and director of online program for the master's in special education. His research interests include transition planning, student-directed individualized education program development, and special education teacher professional preparation. He co-authored a book on transition instruction with Dr. Colleen Thoma and Dr. Christina Bartholomew entitled *Universal Design for Transition* (Paul H. Brookes Publishing Co, 2009), and has served as a contributing author in books and chapters on self-directed IEPs. He is the recipient of the Division on Career Development and Transition, Transition Teacher of the Year award in 2008.
[scottla2@vcu.edu]

Michael Shevlin is a senior lecturer in the School of Education at Trinity College, Dublin. He teaches at both undergraduate and postgraduate level and supervises research at masters and doctoral level. He has participated in a number of funded research projects and published widely in the area of inclusive education and facilitating the participation of disabled young people in mainstream schools and society. Michael has also been involved for many years in statutory, policy making and advisory bodies in relation to inclusive education (Member of Special Education Review Committee 1991-3; National Council for Special Education 2003-6; Expert Taskforce on Individual Education Planning 2006; CHOICE (DES) on entry to teacher education for people with disabilities 2008-9.) [mshevlin@tcd.ie]

Karrie A. Shogren, PhD, is associate professor of special education; associate director Kansas University Center on Developmental Disabilities; and associate scientist, Beach Center on Disability at the University of

Kansas. Dr. Shogren's research focuses on self-determination and systems of support for students with disabilities and she has a specific interest in the multiple, nested contextual factors that impact student outcomes. Dr. Shogren has published more than 50 articles in peer-reviewed journals, is the author or coauthor of five books, and is one of the coauthors of *Intellectual Disability: Definition, Classification, and Systems of Support*, the 11th edition of the American Association on Intellectual and Developmental Disabilities' seminal definition of intellectual disability (formerly mental retardation). Dr. Shogren is a fellow of the American Association on Intellectual and Developmental Disabilities.
[shogren@ku.edu]

Colleen A. Thoma is professor and chair of the Department of Special Education & Disability Policy in the School of Education at Virginia Commonwealth University. Her research interests include preparation of teachers to support self-determined transition planning, student-directed individualized education program development, universal design for transition, postsecondary education transition programs for students with intellectual disability, and the impact of student self-determination on transition and academic outcomes. She has authored or coauthored numerous books and articles on transition including universal design for transition (Thoma, Bartholomew & Scott, 2009); student-directed IEPs (Thoma & Wehman, 2011) and demystifying transition assessment (Thoma & Tamura, 2013). She is a past recipient of a Mary E. Switzer Distinguished Research Fellowship (2011, National Institute on Disability and Rehabilitation Research) and the Oliver P. Kolstoe Award for contributions to the field of transition (2013, Division on Career Development and Transition).
[cathoma@vcu.edu]

Danielle Tracey is a registered educational and developmental psychologist with extensive experience working in the community sector supporting children and young people with learning difficulties. She completed her PhD in psychology in 2002 whereby her doctoral research developed our understanding of the self-concept of students with mild intellectual disabilities and the impact of educational placement. Her professional and research interests focus primarily on the social and emotional wellbeing of children and young people who struggle with learning. She is currently academic course advisor (special education), senior lecturer in educational psychology, and senior researcher in the Centre for Educational Research in the School of Education at the University of Western Sydney.
[d.tracey@uws.edu.au]

Alexander Seeshing Yeung is a professor and deputy director of the Institute for Positive Psychology and Education (IPPE) at the Australian Catholic University. He applies mixed-method approaches in research. His major research area is educational psychology and his expertise includes self-concept, achievement motivation, measurement and evaluation, cognition and instruction, teacher education, and studies with special samples. He has a strong track record of successfully conducting large-scale research in Australia, Singapore, and Hong Kong. [alexander.yeung@acu.edu.au]

Michael L. Wehmeyer, PhD, is professor of special education; director, Kansas University Center on Developmental Disabilities; and senior scientist, Beach Center on Disability at the University of Kansas. He has authored or coauthored almost 300 peer-reviewed journal articles or book chapters and authored, coauthored, edited, or coedited 32 books on issues pertaining to self-determination, positive psychology and disability, transition to adulthood, the education and inclusion of students with severe disabilities. He is past-president and fellow of the American Association on Intellectual and Developmental Disabilities; a fellow of the American Psychological Association, Intellectual and Developmental Disabilities Division; and vice-president for the Americas and Fellow of the International Association for the Scientific Study of Intellectual and Developmental Disabilities. [wehmeyer@ku.edu]

Hua Flora Zhong is a research data analyst at the Institute for Positive Psychology and Education at the Australian catholic University. Her role focuses on undertaking qualitative and quantitative data analysis using advanced statistical techniques, including structural equation modeling, confirmatory and exploratory factor analysis, multilevel modeling, and Rasch analysis. She recently completed her PhD in education, which investigated the construct of vocabulary knowledge in a longitudinal setting among English as a foreign language young learners. Hua has been involved in various research projects covering a wide range of areas, including TESOL, students' motivation and achievement, secondary education, Australian national identity, and LGBTQ. Her current research interests include second language vocabulary acquisition; language testing and assessment; the construct of self-concept and its relationship with students' motivations and achievement. [hua.zhong@acu.edu.au]